CENTER FOR THE STUDY OF THE PRESIDENCY
WASHINGTON, D.C.

TRIUMPHS AND TRAGEDIES OF THE MODERN PRESIDENCY

SEVENTY-SIX
CASE STUDIES
IN PRESIDENTIAL
LEADERSHIP

DAVID ABSHIRE, EDITOR

PRAEGER

Westport, Connecticut
London

About the Center for the Study of the Presidency

The Center for the Study of the Presidency (CSP) is a non-profit, non-partisan 501(c)(3) organization dedicated to serving as a central resource addressing issues affecting the modern Presidency. As the foremost organization in the United States dedicated to the study of the American Presidency, the Center acts as an institutional memory for the White House in a changing national and global environment.

Other CSP publications of interest:

> *Presidential Studies Quarterly* (ISSN 0360-4918)
>
> *Dialogues on Presidential Leadership: The President,*
> *Congress, and the Media* (Washington, D.C., 2000)
>
> *In Harm's Way: Intervention and Prevention*
> (Washington, D.C., 2000)
>
> *Constructing the Presidency for the 21ˢᵗ Century,*
> by David M. Abshire (Washington, D.C., 1999)
>
> *The Character of George Washington,* by David M. Abshire
> (Washington, D.C. 1999)

Library of Congress Cataloging-in-Publication Data and British Library Cataloguing in Publication Data are available.

ISBN: 0-275-97351-4

0-275-97352-2 (pbk.)

First published in 2001

Praeger Publishers, 88 Post Road West, Westport, CT 06881
An imprint of Greenwood Publishing Group, Inc.
www.praeger.com

Printed in the United States of America

The paper used in this book complies with the Permanent Paper Standard issued by the National Information Standards Organization (Z39.48-1984).

10 9 8 7 6 5 4 3 2 1

This document is the first
attempt ever to help prepare
the President-elect by
presenting him with a series
of case studies in Presidential
leadership on the successes
and failures of his predecessors
and the lessons learned.
We are sharing this work with
the wider public in an effort to
inform their expectations and
shape the context in which we
judge our national leaders

PROLOGUE

Triumphs And Tragedies Of The Modern Presidency

By David M. Abshire

IT WAS LINCOLN WHO SAID, "Fellow citizens, we cannot escape history." To his future peers, Lincoln might have added, "Fellow Presidents, we especially cannot escape history."

The President might consider taking a day or two to study how other Presidents walked, stumbled, and climbed up to definitive moments in their Presidencies. This book of case studies, representing the authors' own views, was prepared for just that purpose. Here, organized in nine categories, are studies in Presidential triumph and tragedy. By reading this, a President can be fortified for the long look forward by better understanding the long view backward. This vantage may help nourish the character, wisdom, and vision we associate with Washington, Adams, Jefferson, Lincoln, the Roosevelts, and Truman— all readers of history. These lessons will be different and surely more valuable than the advice of pollsters and spin masters or the evening news.

A noted Harvard Professor, Ernest May, warns Presidents against blindly applying historical analogies to current events, such as the "Munich analogy" once applied to Vietnam. But when one turns to the art and character of Presidential leadership, especially in view of our democratic form of government, wisdom and warnings can be culled from studying the record of the past. The exercise of leadership, especially American Presidential leadership, tends to remain remarkably constant through two centuries in such fundamental things as harmony and conflict with Congress, leading a nation confronting foreign and domestic crises, and trying to transform policies or promote the reform of stagnant institutions.

Certainly the settled judgment of history is quite different from any transient judgment of the moment, of any polls, or indeed, of the initial public judgment, and even that of historians as a President leaves office. Spin masters will try to take over a President the minute he is elected and the information revolution will try to make him live for the moment, with every twist and turn of his ratings. But hewing remorselessly to the popular opinion of the day—rather than to the long look of history—can cost a President his legacy, even his good name.

The Long View Counts

There is an intriguing commonality between the successful Presidencies of Washington, Lincoln, and the Roosevelts, and the unsuccessful tenures of Buchanan, Harding and Andrew Johnson. Most apparently thought that, once elected, they would do well in the Oval Office. Lincoln was an instructive exception, for he was not so sure of his forthcoming performance. His model, George Washington, also thought himself not up to the task of being our first President. So there is a lesson in the value of avoiding hubris. A bit of modesty and indeed awe is salutary for any President-elect. It is no less important for the people around the President, for they do much to set the tone and perception of a new leader.

What we underline is that it is not the public poll or press perception of the moment, but the long-term judgment that counts. In 1948, Truman's poll ratings were so low that he was not considered electable in 1952. Yet during the next two decades, historians elevated him to the near great, as they eventually have Eisenhower and Reagan. Lincoln himself feared for his reelection in 1864. Seeds of Lincoln's exalted reputation in this country, indeed worldwide, were not planted until on his martyred deathbed when Secretary of War Stanton murmured, "Now he belongs to the ages." And indeed, he did.

It's the long view that counts. Presidential advisor Richard Neustadt of Harvard University has written about this in his tribute to the "Nancy Factor," as he labeled it. That Mrs. Reagan constantly looked after her husband's historic standing, and that a President can get into trouble when there is no "Nancy Factor," is a telling comment on the perils of this office. So how did Iran-Contra happen? Mrs. Reagan was cut out of the loop and had no opportunity to comment on the disproportionality of this sad episode. When Iran-Contra broke she felt President Reagan was being isolated. She discreetly invited Robert Strauss, a former Democratic Party Chairman, to the White House quarters in December 1986 to tell the President the trouble he was in. Strauss was direct. He said he had learned from a similar advisory situation with Lyndon Johnson, when he did not speak up but told Johnson what he wanted to hear about the Vietnam quagmire. Strauss later told Reagan that when he left the LBJ White House that night he felt like a $3 prostitute. He would not commit that grievous error again when called upon to give advice. "You, Mr. President," he said to Reagan, "are in deep trouble."

Shortly thereafter, Reagan broke out of the bunker: he eschewed executive privilege, set up an independent board to do an initial investigation, and created for three months an independent Special Counsellor to ensure full cooperation throughout the Executive branch with the investigations by Congress and the independent council.

Mistakes Will be Made

Napoleon Bonaparte once observed that, "Success in war is not with he who makes no mistakes, but with he who makes the fewest mistakes," and so it is with Presidents. Presidents will make mistakes, and perhaps the greatest test of character is how a President deals with the inevitable failures. The lesson for a President who has committed an ethical mistake is to talk it through with an outside advisor, don't cover up, get it all out and quickly.

But this lesson applies to decision-making in general, because, as Robert Strauss noted, people are disinclined to go against the grain in the Oval Office. A dominant Franklin Roosevelt preferred consensus, but how he dealt with and used General George Marshall to give a second judgement is a tremendous tribute to this great wartime President.

As a young general who had just arrived in Washington, Marshall was in a meeting with Roosevelt, who went around the room on a crucial matter expecting approval from his subordinates. He finally came to the newcomer. "George," said he, "I'm sure you agree." "No I don't, sir," responded the general. Everyone in the room thought that was the last of Marshall. To the contrary, it was the last time the President addressed him as George. Marshall wanted his formal rank used not because he was stuffy, but as a symbol of professionalism that was required to give uncolored judgment that was free of familiarity. So it was this man who challenged his judgement that Roosevelt made his chief of Army staff, and upon whom Roosevelt relied to organize the war victory.

Mr. President, you need your "Nancy Factor" and you need your George Marshalls, as best you can find them.

Another lesson in times of crisis is to take full responsibility. Don't say, "Mistakes were made," but rather "It's all my fault," as Kennedy said after the Bay of Pigs disaster. Remember General Eisenhower as Supreme Allied Commander who went into Normandy with a statement written out in case of failure. "It's all my fault," it read.

Reasons for Humility

A word of caution. Since World War II, some of the most able Presidents have experienced both great successes and great catastrophes. Lyndon Johnson used his uncanny ability to move an historic domestic agenda through Congress, as Michael Beschloss's case study explains. Yet that same President led us into the most tragic foreign war of attrition our country has ever experienced, and so tarnished a great legacy. Richard Nixon opened up China and re-balanced power globally (described in Peter Rodman's case study), yet the same man led us into the Watergate trauma. Ronald Reagan re-energized the nation and turned the tide of the Cold War, but the same man allowed the climate that led the to Iran-contra miasma. A talented Bill Clinton created coalitions to dominate the political center and to help foster a transition from budget deficits to an historical surplus. The same man also brought on the second impeachment in American history. These three tragic episodes are found in James Pfiffner's case studies.

It is important to recognize that good intentions don't count. Lyndon Johnson did not want to be the first President to lose a war, and he certainly did not want the war to interfere with his Great Society. Richard Nixon was trying to protect himself as the great peacemaker even as he had phones tapped and investigations blocked. Reagan was concerned about hostages and his freedom fighters, the contras. Clinton strove to protect his wife and daughter.

Leadership with Congress

The first test of Presidential leadership is with the Congress. On the one hand, both President Wilson in handling the Versailles Treaty (related in the case study by John Milton Cooper) and President Clinton in handling the Comprehensive Test Ban Treaty (Carl Cannon), two treaties with some flaws, made similar mistakes in their dealings with Congress, though these events took place nearly 80 years apart. On the other hand, the handling of the Marshall Plan, the original NATO Treaty, and the 1997 Balanced Budget Act are models of Executive-Legislative leadership successes as conveyed respectively by Larry Bland, Elizabeth Spaulding, and George Edwards.

An effective President maximizes his power and influence by reaching out to Congress and building coalitions. Justice Jackson said that, constitutionally, the power of the sovereign is maximized when the Legislative acts together with the Executive. This is not just a sound constitutional principle but the foundation of political strategy: A house divided cannot stand.

Balance this against the advice of the legal advisors who may say, "Don't give an inch, don't give away your power, and remember Article II, Section 2 of the Constitution." Woodrow Wilson didn't give away his power, but he failed to include Republicans in his negotiating delegation to Paris and he failed to reach across party lines in the Senate to obtain ratification of the Versailles Treaty, and so he lost. By contrast, the Marshall Plan, the NATO Treaty, and the Gulf War (James Kitfield) are all examples of power not given away, but gained.

Trust: the Coin of the Realm

The beginnings of building a united house come from Presidential trust. George Washington was consumed by a concern for the reputation of being a trustworthy man. President Eisenhower's superb Congressional liaison, Bryce Harlow (my mentor), offered this maxim, "Trust is the coin of the realm." Creating trust has to be a part of

Presidential leadership with Congress as well as overseas, and this trust can build influence and power.

Congress has sometimes been obstructionist and protectionist, preserving the past, not facing the future. Nonetheless, the new President must recognize that many of the reformist moves that helped the Chief Executive have come from the Congress. In defense, for example, the requirements of the Defense Department Quadrennial Defense Review, the National Defense Panel, the Rumsfeld Commission to Assess the Ballistic Missile Threat all came from Congress. In the previous decade, it was the Congressional Goldwater-Nichols Act that was responsible for giving General Norman Schwarzkopf the authority for a unified command that won the Gulf War. In trade, as Sherman Katz relates in his case study, the Office of the United States Trade Representative was an evolving creature of the Congress and yet added to Presidential negotiating power to open markets.

The President and His Team

But in the end, the President must lead. And to lead, he needs a team. He might start by upgrading his Congressional relations staff—a Bryce Harlow is worth his weight in gold. The new President needs a crack team of top Congressional liaison officers throughout the Executive branch. Remember, it is crucial to select a staff who has an ability to empathize with their contacts on the Hill, and who have stature. Dean Acheson and George Kennan were once Assistant Secretaries of State for Congressional Relations. Recruiting such talent and building teamwork with the departments is a critical aspect of the art of leadership.

But more importantly, a new President, as he assembles his staff, should re-study our first President. After all, the Constitution, especially Article II, Section 2, was written with George Washington in mind. Washington was a truly good chief executive, and, with extraordinary character and dependability, he deliberately built a Cabinet of people far more brilliant and creative than himself. They were people of different views and skills who would not have gotten along without Washington as their leader. Thomas Jefferson opposed the Constitution, but Washington brought this decentralizer into the fold. A brilliant Alexander Hamilton, a centralizer determined to revitalize the credit of the nation, had teamed up with James Madison, a checks and balances political philosopher, along with John Jay, a diplomat, to produce that extraordinary document, *The Federalist Papers*. Their *nom de plume* was the Roman, Publius. Washington captured this "Publius Effect" in his first Cabinet. Hamilton became Washington's Secretary of the Treasury, Jefferson, his Secretary of State, and Madison became the Administration's point man in the House of Representatives. But it was Washington's character that became the fulcrum for them all.

In the early Cold War period, plain-spoken Harry Truman also built a Cabinet of exceptional talent with his character as the unifier—with Marshall, Acheson, Lovett and even with Republican Herbert Hoover, who was brought in to head a commission in 1947 on the organization of the Executive Branch. This suggests not an intelligence quotient but an emotional quotient. Washington and Truman were comfortable with themselves. They harbored no inner demons and no jealousies or fears of being overshadowed. Hence, they could marshal those with greater creativity than themselves and, consequently, both were great institution builders. What better examples for the first President of the 21st Century? Build a magnificent Cabinet, and include the opposite party, as Roosevelt did with Republicans Knox and Stimson during World War II, and as Kennedy did with Republican Douglas Dillon at Treasury.

Right Person in the Right Job

Getting the right people is critically important. Not just selecting a talented man or woman, but matching the right person with the job. In crisis management, as related in case studies by Stephen Barr, President Clinton selected James Lee Witt to head FEMA and John Koskinen to head the Y2K Task Force and we were all spared catastrophes. Clinton showed his wisdom in selecting and constantly backing Robert Rubin, along with Alan Greenspan, on domestic and international finance. President Reagan had Washington-wise James Baker as his first chief of staff. This contrasts with his subsequent selection of Donald Regan, a man of corporate talent and an able Treasury Secretary who was miscast as the Chief of Staff. Jimmy Carter brought primarily Georgia outsiders to the White House and suffered from their inexperience with the peculiar world of Washington. In the Gulf War, George Bush was fortified by triple organizational abilities in Dick Cheney, Colin Powell, and Norman Schwarzkopf. Richard Nixon had Henry Kissinger as his invaluable partner in opening China and rebalancing world power. Great combinations of people in the White House and Cabinet can produce great results.

Discontinuity among policies from one Administration to the next can cause great waste, harm, and loss of opportunity. Consider the Superconducting Supercollider project conveyed in Anne Solomon's case study. After spending $2 billion, this $11 billion high-energy particle accelerator fell through the cracks between the Bush and Clinton Administrations. Because the next supercollider will not be built in the United States, we may lose a generation of expertise in the basic physical sciences—the stuff of which innovative economies increasingly are made. Our economy and national security rest on such innovations. The impact of such Presidential decisions as Kennedy's "man to the moon" (Ted Sorenson), and Clinton's Human Genome Project and Global Positioning System directives (Anne Solomon) are captured in these case studies.

Leadership with Values

These studies also show that it is not enough to be a leader; it is necessary to be a leader informed by values. The President's Cabinet and sub-cabinet can be instilled with the importance of leadership and values, just as these qualities are now taught at business schools, the military academies, and other centers of creative leadership. The Senior Executive Service, the military, and the Foreign Service need to be led in a way that magnifies creativity. We need a President-elect who will subject top appointees to several days' immersion into case studies and exercises in leadership and values. There has been much talk about the importance of this; it is now time to walk the walk.

There is certainly a continuing surge of challenges to Presidential leadership in our time. By the same token, revolutions in demography, finance, technology, and terrorism have combined to produce disarray and unpredictability in the post-Cold War world and to collapse the time available for decision-making while increasing serious chances for missteps. Short-term turnarounds can detract from long-range policies. For example, half of our national prosperity has been driven by past federal investment in basic research. Our capacity to control short-term political, military, terrorist, or financial crises will depend in future years upon our long-range investments in a scientific foundation and in our educational system. The case studies in this area indicate how often there has been a lack of continuity between Administrations, and sometimes a lack of vision for what it takes to grow an innovative society.

There has been remarkable Presidential continuity on trade policy. Opening worldwide markets becomes a strategic lever to build more orderly, more humane, and more democratic societies—if accompanied by equal efforts to strengthen the rule of law and to fight against corruption. But this can only succeed with a Congressional coalition, as was done with NAFTA. The new President must mount the bully pulpit to meet the challenges of globalization as his predecessors did.

An Array of Challenges

The next President is almost certain to face an international financial crisis. It is likely to be as large or even larger than the one Clinton and Rubin encountered in 1997-98. As Roy Smith's case study points out, daily average trading volume in foreign exchange markets now exceed $1.5 trillion in "funds that are capable of moving... far faster than the best prepared IMF-led interventionist effort could." He argues that the changeover of Administrations provides an unusual opportunity for new thinking on the roles and missions of the Fund and the crucial U.S. leadership role in it.

While these case studies make clear the importance of Presidential leadership to obtain Congressional backing, Sidney Weintraub's case study demonstrates where a President correctly acted unilaterally. Clinton had the leadership support of Majority Leader Dole and Speaker Gingrich to save Mexico from a financial crisis, but they could not gain sufficient support from their fellow members. Clinton's action with regard to the use of the Exchange Stabilization Fund was legally ambiguous. But the President's courageous action led to the economic stabilization of Mexico and limited the financial contagion. In extremis, the President was acting, in this swift-moving world of international finance, in a manner somewhat analogous to Article II, Section 2, of the Constitution on the role of the Commander in Chief. He needed what the authors of *The Federalist Papers* called "energy in the Executive," in this case, with or without the Congress or public.

What also complicates the nation's economic future is the way private sector advancements now leave the government far behind. As Henry Owen's study notes, people in leading positions in the U.S. private economy must be brought into an advisory system in order to strengthen our national government's decision-making.

Transformational Leadership

Clearly, the problems and opportunities facing the new President and the nation demand transformational solutions, not business as usual and tinkering at the margin. Historian James MacGregor Burns denotes two kinds of Presidents: transactional and transformational, the latter including President Lincoln and the two Roosevelts, who re-steered history and changed the nation. While he is not an advocate of Reagan's policies, Burns admits that Reagan had transformational qualities. Of course, transformational leadership demands both the Presidential qualities of communication and vision and a good match between the character of a President and the crises of a particular time and place in history.

The section on the "First 100 Days" is especially germane. As Lyndon Johnson once said about a new Presidency, "You've got to give it all you can, that first year. Doesn't matter what kind of majority you come in with. You've got just one year when they treat you right."

As Fred Greenstein and Robert Bowie relate in their respective studies that follow, Eisenhower used his initial period to reorganize the national security process to develop a "Long Haul" grand strategy for the Cold War. The new President should follow that example. A similar reorganization clearly needs to be done for the 21st Century since we coasted from the Cold War to the post-Cold War absent a coherent strategic vision of our national interests and security needs.

The 2000 Presidential campaign placed education, Social Security, and Medicare at the top of the national agenda. Michael Beschloss describes LBJ's remarkable domestic policy success after his election.

Lou Cannon conveys Reagan's skillful passage through Congress of his economic proposals while James MacGregor Burns recounts how Roosevelt improvised during his first 100 days, then planned his masterstrokes during a "second 100 days" in 1935 following a mid-term Congressional election.

Real Perils Ahead

But just as there are examples of a President achieving his promise, these also are examples of the perils—especially the perils of campaign promises—that haunt a new President. For example, President Carter, a former naval officer, promised during his campaign to withdraw troops from Korea, causing consternation in the Pacific. Kennedy, after a masterful inaugural speech, eliminated Eisenhower's national security system and stumbled into the Bay of Pigs disaster.

We move into the 21st Century, fortified in part by the surplus made possible by the end of a draining and dangerous Cold War, but also in need of institutional change. There is a widespread view that we are in an era of good feeling and a budget surplus, an era in which steady transactional or incremental leadership is sufficient.

But we live in a dangerous world. Today, the new President has a freedom of action both domestically and abroad that can rapidly erode. We are the preponderant power, the only superpower, but our greatness can be squandered in the absence of a coherent grand strategy. The information revolution brings promise as well as new perils. Our national security machinery has not been able to adequately anticipate and mold, rather than react to, the strategic environment; the machinery has not been configured for today's borderless but conflictual world. Our tendency to miscalculate and mis-communicate on the eves of conflict has persisted, as Samuel Williamson describes, from Korea to Iraq to Kosovo. Our homeland could now be in danger from miniaturized weapons of mass destruction as well as large intercontinental missiles. Already technology is spinning ahead of policy comprehension, and our commitment to basic research is waning while the digital divide grows wider. Problems in our inner cities will affect new generations, as education often languishes and children are left behind. An aging population unfortunately depends upon an inadequate and insecure Social Security and Medicare system. The times call for dynamic transformational leadership in these key areas.

Presidential History is Lived Forward

So, it is well for the new President to remember George Santayana's oft-repeated warning: Those who do not learn from history are condemned to repeat it. The Center for the Study of the Presidency began this initiative with one formidable goal in sight: to instill an institutional memory in the White House, not only for the President but also for the men and women of his Administration. From one Administration to the next, as papers are dispersed to Presidential Libraries, The National Archives, or The Library of Congress, our country suffers a flushing out of the "old" in favor of the "new" that causes more harm than good.

I personally was exposed to a dramatic case of White House memory failure. On December 26, 1986, while NATO Ambassador, I was phoned by the President and summoned to serve for three months as his Special Counselor to coordinate the White House response to the Iran-Contra investigations and, in effect, to "get everything out." The President had already set up the Tower Board to review the entire national security process as well as what went wrong. I realized how highly relevant was my three-year service on the Murphy Commission on the Organization of Government for Foreign Policy. Its membership was extremely prestigious with persons like Majority Leader Michael Mansfield and Vice President Nelson Rockefeller. When the Murphy Commission report was released, President Ford spoke of its value to future Presidents. So, a decade later, in my new job I asked the White House staff for their copy. And after a search, the response was "Don't have it, never heard of it." We and the authors of these case studies hope that the lessons of history assembled herein will not be lost, but heard.

In this endeavor we may appear to have set ourselves up as smart-aleck judges of the past. But, in fact, we even have some disagreements among authors. Certainly we recognize, with British historian C.V. Wedgwood, that "History is written backward but lived forward. Those who know the end of the story can never know what it was like at the time." With some humility, then, we offer a first attempt ever to outline for the new President-elect key historical lessons on the pitfalls of the Presidency and the opportunities to move towards transformational leadership. This document may not be perfect, for it was done under the pressures of time and Presidential campaign heat. But we have dared to try.

David Abshire

Election Day 2000

David Abshire is President of the Center for the Study of the Presidency in Washington, D.C. He is also co-founder, vice-chairman, and former CEO of the Center for Strategic and International Studies. In government he served on the staff of the House Minority Leader from 1958-1960; as Assistant Secretary of State for Congressional Relations, 1970-1972; member of the Murphy Commission on the Organization of Government in the Conduct of Foreign Policy, 1975; Chairman of the Board for International Broadcasting, 1974-1977; Ambassador to NATO, 1983-1987; and in the Cabinet as Special Counselor to President Reagan in 1987. A graduate of the United States Military Academy, he holds a Ph.D. in American History from Georgetown University. His books include Preventing World War III and The President vs. Congress.

John Milton Cooper — E. Gordon Fox Professor of American Institutions, University of Wisconsin, and author of *The Warrior and the Priest: Woodrow Wilson and Theodore Roosevelt* and the forthcoming *Breaking the Heart of the World: Woodrow Wilson and the Fight Over the League of Nations*

Robert Dallek — Professor of History, University of California, Los Angeles and author of *The American Style of Foreign Policy: Cultural Politics and Foreign Affairs*; *Ronald Reagan: The Politics of Symbolism;* and *Lone Star Rising: Lyndon Johnson and His Times, 1908-1960*

I.M. Destler — Director, Center for International and Security Studies, University of Maryland, author of *Making Foreign Economic Policy*, and co-author of *Our Own Worst Enemy: The Unmaking of American Foreign Policy*

Edwin Dorn — Dean, LBJ School of Public Affairs, University of Texas and author of *After the Zero Option: Now That Reagan and Gorbachev Have Agreed, What Happens Next?*

George C. Edwards III — Director, The Center for Presidential Studies and Jordan Professor of Liberal Arts, Texas A&M University, Editor, *Presidential Studies Quarterly,* and author of *Presidential Leadership: Politics and Policy Making*

Alvin Felzenberg — Visiting Fellow, Heritage Foundation, former Staff Director of the Empowerment Subcommittee (House Small Business Committee), staff member on the District of Columbia Subcommittee (House Government Reform Committee), and co-author of *Evolution of the Modern Presidency*

John Lewis Gaddis — Robert A. Lovett Professor of Military and Naval History, Yale University and author of *The United States and the End of the Cold War: Implications, Reconsiderations, Provocations* and historical consultant for CNN's "Cold War" series

Doris Kearns Goodwin — Former Professor, Harvard University and Pulitzer Prize-winning Presidential biographer and author of *No Ordinary Time: Franklin and Eleanor Roosevelt: The Homefront in World War II*

Matthew Holden — Henry L. and Grace M. Doherty Professor of Government and Foreign Affairs, University of Virginia, author of *Continuity and Disputation: Essays in Public Administration*, and former President, American Political Science Association

Thomas Mann — Averell Harriman Senior Fellow in American Governance, The Brookings Institution, former Director of Governmental Studies at Brookings, Executive Director, American Political Science Association, and Fellow, American Academy of Arts and Sciences, National Academy of Public Administration

Norman Ornstein — Resident Scholar, American Enterprise Institute for Public Policy Research, Director of the Transition to Governing Project, election analyst for *CBS News*, and former Co-Director of the Renewing Congress Project

Roger Porter — Director, Center for Business and Government, John F. Kennedy School of Government, Harvard University and author of *Presidential Decision-Making: The Economic Policy Board*

Stephen Skowronek — Professor of Political and Social Science, Yale University and author of *The Politics Presidents Make: Leadership from John Adams to Bill Clinton*

Richard Solomon — President of the U.S. Institute of Peace, former Assistant Secretary of State for Asian and Pacific Affairs (1992-93), Director of Policy Planning at the State Department (1986-89), senior staff member on the National Security Council (1971-76), and head of the Social Science Department at the RAND Corporation

Shirley Anne Warshaw — Professor of Political Science, Gettysburg College and author of *The Keys to Power: Managing the Presidency*

In early 2000, the Center for the Study of the Presidency (CSP) formed a Council of eminent scholars, for advice and participation in its programs and, later, to promote interactions among themselves on issues and the history of the Presidency. At about the same time, CSP initiated this novel project, a *Report to the President-Elect 2000*, with case studies on Presidential successes and failures with lessons learned. Many Council members have offered advice for authors and some have prepared case studies themselves, and for this we are deeply grateful.

The views expressed in the case studies are, of course, those of the authors and in certain cases authors may not fully agree with each other.

In all cases, authors have worked diligently to produce short studies on cases on which they have written books and articles before. Without this devotion to this project by nearly 60 individuals, *The Report* would not have been possible.

EDITORIAL STAFF

TABLE OF CONTENTS

TABLE OF CONTENTS (Continued)

I. COMMON THREADS AND
LESSONS LEARNED

COMMON THREADS AND
LESSONS LEARNED

"The First One-Hundred Days"
of an Administration

George C. Edwards III
Author of *Presidential Leadership: Politics and Policy Making*

The early months of a new Presidency represent the most important period for establishing the tone and character of the White House's relationship with Congress. It is the time of closest scrutiny and the greatest vulnerability to making major mistakes. Taking the right steps early and avoiding errors can lay the foundation for a productive working relationship. Actions taken early create lasting impressions. According to Max Friedersdorf, the "enemies and mistakes made in the first week will dog a President throughout his term in office." Stuart Eizenstat adds, "I don't think Carter's image ever recovered from some of those early mistakes."

There are four strategic lessons that stand out from examining Presidential transitions since the 1930s:

▶ Understanding Your Strategic Position;

▶ Moving Rapidly;

▶ Setting Priorities; and

▶ Establishing Relationships on Capitol Hill.

Understanding Your Strategic Position

A President must largely play with the hand that the public deals him through its electoral decisions (both Presidential and Congressional) and its evaluations of the Chief Executive's handling of his job. A President is rarely in a position to augment substantially his resources, especially when just taking office.

The first step a new Administration should take to ensure success with Congress is to accurately assess its strategic position so it understands the potential for change. The early periods of the new Administrations that are most clearly etched on our memories as notable successes were those in which Presidents properly identified and exploited conditions for change.

When Congress first met in special session in March 1933 after Franklin D. Roosevelt's inauguration, it rapidly passed, at the new President's request, bills to control the resumption of banking, repeal Prohibition, and effect government economies. This is all FDR originally planned for Congress to do. He expected to reassemble Congress when permanent and more constructive legislation was ready. Yet the President found a situation ripe for change. As James MacGregor Burns described it, "adulation for Roosevelt was sweeping the country." FDR decided to exploit this favorable environment and strike repeatedly with hastily drawn legislation before sending Congress home. This period of intense activity came to be known as the "100 Days."

Lyndon B. Johnson also knew that his personal leadership could not sustain Congressional support for his policies. He had to exploit the opportunities provided by the assassination of President John F. Kennedy and the election of 1964. He told an aide early in his Presidency, "I keep hitting hard because I know this honeymoon won't last. Every day I lose a little more political capital." In February 1965, after his landslide victory, Johnson assembled the Congressional liaison officials from the various departments and told them that his victory at the polls "might be more of a loophole than a mandate," and that they would have to use his popularity to their advantage while it lasted.

The Administration of President Ronald Reagan realized from the beginning that it had an opportunity to effect major changes in public policy, but that it had to concentrate its focus and move quickly before the environment became less favorable. The President and his staff moved rapidly in 1981 to exploit the perceptions of a mandate and the dramatic elevation of Republicans to majority status in the Senate. Moreover, within a week of the March 30 assassination attempt, deputy chief of staff, Michael Deaver convened a meeting of other high-ranking aides at the White House to determine how best to take advantage of the new political capital the assassination attempt had created.

If the White House misreads its strategic positions, the President may begin his tenure with embarrassing failures in dealing with Congress. For example, Bill Clinton overestimated the extent of change that a President elected with a minority of the vote could make. Any President elected with only 43 percent of the vote should not expect to pass far-reaching social legislation without involving the other party, especially when the public is dubious and well-organized interest groups are fervently opposed. A partisan approach was unlikely to succeed; yet this is the strategy President Clinton adopted. For example, the "us against them" approach to policy making encouraged the President to develop his health care plan in Democrats-only secrecy and to pursue a left-in coalition building strategy instead of a center-out one. Failure was inevitable.

Moreover, the greater the breadth and complexity of the policy change a President proposes, the more opposition it is likely to engen-der—and thus the stronger the President's strategic position must be to succeed. In an era when a few opponents can effectively tie up bills, the odds are clearly against the White House. Yet despite his weak under-pinnings, when it came to health care reform—the centerpiece of his Presidency—Clinton proposed perhaps the most sweeping, complex pre-scriptions for controlling the conduct of state governments, employers, drug manufacturers, doctors, hospitals, and individuals in American history. The foundation was lacking for change of this magnitude.

Moving Rapidly

It is not enough for a President to recognize the opportunities in his environment. To succeed with Congress, he must also move rapidly to exploit those opportunities. As Lyndon Johnson put it, "You've got just one year when they treat you right and before they start worrying about themselves." It is also to the advantage of a President if he is ready to replace enacted requests with additional items of his legislative program. In other words, it is best to keep Congress concentrating on the President's proposals.

Kennedy, Johnson, Reagan (and to some extent Jimmy Carter) took advantage of the opportunities provided by the "honeymoon," whereas Eisenhower, Nixon, Bush, and (in important ways) Clinton did not. Further, most Presidents are not ready with a second wave of proposals. The exception, as one might expect, was Lyndon Johnson.

First-year proposals have a better chance of passing Congress than do those sent to the Hill later in an Administration. Thus, the White House should be ready to send its priority legislation to Capitol Hill, and the transition period becomes especially crucial for drafting legislation. The more complex the policy proposal, the more important it is to begin developing it as soon as possible. An organizational structure for drafting the first year's priority legislation should be established before the election, and the President's transition team should begin the drafting of priority legislation as soon as possible following the election.

Although the prospects of passage are enhanced if legislation moves quickly, there are good reasons why many Presidents are not able to ensure that it does. For example, Jimmy Carter's proposals for energy, welfare reform, and the containment of hospital costs were complex and controversial policies that took a long time to draft and to clear relevant offices in the White House. Carter could not turn to a well-established party program as Kennedy and Johnson could. Bill Clinton's health care reform proposal faced similar obstacles.

There is of course an alternative to the methodical, time-consuming drafting of legislation. The President might choose simply to propose a policy without thorough analysis to exploit the favorable political climate of his honeymoon. This appears to have been the strategy of Reagan's White House regarding the budget cuts passed by Congress in 1981. According to Budget Director David Stockman, "None of us really understands what's going on with all these numbers." Although the strategy of "move it or lose it" may increase the probability of a bill's passage and not affront the sensibilities of someone with Ronald Reagan's lack of concern for details, it is not difficult to understand why someone with the temperament of Jimmy Carter may eschew such a process.

Nevertheless, the failure to use the transition period to prepare priority legislation can be costly. A policy vacuum existed in the approx-imately 10 months between Bill Clinton's inauguration and the arrival of a complete health care reform proposal on Capitol Hill. In this vacu-um, issues of relatively low priority such as gays in the military received disproportionate attention in the press and may have cost the Administration vital goodwill that it would need in its search for support for its cornerstone policy. In addition, the President was forced to raise health care reform in the context of major expenditures of political cap-ital in battles on behalf of his budget and the North American Free Trade Agreement (NAFTA).

Setting Priorities

It is best for a new President to resist the temptation to try to deliver on all of his campaign promises immediately following the elec-tion and to accede to the many demands that are made on a new Administration. Instead, it is important to establish priorities among legislative proposals. In addition, because the Washington community pays disproportionate attention to the first major legislative initiatives, it is especially critical to choose early battles wisely.

If the President is not able to focus Congress's attention on his pri-ority programs, the bills may become lost in the complex and overloaded legislative process. Congress needs time to digest what the President sends, to engage in independent analyses, and to schedule hearings and markups. Unless the President clarifies his priorities, Congress may put the proposals in a queue as they are put forward. It is also wise to spread legislative proposals among Congressional committees so that different committees can be working on different parts of the President's agenda at the same time.

Setting priorities is also important because a President and his staff can lobby effectively for only a few bills at a time. The President's political capital is inevitably limited, and it is sensible to focus it on the issues he cares about most. Otherwise this precious resource might be wasted, as it was in 1981 when Jimmy Carter "spent his political capital to a deficit on pork barrel projects," which were not among his priorities.

President Carter has been widely criticized for having failed to set legislative priorities, especially in light of the scale, diversity, complexi-ty, and controversial nature of his initial legislative program. He actual-ly proposed about the same percentage of new and large programs as Kennedy and Johnson and fewer new programs overall than Johnson. Yet Carter's critics argue that his failure to rank his legislative propos-als made his legislative program seem larger than it was. This problem was aggravated because so many aspects of his program, including ener-gy, tax and welfare reform, health insurance, and the financing of Social Security, fell within the jurisdiction of the House Ways and Means Committee and the Senate Finance Committee. Without guidance on priorities, the proposals clogged the pipeline and stretched Carter's prestige too thin. As the President's chief of Congressional liaison put it, "We overloaded the circuits and blew a fuse."

On the other hand, in the early Reagan Administration the White House knew it lacked the political capital to pass a broad program that would include divisive social issues. Thus, it enforced a rigorous focus on the President's economic plan, its priority legislation. As James Baker put it, "We drafted a hundred-day plan and we stuck to it." By focusing its resources on its priorities, the Administration succeeded in using the budget to pass sweeping changes in taxation and defense policy.

It is especially important to set priorities in the early weeks of a new Administration because the first year in office is the period when the President will have the greatest latitude in focusing on priority legislation. After the transition period, other interests have more influence on the White House agenda. The White House can put off dealing with the full spectrum of national issues for several months at the beginning of a new President's term, but it cannot do so for four years—eventually it must make decisions. By the second year, the agenda is full and more policies are in the pipeline as the Administration attempts to satisfy its constituencies and responds to unanticipated or simply overlooked problems.

In addition, the President himself will inevitably be a distraction from his own priorities. There are so many demands on the President to speak, appear, and attend meetings that it is impossible to organize his schedule for very long around his major goals, especially if he has been in office for a while. Finally, Congress is quite capable of setting its own agenda. The public expects Congress to take the initiative, and Members of Congress have strong electoral incentives to respond.

Setting priorities early also can save a great deal of energy in the hectic early months of a new Presidency. "Everybody who came in knew where he stood," David Gergen said about the White House staff who came in to work for President Reagan. "There were no struggles over the soul of the Administration, over the overall direction."

Setting priorities is considerably easier for a President with a short legislative agenda, such as Ronald Reagan, than it is for one with a more ambitious agenda. It is also an advantage if the opposition party is in disarray and lacks alternatives to the President's agenda, a situation enjoyed by the Republicans in 1981 as the Democrats reeled from Reagan's electoral victory and their loss of the Senate.

Establishing Relationships on Capitol Hill

A crucial aspect of a successful strategic plan is a comfortable working relationship with those on the Hill. The Administrations that have been successful have been ones that worked closely with the Congress from its earliest time. Appointing people familiar with Congressional operations to the White House legislative liaison operation and ensuring that Administration officials are acceptable to Congressional leaders is vital.

Consulting with legislators is one of the surest means of demonstrating respect for Congress and building bridges to it. The failure to consult can be a serious irritant to Members of Congress. Jimmy Carter, for example, was criticized by many for his failure to consult with Congress, including Congressional leaders, on some of his most important legislative initiatives. That his plan for a national energy policy came as a surprise to Members of Congress delayed its consideration and affected the final form of the legislation.

Much of this consultation may take the form of touching base with Congressional leaders on the general outlines of legislation and providing advance warning of impending proposals. Such action is likely to generate goodwill and aid in gauging levels of support and in anticipating Congressional objections. It may be possible to preempt some of the opposition with strategic compromises.

Members of Congress appreciate advanced warning of Presidential proposals, especially those that affect their constituencies directly. No official, especially an elected one, wants to be blindsided. Politicians quite naturally want to be prepared to take credit or avoid blame. Moreover, when a policy fails, Members of Congress are unlikely to support the President in the perilous landing if they have not been involved in the take-off of the policy. They also have pride in their work and may be offended if they feel the White House has not taken them seriously.

Naturally, it is easier to consult with and accommodate Members of Congress in a context of consensus than in the more typical contemporary environment of polarization. Yet in times of controversy and conflict regular and open communication is especially important. Although consultation does not guarantee success, during normal times there is little chance of smooth relations with Congress without it. In periods of emergency the President has more leeway, but even then involving Congressional party and committee leaders early can mute and delay potential opposition.

It is also useful for the leader of the White House Congressional liaison office to be involved in choosing or at least clearing the heads of the Congressional liaison teams at the various departments. The chief of the White House legislative liaison team should meet regularly with the department liaison officials, keeping them informed of the President's priorities and heading off agency proposals that the President opposes. This increases the probability of the White House keeping the departments working on its programs and successfully orchestrating the Administration's Congressional relations.

To operate effectively, the chief of the White House Congressional relations office must have direct access to the President. It is essential that Members of Congress know that the head speaks for the President. Other White House aides should channel communications from Congress through him to discourage end runs. Moreover, the chief's status is of symbolic importance to Congress. It reflects the importance the President places on Congressional relations. An office in the West Wing is an eloquent indicator of this.

Executive-Legislative Relations

By James P. Pfiffner
Author of *The Strategic Presidency: Hitting the Ground Running*

The Framers of the Constitution through the separation of powers system ensured that the President and Congress would be vying for control of public policy. So it is unusual for there to be smooth working relations between the two branches. In modern times there have been three exceptional periods in which the President was able to lead Congress and convince its Members to enact much of his legislative agenda: 1933, 1965, and 1981. Immediately after his inauguration, Franklin D. Roosevelt was able to get much of his initial New Deal policies enacted by an overwhelmingly Democratic Congress. In 1965, after being elected in his own right, Lyndon B. Johnson guided through Congress a large number of laws that were part of his "Great Society" efforts. Finally, in 1981 President Ronald Reagan was able to convince a Democratic House to go along with him and the Republican Senate to enact many of his economic policies, including tax and spending cuts and increases in military spending. But it is striking that after these initial victories, Executive-Legislative relations returned to normal, and each of these Presidents was much less successful than he had been in his early months in office.

In the second half of the 20th century a new challenge was added to the separation of powers system with the increasingly common presence of divided government, that is, when one political party controls the Presidency, and the other controls one or both houses of Congress. From 1897 to 1954 divided government occurred only 14 percent of the time, but from 1981 to 2001 it occurred about 90 percent of the time, with a unified government only from 1993 to 1995. Thus Executive-Legislative relations is particularly challenging in the contemporary era. This does not mean that good legislation is not passed, but it does mean that cooperation between the branches is only occasionally successful, as illustrated in the cases in this section.

The failure of a President to deal effectively with Congress is illustrated by the defeat of the Versailles Treaty by the Senate. The treaty was rejected in part because President Woodrow Wilson did not take the care to consult with influential Senators, include them in his planning, or take seriously into account their problems with the treaty that he negotiated. In contrast to Wilson's failure was President Harry S. Truman's ability to win ratification of the treaty establishing the North Atlantic Treaty Organization in 1949. Truman did this with a careful bipartisan approach that included close cooperation with Senator Arthur Vandenberg. Vandenberg argued in a famous quote that partisan politics should stop "at the water's edge." Truman's leadership paved the way for a Cold War policy that was eventually successful for the United States.

Although there are many differences between the two cases, President Lyndon B. Johnson's victory with the 1964 Civil Rights Act and Bill Clinton's failure with his health care reform proposals can be explained by the relationship of the two Presidents to Congress. Johnson had spent years in

Congress and paid close attention to the legislative tactics involved. Clinton developed his health care reform plan mostly within the Executive Branch before presenting it to Congress. Johnson was willing to share credit for the civil rights law with Republicans, especially Senate Minority Leader Everett Dirksen of Illinois. Republicans resolved not to cooperate with Clinton on his health care proposals and to defeat any Administration plan. Johnson ended up with one of his most significant victories, and Clinton was faced with one of his greatest defeats.

But more important than the legislative tactics in these two cases was the difference in the relations between Congress and the President in the two different eras. In Johnson's case the Democrats controlled both houses of Congress, but more importantly the country was ready for a change in civil rights policy. Johnson used that, along with the assassination of President John F. Kennedy to argue that the time was ripe for a change. Clinton also enjoyed unified Democratic control of the government, but the Democrats were not united behind any one solution to the health care problem. The fact that Clinton had been elected with only 43 percent of the vote and enjoyed only moderate public approval ratings was also pertinent. In addition, while most Americans thought health care reform was important, there was no public consensus about how to reform it. The Clinton plan was very complex and called for large changes in the way health care was financed, and the country was not ready for large-scale changes in the health care financing system. During the same 103rd Congress, President Clinton was able to claim a victory with his deficit reduction package in his first budget, but he had to do it with no Republican votes.

The best position for a President to be in is to have large majorities of his own party controlling Congress when he sends his legislative proposals to the Hill, as happened in the first days of the New Deal and Great Society. But if a policy issue is put in the right framework and a President is willing to negotiate with Congress, success is possible. The Marshall Plan was an impressive effort on the part of both parties to assure the economic recovery of Europe after World War II.

In 1986 President Reagan again was able to win passage of an important tax bill even though the House was controlled by Democrats. He backed a tax reform initiative that would close loopholes at the same time it reduced income tax rates. At first, it seemed that the bill would be killed by the many interest groups that lobbied for the tax provisions that favored them. But President Reagan insisted on persevering in closing the loopholes and reducing rates. Similar proposals had been made by Democrats, and when it appeared that the Administration bill had a chance of being passed, it picked up Democratic support in Congress. Despite the difficult politics, Democrats wanted to be able also to share credit for a tax policy reform that economists of both parties had favored for a long time. When the bill passed against great odds, both parties declared victory, and the tax code was greatly simplified. Similarly, President Clinton was able to cooperate with the Republican Congress in 1996 in order to pass the balanced budget bill that gave the United States its first balanced budget since 1969. Only compromises by both sides and a willingness to share credit allowed this important breakthrough to occur.

In sum, the lessons learned from these cases of Executive-Legislative relations demonstrate that, despite the separation of powers structure and divided government, impressive advances in public policy can be achieved. But it takes a willingness to reach across party lines and share credit for victories.

Domestic Policy

By James P. Pfiffner

Although the President is often able to set the agenda and control the execution of foreign and national security policy, domestic policy is the realm of Congress—and Congress is much more assertive about its constitutional prerogatives in the domestic arena. Thus a President must work closely with Congress on policy issues, but he must also be an effective manager of the Executive Branch implementing domestic policy. This sometimes calls for the President to take direct control in crisis situations.

In the creation of the Environmental Protection Agency (EPA), President Richard M. Nixon recognized that there was a large-scale swelling of support for cleaning up the environment. Both sides of the political spectrum agreed that something had to be done, and the President had to decide what approach he would back for confronting the problem of environmental pollution. Nixon opted for a focused approach rather than to propose a large-scale reorganization of Executive Branch agencies into a new Department of Environmental and Natural Resources. The main reason was that Congress has always been vitally concerned with the organization of the Executive Branch, since committee jurisdictions—and thus individual power in Congress—have been closely connected to the Executive Branch. Nixon was able to compromise with the Democratic Congress on a plan to create EPA as an independent agency rather than as a broad-based department.

The issues of Presidential leadership and budgetary constraint played important roles in two cases of mixed success: the superconducting super-collider (SSC) and the international space station. Each of these was a large-scale project costing billions of dollars that stretched over several Administrations. There were compelling scientific arguments for each project and initial Presidential support, but each got derailed over increasing cost projections. President Ronald Reagan supported the building of the SSC, but by 1993 the cost projections had increased significantly and Congressional support had eroded enough to cancel the project. In the case of the space station, the Reagan and Bush Administrations supported its planning and construction. But by 1993 the costs had escalated and Congressional support had eroded enough to scale back its funding to the point where its scientific value was in question.

The lessons to be drawn are that large-scale scientific enterprises need strong Presidential support across Administrations and through times of budget constraint (deficit reduction was a major priority in 1993). But for Presidential support to hold across parties, the coalition in favor of the project has to extend to both sides of the aisle in Congress. These drawbacks were avoided by John F. Kennedy's initiative to put a man on the moon within a decade. He developed bipartisan support for the Apollo program in Congress. So did President Dwight D. Eisenhower in his proposal for the interstate highway system. Both of these cases show how large, costly scientific and infrastructure programs can be successful. The Human Genome Project teaches us that coordination with Congress and the settling of bureaucratic turf fights within the Executive Branch can also be crucial to success.

The case of domestic crisis with a high potential for violence presents some clear lessons about crisis management for Presidents. Often a crisis is provoked by a group with grievances whose interests may stretch beyond the immediate circumstances of the situation. The group may make demands that are not possible to meet realistically, and their actions may be, in fact, illegal. But the lessons of avoiding bloodshed from these cases are that Presidents must be patient and not give in to government officials' demands for immediate action that might easily result in violence. It is often better to give the aggrieved group a full hearing and be willing to grant some of their demands insofar as they have legitimate complaints. In addition, the President may have to take personal control of the situation and make his policy decisions clear so that subordinates do not act precipitously.

President Gerald R. Ford's pardon of President Nixon illustrates the lesson that a President can exercise his constitutional powers, but he should prepare the public for his decision carefully. In the long run, Ford's pardon seems to have been wise, but in the short run it hurt him politically, in part because he did not prepare the public carefully for his decision.

Fiscal Policy and International Economics

By James P. Pfiffner

It is the conventional wisdom in Washington that with divided government—that is, with one party controlling the Presidency and the other party controlling one or both houses of Congress—important policy advances are impossible. Although it is true that divided government makes legislating more difficult, there are several examples of cooperation between the branches and across party lines that produced important breakthroughs in public policy. It is not easy, but it is possible.

In 1983 the Social Security trust fund was running out of money in the short term, and the possibility of default on payments was real if nothing was done. Although both parties recognized the impending crisis and the urgency for some solution, they were not able to agree on what to do.

Democrats, who controlled the House and were led by Speaker Thomas P. (Tip) O'Neill, were dead set against any cut in benefits, while the Republicans (led by President Ronald Reagan) were adamantly opposed to any increase in taxes. President Reagan appointed a blue ribbon commission headed by Alan Greenspan. The Greenspan Commission was able to come up with a compromise solution that included both raising taxes and cutting benefits. But the key to the solution was the willingness of the leaders of both parties to support the compromise and therefore give political cover to members of each of their parties.

In this case the willingness to compromise, share credit, and bargain in good faith was key to policy success across partisan lines—and the public interest was served. In the case of the Mexican bailout, the kind of cooperation in Congress that made resolution of the 1983 Social Security problem possible was not forthcoming, despite the support of Congressional leadership for President Bill Clinton's proposal. So Clinton was forced to shift funds within the authority of the Executive Branch. This was not the optimal solution, but it was necessary for the policy to succeed. When the gambit was successful in restoring confidence in the Mexican economy, the funds were paid back to the United States. If the policy had not been successful, the Administration would have been severely criticized. A better solution would have included support from Members of Congress of both parties, although such support may have been impossible, given the political circumstances.

In the cases involving trade relations with Japan and the International Monetary Fund, optimal policies are not immediately obvious. Perhaps one of the lessons here is that Presidents need to build on past successes in policy and to be clear about U.S. interests. But they need also to realize that small-scale steps may be preferable to attempts at large-scale policy change. It is clear that the United States has a large stake in the fiscal health of Japan, and the President must assure the Japanese that we are fully engaged, when it is appropriate, with assisting Japan to come out of its recession.

One of the important functions of the White House staff is to present the President with alternative policy options so that the most informed decisions can be made. Thus policy development structures in the White House can play crucial roles. For economic policy, both the Economic Policy Board in the Ford Administration and the National Economic Council in the Clinton Administration provide useful models of how to advise the President. The key is for any such structure to ensure that all important bases have been touched in advising the President on important policy choices. In order for this to happen it is useful to have a staff director who is a neutral broker, so that all affected parts of the Administration will have confidence that their perspectives will be presented to the President.

Thus the lessons from the following cases are that Presidents need carefully balanced advice from their White House staffs, and that they need to be willing to share credit with Congress and across party lines if they want to achieve victories in contentious areas of public policy.

National Security Institutions and Decision Making

By James P. Pfiffner

The creation of the North Atlantic Treaty Organization (NATO) was based on the need for collective security in the wake of World War II and the expansive foreign policy objectives of the Soviet Union. But by 1967 Western nations had a growing desire for increasing scientific, cultural, and financial interactions with the Soviets. The problem was how to achieve these positive developments without sacrificing the necessary national security purposes of the alliance. The Harmel Report was a useful way to consider formally both sides of the issue and assure to all members of the alliance that both detente and national security goals could be approached simultaneously.

The expansion of NATO in the late 1990s, however, did not undergo the same level of international negotiation or internal debate as the organization's creation did a half-century before. Although the outcome was positive for the new members of NATO—Poland, Hungary, and the Czech Republic—the reaction of Russia was negative and may have long-term consequences. President Bill Clinton was faced with reassuring Russia and at the same time reassuring NATO allies that the new alliance would be ready for the post-Cold War world.

The newly expanded NATO was able to act in Bosnia, but the future implications for the alliance are not fully clear. Will there be pressure for the entrance of other members who might not be as capable as present members of fulfilling their obligations? What will be the financial and military implications to the United States if new members cannot fulfill their obligations? Multinational alliances are inherently unstable and constant attention must be paid to assure their continued viability. The lessons from our experience with NATO are that continued vitality of alliances is possible, but that major changes have to be approached carefully.

The lessons from the Commissions on the MX missile basing mode (the Scowcroft Commission) and the U.S. policy toward Central America (the Kissinger Commission) are that it is possible to use commissions to resolve difficult partisan disagreements about policy. The necessary ingredients for success include a prominent and widely esteemed chair who can command respect from both political parties. In addition, both parties must be represented on the commission by members who are open to compromise. Third, any major policy issue must take into account Congressional concerns through close consultations. The other major lesson is that if bipartisan approaches and close consultation with Congress are undertaken in the early stages of policy development, there may be no need for a blue ribbon commission to fix a policy that is unacceptable to major interests because their concerns would have been factored in from the beginning.

Presidents have many Executive Branch institutions at their disposal for effective policy making. Even though Congress created the Office of U.S. Trade Representative (USTR) without a request from a President, holders of the Oval Office have taken advantage of the USTR for coordinating U.S. trade policy across the major departments of the Executive Branch. The United States Information Agency has served an important function in international public diplomacy. Its new institutional location in the State Department should not change that historic mission.

The final lesson from this section is that the internal policy making process in the White House and Executive Branch must be deliberate and orderly. President Dwight D. Eisenhower established such a procedure early in his Administration and insisted that all sides of important national security issues be presented to him during decision making. The absence of such a process contributed to President Kennedy's mistakes at the Bay of Pigs and President Johnson's decision to escalate the war in Vietnam. Kennedy's handling of the Cuban Missile Crisis was effective, but it was ad hoc—that is, developed for that crisis rather than being built into an ongoing process for making national security decisions. Presidents also have miscalculated in the cases of Korea in 1950, Iraq in 1990, and Kosovo in 1998-1999. Skepticism and the ability to see a problem from the point of view of our adversaries can help alleviate such miscalculations.

Foreign Interventions and Interactions

By James P. Pfiffner

There are some important lessons to be learned from U.S. interventions in foreign countries, both military and civil. Most importantly, Presidents must be carefully prepared for decision making by thorough staff work. The Bay of Pigs invasion is an example of a President making a fateful decision under the assumption that the plans were fully examined for workability. In fact, the invasion plans had been developed in such secrecy that they had not been analyzed by military professionals. In addition, the assumptions about internal political conditions in Cuba (that is, that Cubans would rise up against Fidel Castro) were wildly unrealistic and not based on hard intelligence.

President Kennedy learned the lessons of the Bay of Pigs and took a much different approach to the Cuban Missile Crisis of October 1962. He was able to successfully avoid nuclear war because of his insistence on careful and thorough staff work, despite the need for the utmost secrecy. Kennedy ensured that all options were aired and considered. He did not act precipitously by taking quick military action but allowed Soviet Premier Nikita Khrushchev time to reevaluate his actions. Kennedy also provided flexibility so that Khrushchev could save face rather than forcing him into a corner in which he might have been tempted to strike out in order not to be embarrassed.

The need for consistency and decisiveness is illustrated by Nixon's opening to China and his orchestration of the reversion of Okinawa to

Japan. The timing of the opening to China had to be kept secret in order to avoid domestic and international attempts to derail the historic diplomatic initiative. But the way had to be prepared by convincing the Chinese that Nixon was serious about a softening of relations, so unilateral signals were sent to China. The international situation, especially relations between the Soviet Union and China were ripe, and the President was able to take advantage of the timing. Once the opening was made, Nixon had to move quickly to reassure U.S. allies in Asia as well as domestic political supporters that their interests would not be abandoned.

The situation in Okinawa was different in that there was building public pressure in Japan for the return of sovereignty over the island that the United States had been using as a military base since the end of World War II. The base had become essential to American war efforts in Vietnam and to the ability to resupply U.S. forces throughout the Pacific region. Thus the American military leadership had to be reassured that its ability to carry out military missions would not be sacrificed in pleasing Japan. Through a series of negotiations, depending heavily on professional diplomatic emissaries to Japan, Nixon was able to construct an acceptable compromise involving U.S. use of Okinawa as a military base but return of the island to Japanese sovereignty. It also included an expected concession on textiles and a secret side-agreement that the United States could base nuclear weapons there in an emergency. Despite the ambiguous dimensions to the agreement, the major issues were settled between the two allies.

The problems of indecisiveness and lack of clear policy direction are illustrated by the U.S. interventions in Lebanon and Panama. In 1982 President Ronald Reagan sent U.S. forces to Lebanon as neutral peace-keepers, which was appropriate at the time. But over the next year the internal balance of power in Lebanon changed and America found itself in the middle of an escalating war around Beirut. At this time the United States should have decided that it was important to leave U.S. forces in the area and therefore reinforced them to reflect the new military risks involved, or it should have decided that any U.S. interest was not worth military risks and withdrawn the forces. Advice to the President was split between the Departments of State and Defense, and President Reagan refused to choose between the two. Thus U.S. forces were left in the area and were vulnerable to the terrorist bombing that killed several hundred Marines. Similarly, the unsuccessful U.S. intervention in Somalia made the United States more skeptical about the ability of military force to solve bitter internal disputes in foreign nations.

In the Panama crisis of 1989 different parts of the U.S. government did not agree about the need to oust dictator General Manuel Noriega. Thus mixed signals were sent, and Noriega resolved to stay in power as long as he could. Noriega and other forces in Panama were not convinced of American backing if they attempted to overthrow Noriega. In addition, the indictment of Noriega by U.S. attorneys was not foreseen by other American policy makers and further convinced Noriega that he could stay in power. Finally, military invasion by the United States became the only way to bring about Noriega's departure from office.

Often it is perceived that decisions made in international relations depend on the strategic interests and the relative power of the nations involved. But in some cases the personal relationships between leaders can make an important difference. Such was the case with President Reagan's relationship with Japan Prime Minister Yasuhiro Nakasone in the contentious area of trade relations between the two countries. But even more importantly, the Reagan-Gorbachev relationship eased the end of the Cold War and the transition of the Soviet Union to a more democratic state.

These cases point to some lessons for the future President. Careful and deliberate advisory systems must be devised and used by the President. There is no substitute for good staff work that fully examines all reasonable options and skeptically evaluates alternative courses of action. But action must also be timely. The President needs to make clear decisions in time to take successful action. Once a decision has been made, clear signals must be sent to allies and adversaries so that U.S. resolve is not in question. But flexibility and compromise with foreign nations is also necessary, as demonstrated in the Cuban Missile Crisis, the opening to China, and the reversion of Okinawa to Japan.

Managing the Executive Branch

By James P. Pfiffner

The Presidency is preeminently a position of political leadership for the nation, where broad visions of the future are shaped into policy agendas that are enacted by Congress and signed into law by the President. Political leadership often obscures the importance of management to the Presidency. Some argue that Presidents have so many important functions to perform that they should not be concerned with the "details" of management. The counter argument is that Presidents have too much at stake to ignore their managerial duties. The Constitution, in vesting the "Executive power" in the President and providing the he "take care that the laws be faithfully executed," gives the responsibility for managing the Executive power to the President. But more immediately, the President's own political interests will suffer if he allows management to slide.

At the first level, the White House has grown into a set of sizable bureaucracies that need to be managed effectively if they are to serve the President. That does not mean that the President personally has to do the managing—that would be an unwise use of Presidential time. But the President ought to make sure that someone, presumably the Chief of Staff, is managing the White House staff and Executive Office bureaucracies.

At the second level, the rest of the Executive Branch, including Cabinet departments and agencies, must be at least coordinated, if not tightly managed from the White House. Micro-management by the President's staff is not desirable, but attention to managerial issues that cut across departments and agencies is necessary. The President should ensure that a managerial capacity is available in the Office of Management and Budget or in a new Office of Executive Management to guarantee that large-scale managerial issues are dealt with in the President's interests.

The bottom line is that the President's own political legacy and fate are at risk when management issues fall through the cracks. Policy coordination must take place at the top, and the implementation of programs must be pursued throughout the Executive Branch. If management is neglected, inefficiency is likely and scandals can easily ensue. Important dimensions of the Watergate, Iran-Contra, and some of the Clinton scandals were due to the failure to enforce sound management practices.

The examples of the Federal Emergency Management Agency and confronting the Y2K potential disaster demonstrate the importance of recruiting hardheaded, talented managers to the Executive Branch. In making political appointments, Presidents should not ignore experience and talent. If they do, it may lead to disaster—but if they make the right appointments, as in these two cases, they can expect to benefit from the success of the programs.

Presidential Continuity:
The Use of Individuals Across
Administrations

By James P. Pfiffner

When control of the Presidency changes to the opposite political party, most often all major appointive offices change to the party of the new President. Occasionally, however, this pattern is broken when Presidents retain exceptional individuals from the previous Administration of the other party. The value of this practice in certain circumstances is illustrated in the cases of Paul Volcker and Alan Greenspan as Chairs of the Federal Reserve Board, Dennis Ross as Middle East negotiator, Mike Mansfield as Ambassador to Japan, and Max Kampelman as Ambassador in Europe.

Virtually all of the Presidential appointees at the top of the Executive Branch serve at the pleasure of the President, and it is expected that they will resign when a new President takes office. The reason for this practice is that each President needs to have his own representatives in place to ensure that his policies will be faithfully carried out. Career civil servants are quite capable of carrying out the law, but political appointees carry with them, as representatives of the President, the legitimacy provided by the election.

Despite this healthy democratic practice, some individuals possess unique dimensions of experience, expertise, and talent—and are not so committed to one political party or ideology so that their talents can be beneficially used across Administrations. Wise Presidents will recognize these individuals and occasionally invite those who have served in the previous Administration to stay on to lend continuity to U.S. policy as well as to take advantage of their individual talents.

Presidential Crises: Watergate, Iran-Contra, and Impeachment

By James P. Pfiffner

Three major crises of confidence have shaken the modern Presidency—Watergate, Iran-Contra, and President Clinton's impeachment—each of them caused not by external threats but by Presidential decisions. Each crisis has led to serious consideration of impeachment and removal of the President from office—Richard M. Nixon resigned in the face of virtually certain impeachment, Ronald Reagan saved himself by getting the truth out, and Bill Clinton was impeached although not removed from office.

Each of the cases illustrates the problem that occurs when a President does not fully face the facts when confronting a crisis. Despite the different situations in each of these crises, a similar pattern emerged when the Presidents refused to get out all of the facts immediately and honestly. Ironically, the risks taken by these Presidents did not achieve the desired results. Each of these initial incidents evolved in a full-blown crisis that threatened the Presidency and distracted the Administration from its policy goals.

The conclusion of the analysis of these cases is that each of the three Presidents was guilty of serious missteps, but that President Reagan handled his crisis better by moving to get the truth out and that President Clinton's transgressions did not present as serious a threat to the Constitution as the other two crises.

II. THE FIRST 100 DAYS OF AN ADMINISTRATION

Franklin D. Roosevelt's "First Hundred Days"

By James MacGregor Burns

The famed "First 100 Days" of Franklin D. Roosevelt are often looked back on as a time when the new President exhibited decisive action and strong purpose in the face of the Great Depression. In fact, FDR entered office with no set program or even a definite philosophy of government. Roosevelt said that he was perfectly aware that he might have to try first one thing and then another—the pragmatic implication was that "what works" would be the decisive question, although it was not always clear what worked. What FDR did promise was "action, and action now"—and that, he certainly delivered.

So the legislative initiatives and executive actions of the "First 100 Days" lacked a central philosophy. On the one hand Roosevelt tried to carry out the promise he had made in the 1932 election that he would lower the cost of government. On the other hand he began the big spending programs that would characterize his first term. FDR even cut down on benefits to veterans, saving, he claimed, several hundred million dollars. On the other hand, he began the Civilian Conservation Corps and other New Deal measures that would have a significant impact on the economy. It was, in short, a period of experimentation and trial by error, but at the same time the start of significant increases in governmental action and responsibility.

What I like to call the "Second 100 Days" took place in 1935, following the Congressional elections of 1934, in which, on a rare occasion, the President actually found his party's support in Congress significantly increased. Armed with that support, and with backing from millions of Americans with whom he had communicated so effectively on the radio, Roosevelt turned "sharply left" in 1935, the year when much of the enduring New Deal, the Social Security Act, the Wagner Act, tax reform, increased spending, and other measures of the same philosophy were enacted. This turn to the left also was prompted by the rise of much more protest among the people than usually is remembered by historians of the Roosevelt era. So-called demagogues such as Huey Long and Father Coughlin were attacking Roosevelt for insufficient re-employment and other reform measures, but he so successfully headed them off that the protest in the 1936 election resulted in relatively few votes against the President.

The significance of this experience for other Presidents—and for future Presidents—may be somewhat limited by virtue of the state of crisis in which the country found itself in 1933, compared with other inaugural years. Perhaps one implication of 1933 is that the American people were willing to give a President a chance—even over two or three years—to show what he could do. Another lesson might be that a President cannot necessarily establish his enduring direction or program until after the mid-term election two years into his term. However, this could be a danger for Presidents, because virtually every mid-term election in this century, and even before, has produced a Congress more hostile to the President; so waiting for the third year might entail a great risk for the 21st century President.

My main point is that 1933-35 was a more complicated period, a more jumbled executive and legislative program, and a more pragmatic and experimental approach than some of the histories indicate today, with their emphasis simply on "bold Presidential action." So this is another reason for us to study the Presidency more deeply and in greater detail.

★　★　★　★　★

Dwight D. Eisenhower's "First Hundred Days"

By Fred I. Greenstein

The Rooseveltian notion of the "First 100 Days" of a Presidency as a time for highly visible policy achievements did not work for Dwight D. Eisenhower. He spent his "First 100 Days" in a highly deliberate process of reorganizing the Presidency and beginning the process of creating what proved to be the national security strategy of the United States over the course of the Cold War. Still, any new President could profit from studying Eisenhower's assumption of the Presidency. Here is a brief account, going back to Election Day 1952.

Dwight D. Eisenhower was a highly policy-oriented Chief Executive with a sophisticated sense of how to organize collective endeavors. He reluctantly agreed to run for President when he concluded that the Truman Administration did not have a strategy for conducting the Cold War that would be in the nation's interest over the long run. Further, the almost certain Republican nominee, Ohio Senator Robert A. Taft, was unwilling to commit the United States to participate in the collective security arrangements Eisenhower had helped to forge as the first military commander of the North Atlantic Treaty Organization (NATO).

Eisenhower presided over a seamless process of constituting his Presidency and initiating its important, but not highly visible, first year accomplishments. Once the votes had been counted on Election Day 1952, Eisenhower promptly began constituting his Presidency, naming his Budget Director and his White House Chief of Staff, an office that he created. He then promptly selected his Cabinet-to-be, including both Republican internationalists and representatives of that party's isolationist-leaning Taft wing. Eisenhower also named his White House staff, relying heavily on experienced Washington professionals with whom he had worked as Chief of Staff of the Army and NATO Commander. Included were the first Congressional Liaison Director and the first Presidential Special Assistant for National Security in the history of the Presidency.

New Look Strategy

Thereupon Eisenhower forged an impressively cohesive team out of big disparate appointees. Two notable team-building and policy-planning activities occurred before he took office. In late November, Eisenhower embarked on the trip to Korea that he had promised to make in his campaign. Making it do double duty, he arranged for his appointees to convene on a naval ship at Wake Island, and they spent the voyage to Honolulu engaged in policy deliberations. On that trip Eisenhower impressed on his aides the concept of the nation's national security needs—which was to emerge full blown late in 1953 as his Administration's New Look strategy. The concept was one in which the United States would build sufficient military strength (especially in the realm of nuclear weapons) to prevent the Soviet Union from expanding its sphere of influence, but would minimize military expenses in order to foster a vibrantly expanding economy. Early in January 1953, Eisenhower convened his aides-to-be at his New York City campaign headquarters for a similar discussion and to make practical preparations for the inauguration and early period of the Presidency.

There was no rapid assault on Capitol Hill in the first months of the Eisenhower Administration. Indeed, Eisenhower chose not to send a first-year domestic program to Congress, departing from a practice that had begun under Truman. Late in his first year, however, Eisenhower assembled his aides for a two-day conference on domestic policy and hammered out a program that was dispatched to Congress in 1954. Consistent with Eisenhower's hidden-hand leadership style, the early months of his Administration were marked by productive, low-profile accomplishments.

By mid-spring, Eisenhower had presided over the creation of an impressively deliberative national security policy planning and policy making process. Meanwhile, he had begun the deliberations that were to lead to the official enunciation of the New Look later in the year. Finally, he was closely involved in the steps that led up to the agreements in the summer of 1953 that in effect ended the Korean War. In short, the Eisenhower Presidency was not ranked by a conventional "100 Days," but Eisenhower made impressively systematic use of the full period from his election through the end of his first year. He laid the cornerstone of his Presidency and created the national security stance that his and later Presidencies were to employ for the remainder of the Cold War.

John F. Kennedy's "First One Hundred Days"

By Charles Bartlett

His oft-repeated campaign pledge to "get America moving again" was a running theme in John F. Kennedy's preparations to take control of the government in January 1961. But he nevertheless urged his aides to discourage the notion that he intended to emulate the whirlwind pace of Franklin Roosevelt's "First 100 Days" in 1933. Unlike FDR, Kennedy reasoned, he was not assuming the Presidency of a nation in the grips of a dire crisis. It was true that the economic recession that began in April 1960 needed attention. It had caused unemployment in industrial states, which had hurt the cause of his opponent Richard M. Nixon and helped Kennedy politically. It promised, however, to be a shallow recession that would serve the great purpose of dampening the inflationary fires.

So the President-elect had time, in his pre-inaugural days, to relish his victory, to bathe his fatigue in the Florida sun, and to celebrate the birth of his son, John F. Kennedy, Jr. He had the reassuring support of staff aides who had proven themselves in the heat of political battle. They were now launching task forces of distinguished citizens to propose solutions to the problems that the Administration would face. It was wisely decided to protect members of these advisory committees from political pressures by neglecting to disclose their identities.

Kennedy had been advised by Harvard's respected expert on the Presidency, Richard Neustadt, that he should announce, as soon as he was elected, his intention to retain in office two men whose roles would convey a sense of continuity and assurance to the public. The two men were J. Edgar Hoover, Director of the FBI, and Allen Dulles, Director of Central Intelligence. Kennedy followed Neustadt's advice, and it is interesting and ironic to recall that these two appointments caused him more difficulties than any that he subsequently made.

Staffing

In fact the staffing of the Kennedy Administration went amazingly well. The key figures in the Senate and campaign staffs fit neatly into White House niches. Theodore Sorensen was nominally to be the top aide with the title of Special Counsel to the President, but there was to be no commanding figure on the staff.

President Eisenhower had argued for the creation of a post to be known as "First Secretary of the Government." But Kennedy had decided to make a sharp turn away from Eisenhower's structured staff. There was to be no Sherman Adams, no top assistant empowered to filter all matters relating to the President. There were no plans for regular staff meetings or for the elaborate structures that the Eisenhower team had erected to conduct national security business.

Cabinet meetings and sessions of the National Security Council were to be rarely summoned by Kennedy because he felt they were, for most of those involved, a waste of time.

Kennedy's instinctive preference for Secretary of State was a fellow Senator, J. William Fulbright of Arkansas, but this choice was heatedly opposed by his brother, Robert Kennedy, who argued that Fulbright's record on civil rights would not conform to the President's commitments in that area. The President-elect then turned to his two most eminent advisers, Robert Lovett and Dean Acheson. They urged the appointment of Dean Rusk, an establishment figure who had supported Adlai Stevenson for the nomination. It was hard to find a Democrat with the credentials that would reassure the financial community. The best perceived to be available was a Chicago banker, David Kennedy, but the argument was made that the President would then have too many Kennedys in his Cabinet. With no Democratic possibility in sight, Kennedy turned to a respected Republican, Douglas Dillon, who had served in the Eisenhower Administration and had contributed substantially to the Nixon campaign.

Robert Kennedy deserved any reward his brother could give him for his tireless and frequently brilliant exertions in the campaign. He had not been inspired, by his training and experience as a lawyer, to look to the post of Attorney General—and the President-elect was keenly aware of the critical reaction that appointment would generate. But this was not to be their decision because their father weighed in heavily, arguing strongly and, as it turned out, wisely that Bobby deserved the post and would do well in it.

Nothing matches the exhilaration and optimism of a President taking office with confidence in his team and his intentions. One had the feeling, in talks with the President in those early days, that there was no wrong he did not intend to right, no move he would not make to brighten the luster of the United States. A Presidential transition provides a brief euphoric period before the harsh realities of dealing with 535 elected legislators set in. Great accomplishments seem possible and, in that spirit, Kennedy and his able staff managed to lay before Congress a welter of proposals covering a range of national concerns. By Sorenson's count, there were 277 separate proposals.

The sobering blow in Kennedy's baptism as President was not how-ever dealt by Congress but by a tragically short and bloody battle in Cuba's Bay of Pigs. This was a huge miscalculation by the intelligence community, but it carried the stamp of Kennedy's approval. Kennedy softened the public's reaction with a manly assertion of his responsibility. He seemed later, reviewing the episode in private, to count this as an occasion on which he had leaned too heavily on his staff. But he and his staff, when severely tested in later days by the Cuban Missile Crisis, demonstrated that they had drawn wisdom and strength from the humiliation they suffered in the Bay of Pigs.

The "First One Hundred Days" of Lyndon Baines Johnson

By Michael Beschloss

During the first six months after his inauguration in January 1965 as President in his own right, Lyndon Johnson achieved one of the richest legislative records in American history. LBJ's Medicare and Voting Rights bills, and other strides toward strengthening education; health care; the fight against crime; the arts and humanities; highways; the environment; and job training all came within this crucial half-year, forming much of what we now admire as his domestic legacy.

In September 1965, the historian William Leuchtenburg told Johnson, "This has been a remarkable Congress. It is even arguable whether this isn't the most significant Congress ever." Irritated, Johnson replied, "No, it isn't. It's not arguable. . . .Never has the American system worked so effectively in producing quality legislation."

How did it happen? LBJ started with a gift that few Presidents enjoy. He had been elected with 61 percent of the vote against Barry Goldwater, in the greatest Presidential landslide in American history. The Johnson landslide gained 39 seats in Congress. Thus the Democratic majority in 1965 was 68 Senators and 295 Members of Congress. Only FDR in 1936 had attracted greater Congressional support. Many of these Democrats knew that they owed their election to Johnson and acted accordingly.

From his long history in Congress, Johnson knew that his influence would never be so great as at the beginning of the first year after his election. From the start, he was running against the clock. In January 1965, LBJ told his Congressional liaison men that since Goldwater was no longer around to scare people, he had probably already lost about three million of his 16 million popular vote margin: "After a fight with Congress or something else, I'll lose another couple of million. I could be down to eight million in a couple of months." The message: work fast. Even with his majority, Johnson thought it would be "a hard fight every inch of the way."

In May 1964, Johnson had announced his "Great Society" in a University of Michigan commencement speech. That July, he secretly established 14 task forces made up of experts to flag urgent problems and suggest solutions. "It is very important that this not become a public operation," he told his Cabinet. Premature leaks would generate opposition even before his programs were announced. And during the 1964 campaign, while Johnson suggested to Americans that he wanted to launch a sweeping attack on national problems, he wished the voters to think of him more as a frugal centrist than the big-spending champion of Big Government he would suggest himself to be once elected.

Six Keys to Leadership

Within this framework, there were six keys to Johnson's leadership at the outset of his elected term. First, conviction. As with President Reagan two decades later, members of the Johnson Administration, Congress, and the American people understood that LBJ had strong ideas about the role of government; that these ideas were consistent (allowing lower-level bureaucrats, for example, to imagine with reasonable assurance how the President's philosophy should be applied to a minor matter); and that he would move heaven and earth, if necessary, to carry them out.

Second, timing. Not only did Johnson realize that he would never again have such power over Congress as he did in early 1965, he also knew that 1965 was a liberal moment that would come only once in a generation. The nation was at the apogee of its postwar economic boom. Americans were feeling tolerant, generous, and eager to attack nagging problems like discrimination, health care, education, and poverty. Johnson knew that the moment was rare and that it was not likely to last long. (He was right; the 1966 Congressional elections brought a Republican landslide, which was a stinging backlash to the Great Society's spending and social reforms.) LBJ wanted to strike while the iron was hot.

Third, personnel. In the spirit of his hero FDR, Johnson had an uncanny eye for young, fresh talent and the self-assurance to bring strong-minded, independent people into government who in many cases, he realized, knew more than he did. Much of the national Democratic establishment of the late 20th century—individuals like Joseph Califano, Bill Moyers, John Gardner, Cyrus Vance, and Barbara Jordan—consisted of people that LBJ discovered and promoted.

Fourth, legislative skills. It is almost impossible to overestimate how much LBJ benefited from having served in Congress for 27 years, 6 years of which he spent as Majority Leader of the Senate. Having witnessed numerous Presidential failures with Congress, Johnson designed his programs from the ground up in concert with influential Members of Congress. Having worked intimately with most party leaders, committee chairmen, and ranking Republicans, he had a deep wellspring of personal relationships and knowledge of the players on which to draw. For instance, in 1964, when Johnson had needed the votes of Republican Senators to overcome the opposition of Southern Democrats to his Civil Rights bill, he knew just how to appeal to his old friend Minority Leader Everett Dirksen to overcome Dirksen's doubts about the measure and bring the Republican party along. Once Johnson submitted his programs to Congress in 1965, he was as personally involved in twisting arms as he had ever been as Majority Leader. "Make an effort to get to know the men who sit on the committees that oversee your operations," he ordered his Cabinet. "The job of day-to-day contact with Congress is the most important we have. Many battles have been won, and many cases settled 'out of court,' by the right liaison man being there at the right time, with the right approach."

Fifth, Johnson knew how important it was for him to use his bully pulpit to bring the American people along. He was always striving to explain more eloquently how and why he wanted to improve life for Americans. Some of his efforts were failures, because orchestrating speechwriters and reading from prepared texts were not Johnson's strengths. Despite the contributions of John Steinbeck, his 1965 inaugural address was forgettable. So was that year's State of the Union speech. But in March 1965, when LBJ went before Congress to demand a Voting Rights bill declaring, "We shall overcome," he showed how powerfully he was able to move public opinion. In what was probably his best speech, Johnson used the Voting Rights address to campaign for the rest of the Great Society, saying, "I want to be the President who educated young children to the wonders of the world. . .who helped to feed the hungry. . .who helped the poor to find their own way." LBJ went on to say that when he had taught poor young Mexican Americans in 1928, "it never even occurred to me in my fondest dreams that I might have the chance...to help people like them all over this country. But now I do have that chance—and I'll let you in on a secret: I mean to use it!"

Sixth, flexibility. In the wake of the 1964 election, Johnson had hoped to give the South and other areas resistant to integration some breathing space as the Civil Rights Act of 1964 was implemented. In 1965, when Martin Luther King and other leaders demanded a separate bill to ensure voting rights, LBJ—although he thought the bill was possibly even more vital than the previous measure banning discrimination in public accommodations—did not want to force another showdown so soon. Nevertheless, when King and other leaders pressed for action at Selma and elsewhere, generating a public groundswell, LBJ was responsive enough to give in and throw himself into an immediate bill, which Congress passed in the summer of 1965.

Richard Nixon's "First One Hundred Days"

By Lee Huebner

Even as Ray Price was helping to draft Richard Nixon's Inaugural Address, in which the new President would call upon his countrymen to "lower our voices" and to reach "beyond government," this senior Nixon speechwriter was also urging the President-elect to lower public expectations by avoiding "those 100 day stunts" that he felt had misserved earlier Presidents.

"The critics' scoring rules are wrong," Price argued in a spirited internal memo. Their approach, he said, had only led to "grandstanding[. T]heir frenzies of activity for activity's sake, their extravagant rhetoric, their wars on every real or imagined social ill, their piling of promise on over-promise, their rush of half-baked legislative proposals, their substitution of emotion for reason, their basic premise that to pass a law means to solve a problem," were all counterproductive.

Price's viewpoint was shared by many within the Nixon camp during the transition period, including—in some of his many moods— Richard Nixon himself. Many outside voices agreed that what the nation needed most in 1969, as Walter Lippmann later put it, was "to liquidate, defuse, deflate the exaggerations of the romantic period of American imperialism and American inflation." Even Nixon's most liberal advisor, Daniel Patrick Moynihan, urged that the first Nixon year be one of "consolidation," a time to accumulate new political capital, rather than to launch a host of new initiatives or even to eliminate failed but symbolic old programs.

On the other hand, as Price noted, another side of Nixon was "like a bull at the rodeo gate, wanting to charge out," eager to assert command, to make a splash, to surprise his critics, to shape history. Nixon could be romantic about "creative and innovative" ideas—styling himself as a new Disraeli, a "Tory man with Whig principles." And he had assembled a talented, diversified governing team that wanted to make a difference.

Nixon's record in his first months in office reflected the tension between these two sensibilities. It was on the whole a cautious, often reactive period—characterized both by frustrating indecision and by wise restraint. But the deliberative atmosphere was punctuated by bold (and sometimes inconsistent) bursts of action.

Many of the bold strokes were Nixon's doing. Others happened while he looked on—or while he looked away. Some of these steps were taken secretly and came to light only later. Others happened in full public view.

A Challenging Time

The context in which Nixon launched his Presidency was perhaps the most challenging to face any President since Abraham Lincoln. In addition to an interminable foreign war, Nixon, like Franklin Roosevelt, inherited a perilous domestic crisis, one that he described as a "crisis of the spirit"; a questioning of national will; a dangerous sense of racial, social, and generational division. But unlike Roosevelt (or Ronald Reagan, or Dwight Eisenhower, or Lyndon Johnson) Nixon came to office in the weakest political position of any President in a century. Only 43 percent of the electorate had supported him. His controversial career still marred Nixon's credibility—his poll ratings as he took office were the lowest of any President before or since. More than that, the credibility of the Presidency itself was at a low ebb. When Nixon's daughter Julie returned to Smith College in January of 1969, the campus newspaper featured a picture of her father over a banner headline that read "A Crisis of Legitimacy."

Compounding all of this was Nixon's sense—partly justified and partly exaggerated—that the press, the Congress, and the federal bureaucracy were strongly against him. This disposition turned into a self-fulfilling prophecy. The President compounded his press relations problem, for example, by appointing a young non-journalist as Press Secretary, freezing out establishment reporters, and creating an over-weening public relations machine to fashion a favorable "image." Facing the first Congress in 120 years in which neither chamber was of the same party as an incoming President, Nixon's Congressional relations strategy focused defensively on his hard core supporters and failed to build effective bridges to the Democratic majority. He quickly forced a harsh showdown with the Senate over anti-ballistic missile deployment, winning by one vote but further straining long-term relationships. Meanwhile, perceiving the federal bureaucracy as "the enemy," Nixon expended enormous energy trying to end-run the departments and agencies.

Nixon did not even have the advantage, in many areas, of clearly delineated programs. In this respect he resembled the pragmatic, exper-imental FDR and stood in sharp contrast to Johnson and Reagan. His campaign had presented a polarized electorate with sharply described problems, but often with fuzzy solutions.

One result was that "process," initially, became more important than "programs." An old cliché argued that "Democrats tend to be fascinated by programs while Republicans are fascinated by structure"—and this was at least partly true in 1969.

An Expanded NSC

Restructuring the foreign policy making process was the most important of Nixon's early actions. Foreign affairs were his passion and preoccupation. ("You don't really need a President for domestic policy," he often declared.) He wanted to be "his own foreign secretary," in part because of his antipathy to the State Department and Central Intelligence Agency. And his National Security Advisor, Henry Kissinger, knew precisely how to act on this ambition. In what was later called "the coup d'etat at the Hotel Pierre" (headquarters for the transition), Kissinger designed a series of orders that put him at the center of the policy making machinery. Later a "back channel" was set up so that the White House could deal directly with the USSR through Soviet Ambassador Dobrynin—without bureaucratic knowledge. These and similar measures allowed the President and his expanded National Security Council staff to keep the rest of the government, including the Secretaries of State and Defense, in the dark on many matters. The new procedures undoubtedly enhanced both the confidentiality and the creativity of Nixon's foreign policy, but they also led to errors, omissions, and a "cult of secrecy" in which wiretapping became a frequently used and sometimes misused instrument of power.

From the start, Nixon employed the new machinery to advance a clear set of priorities. Vietnam came first. He quickly eliminated two possibilities—the war was not winnable on the one hand, but he would not "bug out" on the other hand. The President felt that he could end the war quickly through a negotiated settlement, and even expected at first that a "peace dividend" would soon allow him to balance the budget and finance his other programs.

To this end, even more than Kissinger, Nixon immediately began to pressure Moscow to push Hanoi to cooperate (seriously overestimating Soviet influence). Further, he worked to "link" progress on arms control with Soviet cooperation on Vietnam and other matters. The President also made an early commitment to phased unilateral troop withdrawals, hoping to turn the South Vietnamese army into a credible long-range force, while calming U.S. domestic opposition. To help in the calming, Nixon moved speedily on a program of draft reform (and eventual draft elimination). But this peace strategy did not foreclose continued military pressure, largely through a 14-month bombing campaign in Eastern Cambodia that was launched in response to North Vietnam's offensive in March 1969. (Protecting its secrecy is what motivated the first wave of wiretaps.)

Vietnam was not Nixon's only priority. In his first press conference on January 27, he signaled a considered new posture on arms control by calling for "sufficiency" rather than "superiority." Going against most advice, he insisted on making a February trip to Europe. This not only burnished his Presidential image but also signaled the priority Nixon placed on what he called our "blue chip" European alliances—and especially on close ties with French President Charles DeGaulle. Perhaps most importantly, and despite Kissinger's initial caution, the President quickly signaled his desire for rapprochement with China.

In domestic affairs, structural reform was also an initial priority, as was evidenced by Nixon's early appointment of the highly effective Ash Council to study government reorganization. Other early innovations included the Urban Affairs Council (which evolved into the Domestic Council), the Cabinet Committee on Economic Policy, the Office of Inter-governmental Relations, the Office of Minority Business Enterprise, and the privatization of the Post Office. Meanwhile, Nixon and his Chief of Staff Bob Haldeman spent endless hours chewing over questions of White House staff structure. (Nixon later said he regretted the personal isolation that these early decisions produced.)

Specific policy choices proved harder to make in the domestic than in the foreign arena. At first, Nixon's inclination was to leave policy choices to the Cabinet. He appointed a politically moderate Cabinet, made up mostly of people he scarcely knew, and convened it with diminishing frequency. (Nixon said he saw no obligation "to be bored for my country.") At first, he gave Cabinet Secretaries a free hand to appoint their own subordinates, but he quickly came to regret this move—especially as the Cabinet failed to clear out bureaucratic enemies. Nixon spent the latter part of his Presidency overcompensating for his initial permissiveness.

The President's obsession with foreign affairs, the absence of a clear philosophy, and a challenging set of political constraints (including the so-called Southern Strategy) all contributed to a slower domestic pace. Internal conflicts also slowed things down, epitomized by both the clash over welfare reform between the Moynihan camp and that of the more conservative Arthur Burns, and by the tussle over school desegregation policy between John Mitchell's conservative Justice Department and Robert Finch's more liberal Department of Health, Education and Welfare. In both of these areas, however, the tension would eventually prove to be creative, resulting in the boldest of all of Nixon's domestic initiatives (welfare reform), as well as the quiet but effective desegregation of most southern school districts by the fall of 1970.

Domestic Initiatives

In the "First 100 Days," however, bold domestic initiatives were relatively few. One exception came in the first week, when Nixon, angered by newspaper crime stories and in his "bull at the gate" mood, demanded that a program to combat crime in the District of Columbia be on his desk in 48 hours. The need to submit a revised budget in March also forced some early economic decisions, including Nixon's determination not to risk sharp spending reductions that might trigger a recession. The budget review also reflected the Administration's inclination to keep popular Great Society programs like the Office of Economic Opportunity and Model Cities—much as Nixon personally disliked them.

As he completed his "First 100 Days" in April, an impatient President—having decided at the outset not to give a State of the Union address (which would have forced more early decisions)—now issued an omnibus statement on domestic affairs. The message promised a series of later, detailed proposals in areas like tax reform, Social Security, organized crime, revenue sharing, home rule for the District of Columbia, and manpower training. By summer, despite its piecemeal emergence, the domestic program was, in Bill Safire's words, in "real danger of being described as liberal." And by late 1969, with the emergence of John Ehrlichmann as the arbiter of domestic initiatives, the Administration had achieved a fairly dynamic domestic rhythm. Enough was happening, in fact, to allow the PR team to plausibly present a host of domestic initiatives under the title "Reform is the Watchword." And Nixon's State of the Union addresses in 1970 and 1971 would present an aggressive domestic program (including major reforms in areas like health and the environment) that Nixon claimed would usher in "a great age of reform" and a "New American Revolution."

One factor that prevented this perception from being generally accepted, at the time and since, was the inconsistency of the Administration's rhetoric. Even the bolder presentations mentioned above emerged only from a concerted effort—after the fact—to fashion an overarching domestic philosophy that would explain and connect the wide variety of Presidential initiatives. Policy in this case preceded philosophy, rather than following it. And it was also true that bursts of progressive language were more than offset by the distinctly conservative cast of much of what the Administration had to say. When a liberal group complained to John Mitchell about a lack of progress on civil rights, the Attorney General candidly advised them to "watch what we do and not what we say."

This disparity between rhetoric and policy was another early habit that persisted in later years—helping the Administration resolve some of its tortuous political dilemmas, but also obscuring, from that day to this, the scope of its accomplishments.

Nixon's decision not to play the "100 Days" game was certainly consistent with this rhetorical strategy. On the other hand, in the record of those "First 100 Days" one can now discern the foundations of many of the Administration's most notable successes. And one can also trace some of the attitudes and actions that would lead to its most conspicuous failures.

★　★　★　★　★

Jimmy Carter: Transition and Early Presidency

By John P. Burke

Jimmy Carter's preparation for the Presidency in 1976 was the most ambitious to date. Eisenhower had done little before Election Day; Kennedy had enlisted the services of Clark Clifford and Richard Neustadt to craft some memos to him; while Nixon was practically forced by his advisers to undertake a personnel operation, yet these efforts proved useless. Carter, however, began preparations following his victory in the Pennsylvania primary, and after the Democratic convention a transition-planning operation was in full swing.

The effort was organized and led by Jack Watson, who had worked in a number of capacities with Carter during his governorship and was then a partner in the law firm of Charles Kirbo, a close Carter confidante. Watson quickly set up an ambitious operation with a broad mandate. The work of Watson and his group encompassed an elaborate personnel operation, teams to delve into agency and departmental matters, a staff to develop policy options and an agenda for the new Administration, groups to deal with the press and Congress, while still others were charged with studying White House organization and executive branch reorganization. No prior effort could even begin to match the work of Watson's operation—and it would set, in varying degrees, the parameters of Presidential transitions to follow.

Yet operating separately from the campaign, and with little coordination with its staff, Watson's efforts quickly generated conflicts and tension with those still busy at work trying to elect Jimmy Carter. Following Carter's victory, disagreements and personality differences emerged full force; not only would this hamper the transition—valuable time was lost in resolving conflicts and getting the post-election transition up and running—the differences were carried forth into his Presidency. Carter, for his part, provided little direction; trusting in his inner circle of fellow Georgians, he preferred that they resolve their differences among themselves.

The Carter transition set the groundwork for a White House staff that was at best loosely organized and lacked coordination and discipline. Carter's own sense of staff operations was largely framed in reaction to the Nixon Presidency—fewer staff, less hierarchy, and, at least initially, no Chief of Staff. It might have worked a decade or two earlier, or with a President who was attuned to staff management and better skilled at bringing forth the best from a collegial system—for Carter it proved frustrating. Carter's difficulties were also compounded by his selection of fellow Georgians to fill key staff positions. It gained him loyalty (although that was often strained by internal competition), at the cost of experience.

Policy and Politics

Oddly, given its collegial design, the staff began to fall into compartmentalized niches. Jack Watson would later reflect, "We regarded ourselves and President Carter regarded each of us, too categorically." This division especially affected the integration of policy analysis and political feasibility. As aide Peter Bourne recalls, "Policy recommendations were forwarded independently to Carter and without assessment of their political implications, and political advice was given by people who had little grasp of the issues involved." Policy and politics, in Watson's view, were "tracks that went separately all the way up to the top."

Carter's hopes to devolve policy making from the White House to the Cabinet (another reaction to a perceived Nixon legacy) were compromised by the lack of attention to how advice from the Cabinet would be structured into policy deliberations. Cabinet meetings quickly proved unproductive, problems of discipline and loyalty emerged, relations with the White House staff became strained, and policy efforts led by Cabinet members proved disorganized and frustrating. Lacking a White House staff that could effectively coordinate and fill the breach, the job often fell to Carter himself. What developed was almost the opposite of what was intended—compartmentalized rather than collegial, micro-managed rather than delegated.

The Carter transition is especially important in understanding the early travails of the Carter Presidency. Although policy proposals were churned out, little effort was given to prioritizing them or reckoning their political feasibility. The infamous Carter "laundry list" was one result, and it did not sit well with the Democratic leadership in Congress. Just the top of Carter's agenda included such hefty items as an economic stimulus program, welfare reform, hospital cost containment, a new urban policy, new minimum wage legislation, an ethics-in-government bill, changes in Social Security, creation of a department of energy and a consumer protection agency, and a request for executive branch reorganization authority.

Congress

Carter's relations and those of his staff with the Democratic leadership in Congress also did not get off to a happy start during the transition, as House Speaker Tip O'Neill well related in his memoirs. Those difficulties would continue. The transition was the source of three policy proposals that particularly strained Carter's relations with Congress once he was in office.

The first was a $50 tax rebate for each taxpayer. Designed as the centerpiece of Carter's economic stimulus package (its $11 billion price tag was two-thirds of the package's first-year cost), it passed the House. But as the economy picked up, the Administration began to back off from the proposal, and by April 14, 1977, Carter abandoned it. The decision met with some relief in the Senate, but it did not help Carter in the House. Congressman Al Ullman, then the chairman of the Ways and Means Committee through which much Carter legislation would have to pass, noted at the time that, "I and lot of other members put our necks on the line. [Carter] was a little less than fair to those of us who supported the rebate against our better judgment and worked hard to get it passed."

The second source of tension stemmed from Carter's efforts to eliminate a number of pork-barrel water projects. Carter announced his opposition in late February without much consultation with Congressional leaders or the Members from states and districts affected by the cuts. For Carter, the cuts symbolized the kind of new politics he wanted to achieve; for Members of Congress, they were crucial "credit claiming" projects useful to their reputations with the folks back home— and in some cases were the result of years of legislative logrolling and personal lobbying. In the view of OMB Director Bert Lance, a close Carter confidante, it was "Carter's first decision" and "it alienated as many Members of Congress that you possibly can do." Although Carter eventually achieved a compromise on the projects, in his memoirs he stated that the lesson he drew was not to recognize the realities of Congressional politics and factor that in as a cost for important policy goals, but that he should have been more steadfast in his opposition.

Energy Program

Perhaps the most important Carter policy effort of his early Presidency was his comprehensive energy program. Here he chose to play his cards close to the vest initially by commissioning James Schlesinger to craft a proposal, in secret, during the transition. Congress, the affected agencies and departments, and Carter's own policy staff were kept in the dark. Clad in a cardigan sweater, Carter unveiled the plan in a televised "fireside chat" on February 2, 1977, followed by another televised address on April 18, and a speech to a joint session of Congress two days later. Concerns were raised within the Administration about some of its provisions, and although it passed the House largely intact, Senate action resulted in a number of major changes. Carter was successful in gaining assent to the creation of a Department of Energy, but his pricing plan for natural gas, a gas-guzzler tax on cars, and levies on crude oil were all defeated. It took until November of 1978 for both houses of Congress to agree on a final bill. According to one study of the effort by John Barrow, Carter's plan "...had been compromised almost beyond recognition...the plan's most important conservation measure effort (higher oil prices) was abandoned...it served to make more severe the oil shock of 1979."

In sheer numbers alone, Carter was in an enviable position in his dealings with Congress, which had 61 Democrats in the Senate and 291 in the House. But the numbers belie the political reality. This was the first newly elected President following the McGovern-Fraser reforms in the nomination process—few in the party and Congressional leadership supported Carter's nomination bid, and only 14 percent of the Democratic Members of Congress were delegates at the party's national convention. The general election was extraordinarily close, and through-out Carter largely ran on his own personal qualities and against Washington and the traditional liberal ideology of his own party.

That stance, coupled with Carter's own unpretentious style, initially appeared to have struck a responsive chord with the American public. At the milestone of his "First 100 Days," he enjoyed a 64 percent approval rating. However, the test was yet to come as to whether Carter's originality and style could meet the challenges facing America in the late 1970s.

Carter may have sought to redefine the nature of the American Presidency—a "trusteeship Presidency" (as Charles O. Jones has phrased it) and one embracing a politics of the larger "public good" rather than the compromise of particular interests (Erwin Hargrove's view). Although well intended in that effort, Carter may have been a bit ahead of the times or perhaps, as some critics have argued, just a bit out of his element. Where Carter could take the lead and serve as America's trustee he was on safer ground—pardoning draft evaders the day after his inauguration, emphasizing human rights, nurturing the Camp David Accord, and securing the Panama Canal Treaty. Where normal politics prevailed, as it did on most domestic initiatives, the road proved rockier.

Ronald Reagan's "One Hundred Days"

By Lou Cannon

The agenda of Ronald Reagan's "First 100 Days" in office—indeed, in large measure, the agenda of the first year of his Presidency—was defined by the promises of his 1980 election campaign. During that campaign, in which Reagan defeated incumbent President Jimmy Carter and independent candidate John Anderson, he repeatedly pledged to cut taxes, boost military spending, and balance the federal budget by reducing domestic spending. Anderson famously scoffed that these promises could be accomplished simultaneously only with "mirrors," but Reagan was serious about them. The clarity of Reagan's policy intentions and the electoral mandate he had received for them were decisive in giving the new Administration a running start.

Reagan's transition teams had studied Carter's 1976 transition and learned from its mistakes. For instance, Carter had named separate campaign and transition staffs. The two staffs soon developed intense rivalries and competed for jobs and influence. In contrast, most of Reagan's pre-election planning was conducted by members of his top campaign hierarchy, and Reagan reached relatively quick decisions on the composition of his Cabinet and White House staff. Conflicts later developed between this staff and key members of the Cabinet— and within the staff itself—but their initial teamwork and focus on Reagan's well-defined objectives helped get the Administration quickly off the mark.

Reagan's running start was aided by a compilation (later called "the Holy Scrolls") directed by chief domestic adviser Martin Anderson of every policy statement that Reagan had made during the campaign. New appointees were given copies of these statements and were told that they were the blueprints of Administration policies. Also useful was the Initial Actions Project, a political guide to action prepared by pollster-strategist Richard D. Wirthlin, and his associate, the late Richard Beal, aided by David Gergen. This 55-page report, known as the transition's "Black Book." was presented in draft form to Reagan a month before he took office. "How we begin will determine significantly how we govern," the report said.

Inspirational Leadership

Taking his cue from his first political idol, Franklin D. Roosevelt, Reagan saw his own role as providing inspirational leadership to reverse what he believed was a crisis in public confidence. As a college student, Reagan had thrilled to the inaugural address delivered by FDR in 1933 during the depths of the Great Depression and he memorized its stirring perorations. "My firm belief is that the only thing we have to fear is fear itself..." Emulating FDR in manner, despite their considerable policy differences, Reagan displayed a sunny optimism in his meetings with Congressional leaders and other Washington power brokers, and especially in television and radio speeches to the American people. Reagan's poll ratings rose notably between the time of his election and his inauguration. After Reagan delivered his economic message on February 18, 1981, a *Washington Post-ABC News* poll showed two-to-one support for the policies that would become known as Reaganomics.

It should be noted that Reagan did not regard all of his campaign promises as equal. During the transition and the first months of his Presidency, he gave primacy to economic issues. Reagan had been advised to emphasize the economy and to put everything else on the back burner by former President Richard Nixon (in a memo disclosed in my book, *President Reagan: The Role of a Lifetime*), but it is likely that Reagan would have done so anyway. "If we get the economy in shape, we're going to be able to do a lot of things," Reagan confided to a friend soon after reading the Nixon memo. "If we don't, we're not going to be able to do anything." This emphasis drove social issues such as abortion and school prayer, which were important to religious conservatives, off of the Administration's political radar screen during Reagan's first months in office—and to some degree throughout his Presidency. The Administration's approach was summarized by James Baker, the practical White House Chief of Staff, who said, "We ought to have three goals, and all three of them are economic recovery."

Two Caveats

Two caveats are necessary in any discussion of Reagan's beginnings as President. The first is that the Administration was able to hew to its preferred emphasis on the economy because the 52 Americans who had been held hostage for 444 days in Iran were released in the first moments of Reagan's Administration, as he was giving his inaugural address on the west front of the Capitol. (The details of this action do not concern us here—my research credits both the outgoing and incoming Administrations, who sent a unified message to the Iranian regime, "Do not expect a better deal from Ronald Reagan.") Had the hostages remained in captivity, the American people would have demanded action, and the Administration would have faced a difficult and sensitive foreign policy issue with the potential of becoming a crisis.

The second caveat is that Reagan's "100 Days" in one sense lasted only 70 days—but in another lasted six months. On March 30, 1981, Reagan was shot and nearly killed in an assassination attempt. He was incapacitated for several weeks during which his aides of necessity did the day-to-day decision making. This probably reinforced Reagan's proclivity for excessive delegation, which later in the Presidency had harmful consequences. But Reagan's courageous conduct in the face of death ("I hope you're all Republicans," he quipped to the doctors who were about to operate on him) made him a hero to the American people and yielded political dividends. Influential columnist David Broder wrote that the wit and grace displayed by Reagan after the assassination attempt elevated his "appealing human qualities to the level of legend." Baker and other White House aides took advantage of Reagan's mythic status to advance his tax and budget bills, as did the President in a memorable address to a joint session of Congress less than a month after he was wounded. Although the Democrats (led by House Speaker Thomas P. (Tip) O'Neill) put up a stiff fight, a coalition of united Republicans and conservative Democrats from the South and West won a series of legislative victories culminating in a seven-vote victory on a key budget bill on June 26, 1981.

This marked the real end of Reagan's "100 Days."

★　★　★　★　★

Ronald Reagan: Putting Together an Early Action Plan

By David Gergen

He wasted no time getting ready for the presidency. The day after he won, he began moving swiftly.

Reagan named Jim Baker his incoming chief of staff, and Baker in turn invited a number of us in Washington to sign up for the transition and for early duty in the administration. As I took up my assignment at the transition, it was readily apparent that Reagan's campaign gave us two immediate advantages. First, neither he nor his staff had to spend transition time trying to figure out his main substantive agenda. That was mostly done, rooted in the plan laid out in Pittsburgh. The staff could thus concentrate on ways he could quickly take charge the moment he was inaugurated. Second, he could work with a small group of trusted advisers to focus on personnel selection—a subject we will turn to in a moment.

In order to hit the ground running, Reagan needed his own budget that would flesh out the details of his overall plan. If he were slow on that front, Jimmy Carter would send his own budget to the Hill as he was leaving office and that would shape congressional action for months. Reagan could not afford to wait; he had to make his imprint fast. Early in the transition, he appointed Stockman as his budget director and gave him leeway to move. Stockman took up the spending shears with relish, pruning back every Great Society program he could get his hands on. Reagan had signed off on a raft of spending cuts before most new cabinet officers were on board. Many of them screamed—they had been deballed before they even put their pants on—but they had to go along. The Stockman plan, to which Dick Darman also contributed significantly, was an aggressive exercise of power, but it gave Reagan a head start as president.

My task in the transition was to work with Richard Wirthlin in co-drafting an "Early Action Plan" for the First Hundred Days of the Reagan presidency. Dick, a Ph.D., provided most of the conceptual framework for the plan that emerged. We were both helped by one of his assistants, Richard Beale, along with a team of young researchers.

The researchers assisted me in pulling together a study of the First Hundred Days of the past five presidents who had been freshly elected, just like Reagan: Roosevelt in 1933, Eisenhower in 1953, Kennedy in 1961, Nixon in 1969, and Carter in 1977. Given the hallowed reputation of FDR's First Hundred Days, we felt it important to plot out precisely what each man had done during each of his days— his legislative proposals, executive orders, symbolic gestures, meetings with Congress, introductions to the Supreme Court, speeches, press conferences, trips, and the rest. We then reviewed the press clips and historical accounts that appeared after each "new beginning," assessing what seemed to work and what didn't. From there, we could begin to map out how Reagan might successfully master his own moment.

Three Lessons

I drew three conclusions from that study of the past:

First, the public makes a fresh evaluation of a president the day he takes office. Until then, people have known him only as a candidate. Now he finally holds the reins for the first time, and people must judge anew: Is he really up to the job? Can we trust him? Does he know where he wants to go? Do we want to go there, too? Does he have a central focus? In short, do we like what we see—or suffer from buyer's remorse?

Carter's experience convinced us that focus is essential for a new president. Taking over in 1977, he had tried to emulate Roosevelt by sending up stacks of legislative proposals in his early months. But his ideas had no internal coherence and, in the absence of crisis, struck many observers as hurly-burly. By the end of Carter's First Hundred Days, puzzled reporters wrote they couldn't make sense of what he was trying to accomplish. "He seems to stand for everything and believe in nothing," was their basic story line. Obviously, we weren't going there.

Second, those early months provide an opportunity for a president to put a firm thematic stamp upon his entire administration. Roosevelt had become "Doctor New Deal," as he called himself, helping a sick patient recover. Eisenhower slipped away from reporters and flew off to the Korean War front during his transition becoming a president in search of peace. While Nixon spoke in his inaugural address as a man who wanted to "Bring Us Together" at home, he showed quickly that his attentions were elsewhere as he flew off to Europe. People soon realized that he would mostly be a foreign policy president. At the end of a Hundred Days, Americans were less sure what Kennedy was all about, though they liked and admired him, and even less certain about Carter, who left them scratching their heads. Clearly, Reagan had to put his own stamp on his presidency.

Third, it was obvious that the First Hundred Days were also a time of great peril, when presidents made some of their biggest mistakes. Kennedy had his Bay of Pigs in the First Hundred Days; Ford had his pardon of Nixon; Carter had a small disaster over a proposal to cut water projects and a bigger one with announcement of his energy plan.

Because Carter was still so fresh in our minds, his presidency was particularly instructive: he had promised during his 1976 campaign to make the United States "energy independent," but his ideas were vague. They lacked the specificity that might have allowed him to claim a mandate. Taking office, he called in one of Washington's smartest men, Jim Schlesinger, and instructed him to come up with an energy plan within ninety days. His work was to be secret. Schlesinger obediently pulled down the shades, ignored the Congress, and, with a few aides, produced a comprehensive energy proposal. On the merits, the Schlesinger plan had much that was ingenious, but the process had so shut out Congress and the lobbyists that they were steaming mad. They refused to sign on quickly.

Appearing in cardigan sweater by a log fire in the Oval Office (another mistake, in my judgment, since presidents in their early days are still trying to identify themselves with the dignity of the office), Carter unveiled the plan. It hit with a thud. As the late-night shows said, Carter gave his first fireside chat—and the fire died.

Reagan looked over all this history, reviewed our recommendations, and soaked up some additional thoughts from Wirthlin. When he and Nancy came to Washington for a transition visit, we gathered at the Blair House where he gave his blessing to the Early Action Plan. Once in the White House, Reagan did not try to follow it to the letter, but it proved to be an important road map for his first weeks in office. It is important to reiterate that a plan for those early days in office would not have been possible had not Reagan—along with Meese, Anderson, and other policy advisers—first worked out a substantive agenda for his presidency long before he was elected. We could build on their foundation.

The Early Action Plan was also but a piece of a much larger organizational effort during the transition. Dozens of men and women, many of them veterans of the Nixon and Ford years, joined in teams to study each of the departments inside out and make recommendations for changes in policy, process, and personnel. Another large group planned out the inauguration. Still another group planned the physical move into the White House. I was particularly proud because a wonderful young man who had worked with me over the years, John F. W Rogers, had risen in the ranks and was now helping to plan the physical takeover.

Excerpted from *Eyewitness to Power: The Essence of Leadership* (New York: Simon & Schuster, 2000), 165-196.

TRIUMPHS AND TRAGEDIES OF THE MODERN PRESIDENCY

George H.W. Bush:
Transition and Early Presidency

By John P. Burke

The George H.W. Bush transition to office in 1988 presents the only instance of an electoral transition within the same party since the passage from the Coolidge to the Hoover Presidency in 1929. Further, it is the only electoral transition by a sitting Vice President since Martin Van Buren took office in 1837. President Bush began a modest pre-election transition effort well before the November election. It was aimed almost exclusively at planning a personnel operation and was under the direction of longtime associate Chase Untermeyer. Bush had also given some personal thought to what his Presidency might look like, and immediately after the election he not only set up a transition operation but announced the appointment of James Baker as Secretary of State, Untermeyer as Director of White House Personnel, and another close aide, Boyden Gray, as his White House Legal Counsel. These latter appointments were especially useful in preparing for a personnel process that had become increasingly complex and time-consuming.

In filling both staff and other positions, Bush and his associates moved quickly for the most part, and were able to draw upon a pool of talent that often had both close personal connections to George Bush and a variety of "inside the Beltway" experience. There was a bit of intramural politicking concerning John Sununu's role as Chief of Staff, especially whether a way could be devised to bring campaign strategist Robert Teeter on board. There were also delays in naming the White House economic and domestic advisers. Some of the organizational decisions made—particularly in downgrading White House units that would play a major role in "marketing and selling" policy proposals—would also have repercussions once the Administration was in office.

But for the most part Bush had a well-organized and managed transition. It benefited from the good auspices of the Reagan Administration. Advice and information were quickly conveyed—both before and after the election—giving the Bush team an easy head start. Many of those tapped to serve could also draw on their own past experiences in Republican Administrations. Moreover, a number of soon-to-be White House aides had not only served in the Reagan White House, but they had easy access to the present occupants of the positions they would soon hold. It was not only a friendly takeover, it was a familiar takeover.

Throughout the transition Bush played an active role, which was quite a change from Reagan's indifference to staff and organizational matters, and President Carter's preference for letting his fellow Georgians work things out among themselves. Bush was directly involved, not just in selecting the Cabinet but also in choosing the key players on the White House staff, and he was attentive to the issues of organization, process, and management that are crucial to an effective staff and advisory system.

Yet neither during the campaign nor in the early months of his Presidency did Bush present a bold new agenda to Congress and the nation, as Reagan had done eight years earlier. As a friendly takeover by a sitting Vice President, Bush was perhaps hampered by a sense of continuity rather than radical change. As John Sununu told the press in late January 1989, "Everyone is looking for some drastic change or redirection [but] this is a conservative Republican President taking over from a conservative Republican."

Nor had the election conveyed a mandate. Bush's margin of victory over Dukakis was certainly respectable (53.3 percent to 45.6 percent), but it was well short of a landslide and was accompanied by GOP losses in both the House and the Senate. Bush was only one of two postwar Presidents elected to office (the other was Nixon) who had to contend with both houses of Congress being controlled by the other party. In fact, Bush faced a House with fewer Republican members than any newly elected Republican President in the 20th century.

President Bush sought to foster a cordial relationship with Congress, an effort that he even incorporated into his inaugural address. But his attempts were complicated in the Senate by his decision to pursue John Tower's increasingly troubled nomination as Secretary of Defense. In the House, Bush and the GOP continued to face partisan opposition under House Speaker Jim Wright, especially as Wright struggled with the ethics allegations that would lead to his resignation as Speaker in May. Within the ranks of House Republicans, comity was further attenuated by the increasingly partisan stance of Minority Whip Newt Gingrich and his followers.

The early days of the Bush Presidency were not without their achievements, however. Especially in foreign policy, the team of Bush, Secretary of State James Baker, and National Security Council Adviser Brent Scowcroft developed a close working relationship that contrasted with the infighting of the Reagan years. During the transition period, Bush and his advisers successfully sought to defuse the contentious issue of aid to the Contras in Nicaragua (an issue that had bedeviled his predecessor), by crafting a bipartisan plan to extend humanitarian but not military aid. They also took steps to deal with mounting Latin American debt, which eventuated as the Brady Plan, named after Treasury Secretary Nicholas Brady. Bush's late November meeting in Houston with Mexican President Carlos Salinas set the stage for what would become the North American Free Trade Agreement (NAFTA).

Savings and Loan Crisis

The transition period also saw a concerted effort to develop a plan to deal with the savings and loan crisis, which Bush presented to Congress on February 6 and was finally passed in early August. But like the Brady Plan, although it was an important policy achievement, the savings and loan plan did little to capture the public imagination. The kind of proactive effort on the domestic front that might have provided the "vision thing" that Bush appeared to lack, moreover, was handicapped by worsening deficit projections. From December 1988 on, Richard Darman, the new Director of Office of Management and Budget, sought to craft a solution. Bush's hope, articulated during the campaign, of a "flexible freeze" (freezing total spending, adjusted for inflation, while flexibly increasing or decreasing particular programs) would not work in Darman's view. Instead, he developed a two-step approach: a first year budget that would avoid new tax increases and force Congress to make difficult cuts, with the issue of raising taxes postponed until the next year. With the "big fix" and the problem of dealing with Bush's "read my lips" election pledge to come later, it was a decision that led to the 1990 budget agreement and would have repercussions on Bush's chance for re-election. Given that the deficit issue and how to deal with it would loom large over this Presidency, the Administration's choices here raise some important "What if?" counterfactuals. Would Bush have been better off to bite the tax bullet early on, perhaps taking a political hit but striking an agreement with Congress during the more favorable "honeymoon" period rather than on the eve of a mid-term election? Or, conversely, should Bush have pushed harder on retaining a "flexible freeze" approach?

The early Bush Presidency was not bereft of domestic initiatives, but they often lacked fiscal commitments and suffered from poor marketing and selling. Media events were staged in the early weeks of the new Administration to demonstrate Bush's commitment as the "Education President," the "Environment President," the "Anti-Drug President," and so on. Yet the Administration's policy proposals in these areas emerged piece-meal in subsequent months, with little thematic continuity and waning media attention: a merit schools proposal (April 5), ethics-in-government legislation (April 12), expansion of Medicare (April 18), child care legislation (May 9), a crime bill (May 15), and a major revision of the Clean Air Act (June 12).

Media Access

Interestingly, Bush was highly accessible to the press throughout his Presidency. In his "First 100 Days" as President he held 11 press conferences, about one per week, and had nine additional question-and-answer sessions with groups of reporters. But these were often impromptu events, and informal as well: Bush preferred to brief reporters in the White House press room rather than stage the more formal events Reagan would hold in the East Room. It was a venue in which George Bush was more comfortable, but it did not result in a more favorable media. In one study of media coverage of the first 60 days of the new Administrations, Bush garnered only 505 references on the evening news broadcasts compared to 832 for Carter and 1,030 for Reagan.

Bush clearly wanted a different kind of Presidency from that of his predecessor—less emphasis on pomp and public presentation, more on quiet achievement and in a lower key. Yet he and his advisers failed to lay the groundwork to ratchet down or otherwise alter public and press expectations. At least initially, the public appeared to like this President and his early performance in office: in June 1989 his approval rating stood at 70 percent, higher than Reagan's 58 percent rating eight years earlier and second only to Kennedy's in 1961. But Bush's standing in the polls might have fostered a false sense of security, as problems would mount and other perceptions would build later in his Presidency.

On March 7, 1989, six weeks into his Presidency, Bush personally addressed the issue that his Administration was adrift: "So I would simply resist the clamor that nothing seems to be bubbling around, nothing is happening." He told reporters, "A lot is happening, not all of it good, but a lot is happening." On March 16, he told the press that "more is going on than meets the eye or makes headlines." In late April, Bush's "100 Day" mark passed with less notice and media fanfare than had occurred in the Carter and Reagan Presidencies.

★　★　★　★　★

The Clinton Presidency: The "First One Hundred Days"

By Charles O. Jones

The success of a President's "First 100 Days" is typically determined by how effectively he and his team have managed the transition from campaigning to governing. This view was well summarized by a senior aide to President Ronald Reagan: "In my view, [the transition is] hands-on management in operation. It's not so thematic and it's not so visionary except the crafting of the 100-day plan....What was it you said during the campaign? And how does that fit with your 100-day plan?" The Reagan transition through to the "First 100 Days" was, for the most part, linear. Benefiting from a clear agenda and substantial political advantages, Reagan advisers could and did proceed to organize effectively so as to "hit the ground running."

It would be hard to imagine a more stark contrast than that between the Reagan and Bill Clinton transitions. Pre-election transition planning for Reagan was integrated with the campaign organization; the two were separated for Clinton. Dismantling the campaign organization and creating the new Presidency were separated for Reagan; they were integrated for Clinton. Principal White House staff appointments were made early for Reagan; they were made later for Clinton. Reagan's Chief of Staff was a Washington insider; Clinton's was a friend from Arkansas. The transition was not "hyped as a big separate thing" for Reagan (quoting a Reagan aide); it was in the news almost every day for Clinton. Reagan left for his ranch in California after the election, and aides announced his Cabinet appointments; Clinton continued to be involved daily in the transition—announcing appointments, conducting a conference on the economy, holding press conferences, giving speeches. The Reagan team managed expectations; the Clinton team raised expectations.

It is true that the Clinton campaign had been about "The economy, stupid," James Carville's reminder to the campaign organization. But Carville had other advisories: "Change vs. more of the same" and "Don't forget health care." That the Clinton agenda was about more than the economy was evident from their book of promises, *Putting People First*. It contained 35 proposals for the Clinton national economic strategy and 577 proposals for other crucial issues. Clinton was said to admire Reagan's concentration on a limited agenda, but his interest and involvement in this huge catalog of issues suggested a very different intention. Having an agenda with many items need not preclude setting priorities. Unfortunately, however, the Clinton Presidency began with more uncertainty than certainty in regard to priorities. A re-reading of Bob Woodward's, *The Agenda,* and Elizabeth Drew's, *On the Edge,* provides the details.

An effort to focus on priorities by the new Clinton Presidency was made difficult very early on by the President-elect having violated the rule against making policy pronouncements before taking office. At an early news conference he discussed his intention, by executive order, to lift the ban on gays in the military. That issue then came to be more prominent than the new President would have preferred. Among other developments with the issue, President Clinton was unable to fulfill his commitment to act quickly by Executive Order. Rather, the matter extended well into the first year of his Administration.

The President-elect had also announced that he would appoint a Cabinet that would represent the diversity of the nation. Although a laudable goal in many respects, it had the effect of encouraging the press and various groups to keep score and to rate selections as much by who they represented as by their own talents. Such attention also sometimes distracted from the larger purposes of the new Administration.

Limited Political Capital

In fairness to Clinton and his team, they faced extraordinary pressures. Their political capital was limited (with a 43 percent win and reduced majorities in Congress), and yet expectations were high and cross-pressures abundant. This was the first all-Democratic government in 12 years. Liberals were expectant and centrists were eager (Clinton had chaired the Democratic Leadership Council at one point). Further, he had been reassured by Democratic leaders in Congress that they could deliver on Clinton's program.

As it happened, those immediate actions that Presidents take to demonstrate their "take charge" style were more likely to satisfy liberals than centrists. Clinton signed Executive Orders regarding abortions performed in military hospitals, federal funding of fetal tissue research, and the importation of RU-486, the so-called abortion pill. As promised, he also signed the Family and Medical Leave Act, along with other legislation that President Bush had vetoed in the last Congress. Clinton announced the formation of a health care task group to be headed by the First Lady (suggesting that welfare reform lost out as an immediate priority). The promised middle-class tax cut was dropped.

These and other early actions strongly hinted that the Clinton Presidency would be more liberal and confrontational than might have been anticipated from the campaign and the election results. Accordingly, Congressional Republicans found it easy to unite in opposition to a full menu of Clinton initiatives. Even the pacing of the economic proposals played into the hands of Republicans. An economic stimulus package was forwarded early. An effort by certain centrist Democratic Senators to fashion a bipartisan compromise was turned down by the White House and so the package was killed by a filibuster. Republicans labeled it classic Democratic spending. The President's reaction to this defeat came at a news conference: "I just misgauged it and I hope I can learn something. I've just been here 90 days." Alas, those 90 days are important for any Presidency in setting a style and tone.

I summarized the Clinton transition and "First 100 Days" this way in my book, *Clinton and Congress, 1993-1996: Risk, Restoration, and Reelection:* "First, expectations had been raised, not moderated, thus inviting accountability early and often. Second, postelection statements and priorities by the President and his staff, as well as initial actions once in office, were markedly more liberal than conservative or centrist in character. Third, congressional Republicans therefore had incentives to unify in opposition to the new Administration on ideological and procedural grounds. Fourth, it came to be impossible for the Administration to meet its optimistic timetable in regard to health care, welfare reform, and the elimination of the ban on gays in the military, thereby permitting opposition to develop and the 'L' word to be affixed to the President and his aides" (p. 77).

The Clinton experience offers lessons for future Presidents during their "First 100 Days." First and foremost is the need to comprehend fully who you are, where you are, and how you got there. The "who" refers to your experience and that of your aides. The "where" refers to the fact that Presidents enter a government already at work—in Congress, in the departments and agencies, throughout the nation and the world. The challenge is to fit yourself in effectively enough so as to lead. And the "how" refers to the political capital you have available to assist in convincing others that what you want is what they should want (a Richard E. Neustadt formulation). It is fair judgment that Clinton and his team deserved the poor marks they received by these tests. They did, however, "learn something," as the President had hoped they would. It is preferable, nonetheless, to be educated in advance. And it is certain that requirement will be just as important for the next President as it was for Bill Clinton.

The Presidential "One Hundred Days:" An Overview

By Richard E. Neustadt

The "100 Days" of 1933, a term the American media had borrowed from French history, was used to denote Franklin D. Roosevelt's great success with Congress in and after that year's banking crisis. Ever since, the term has been used analogically by journalists to measure the effectiveness of newly elected Presidents in their first legislative session, and also it has been used by certain Presidents-elect to plan their post-inaugural strategies.

The analogy, however, is not apt. Roosevelt's Congress had come into special session at his call amidst emergency conditions. Subsequent Presidents have dealt with Congresses in regular session, facing lesser problems. "One Hundred Days" reaches only to Easter recess of a modem Congress, which is not a date for finishing most bills. Even President Lyndon B. Johnson in 1964, although not a President then elected, faced only a psychological emergency created by his predecessor's murder. He rode to early legislative triumphs at the later cost of escalation in Vietnam, imprisoned by his own initial pledge of "let us continue." The next year, newly elected in his own right, Johnson's coattails carried with him the largest Democratic majorities in both Houses since Roosevelt's heyday. With these, in the course of two regular sessions, Johnson launched and carried through the measures for his Great Society.

The original "100 Days" had nothing whatever to do with the United States. In the spring of 1815, the former Emperor of the French, Napoleon I, escaped from Elba, where he had been exiled after his abdication of the year before. Returning to France, he rallied the army, regained Paris, restored his rule, prepared to fight the rest of Europe (still arrayed against him), and at Waterloo in Belgium he was decisively defeated. Thereupon he had to abdicate again and this time was transported far away, to St. Helena in the South Atlantic. This coda to his reign in France lasted 100 days, and was so labeled by historians.

FDR's First One Hundred Days

In 1933, when Americans swiped that label, FDR had been sworn in on March 4 (under constitutional provisions before the 20th Amendment), while the "lame-duck" session of Congress had adjourned the day before, and the new Congress was not scheduled to meet until the following December. But in March, the country was gripped by financial disaster crowning three years of deepening depression. Banks were failing on every hand. Desperate depositors were losing their whole savings. Desperate businesses were short of cash. Roosevelt at once took Executive measures, but he needed legislative authority for more, and so called the new Congress in special session. Somewhat to his surprise, he found it so compliant in the face of the emergency that he kept it in session for three months. Roosevelt bargained through Congress 16 major bills, many of them newly improvised (such as the National Industrial Recovery Act), and some previously kicked around for years (like the Tennessee Valley Authority). In sum, they constituted what became known as the "First New Deal."

When FDR ran low on measures and found members running out of steam, he prudently dismissed them, and from June until December governed with the Congress out of town. From his call until adjournment, that special session had lasted "100 Days." The press affixed to it the napoleonic designation.

Ever since, journalist have speculated in advance, and summed up after, about a new President's "First 100 Days"—now that Congress is routinely in session (thanks to the 20th Amendment). The new President's legislative success, compared to Roosevelt's, is often at the heart of their stories. And not journalists alone—incoming Presidents, and even more their staffs, have often adopted this yardstick, prospectively, before their inaugurations, in commenting on what they hoped to do. Bill Clinton was notorious for this after the 1992 election. Some of them, moreover, have centered their planning on the first three months in office. Ronald Reagan's staff is a notable example. Scholars, too, have tended to generalize: claiming the early months of a new term as the most advantageous time for Presidents to make their mark on Congress. Avowedly or implicitly, Roosevelt—and Reagan—are frequently invoked.

Journalists and scholars read each other, while Presidents-elect, or at least their aides, read both. Accordingly, in Rooseveltian, not Napoleonic terms, the tag "100 Days," as measurement and opportunity alike, now seems to be entrenched in the conventional wisdom of our politics.

Analytically this is unfortunate, for at least three reasons. The first relates to conditions produced by the 20th Amendment itself. The second involves the character and timing of Congressional "honeymoons" with newly elected Presidents. The third pertains to their usual ignorance about the ways and means of some (or all) institutions "inside the beltway." Let me take these three in turn.

Congress Meets Early

The 20th Amendment to the Constitution was designed to assure that the four months of Herbert Hoover's lame-duck status after FDR's election, in the midst of a burgeoning financial crisis, would never occur again. Henceforth, the new Congress would meet in regular session on January 3 of the year after November's election, with the new President inaugurated January 20. This might have helped cope with the banking emergency of 1932-1933. It also put an end to lame-duck sessions of the outgoing Congresses, which had long been thought unsatisfactory. But in other respects the new timing was profoundly disadvantageous for incoming Presidents.

Formerly, elected Presidents had four months before inaugural to choose their Cabinets and personal aides while appraising the condition of the country. They would then have nine months in office to accustom themselves to one another, to learn the ropes in the Executive establishment (and in press relations), to review policies, and to ponder budgets—all before Congress and its committees hove on the scene. If Congress arrived earlier, it would do so only in special session on the President's call, for the limited purposes he chose. Even Abraham Lincoln, with the Union dissolved and hostilities beginning, gave himself and his associates from March to June before calling Congress into special session.

How good that looks now, from the standpoint of an incoming Administration, and how unattainable! Instead, the new Congress is in session three weeks before inaugural, with its committees organized, impatiently awaiting the new President's initiatives. Moreover, since for half a century, one or both Houses has usually been organized by the political party opposed to the President, that impatience has an undertone of negativity.

This brings me to my second point. Congress, institutionally, is suspicious of "downtown," competitive with the White House for control of federal agencies, their programs and their budgets, and licensed by the Constitution to compete. So Congress does, in modem times most notably through its extensively staffed subcommittees and its partisan floor leaderships. Since the latter are so frequently opposed to the White House in national politics, the competition is necessarily heightened, with party enhancing institutional motives. Constituency motives increase competition still more. "All politics is local" as a recent Speaker said, and all Congressional constituencies differ, not alone from one another but also from the President's.

Public Opinion Creates Honeymoon

Thus the presumed advantages, in legislative terms, of the "First 100 Days" for new Administrations cannot be said to rest on any special institutional, partisan, or constituency preferences binding Members of Congress and Senators to newly installed Presidents. On the contrary, those underlying motives to compete with the White House seem as much a factor in Congressional life at the outset of a Presidency as later. What then explains the widely reported, readily observable "honeymoon"—by way of courteous manners and procedural accommodations—most incoming Presidents appear to get from Congress? The answer seems to lie in public opinion, or more accurately in public sentiment as gauged by Members of Congress themselves and by their party leaders, drawing upon polls and on press treatment of the new regime downtown.

From long experience, the judgment on the Hill appears to be that in the first weeks after an inaugural, most Americans wish their new President well and want him to succeed. Partisanship is relatively low and interest in him relatively high, an interest fueled by curiosity about the President in his new, never-before-seen capacity, not as one party's candidate but as the country's magistrate. The Congressional instinct therefore, crossing party lines, is to repress most overt signs of rampant competition until that public mood is seen to fade, as judged by media reactions and constituent expressions, and by polls. Then as an institution, Congress bounces back to its accustomed stance of vocal, procedural, and substantive competitiveness with the President.

In modern times, the Congressional reflection of a public "honeymoon" has not endured for more than about six months. In the air-conditioned era, the first session of a Congress far exceeds six months, with final action on most controversial bills occurring later. So "honeymoons" are marginal, at best, in deciding a new President's success with legislation. The Reagan case, so often cited as exceptional, is less different than it seems—although his gallant response to attempted assassination, coupled with his concentration on a nominally single target (the budget), and with Democratic shock after losing the Senate, changed both public and Congressional parameters for the time being.

The third reason to discount the efficacy of a newly elected President's "First 100 Days" is ignorance, his own and that of his associates. If he has not already held high Executive office at the federal level—as only Dwight D. Eisenhower, Richard M. Nixon, and George H.W. Bush have done since FDR—the President will be ignorant of many things he urgently needs to know, yet can learn only by experience all through the "100 Days" and for months after. So those early months are exceptionally hazardous as well as marginally advantageous. Hazards transcend the legislative sphere and include Executive operations, where even a Vice President's experience is not a certain guide to Presidential knowledge.

A classic case of ignorance-as-hazard is that of President John F. Kennedy in planning for the Bay of Pigs, the covert invasion of Cuba that exiles attempted under CIA direction on the 87th day of his incumbency. When the Director of the Agency urged his approval, Kennedy did not know that the man spoke for only one part of it, the covert operators who had made the plan and loved it. The Agency's analysts, who would have scoffed, had been kept uninformed, as not needing to know. Moreover, being told by the Joint Chiefs of Staff (JCS), to whom he had insisted on referring the plan, that it had a "fair" chance of success, he took "fair" as next to good, whereas the Chiefs, evidently, meant next to poor. When Kennedy then changed the plan, moving the landing site to lessen the "noise level" (thereby unintentionally placing it on the wrong side of a swamp from the mountains the invaders were to use as their escape hatch), he assumed that the Chiefs would comment on the change without being asked. Since it was not their operation, they wouldn't and didn't. Finally, JFK thought that when he barred use of American forces, the CIA and JCS would take him at his word. Having dealt some years before with Eisenhower, who had been prepared to eat such words, if necessary, they assumed that Kennedy would do the same, and acquiesced in further changes that made overt U.S. intervention all but essential. Thereupon, to their horror, Kennedy pretty much kept his word, and let the invasion fail.

From all that, Kennedy learned a great deal, which was and is important compensation. Ignorance, in this sense of personal not knowing, is complemented by ignorance in the sense of institutional inexperience. With the Bay of Pigs, the CIA had never before attempted a covert operation on such a scale, and the JCS had never been called upon to comment hastily on someone else's war plan.

Ignorance in this second sense is no respecter of the line between the Executive and Legislative Branches. In June 1977, when President Jimmy Carter let his Budget Director, Bert Lance, go to a Senate Committee to seek modification of the terms of his confirmation, neither they, nor indeed the Committee Chairman, seemed to be aware of how exceptional such a request would be, and thus how likely to intrigue at least some journalists in an otherwise slow summer.

And in February 1981, when Reagan sent to Congress the most sweeping revisions of the budget and of taxes ever attempted by an incoming Administration, he rationalized it with an economic scenario, termed "rosy" by associates, that suffered from the haste with which the package had been put together. Within weeks the plan was acknowledged by his Budget Director as plain wrong. Faced by the choice of repudiating that scenario, hence modifying his proposals, Reagan understandably decided to stick with both. This set the stage for outsized budget deficits in later years. He then found virtues in them, but would not have planned budget deficits consciously. They were the unintended consequences of a huge and novel effort, pursued in haste by his incoming aides on top of hard-pressed civil servants.

Ignorance-as-hazard (personal not knowing) will be inescapable for many, or most, Presidents-elect. This is all the more reason why ignorance of institutions should be avoided wherever possible by new Administrations. Innovations, to be sure, will be desired and desirable in the first months. But those requiring the relevant parts of government to act in wholly unfamiliar ways, perhaps should be delayed at least until the personal ignorance of major players has been overcome. How else deal with the shortcomings of Reagan's Budget Director?

As for that rarity, a newly elected President with Vice Presidential experience, if, as in Nixon's case, there has been a long interval between the one post and the other, past experience is not a guarantee of understanding every facet of the Presidency he inherits. If the Vice Presidency has been the incoming President's immediate preceding office, separated only by his campaign, he may know everything about his new job except how it feels to be in it. The President undoubtedly will have imagined what it's like, sitting on the side, watching mistakes being made, but perhaps he imagined wrongly, as compared with how he would perform if actually in- and on-the spot. His early months will thus involve not "learning" so much as adjustment of perspective—which is best done consciously.

For the newly elected President fresh from the Vice Presidency there is, besides, a special hazard in his "First 100 Days" and even after. At least I judge so, on the strength of tales told by associates of our sole modern example, George H.W. Bush. In late 1988 and early 1989, all sorts of people in the Reagan Administration, cheered by their party's victory, with all sorts of views and plans for their departments or their own next steps, had to be disappointed, gently moved aside, or quietly disposed of so the incoming President could interject his views and plans with the people of his choice. What for new Presidents of other sorts is an open changing of the guard, was for Bush an almost covert one, involving far less brashness and decidedly more tact than usual—and stretching far into the spring. Coping with his problems is presumably a challenge for any successor in a comparable situation.

III. EXECUTIVE-LEGISLATIVE RELATIONS

The Versailles Treaty

By John Milton Cooper

President Woodrow Wilson's unavailing effort in 1919 and 1920 to gain Senate consent to the Treaty of Versailles—which provided for full membership in the League of Nations—stands to this day as perhaps the greatest Presidential failure in the politics of foreign policy. Many factors beyond his control contributed to Wilson's defeat in this supreme effort of his career, but the incident supplies a number of lessons for any future President who tries to sell a major departure in foreign policy to Congress and to the public.

Wilson's first mistakes came early. He had endorsed the idea of a league of nations to maintain peace (by force if necessary) in 1916. The next year the President proposed that the United States become a charter, full-fledged member of such a league and a guarantor of the peace. At the same time, Wilson's Presidential predecessor, William Howard Taft, headed a major organization, the League to Enforce Peace (LEP), which had been lobbying for the same things. Unfortunately, with American intervention in World War I in 1917, Wilson retreated from the public arena and did not explain his thinking adequately, partly on the excuse of the pressures of war leadership. Even more unfortunate, he kept the LEP at arm's length and did not allow the organization to promote his thinking. As a result, although there was widespread public support for some kind of league and maintaining the peace, it was never firmly based beyond Wilson's loyalists in his own party. Later at the height of the debate over the treaty, Wilson undertook a whirlwind speaking tour to educate the public, but this was a case of too much too late—too much public persuasion and education compressed into a small, abortive campaign.

With victory in the war assured in November 1918, Wilson made further mistakes. Some have argued that he was wrong to go to Paris as the head of the American delegation to the peace conference—and to spend the first half of 1919 out of the country. Given the summit meeting character of that conference, it is hard to see how Wilson could have avoided being there for at least some of it. What he had not done, however, was to develop a cadre of able, trusted lieutenants who could negotiate for him and take some of the burden of diplomacy off of his shoulders. This meant that, unlike the other national leaders present at Paris, Wilson operated almost entirely on his own.

The President also failed to reach out to other interested parties when he went to Paris. The role of the Senate in treaty making made it advisable to include members of that body in the peace delegation. In 1898, at the end of the Spanish-American War, President William McKinley had appointed three Senators to the delegation to negotiate the peace treaty, and they helped win consent when they returned to the United States. Wilson's problem was his bitter enemy Senator Henry

Cabot Lodge. He could not include any Senators without inviting Lodge. Since there was a good chance that Lodge would have declined an invitation in order to preserve his freedom to oppose the treaty, Wilson might have done well to take a chance on inviting him—and then been free to include any Senators he pleased.

Likewise, Wilson failed to practice bipartisanship in appointing members of the peace delegation. Several top Republicans seemed to be good picks, including former President Taft, former Secretary of State Elihu Root, and the party's last nominee for President and Wilson's opponent in 1916, Charles Evans Hughes. They were all strong, able men, who might have helped to sell the peace treaty and the League of Nations to their party brethren.

Like most strong Presidents, Wilson committed these errors out of the defect of his virtues. He was a singularly bold leader and one who wanted to preserve as much freedom of action as possible. He could not be sure until the war was won and he got to Europe whether conditions favored the kind of strong, peace-enforcing league that he wanted. He surprised nearly everyone by producing the Draft Covenant of the League in less than a month and unveiling it to the world. At first and later, public reaction to this move was so strongly positive that it looked is if Wilson could ride a wave of popular acclaim to victory.

The major source of opposition did not lie in isolationism (the outright rejection of overseas security commitments). Rather, it was contained in strongly held Republican views that favored a traditionally nationalistic, great power approach. This philosophy jealously guarded American sovereignty and approved of only limited security arrangements. A wide gulf separated this mainstream Republican position from Wilson's more sweeping vision, but there were plenty of opportunities for compromise.

The issue came down to reservations on American ratification of the treaty. Lodge and most Republican Senators favored "strong reservations," which would particularly have circumscribed American pledges under the League's collective security clauses.

Wilson wanted a broader pledge that amounted to some kind of guarantee to maintain world peace. Inasmuch as future cases would have to be decided based on their own circumstances anyway, there should have been ways to satisfy both desires to some degree. Most responsible communicators at the time believed that some accommodation could have been reached between the two sides, regardless of the bad blood between Wilson and Lodge.

Complicating this incident was the worst crisis of Presidential disability in American history. At the climax of the League of Nations controversy, Wilson suffered a massive stroke, and he should have been removed from office. Instead, with his wife assuming a shadow regency, he served out the rest of his term (although the country effectively did not have a President). For the treaty controversy, the stroke had two particularly adverse consequences. First, Wilson's severe incapacity immediately following the stroke removed him from negotiations with Senators at a particularly critical stage. Second, after he recovered to a degree, the psychological and emotional effects of the stroke rendered him incapable of judging political reality correctly and contemplating responsible compromise. It is highly unlikely that the debate over the Versailles treaty would have ended as it did in stalemate and defeat if Wilson had not suffered his stroke.

Whether the failure of the United States to ratify the treaty and join the League "broke the heart of the world," as Wilson said, remains highly debatable. Without question, the sour outcome of this great crusade for peace made international relations worse during the next two decades. A strong League of Nations with the United States as its leading member might or might not have prevented World War II, but it would surely have made dealing with the crises of the 1930s more constructive and responsible. Wilson's defeat was a sad hour in the history of this nation and the world, and he could have helped things to turn out better.

★　★　★　★　★

Creation and Implementation of the Marshall Plan, 1947-1948

By Larry I. Bland

The European Recovery Program, better known as the Marshall Plan, is popularly but incorrectly regarded as a giant welfare program that helped Western Europe. Consequently, there are periodic calls for "a Marshall Plan for _____" (fill in the blank), most recently East Europe. Experience has shown, however, that the particular circumstances of the period and place are not easily replicated.

In Europe after World War II, the prestige of the Communists was high and their political clout was rapidly growing at the expense of parties representing the moderate left and right. International trade was stagnant, despite great demand, because the West Europeans had inadequate purchasing power. Imperial powers such as France, Britain, and the Netherlands sought preferential treatment. There was pressure on all West European governments to increase social welfare spending and raise defensive tariffs against the undamaged United States, which held almost 50 percent of the world's wealth.

Americans reacted with concern to media images (newsreels, *Life* magazine, etc.) of European destruction and suffering. Bilateral loans, International Monetary Fund currency stabilization efforts, and U.S.-financed UN-sponsored relief and reconstruction activities ($9 billion between 1944 and 1946) were clearly inadequate for the challenges. Thus, political and social leaders in the United States in the winter and spring of 1947 engaged in a serious discussion on what to do. They connected the too-little, too-late U.S. response to the 1929-1931 European economic crisis with the rise of Hitler, and feared the consequences of another such failure. Truman Administration advisers were convinced that a new approach was needed.

Top Truman officials focused on American beliefs in the value of a federalist system, the New Deal's free-trade ideas, and the tendency to seek to transform seemingly intractable political problems into technical ones that are solvable. In a June 5, 1947, address at Harvard University, Secretary of State George C. Marshall delivered a 10-minute, low-profile speech that avoided specifics but outlined the issues. Marshall made a dramatic statement of Europe's economic plight, and argued that the United States could do something about it. He said that Europeans should assume the responsibility for initiating the program, and that the offer was open to all European nations (it was assumed that the openness requirements would cause the USSR to reject the idea). Finally, Marshall made a decisive statement on the need to rehabilitate the German economy. The press named the idea after the nonpartisan Secretary Marshall. The name was useful to the Truman Administration, which had lost control of both houses of Congress in the 1946 elections. (Truman noted in his memoirs that the Plan would never have passed if it had been labeled the "Truman Plan.")

Marshall's Harvard address was short on specifics (such as dollar amounts) in order not to galvanize opposition in the United States (particularly from the Robert A. Taft-Herbert Hoover wing of the GOP) before the Europeans could react. During the summer of 1947, the Committee of European Economic Cooperation began meeting in Paris. The Soviet-dominated countries rejected the idea, and a program by the United States was proposed. To speed consideration and emphasize the Plan's importance, President Truman called a special session of Congress in November.

Nonpartisan Approach

Marshall was careful to emphasize the proposal's nonpartisan nature. He made a special effort to cultivate Senate Foreign Relations Committee Chairman (and potential Presidential nominee in 1948) Arthur Vandenberg (R-Mich.) to counter the Taft opposition. To help mobilize public support, nongovernment supporters established the Committee for the Marshall Plan (headed by Republican Henry L. Stimson, who was a former Secretary of State and War, with a Women's Division under Mrs. Wendell Wilkie).

Marshall led off the Congressional hearings in early January 1948. He then personally campaigned nationwide, making major speeches to targeted audiences of labor-intensive industries (capital-intensive businessmen were predisposed to support the Plan), export-oriented farmers (for example, cotton and corn growers), and those concerned with the moral dimensions (such as church and women's groups). Increasingly, Marshall warned that the choice was between good and evil and that the United States had to lead the forces of good.

Moderates were insistent that the Marshall Plan not permanently increase government bureaucracy and financial commitment. To meet these concerns, the Plan was limited to four years' duration. A new operating agency was created called the Economic Cooperation Administration (ECA). Vandenberg insisted—and the Administration agreed—that Republican businessman Paul Hoffman of the Studebaker Corporation would head the ECA, but the key office in Paris would be under W. Averell Harriman, a financier identified with the New Deal.

After intense but not prolonged debate, the authorization bill passed easily (Senate, 69-17; House, 329-74) and was signed by President Truman on April 3, 1948. The initial appropriation was $5.3 billion for the first 12 months. The four-year total was $13.3 billion ($11.8 billion in grants, $1.5 billion in loans) to the 16 nations receiving assistance. (To get modern cost equivalents, multiply by 8; to equate it to modern economic impact, multiply by 20.) Most of the money went to finance morale-raising imports of fuel, food/feed/fertilizer, raw materials, and machinery. But an important, if little-known, aspect was the transfer of technical and managerial knowledge aimed at improving the quality of European capitalism. The AFL-CIO was influential in containing opposition to the Plan from European unions and coaxing them away from left-wing socialism and toward American-style unionism.

Passage of the Marshall Plan was not a sure thing. Although the idea of helping suffering Europeans was popular, it was rather media-driven and amorphous. Moreover, following a combined 16 years of economic depression and war, a good number of Americans were opposed to the Marshall Plan's requirements. To achieve Congressional approval and implementation, President Truman and his advisers: (1) converted West Europe's seemingly intractable socioeconomic problems into solvable technical ones (trade, aid, currency, management technique, etc.) with reasonably well-understood parameters; (2) cultivated a bipartisan political approach, thereby marginalizing opposition from the left and the right; and (3) co-opted or divided by careful lobbying those large groups that might have become the locus of serious opposition (i.e., agriculture, business, labor). One intended consequence of the Marshall Plan was furthering America's national interest in a peaceful Europe by forcing the West European nations into supra-national cooperation. The Marshall Plan thereby helped lay the foundation for the modern European Union.

The Ratification of NATO: Executive-Legislative Cooperation and an Unprecedented Commitment in U.S. Foreign Policy

By Elizabeth Edwards Spalding

The case of Senate ratification of the North Atlantic Treaty Organization (NATO) in 1949 shows well how President Harry S. Truman relied on his Congressional background and his trusted White House advisors in order to achieve his policy goals. Most of Truman's foreign policies were truly revolutionary. In the mid-1940s, Truman established precedents in American foreign policy under the extraordinary circumstances of the Cold War; in so doing, he committed the United States to extensive involvement and leadership in global affairs—an approach that we still live with and lead by in the post-Cold War world.

Before becoming Vice President under Franklin Roosevelt in 1945, Truman served in the U.S. Congress for 10 years as a Senator from his home state of Missouri. As Chairman of the Senate Special Committee to Investigate the National Defense Program—better known as the Truman Committee—he was widely respected for his work to make the U.S. war effort more rapid and efficient. When he became President after FDR's death in April 1945, Truman steered his policies through Congress by drawing on his Senatorial experience and his relationships with Members of Congress.

Truman followed a popular President, and it is common to refer to him as walking "in the shadow of FDR." Despite enjoying a short honeymoon period with Congress, Truman was often perceived as lacking in foreign policy experience and charisma.

Initially surrounded by Roosevelt's advisors, Truman moved steadily over the course of his first year and a half as President to put his own people in the Cabinet. During much of the negotiations leading up to the North Atlantic Treaty in 1948 and 1949, General George C. Marshall was Secretary of State and Robert Lovett was Undersecretary. By the time of the Senate vote on the ratification of NATO in 1949, Dean Acheson was Secretary of State and James Webb was Undersecretary.

The Truman Cabinet

Truman chose well. Marshall was greatly admired for his World War II record and was viewed as a man who remained above politics, while Lovett, his trusted aide, respected Truman and had close relationships with the Republicans in Congress. Although Acheson exhibited a demeanor that often grated on various Members of Congress, he was most impressive behind the scenes and in his abilities to testify before Congressional hearings and convince his audience to approve the President's policies. Truman had learned from past poor choices (i.e.,

Henry A. Wallace and James Byrnes) and was smart in choosing these men for additional reasons. Although strongly committed to their own convictions and opinions, Marshall, Lovett, and Acheson always stood by Truman publicly even if they disagreed with him privately; worked unceasingly to pass and implement the President's policies; and agreed with Truman that the Soviet Union presented the gravest threat to the world's freedom and security.

Vigorous debate in Congress met all of Truman's Cold War policies. Many in Congress who supported the largely political and economic aid of the Truman Doctrine[1] and the Marshall Plan[2] looked at the North Atlantic Alliance a bit differently. In 1949, there was a debate as to whether the United States should become a member of a defensive alliance that might not be temporary in nature and how much such a long-term association would cost.

Facing a Republican Congress from 1947 until 1949, Truman forged a bipartisan partnership with Senator Arthur Vandenberg that was crucial to successful passage and funding of the Truman Doctrine and the Marshall Plan. When it came to NATO, Vandenberg again was essential. Some Senators, especially a Republican contingent under Robert Taft, objected to the idea of NATO on the grounds that it violated national sovereignty; infringed on the Congressional power to declare war; and would be an excessive commitment on the part of the United States. Other Senators (Republicans and Democrats alike) were concerned that NATO would undermine the United Nations. These Senators were committed to making the UN a "going concern," as the popular phrase of the time went. Under Truman, Marshall and Lovett cultivated both bipartisanship and smooth Executive-Legislative relations. Vandenberg, for his part and with Truman's support, won Senate approval of the Vandenberg resolution of June 1948, which reconciled U.S. membership in the North Atlantic Pact with the principles of the American Constitution and the United Nations Charter.

By the time of the heart of Senate debate on NATO ratification, the Democrats had taken control of Congress. Senator Tom Connally replaced Vandenberg as Chairman of the Senate Foreign Relations Committee, although the latter was still an important minority figure. Connally did not oppose the North Atlantic Treaty, but he insisted on— and got from Secretary of State Acheson—a guarantee of Congress's primacy in committing the United States to war. It helped that Truman knew Connally personally, because at times Acheson showed great impatience with the Senator and the rest of the Committee. During 10 days of Senate debate, Vandenberg and Connally promoted NATO and its purpose vigorously and were ultimately successful. In July 1949, the Senate approved the North Atlantic Treaty by a vote of 82 to 13.

President Truman kept an appropriately low profile during the debate and depended on Vandenberg, Connally, and Acheson to win the day. The ratification of NATO embodied Vandenberg's famous formulation that bipartisan unity should begin "at the water's edge," an important foreign policy lesson for all those who serve in the Executive and Legislative branches. In agreement with Vandenberg, Truman also viewed NATO as the logical and necessary complement to the Truman Doctrine and the Marshall Plan, and proclaimed the treaty "an historic step toward a world of peace, a free world, free from fear, but it is only one step."

Conclusion

President Harry S. Truman clearly and consistently defined the challenges facing the United States and the free world in the Cold War, what was essentially the "new world order" of the postwar era. At the same time, Truman was able to work with two different Congresses with two different majorities in achieving his foreign policy agenda. As a result, he won Congressional and public support for his major policies of containment—policies that committed the United States to unprecedented involvement in global affairs. The establishment and Senate ratification of the North Atlantic Treaty Organization is a successful example of Truman's approach.

Truman picked able advisors and, although he was a Democratic Party stalwart, he was not afraid to cut across party lines. Secretary of State George C. Marshall—who steadfastly referred to himself as nonpartisan—was almost universally admired by the American people. He was an intimate friend of Republican Senator Arthur Vandenberg, whom Truman relied on for bipartisanship in Cold War foreign policy. Undersecretary of State Robert Lovett was a Republican who agreed with Truman's Cold War policies, and he was also close to Vandenberg. And Secretary of State Dean Acheson, a staunch supporter of Truman in 1946 when others had abandoned the President after the Democrats lost Congress, was sometimes too sardonic for his own good but undeniably possessed a keen sense of the tactics needed to gain Senate approval of NATO. Truman surrounded himself with those who became known as the "wise men," suggesting that he too was not lacking in this virtue. More precisely though, Truman aimed to apply America's principles of freedom and equality to what he viewed as a global struggle between democracy and totalitarianism. He looked to like-minded men such as Vandenberg, and forged partnerships with them, even though they disagreed on many domestic policies and on other foreign policy issues.

---

[1] The Truman Doctrine helped to fund the Greek and Turkish militaries, rather than the United States participating directly.

[2] In the Marshall Plan American money was used by the West Europeans to help themselves recover from World War II's devastation.

Passage of the Civil Rights Act of 1964

By James P. Pfiffner

For the 80 years since the withdrawal of Union troops from the South in 1876, Congress had passed no Civil Rights legislation. Southern conservatives, all Democrats, had been able to prevent any consideration of legislation through the skillful use of parliamentary tactics—even when there was a majority in favor of passage. As Senate Majority Leader, Lyndon Johnson had helped pass the Civil Rights Act of 1957, although its provisions were substantially watered down by conservatives to allow for its passage. The 1960 Civil Rights Act was passed in a similarly weakened state.

Neither John Kennedy nor Lyndon Johnson had records that suggested that they would take up the banner of civil rights for African Americans as a major political priority. But as Kennedy saw the brutal repression of nonviolent civil rights demonstrators in the South in the early 1960s, he became publicly committed to reform. In May 1963 his Administration proposed legislation that would become the Civil Rights Act of 1964. At the time that Kennedy was assassinated in November 1963, the bill had passed the House Judiciary Committee and was before the House Rules Committee.

The bill would outlaw discrimination based on race in public accommodations, in voting, and in employment and training programs. It also empowered the federal government to go to court to enforce desegregation in schools throughout the country by cutting off federal education funds. In addition to outlawing race as a basis for discrimination, the bill included religion, national origin, and sex.

When Johnson became President after Kennedy's assassination, he was in a relatively weak position, having inherited his office and having no electoral mandate. In addition, Johnson faced the same Congressional situation as Kennedy—with powerful southern committee chairmen skillful at procedural legislative tactics and able to activate the "conservative coalition" of southern Democrats and the majority of Republicans that had united so often to defeat Civil Rights legislation. Yet Johnson was committed to get the bill through Congress and he marshaled all of his own prestige, power, and skills to do it. When Johnson brought ardent segregationist Senator Richard Russell of Georgia to the White House to warn him that, despite Johnson's affection for him, if Russell got in the way of Johnson's bill, "I'm going to run over you." Russell replied: "You may do that. But by God, it's going to cost you the South and cost you the election." Johnson's answer was, "If that's the price I've got to pay, I'll pay it gladly" (Dallek, *Flawed Giant*, p. 112).

The first challenge on the bill that Johnson faced as President was to pry it out of the House Rules Committee. The roadblock there was Virginia Congressman Howard Smith, who had used his legislative wiles in the past to block much of the Civil Rights legislation. To get the bill out of committee for floor consideration without Smith's consent required a discharge petition. By Christmas Johnson and the House leadership were still 50 votes short, but they put so much pressure on individual members that Smith finally bowed to the inevitable and allowed the bill to go to the floor before the discharge petition would force him to do it. On the floor of the House the bill's proponents were able to defeat every amendment in the 10 days of debate, and it passed on February 10, 1964, by a 290-130 vote.

The Senate, however, promised to be an even tougher battle. Senator James O. Eastland of Mississippi was Chairman of the Judiciary Committee and had been able to use his powers to kill more than 100 proposed Civil Rights bills in the 1950s and 1960s. But Eastland's powers as Chairman were effectively evaded when the Senate leadership, which held much of the same scheduling power as the Rules Committee had in the House, was able to place the bill directly on the Senate calendar, thereby bypassing the Judiciary Committee completely.

The Filibuster

Since the Civil Rights bill was likely to pass on the floor if it came to a vote, the only way to block consideration of the bill was to filibuster—a tactic that had been used very effectively to block Civil Rights legislation over the past decade in the Senate. Rule XXII in the Senate allowed for unlimited debate by members before a vote. The only way to stop a filibuster and have a vote on the floor was a cloture motion that required a two-thirds majority (later changed to three-fifths). The Senate had never before, despite many attempts, been able to invoke cloture to end a Civil Rights filibuster. Johnson knew that the southerners would use the filibuster, and so he arranged for all of his important legislative proposals to be cleared in the first months of 1964. By taking this action, the filibuster would not create pressure to give up the Civil Rights fight merely to get other legislation considered. "They can filibuster until hell freezes over," Johnson declared (Dallek, p. 116).

So Johnson let the filibuster drone on through April and the beginning of May before he made his move to get the necessary votes for cloture. In his move, Johnson called in favors from his years as Senate Majority Leader and used all of his leverage as President. To get the necessary votes Johnson knew he had to enable moderate Republicans to vote for the bill. To convince them and to provide them with political cover, Johnson courted his old colleague, Minority Leader Everett McKinley Dirksen of Illinois. Johnson appealed to Dirksen's sense of history, and used the example of Michigan Senator Arthur Vandenberg—who in the 1940s became known as a statesman because of his rejection of his previous isolationism and subsequent bipartisan efforts for U.S. engagement in the world. Johnson was willing to share credit for passage of the bill with Dirksen, and also made several small changes in the bill to satisfy him and Republican moderates.

Passage

After 75 days of debate the Senate, for the first time in its history, used a cloture vote to force consideration of a Civil Rights bill (on June 10, 1964 by a vote of 71-29). On July 2, 1964, President Johnson signed the bill into law. In the evening after the signing ceremony Johnson was pensive, and when he was asked by his aide, Bill Moyers, what was bothering him, Johnson replied, "I think we just delivered the South to the Republican party for a long time to come" (Dallek, p. 120). Johnson's prediction came true as Republicans steadily gained strength in the South over the next several decades. By the 1990s, in the former "Solid South," Republicans held majorities in governorships, as well as in Senate and House representation. But the intent of the Act was also fulfilled in that racial discrimination in public accommodations, schools, and voting has been largely eliminated (even though all vestiges of racism have not been erased from American society).

The passage of the 1964 Civil Rights Act was impressive because Johnson achieved it with the same Congress that had given John Kennedy so much trouble—and before Johnson's large victory in 1964 that brought huge Democratic majorities to the House and Senate. The lessons that can be learned from Johnson's victory include his willingness to share credit for victory, his patient use of the legislative tactics that he learned in the Senate, and his willingness to work closely with Members of Congress from both parties. But most importantly, victory was due to the Presidential commitment to the ideals of justice embodied in the Act, and for the willingness to take serious political risks to achieve those ideals.

Lessons from the Tax Reform Act of 1986

By Timothy Conlan

The Tax Reform Act (TRA) of 1986 was the principal domestic legislative accomplishment of President Ronald Reagan's second term and a landmark achievement in the history of U.S. tax policy. The TRA comprehensively restructured the nation's individual and corporate income tax laws. It simplified the income tax structure by reducing the number of individual brackets from 15 to 3. It lowered both personal and corporate tax rates, bringing the top effective rate for individuals down from 50 percent to 33 percent. To compensate for the reduction in proceeds from lower tax rates and to maintain "revenue neutrality," the TRA broadened the income tax base—and it closed, shrank, or limited scores of loopholes, deductions, credits, and exemptions. To further assure that no affluent individuals could avoid paying at least some taxes, the bill added a new alternative minimum tax. Finally, although different companies and industries were affected very differently by the changes, overall corporate tax revenues were substantially increased by the tax law changes, while six million poor people were removed entirely from the income tax rolls.

Because these changes were so substantial and upset so many established interests and practices, most observers doubted that the TRA would be successfully adopted, right up to the point of final passage. Unprecedented numbers of lobbyists and constituents, seeking to block or amend the legislation, swarmed Capitol Hill and organized grass roots campaigns. The task of overcoming tremendous interest group opposition was made even more difficult by divided party control of the executive and legislative branches.

The way the Reagan Administration and other tax reform advocates overcame these obstacles and won enactment suggests several lessons about Presidential leadership strategies in the legislative arena. First, President Reagan's proposal built upon an established consensus among tax policy experts concerning what would constitute true tax reform. Professionals in the Treasury Department, including both political appointees and senior career civil servants, were given wide latitude to design a reform bill that met widely accepted economic and legal principles of "good policy." Although politically inspired adjustments were subsequently made in both the President's last submission to Congress and the Congress's final tax bill, this original proposal (dubbed "Treasury I") determined the basic structure of tax reform legislation. The proposal also remained the standard of good policy (for the mass media and others) against which all other changes and proposals were measured throughout the process. Interest groups opposing tax reform were forced to adopt a "yes, but" stance, expressing support for tax reform as a general concept but seeking to exclude their favored preference from the package. In addition, Treasury I's principle of revenue neutrality set groups seeking to restore tax benefits under the plan against one another as they sought to find compensating sources of new revenues for their proposed changes.

Turning Obstacle to Advantage

Another important factor in this case was the transformation of divided party government as an obstacle to an advantage. Normally, one would expect that Republican control of the White House and Senate, and Democratic control of the House, would heighten the difficulty of enacting a Presidential proposal—and in some respects this was true in the case of the TRA. Yet President Reagan was able to generate enough interest in and support for the idea that Democrats in Congress began to compete for ownership. This launched a process of interparty competition to pass reform legislation that helped greatly to overcome the obstacles to passage.

Two final lessons are extensions of the conventional virtues of perseverance and humility. The Administration's perseverance in the face of repeated obstacles and difficulties was crucial to the eventual passage of the legislation. Many times during the process the bill appeared to be dead and buried. It looked at times as if no bill would be reported from the House Ways and Means Committee. When it was reported, the rule needed for House floor consideration was defeated on the first attempt. Only an all-out lobbying campaign by the White House, including a trip by President Reagan to Capitol Hill to appeal for more Republican votes, reversed that outcome. Later the bill appeared to be stymied in the Senate and again in the conference committee. The President's refusal to give up, along with constant pressure and skilled assistance by his Administration, were crucial in keeping the legislation alive when the situation appeared to be lost.

Finally, the tax reform saga underscores the need for humility in political strategizing. In particular, translating legislative success into political advantage is a difficult and unpredictable affair. Starting out, some White House strategists held great hope that tax reform would help secure a Republican realignment among the voters. They reasoned that realignment would provide tangible benefits to millions of taxpayers and counteract negative stereotypes of the Republicans as the party for the rich and for corporate America. In large part the legislation did these things. However, credit had to be shared with the Democrats, and many benefits were not immediately felt, so Republicans received little advantage from the outcome. In the 1986 elections, soon after the successful adoption of the TRA, the Republicans lost control of the Senate to the Democratic party. Although tax reform played little role in the defeat—and it may well have helped certain candidates—it was not seen in the end as a partisan victory. It was an accomplishment for which the Administration could be proud for policy rather than political reasons.

Deficit Reduction in 1993: Clinton's First Budget

By James P. Pfiffner

The major theme of Bill Clinton's 1992 Presidential campaign had been the state of the economy. Clinton had promised to stimulate the economy, cut the deficit, invest in worker training and infrastructure, cut taxes for the middle class, and reform health care financing. But immediately after the inauguration the unveiling of his budget policy was delayed because the President was not sure whether the economy needed to be stimulated to pull it out of the recession or whether the deficit had to be attacked to ensure the longer-term health of the economy. The first several months of the Administration were a fight for the mind of the President over this issue.

In one corner of the budget policy debate were Clinton's campaign advisers who argued that the President should stick to his campaign promise for a middle-class tax cut and investments to help people deal with economic dislocations caused by a globalizing economy and layoffs. In the other corner were the "deficit hawks" who believed that the long-term health of the U.S. economy was dependent on reducing the deficit. The national debt had climbed from $1 trillion in 1981 to $4 trillion in 1993, the annual deficit would be nearly $300 billion if no changes were made, and interest on the debt approached $200 billion per year, which amounted to 14 percent of budget outlays. The country was eating the seed corn rather than investing it in the future.

The deficit hawks argued that in the short term an economic recovery depended upon keeping interest rates down and inflation in check. If the bond markets (moneylenders) thought that the Clinton economic plan would encourage inflation by continuing to increase the deficit, they would demand higher interest rates to loan money, and the recovery would be cut short. On the other hand, steep deficit reduction would not guarantee a robust recovery in the short term. Federal Reserve Board Chairman Alan Greenspan was reinforcing the same message that the deficit hawks were arguing. Clinton understood both sides of the economic arguments well and was clearly ambivalent, realizing the necessity of deficit reduction but not being eager to sacrifice his other policy initiatives and devote much of his initial political capital to fighting the deficit battle. For a while he thought he could do both at the same time.

One of the key turning points came during the transition in a meeting between Clinton and his main economic advisers on January 7, 1993. They warned that the deficit would soar to $360 billion in 1997 and $500 billion in 2000 if nothing was done to curb it. The advisers admitted that in the short term the cuts and taxes might slow the economy but in the longer term the economy would benefit. Clinton was facing the unfortunate dilemma that he was being forced to impose economic pain during his Presidency so that economic benefits would accrue in the future under his successors.

In a series of all-day sessions in early February, the outline of the Clinton economic plan was hammered out. The President decided to drop his promise for a middle-class tax cut, increase tax rates on the affluent, and propose a broad-based energy tax. The combination of tax increases with spending cuts would reduce the deficit by about $500 billion over five years. The first Congressional votes on the package came with consideration of the budget resolution, which set the outlines and totals of the budget. On March 18 the House passed the budget resolution on a party line vote of 243-183, with 11 Democrats defecting to vote no. The vote in the Senate was tougher for the Administration, but after six days of lobbying and 45 roll call votes to defeat Republican amendments, the Senate passed the budget resolution 54-45, with only one Democrat voting against the President's proposal.

A Democrat-Only Strategy

The Clinton Administration was criticized for its strategy of failing to appeal to moderate Republicans in Congress and to seek only Democratic votes, but in choosing this strategy the Administration was responding to Congressional signals. In late January 1993 Senator Robert Dole told Clinton at a White House meeting that the Republicans probably would not vote for his economic proposals since they included tax increases, thus giving Republicans a campaign issue. Another factor pushing the White House toward a Democrats-only strategy on the Hill was the polarization between the parties in the House. In order to get a budget bill through the House, the Administration had to hold most of the liberal Democrats and could not afford to lose them by appealing to Republicans. This strategy was encouraged by the Democratic leadership.

In late May the Clinton budget was considered in the House. Although both chambers had passed the budget resolution that set out the totals and general outlines of the plan, the reconciliation bill was the enforcing document that laid out the details of spending cuts and tax increases that would be used to reach the totals. After a grueling fight in the House and the granting of many political favors, the President won the battle on May 27 by a vote of 219-213, with 38 Democrats voting against the bill and no Republicans voting in favor. On June 24 after another exhausting fight, during which the BTU tax was dropped and replaced with a 4.3 cent per gallon gas tax, the Senate passed its bill with Vice President Al Gore breaking a 49-49 tie.

But the fight was not over. Both Houses had passed different versions of the reconciliation bill and the differences had to be ironed out in conference committee and brought back to the floor of both chambers for final votes before it could go to the President for his signature. In July, in preparation for the final reconciliation votes Clinton again became intensely involved in lobbying House Members for their votes. At one point Clinton had five Members of the House on separate phone lines at the same time. The President's personal involvement may have been excessive, but it was necessary to win the votes of wavering Members. When the Members saw how desperate the Administration was for votes, they held their commitments in order to bargain for special deals for their districts. The House vote again was extremely close, with a 218-216 win. The final Senate vote was 51-50, with the Vice President again casting the tie-breaking vote.

The budget votes were important in that they made a significant contribution to deficit reduction, but they also demonstrated how fragile support for the President was in Congress. The reconciliation packages were the only major pieces of legislation since World War II that were adopted without one vote from the opposition party.

Lessons Learned

At times it is necessary for the President to become personally involved in active trading for votes in order to win a closely fought, important policy battle. A closely divided Congress makes coalition building difficult, and seeking votes from only one party in Congress makes a President vulnerable to offering concessions to his own party.

Insofar as the deficit reduction package helped (along with President George H.W. Bush's 1990 budget package) to lay the groundwork for the historic economic expansion of the 1990s, it may be appropriate to break campaign promises because of changing circumstances.

A President will probably not get much political credit in the short term for fiscal prudence.

President Clinton's Health Care Reform Proposals of 1994

By James P. Pfiffner

The major legislative initiative of President Bill Clinton's first year in office was the reform of the United States health care system. As Clinton had argued in his campaign, 37 million Americans were without health care insurance, and the United States was unique among modernized democracies in its lack of universal health care coverage for its citizens. Thus, in late January 1993, President Clinton announced a major Administration health care policy initiative that would be headed by Hillary Clinton. He gave the task force a 100-day target to produce the Administration proposal.

Although the group was not ready with a plan within 100 days, by the end of May it had talked with more than 500 separate organizations and had held several hundred meetings with Members of Congress. Despite the felt need to move quickly with one of its most important priorities, the Administration proposal was not ready for several reasons. The task force could not come to terms with the concerns of Clinton's economic team—who thought that sweeping changes might cost too much and favored a more incremental approach.

Clinton finally gave his key kick-off speech on health care to Congress on September 22, 1993. The speech spelled out the principles of universal coverage and managed competition; it was a great success with Democrats in Congress and in public opinion. A majority of the public approved of the President's plan in October 1993 Hillary Clinton received a respectful (Republican) and enthusiastic (Democratic) reception when she went to Capitol Hill to testify for the Administration's health care package. But the actual text of the bill was not yet ready and did not make it to the Hill until October 27.

President Clinton had considered and rejected a single-payer plan (as Canada has) because it seemed too much like "socialized medicine." He thus decided that his plan would rely on private insurance companies and employer mandates. But in order to guarantee that those without insurance would be covered by competitive prices, it would be necessary to create health insurance cooperatives from scratch.

Universal Coverage

Clinton argued that the bottom line of his health care plan was universal coverage, and he threatened to veto any bill that did not provide it. Although the added coverage would be expensive, the cost for the poor of a lot of treatment in emergency rooms was more. But the combination of universal coverage with cost control—two essential elements of the plan—necessarily entailed some coercion. This came in the form of premium caps, mandatory participation in the cooperatives, and mandates for employers to purchase coverage.

These factors added up to a bill of sweeping scope and complexity. The United States had a mixed system of health care, with most doctors and insurance companies in the private sector, and with the federal government financing Medicare and Medicaid. Combine these realities accepted by Clinton, with his goals of universal coverage and cost containment, and you have inherent complexity and some government coercion in any plan to deal with all of these factors at once.

To ask for a simpler approach would mean abandoning some major elements of the plan. So the complaint of complexity, while true, was not so much the issue as were the major parts in the plan. No one else came up with a simpler idea that would accomplish all of the goals of the Clinton plan. Nevertheless, the complexity issue did play a major role in its defeat. But the complexity was real in that the proposed changes would have resulted in huge alterations affecting up to one-seventh of the U.S. economy—changes that would have entailed many unintended consequences. Even though most of the elements of the package already existed in various forms (employer provision of insurance, cost controls through Medicare, managed care, HMOs, etc.), the combination of all of the elements into a sweeping overhaul of such a large portion of the economy was unacceptable to the U.S. political system in 1994.

In December 1993 allegations about the Clintons' investment in the Whitewater development were raised in the press. The possibility of shady or illegal activities on behalf of the Clintons in Arkansas, and the Administration's inability to defuse the issue, rose to the proportions of a major scandal in the spring. The unproven allegations undercut the confidence of the general public in the President, and Clinton's approval ratings began to fall from the almost 60 percent level he had at the end of 1993.

Too Large, Too Complex

At the same time Republicans were able to label the health care plan as too large, too complex, too costly, and too much government. Public opinion about the health care plan was crucial and began to shift in the spring of 1994 as the majority who had approved of the plan became the minority. There may have been a public consensus that health care needed fixing, but there was no consensus on how to fix it.

The complexity of the plan meant that citizens would have to trust the President's judgement that it was good for the country. Thus when the Republicans were able to frame the issue as one of trust in President Clinton on the policy issues, and trust of the federal government on the implementation issues, the answer to the American public was obvious. Interest groups were mobilized in opposition to the Clinton plan.

The Administration was criticized for adopting a partisan approach to the health care bill. The criticism is legitimate, but it is not clear that there ever was a bipartisan coalition that could have been forged to pass a bill remotely resembling the principles laid out in Clinton's popular speech of September 22, 1993.

The failure of the health care campaign highlighted several things. Clinton did not completely understand his vulnerability on the Hill with such a huge piece of legislation. With a 43 percent plurality in the 1992 election, a divided Democratic party, and a contentious and intractable policy issue, how could he have expected to win? The consequences of the failure were the loss of the Administration's major policy initiative, as well as the loss of a number of other bills that were pending in Congress when health care went down.

In sum, health care reform failed because of divided Democrats, emboldened Republicans, high interest group spending against reform, an overly ambitious proposal, Clinton's 43 percent plurality, declining public approval, the Whitewater scandal, the complexity of the proposals, and the resistance of Americans to large governmental programs in the 1990s.

We can learn from the health care experience that large-scale, complex, and costly changes in public policy must have broad-scale support and be developed in close cooperation with Congress. Policy changes may be perceived as expanding benefits, but will lose support if they are seen as potentially taking away benefits from powerful constituencies.

The Balanced Budget Act of 1997

By George C. Edwards III

Throughout his first term, budget battles were at the center of conflict between President Bill Clinton and Congressional Republicans. The President's fiscal year 1994 budget, his first, passed Congress without a single Republican vote.

The Republican Congressional majority that came to power in 1995 was determined to make a balanced budget and tax cuts their vehicle for radically reshaping the federal government. But they underestimated Clinton's will and his ability to stymie them. By the time the Republicans conceded defeat in budget talks that dragged into 1996, they had triggered two federal shutdowns that closed much of the government and brought them a drubbing in the public opinion polls. They also made it easier for the President to present himself to the public as a moderate protecting the country from irresponsible reversals in well-established policies.

The residue of these battles—and of the ensuing fall 1996 elections, in which Democrats tarred Republicans as Medicare killers—was a deep bitterness that seemed likely to poison the relationship between the White House and Congress indefinitely. Yet within a few months both sides reached an historic agreement on achieving a balanced budget within five years.

Foundations of an Agreement

Several environmental factors contributed to this success. In the first place, a balanced budget was achievable only because of the plummeting federal deficit. The primary cause for the deficit's dramatic drop was the surging economy. Also essential to the agreement was the groundwork laid by the budgets of 1990 and 1993. Both budgets structured decision making on taxing and spending in a way that substantially constrained deficit spending.

This foundation had been costly for Presidents, however. In 1990, President George H.W. Bush bit the bullet and reversed his election pledge not to raise taxes. He agreed to a budget deal with the Congressional Democrats that succeeded in reducing the deficit and limiting spending. In 1992, he lost his bid for reelection. In 1993, President Clinton followed Bush's precedent and reversed his promise to lower taxes with a program of higher taxes and spending constraints. In the 1994 elections, Republicans castigated Clinton and the Democrats for increasing taxes in support of a bloated federal government. In the end, they won majorities in both houses of Congress for the first time since the election of 1952.

Yet despite the unsettling history of recent budget battles, efforts to obtain a budget agreement succeeded. First, everyone was exhausted from brutalizing each other over the past four years. The fighting was an obstacle not only to dealing with the budget but also to accomplishing anything else.

In addition, both sides needed an agreement. The President needed a legislative achievement for his legacy, and the Democrats needed credibility on the issue of fiscal responsibility if they were to retake Congress and retain the White House in 2000. The Republicans needed to show that they could govern as a majority party and make moderate rather than radical changes in policy.

In this environment, both sides departed from the warfare over the budget that had preoccupied Congress for most of the previous generation. Low-keyed, good faith negotiations began shortly after the President submitted his budget, and senior White House officials held a series of private meetings with Members of Congress. Unlike the political posturing in late 1995 and early 1996, neither side focused on moving the negotiations into the public arena. In the end, this made it easier for them to reach an agreement.

Equally important, both sides were willing to compromise, and they each gained from it. The negotiations culminated in an agreement to balance the budget by 2002 and Congress adopted a broadly supported, bipartisan budget resolution to guide its tax and spending decisions. This in turn paved the way for two reconciliation bills, including the Balanced Budget Act of 1997, and 13 fiscal year 1998 appropriations bills.

For Republicans, the budget agreement capped a balanced-budget and tax-cutting drive that had consumed them since they took over Congress in 1995. They got tax and spending cuts, a balanced budget in five years, and a plan to keep Medicare solvent for another decade. Thus, although they did not win a radical overhaul of entitlement programs, they did make substantial progress toward their core goals.

For Clinton, the budget agreement represented perhaps his greatest legislative triumph. He left the bargaining table with much of what he wanted, including an increased scope for the child tax credit, a new children's health initiative, restoration of welfare benefits for disabled legal immigrants, increased spending for food stamps, and a host of other incremental increases in social spending.

These compromises did not satisfy everyone, of course. Clinton had to walk a fine line between compromising with Republicans and maintaining the support of Democratic liberals who did not like budgetary constraints and did not want to hand the Republicans a positive accomplishment. They were also upset that they were not included in the negotiating process. Similarly, Republican leaders had to deal with die-hard conservatives, who did not want to compromise at all with the President.

Lessons Learned

The dramatic shift from the rancorous partisan warfare that had dominated the consideration of the budget in the 104th Congress to the bipartisan compromise of the 105th Congress paid substantial dividends. Building on a strong economy and two earlier rounds of deficit reduction, President Clinton and the Republican majority in Congress struck an historic agreement to balance the budget in five years, while cutting taxes and increasing spending for some Administration priorities such as children's health care.

To succeed, all leaders must accurately identify the possibilities for accomplishing their goals. In 1997, President Clinton recognized that it was in the interest of both Democrats and Republicans to reach an agreement on the budget, and that such an agreement was possible. He also concluded that it was worth taking the political risk of antagonizing liberals on the left and being outmaneuvered by his heretofore implacable opponents on the right to attempt to reach a notable agreement.

Leaders must also adopt a strategy for governing appropriate to the environment in which they are operating. When political leaders take their cases directly to the public, they have to accommodate the limited attention spans of the audience and the availability of space on television. As a result, the President and his opponents often reduce choices to stark black and white terms. When leaders frame issues in such terms, they typically frustrate rather than facilitate building coalitions. The positions are difficult to compromise, which hardens negotiating positions as both sides posture as much to mobilize an intense minority of supporters as to convince the other side. Going public is often antithetical to governing.

Traditionally, Presidents attempted to form coalitions in Congress through bargaining. The core strategy was to build a coalition by providing benefits for both sides, allowing many to share in the coalition's success and to declare victory. Going public is fundamentally different. The core strategy is to defeat the opposition, creating winners and losers in a zero-sum game. In going public, the President attempts to intimidate opponents by increasing the political costs of opposition rather than attracting them with benefits. Yet going public may actually make coalition building more difficult. Polarization, gridlock, and public cynicism, which characterize American politics today, are the likely results.

The decision of President Clinton and the Republican Congressional leaders to quietly negotiate and compromise, letting everyone claim victory, made the budget agreement possible. In addition, the success of these executive-legislative negotiations paved the way for additional talks of a similar nature on Social Security and Medicare that may have ultimately proved fruitful if it were not for the confounding influence of the impeachment inquiry in 1998.

The 1999 Comprehensive Nuclear Test Ban Treaty

By Carl Cannon

On September 24, 1996, President Bill Clinton went to the United Nations in New York to sign the Comprehensive Nuclear Test Ban Treaty (CTBT), an elusive pact that the President called "the longest-sought, hardest-fought prize in arms control history."

The verbiage may have been grandiose, but in truth Clinton wasn't far off. The test ban treaty was originally proposed by President Dwight D. Eisenhower and had long been seen by arms control advocates as a step toward reducing in nuclear arsenals, and more importantly, as a tool of non-proliferation.

In 1963, a watered-down version of the ban was passed, amid great fanfare, in a treaty that prohibited atmospheric testing of nuclear weapons. Underground explosions, as well as some other limited forms of tests, had been conducted in the previous decade by the Soviet Union, China, Great Britain, France, and of course, the United States. India joined the nuclear fraternity in 1974. But the end of the Cold War rekindled the hopes in the arms control community for a more complete ban. In 1992, President George H.W. Bush signed a moratorium on such testing, and Clinton eagerly picked up on this theme once he took office. On that autumn day in 1996 when he visited the UN, in fact, Clinton used the same pen that President John F. Kennedy had used to sign the 1963 pact. CTBT was a treaty, he said, that would guide the world "toward a century in which the roles and risks of nuclear weapons can be further reduced, and ultimately eliminated."

It didn't exactly work out that way. In our system, of course, the United States Senate must ratify any treaty negotiated by the President. And the subsequent inability of President Clinton to even get a majority of votes for this treaty, let alone the two-thirds needed for ratification, is a case study in failure. Whose failure, exactly, is still a point of disagreement. What isn't in dispute, however, is that when the dust settled three years later, on October 13, 1999, the U.S. Senate had decided a matter of national security on a virtual party-line vote. Only four Republicans—Arlen Specter of Pennsylvania, James M. Jeffords of Vermont, John H. Chafee of Rhode Island, and Gordon Smith of Oregon—voted with the Democratic President. Of the 45 Democrats in the Senate, 44 of them voted in favor of the treaty—Robert C. Byrd of West Virginia voted present. It was the first time the Senate had rejected a major international treaty pushed by the President in almost 80 years—and it had a distinctly partisan flavor to it.

This unhappy event was the result of mistrust between the Executive Branch and key Senators, of the excess partisanship that characterizes Washington these days, and of uncertain Presidential leadership. The question is whether, and how, it could have been avoided.

Under the two-term tenure of Bill Clinton, the White House struggled from the start to forge even a cordial working relationship with Senator Jesse Helms, the North Carolina Republican who heads the Senate Foreign Relations Committee. This turns out to be highly relevant to the fate of CTBT. On November 21, 1994, even before he assumed control of the committee, Helms said in an off-the-cuff comment to his hometown newspaper that President Clinton "better have a bodyguard" if he visits military bases in North Carolina.

Democrats in the Senate, stung over losing control of their committees, lashed back at Helms' intemperate comment with rhetoric that was equally personal in nature. Senator Christopher J. Dodd of Connecticut, mistakenly saying that Helms had made the comments on the anniversary of JFK's assassination, said, "To suggest on this day of all days, November 22, that an American President's life might be in jeopardy because [he] visited an American military base suggests my colleague from North Carolina doesn't seem to know what country he's in. This is not a banana republic."

Helms probably thought he was in the United States of America, which cherishes free speech, but over in the White House, officials were in no frame of mind to calm down their Democratic allies on Capitol Hill. In fact, they threw fuel on the fire. In a grandstanding move, the Secret Service announced that it was launching an investigation, not into Helms, but into what information he might have received to prompt such a comment. White House Chief of Staff and former Congressman Leon E. Panetta raised the decibel level when he told reporters that Helms' comments were "not only reckless but they are dangerous and irresponsible. I think they raise a very serious question as to whether or not he should assume the chairmanship of that committee."

This was a retaliation of sorts: Helms had, days before, said in answer to a question from the press that he didn't believe Clinton was up to serving as Commander in Chief. Helms added that "the people in the armed forces" agreed with him. The Commander in Chief did not let these comments roll off his back. At a press conference a day later, a seething Clinton called Helms' comments "unwise and inappropriate."

"The President oversees the foreign policy of the United States and the Republicans will decide in whom they will repose their trust and confidence," Clinton added tersely. "That's a decision for them to make, not for me."

These personal differences between Helms and the Clinton team, of course, are rooted in policy differences so vast that an attitude of abiding civility was a prerequisite for constructive discussion, let alone compromise. Instead, the seeds of disaster were sown from the beginning.

The 1994 Law of the Sea treaty disappeared into the abyss of Helm's committee, as did the nomination of the Republican Governor of Massachusetts, William Weld, to be Ambassador to Mexico. Hanging in limbo were, in addition to CTBT, the Administration's proposed amendments to the 1972 Anti-Ballistic Missile (ABM) Treaty and the Kyoto (Environmental) Protocol. Helms was on record as saying he wasn't kindly disposed to any of them.

Into this mess stepped Madeleine K. Albright. When she became Secretary of State in early 1997, she vowed to repair the damage with Helms, and to form a working relationship with him. Helms went along, although his motto seemed to be "trust, but verify." For awhile, the new detente seemed to be working. In April of that year, on a bipartisan vote, the Senate ratified the Chemical Weapons Convention. But this occurred only after Senate Majority Leader Trent Lott, a Republican from Mississippi, prevailed on Helms to bring it up for a vote—and only after Helms had extracted some 28 concessions and clarifications in interpretation of the treaty.

On June 1, 1999, Helms noticed that the Clinton Administration had not adhered to one of the markers he had put down. For two years, Helms had insisted that he wouldn't proceed with CTBT unless his committee received the amendments to the ABM treaty, as well as to the Kyoto accords. And now, in early summer of 1999, Helms concluded that the Administration was no longer dealing with him in good faith.

This conflict, too, was rooted in philosophical differences. On the ABM issue, Helms and most Senate Republicans had long maintained, with some plausibility, that treaties with the Soviet Union are no longer valid and must be renegotiated with Russia and the other former Soviet republics. But having committed themselves to a different direction in arms control, namely President Ronald Reagan's Strategic Defense Initiative, Republicans hoped to defeat those amendments to the ABM treaty and, in the process, scuttle the treaty itself. (The amendments concerned the definitions of "theater" missile defenses, which the treaty permitted, and strategic defenses, which it did not. In 1997, the Clinton Administration agreed with Russian officials on a working definition for these two types of missile defenses, but Helms and other Senate conservatives signaled that they were not inclined to do anything that limited the United States.) Clinton, ambivalent about ABM and lacking the votes to change it anyway, ignored the law—and Helms' deadline. This did not make the chairman overly receptive to CTBT.

To make matters more contentious, Democrats, as they had in 1994, upped the ante in the face of Helms' prickliness instead of trying to cool things down. On September 8, 1999, Senator Byron Dorgan, a North Dakota Democrat, stood on the Senate floor and vowed to obstruct all Senate business—"I intend to plant myself on the floor like a potted plant," he said—unless Helms agreed to let CTBT come up for a vote.

This was a strategy that backfired. In a drama that was extensively covered by the media, Lott and Helms outflanked Dorgan and embarrassed the President in the bargain. As it turns out, neither the Senate Democrats nor the White House had done their homework—or enlisted powerful Republicans to help them make their case the way Clinton had done in 1993 while fighting for passage of the North American Free Trade Agreement. The White House didn't even appear to absorb the lesson learned just two years earlier when the Administration successfully cajoled the Senate into passing the Chemical Weapons Convention. For passage of that accord, Clinton had built support in public by speaking about the pact for months, privately made more than two dozen concessions to Helms, made sure that Lott was aboard, and furiously worked the phones to educate Senators and round up votes.

Two years later, the White House did almost none of that for a treaty that the President himself characterized as more important. In fact, it was the opponents who lined up former Secretaries of Defense—of both parties—in public opposition to the treaty. After the vote, Democrats, including the President, all but accused GOP leaders of being unpatriotic—of indulging their hatred of Bill Clinton and their bitterness at losing the impeachment vote to the detriment of peace and world stability.

Clinton, in a fiery session on the White House lawn, denounced the Senate's action as "reckless" and "partisan." Top Clinton advisor Rahm Emanuel also revealed the White House mindset—that this vote was all about politics. "This just reinforces the hardened, partisan, ideological image that exists of this Congress," Emanuel told *The New York Times*. "These people are hell-bent on their own political destruction. The only thing that unites them is their antipathy to Bill Clinton."

In this instance, however, there was something else that united the Republicans (even foreign policy moderates, such as Senator Richard G. Lugar of Indiana, who care a great deal about international affairs and not very much about Bill Clinton's affairs). The Republicans, urged on by Senator John Kyl of Arizona, had come to the conclusion that CTBT was a bad deal for the United States. For months Kyl had quietly been buttonholing his colleagues to make this point. His objections were five-fold:

1. Although the treaty banned low-yield explosions, the United States would not be able to detect such tests, thus leaving America at a disadvantage to nations that had proven they would cheat on such accords;

2. Without any testing at all, the reliability of the American arsenal would degrade over time;

3. The United States needed this nuclear deterrent all the more because, in part, it had now forsworn the use of chemical and biological weapons;

4. CTBT, although promoted as a force for non-proliferation, would not prevent the transfer of technology from one country to another—it would not even block a rogue nation; and

5. If America's non-nuclear allies lost faith in the efficacy of the U.S. arsenal, CTBT would prove to be an incentive for them to acquire such technology.

These, ultimately, were the arguments that carried the day. Could they have been rebutted? Could compromise have occurred? Not in the rhetorical environment of the time. One lesson of the CTBT vote, the merits of the treaty aside, is that words *do* matter—and so does leadership—and that sometimes the mark of a true leader is knowing what not to say and when to turn the other cheek. And that in a hothouse, partisan rhetorical environment, the spirit of compromise that makes government work is a quick casualty. This time, one side got what it wanted-scuttling of a treaty it found flawed-but the next time it might be the Senate that needs something from the White House. And loose talk about bodyguards, potted plants, and being quick to accuse the other side of being unpatriotic is not conducive to such give and take.

IV. DOMESTIC POLICY

The 1956 Federal Highway Act

By Geoffrey Perret

Dwight D. Eisenhower's first important achievement as President was to bring an end to the fighting in Korea. In June 1953, five months after his inauguration, he secured an armistice that remains in force to this day. Yet even as the armistice went into effect, he was worried about the economic implications of peace.

Eisenhower was deeply troubled that deficit financing on a prodigious scale was paying for the war, and he had pledged during the campaign that he would seek a balanced budget. If Eisenhower stuck rigidly to that goal however, the end of the Korean War would be followed by a severe and prolonged recession, something that every modern President has a duty to avoid.

Eisenhower's solution was entirely pragmatic. The budget remained in deficit in 1954 and the recession proved to be short lived and shallow. Eisenhower meanwhile looked for a public works project that would act as a counter to future recessions. Hastily improvised New Deal make-work projects like the Civilian Conservation Corps— "raking leaves," in his words—were not for him. What Eisenhower wanted was a wide range of public works projects that could be initiated when the economy was functioning successfully, when there was still time to think carefully about national needs and devise programs that could be justified over the long term.

Eisenhower had in mind new highways, urban redevelopment, land reclamation, hospital construction, and water conservation. Such projects could move forward in low gear while the good times lasted, but when the economy turned down—most, if not all—could be rapidly accelerated, and together might provide work for millions, if necessary.

Cold War Considerations

There was already a federal highway system and most people considered it adequate for their needs, but Eisenhower was anticipating future demands, including those of national defense. This was, after all, the height of the Cold War. "If I had all the money I wanted right now," he told Senator Styles Bridges, "I wouldn't use it to keep men in the Army. I would much rather put that money into new highways and roads so we could get around this country in a hurry in case of attack."

He created a committee, chaired by an old friend and Army engineering officer, General Lucius D. Clay, to decide whether such a venture made economic sense. The committee's report, issued in January 1955, recommended 41,000 miles of divided highways, built over a period of 10 years, and costing as much as $101 billion.

The Democrats—and Lucius Clay—expected the federal government to finance the project. However, Eisenhower could not accept this and still achieve a balanced budget. He also was convinced that the states, as major beneficiaries, must bear part of the cost. Legislation was introduced in Congress in the spring of 1955, passed the Senate, but was rejected by the House—mainly because of disagreements over financing. Forced to think again, the White House reintroduced the measure in 1956, with a self-financing proposal: a tax on gasoline of four cents a gallon and a small federal tax on new cars and trucks. The states would cover 10 percent of construction costs; the new taxes would allow the federal government to cover the remaining 90 percent.

As the legislation moved through Congress in 1956, the annual Governors' Conference met. The governors inevitably turned their attention to Eisenhower's highway project. A draft resolution was drawn up in which the governors commended the program as being "bold and imaginative" and proposed naming it in Eisenhower's honor. Governor Averell Harriman of New York, a highly partisan Democrat, got "bold and imaginative" struck out, along with the compliment to Eisenhower.

When this was drawn to his attention, Eisenhower laughed it off. "A project as good as this doesn't need to carry my name," he told his staff. It was enough for him that the Congress enact his legislation, which it did.

It was an extraordinary achievement. The Democrats controlled both the Senate and the House and his own party—which contained a powerful and vociferous anti-New Deal element—hardly seemed to notice that Eisenhower's highway program amounted to the biggest public works project in American history. It was the biggest, some writers have even claimed, since the Pyramids.

The Federal Interstate and Defense Highway came into being because Eisenhower was making an investment in the future of the country, rather than an investment in the next election; because his approach was nonpartisan yet persistent; because he had a clear idea of where he wanted to go and was flexible about how he got there; and because he did not seek to capitalize, either personally or as the leader of his party, on this legislative success. Nearly all the benefits, he knew, would accrue to the nation after he left the White House, not while he occupied it.

JFK's "Man To The Moon"

By Theodore C. Sorensen

Senator John F. Kennedy spoke often about a "space gap" during his 1960 Presidential campaign. He did so, he felt, with good reason. The Soviets were the first nation to launch a space satellite—in 1957—

and also the first to put living animals into orbit. Our failure to respond in kind, he felt, clearly demonstrated a lack of initiative, ingenuity, and vitality under Republican rule. Kennedy also was convinced that Americans did not yet fully grasp the worldwide political and psychological impact of the space race. Kennedy feared that these dramatic achievements would create the dangerous impression among nations choosing between capitalism and communism that the United States had ceded to the Soviets unchallenged world leadership and scientific preeminence.

Once he was elected, Kennedy faced the challenge of fulfilling his campaign promises, and he knew that making the space program competitive with the Soviet Union would be a daunting task. The President was more convinced than any of his advisors that a second-rate effort would be inconsistent with U.S. national security, global leadership, and his "New Frontier" spirit of discovery. In his Inaugural and State of the Union addresses, Kennedy declared the space race to be a top national priority. He asked Vice President Lyndon B. Johnson to chair the National Advisory Space Council (NASC). As the Democratic Majority Leader in the Senate, Johnson had been instrumental in the creation of NASA and could draw on his Capitol Hill contacts and long-standing commitment to the increased U.S. presence in space to help the President realize his objective. Kennedy would use his own power as Chief Executive to shape the budget and public relations processes.

Kennedy then asked James Webb to head the National Aeronautics and Space Administration (NASA). Webb was noted for his political savvy and strong managerial skills when he served as Under Secretary of State and, prior to that, as Director of the Bureau of the Budget in the Truman Administration. However, Webb recognized the political pressure and technical issues facing a first-rate U.S. space program and at first was reluctant to accept the position. Kennedy persisted, first directing Johnson to talk to Webb, then bringing Webb to the White House for a face-to-face conversation.

With Webb on board, Kennedy directed the Vice President and NASC to assess current U.S. space capabilities, including the need for additional manpower, scientific talent, long- and short-term facilities, alternative fuels, agency cooperation, and money. Following a series of intense meetings, the NASC offered its recommendations to the President. Kennedy then made what he later termed one of his most important decisions as President: "to shift our efforts in space from low to high gear."

Russian Orbits Earth

However, on April 22, 1961, well before Kennedy had completed his "First 100 Days" in the White House, Moscow announced that Cosmonaut Yuri Gagarin had orbited the earth in less than two hours. Kennedy publicly congratulated Soviet Premier Khruschev and redoubled his efforts to create a successful U.S. space program.

In a special second State of the Union Message in May 1961, Kennedy made a determined and dramatic pledge to land a man on the moon and return him safely to earth before the end of the decade.

At the recommendation of Webb, the President avoided promising a specific year, understanding that the end of the decade could be interpreted as either 1969 or 1970. An extra year could provide NASA with political leeway if it needed additional time for a moon landing. More importantly, the pledge provided a much-needed urgency for the entire space program.

In the following months Kennedy repeatedly employed his influence as President, and the lobbying expertise of Webb and Johnson, to advance the space program on Capitol Hill. "No single space project in this period," the President told the Congress, "will be more impressive to mankind or more important [or] so difficult or expensive to accomplish." Kennedy explained that the United States could only reach the moon if Congress made the space program a national priority; diverted scientific manpower and funds from other important activities; maintained disciplined program efforts; and ended all the petty work stoppages, rivalries, and personnel changes that had long troubled the space program.

Even with the President's full support, the space program was not without conflict. During the long intervals between flights, some of his political and editorial supporters argued that the space budget should be cut back and its timetable expanded. Taxpayers complained about the cost, and a number of scientists complained that more important activities were being slighted. Republicans soon characterized the effort as a "boondoggle" and "science fiction stunt."

President Kennedy refused to bend. He firmly believed that the space program was vital to American interests. To those who said that the money could be better spent relieving ignorance or poverty on this planet, Kennedy pointed out that America had the resources to do both, and that Congress seemed unwilling to increase welfare expenditures regardless of the size of the space program. To those who criticized his decision to concentrate America's research capabilities on the moon shot, he argued that this broad-based scientific effort included 60 unrelated projects that accounted for nearly one-quarter of the space budget. To those who feared that a failed launch would embarrass him as the President and the nation as a superpower, Kennedy replied that the risk not only demonstrated devotion to freedom but enhanced our prestige among other nations because we refused to accept being second-best.

Kennedy's personal daring and tenacity carried the day. He gained the needed funding from Congress and the support of the media and public. He also delegated many of the details to powerful, politically savvy assistants, most notably Vice President Johnson and NASA Administrator James Webb.

The Creation of the Environmental Protection Agency

By John C. Whitaker

The Environmental Protection Agency (EPA) was created under a Nixon Administration government reorganization plan submitted to Congress on July 9, 1970. The mandatory 60-day waiting period for Congressional objections, which then existed under government reorganization authority, expired in September and the new Agency came into being on December 2, 1970.

The Setting

The creation of the EPA was in response to an astonishing national outpouring of concern and a call for action by the public to clean up the environment. The issue seemed to come out of nowhere. During the 1968 Presidential campaign, the press and candidates Richard M. Nixon and Hubert H. Humphrey showed little interest in this emerging issue. Yet only 17 months after the November 1968 election the new Administration watched with amazement the first Earth Day on April 22, 1970, when literally millions joined in a spontaneous celebration. Earth Day had stirred the nation and there was an immediate clamor for action on the part of both Congress and the new Nixon White House. So many politicians were on the stump on that first Earth Day that Congress was forced to close down as most members returned to their districts to take part in the celebration. The oratory, *The Washington Post* observed, was "as thick as smog at rush hour."

A comparison of White House polls (by Opinion Research of Princeton, NJ) taken in May 1969, and just two years later in May 1971, showed how concern for the environment had leaped to the forefront of the national psyche. In May 1971, fully a quarter of the public thought that protecting the environment was important, yet only one percent had thought so two years earlier.

It was clear to both Congress and the White House that the Executive Branch could not respond to the public's demand to clean up the environment without first creating an organization to do the job. At the time there were 44 agencies, offices, and bureaus located in nine separate departments that claimed some responsibility in the field of "environment/natural resources" programs. Yet no single department had enough expertise to take charge.

The fragmented responsibility and disarray was clearly evident at Cabinet meetings. For example, Nixon watched Secretary Robert Finch at Health, Education and Welfare, the department that then had air pollution monitoring responsibility, and John Volpe, Secretary of the Department of Transportation, argue over which department should take the lead in developing a low-emission automobile. On pesticides, Interior Secretary Walter Hickel and Secretary Finch argued for tighter

pesticide controls, while Agriculture Secretary Clifford Hardin emphasized increased crop productivity resulting from the application of pesticides. Secretary of State William Rogers was concerned that one effect
of a ban on the use of DDT in the United States might be to restrict the
supply of DDT to developing countries. Hickel, whose Interior
Department then had responsibility for water quality, wanted vastly
larger amounts of money and a new method of financing for water pollution control, but was opposed by Robert Mayo, Director of the Bureau
of the Budget, and other economic advisors. Secretary Maurice Stans at
the Commerce Department was wary of tighter environmental standards and what effect this might have on corporate profits. The
Chairman of the Council of Economic Advisors, Paul McCracken, had
the same concern plus another one: Would the United States be at an
economic disadvantage competing in the international marketplace if its
product prices reflected the cost of pollution abatement standards that
were more stringent than those of other countries? And so it went. There
was hardly a Cabinet officer around the table who did not have a stake
in the decision of how to reorganize the government to effectively tackle the environmental cleanup. In the end the decisions were made within the White House staff since the Cabinet largely "went native" and
responded to the parochial bureaucratic concerns by trying to retain
whatever environment/natural resource programs were already lodged
in their departments.

Option 1

Two basic options were hotly debated. The first option was to form
a Department of Environment and Natural Resources (DENR), which
was not a Cabinet department but would draw many of the environ-
ment/natural resource programs into an enlarged Department of the
Interior. This involved two politically tough decisions. Forming a DENR
required moving the forest products and cattle grazing-oriented U.S.
Forest Service (in the Agriculture Department) into the Interior
Department, which already housed the pro-environment National Park
Service and the Fish and Wildlife Service. The other controversial organizational discussion was to combine all of the water policy agencies of
the government—the civil functions of the Army Corps of Engineers, the
Agriculture Department's Soil and Conservation Service, and the
Interior Department's Bureau of Reclamation. This would bring to one
department central control over national water policy and the planning
of water projects.

The DENR proposal was certain to rile Congress by muddling the
traditional jurisdictional authorities of the Congressional oversight and
appropriations committees. The plan threatened the long-established
relationships within the "iron triangle," composed of the special
interests, selected Members of Congress, and the civil service leadership within the departments—which together pretty well run the
federal government unless very strong leadership is exerted by the
White House.

To attempt fundamental government reorganization by taking on the "iron triangle" is a political fight nearly impossible to win. The special interest lobbyists do not want change. After all, many have spent their adult lives getting to know the players in the other two corners of the triangle. And civil servants do not look forward to an uncertain future with new bosses in a strange new department. Finally, members of Congressional committees resist change since the longer they hold their committee assignments the more influence they can exert in the departments under their jurisdiction. Even more disturbing, if new committees of Congress must be established to mirror the proposed organizational changes in the Executive Branch, is there a chance their position on the seniority ladder could be challenged?

Yet the DENR option had strong appeal, largely because it would insure that the new department leadership would not have the option of responding to one unified constituency (for example, environmentalists or natural resource developers), but instead they would have to make balanced decisions that would not only enhance the quality of the environment but continue the vital development of the nation's natural resources.

Option 2

The second option, creation of the EPA, had two basic advantages. First, it would allow for single-minded attention to the task of pollution abatement and enhanced environmental quality. Second, it was politically popular and preserved more closely the traditional Congressional committee jurisdictions.

However, there was one major disadvantage. EPA would clearly have the luxury of serving just one constituency, the environmental community. As a result, EPA leadership would almost certainly propose regulations of the very highest environmental quality (some would even label them draconian) and tend to disregard other considerations (such as the effect on the economy and the development of natural resources). As a result, EPA's proposed environmental regulations and standards would not tend to be balanced or cost effective. Because of the organizational bias built into the EPA, the Agency to this day tends to propose cost-ineffective regulations and standards. This alarms other departments with competing constituencies and that leads to a series of endless meetings, usually sponsored by the Office of Management and Budget, until the EPA is eventually forced to revise its proposals in a more moderate and cost-effective manner.

Lessons for the Future

Past Administrations, without a great deal of success, have tried to moderate the EPA's tendency to propose cost-ineffective environmental regulations. The new Administration would do well to focus on building into EPA's leadership a strong cost analysis capability with a highly regarded professional standing that would also earn the trust of the environmental community.

In the end President Nixon opted for EPA over DENR largely because it was more popular, did not threaten Congressional jurisdictions, and was more likely to quickly become law under the then-existing authority that allowed the Executive Branch to propose a reorganization plan of an Agency, but not a large established department. If Congress did not object within 60 legislative days, then the plan would become law.

Along with the EPA plan, Nixon sent to Congress the same day a reorganization plan creating the National Oceanic and Atmospheric Administration (NOAA) within the Department of Commerce.

But Nixon's interest in a Department of Natural Resources continued. In 1971 he submitted legislation for creation of a Department of Natural Resources (not including, of course, those programs that resided in the newly formed EPA). This was part of an ambitious, nearly government-wide reorganization plan proposing that the departments of State, Defense, Treasury, and Justice, and a smaller version of Agriculture, be retained, and that the remaining seven departments and several agencies should be combined into four new ones: Community Development, Human Resources, Natural Resources, and Economic Development.

This vast plan reflected Nixon's belief that government should be organized around functions rather than on the basis of programs heaped upon programs, with many of them outmoded and often unconnected. Nixon wanted his Cabinet officers to be less special pleaders, reflecting narrowly based interest groups, and more the broad-based officials setting priorities. This mega reorganizational plan brought the " iron triangle" to "red alert" and the plan died in Congress.

Later, the Carter Administration resurrected the Nixon plan, made several constructive changes (there are only so many ways to move the boxes around on the organizational charts), but in the end President Jimmy Carter decided that the cost in political capital was too high and he did not send his plan to Congress. Both the Nixon and the revised Carter reorganization plans remain in the archives of the Office of Management and Budget for the study of the next President and his staff, with a still robust "iron triangle" ready to do battle.

Trio of Native American Uprisings During the Nixon Presidency

By Bradley Patterson

The "cause" of righting three centuries of highly unjust treatment of Native American peoples bubbled in the 1960s and boiled over in the 1970s. Militant Native Americans staged three very visible occupations: of Alcatraz Island (November 1969-June 1971), of the Bureau of Indian Affairs (BIA) building in Washington (November 1972), and of Wounded Knee, South Dakota (February-April 1973). Below is a snapshot of each of the three incidents and how the White House acted.

The Seizure of Alcatraz Island

The Administrator of the General Services Administration (GSA) is the titleholder to Alcatraz Island (as excess federal property). When Native Americans occupied the island in November 1969, the GSA Administrator called for federal marshals to evict them "by noon tomorrow." Senior Nixon White House official Leonard Garment, knowing that the world was watching this escapade and acutely remembering history, flatly countermanded the agency head's instructions. An interagency group was formed to look into the legitimate needs and grievances, particularly of the Native Americans of the San Francisco Bay area. Another Bay area group was given a planning grant to examine these issues. The Vice President sent a negotiator to meet with the occupiers, and the negotiator made several trips to the island. During one of these visits, the Native Americans put mescaline in his coffee. Fearing for the safety of its personnel, the government withdrew the GSAcustodians from, and cut off power to, the island. However, *The San Francisco Chronicle* responded by supplying the Native Americans with a generator. Food and financial donations were sent, and soon the Alcatraz "theater" was studded with Hollywood luminaries. When the activists burned down the lighthouse, maritime interests pressured the government to act more forcefully. After 16 months of fruitless negotiations most of the occupiers finally drifted away and the rest were peacefully escorted off of the island. *The Chronicle* commented: "The federal government wisely let the Indians play out their string."

The Occupation of the BIA Building

Six days before the election of 1972, several hundred Native American activists converged on the Bureau of Indian Affairs building in Washington to protest a "Trail of Broken Treaties." When the BIA staff went home, the activists took over the building. This was a hard-shelled group: typewriters and gasoline were stored at the top of the stairwells, file cabinets were ripped open, exhibition cases were looted, and lavatories were smashed. Not knowing of these developments, on the first night two White House officials met with the activists' leadership and heard them assert, "You know we are going to die tonight!" What did the White House agents do with that? They listened—and through listening bought time and cooled tempers.

The police wanted to storm the building, but late in the evening President Nixon rejected such a course of action. Instead, he decided that the government would go to court the next morning. In a week government attorneys appeared eight times before two federal courts and were granted restraining orders. Five times officials asked for delays so that the actual negotiations could proceed.

The White House promised to form an interagency task force to examine and respond to the "Trail's" 20 "demands." The Indians were told that they would not be prosecuted just for the act of occupying the building, but that they might be charged for vandalism or theft (in the end, few were). The Director of the Office of Economic Opportunity (OEO) finally provided federal funds to buy the protesters transportation, and they left Washington.

The government licked its wounds and took the press on a tour of the trashed building, but kept its end of the bargain. White House Special Counsel Leonard Garment responded in detail to the "Trail's" 20 propositions: many of them would require Congressional legislation that did not have the faintest chance of passage. OEO Director Frank Carlucci later reminded a vexed Congressional committee: "To those who question our administrative procedures, let me assure you that this was no situation for modern textbook practices....We avoided a bloody confrontation."

The Takeover of Wounded Knee

The same group of Native American militants who occupied the BIA building in Washington occupied the Wounded Knee village the following year. They were heavily armed, 200 strong, and violently opposed to the tribal government on the Pine Ridge Sioux Reservation. The protesters selected a spot to occupy in Wounded Knee village, they broke into the local trading post, took its owners hostage, and appropriated the local church. Three hundred BIA police, U.S. marshals, and FBI agents surrounded the site. Although shots were exchanged, the Nixon White House, again in charge of the crisis, made sure that there was no violent counterattack. The well-trained federal law enforcement personnel acted with professional restraint. The press came in droves— 300 newspeople from all over the nation and a dozen foreign countries (including the Soviet Union) watched everything that happened.

An Assistant Attorney General "commanded" the U.S. team on the spot and received his instructions via a speakerphone to meetings between the Deputy Attorney General, Leonard Garment, and other White House colleagues. Garment's word carried the most weight. The 82nd Airborne was asked to estimate what kind of a military operation would be required to dislodge the occupiers. A colonel reported a grim estimate and said that the Army wanted no part of any such action. The

White House vetoed any thought of an armed response. After 71 days of patient, trying, persistent negotiations on the scene, the crisis wound down. The government sent five White House representatives (who sat for hours underneath the pine boughs of an Indian camp) to hear the Indians' case. The protesters wanted the Black Hills given back to them immediately. The White House officials sadly told them that yes, the Congress did violate the Treaty of 1868—after Custer's defeat and the discovery of gold—but no President, only the Congress, could redress that ancient injustice.

Nine years later, a federal court reviewed both the BIA building occupation and the Wounded Knee denouement. The judge ruled:

> The government...acted reasonably, with praiseworthy restraint and concern for the lives of all involved and with remarkable imagination and constructive creativity in handling the occupation and dispossession of the BIA building....Federal officers were persistent, determined and reasonable in their efforts to effect a peaceful resolution of the [Wounded Knee] occupation crisis....

The lands were not returned.

Lessons Learned

When confrontational ire over a domestic policy issue or "cause" escalates into a crisis—a crisis that can arguably be suppressed by taking strong federal law enforcement actions—the President should:

▶ Move tactical as well as strategic governmental management of the crisis promptly into the White House;

▶ View with great suspicion quick calls for the drastic use of federal force;

▶ Not seek court action. Courts issue orders and set deadlines—which are precisely the wrong tools to use because they inflexibly tie the hands of crisis negotiators. The right tools turn out to be improvisation, finesse, judgment, and experience;

▶ Insist on using every conceivable communications method to obtain the best available information directly from the crisis scene;

▶ Use federal force with the maximum restraint (consistent with the real need for action) while evaluating how much of the contretemps may be guerrilla theater designed to tempt federal overreaction in order to give the players greater visibility; and

▶ Initiate moves aimed at peaceful dispute resolution—based on a factual and historical understanding of the pros and cons of the "causes" being advocated—and toward reconciliation.

The Nixon Administration Implements School Desegregation

By Bradley Patterson

On October 30, 1969, a unanimous Supreme Court mandated that "the obligation of every school district is to terminate dual school systems at once, and to operate now and hereafter only unitary schools." The deadline for compliance was the fall of 1970. Southern leaders were apoplectic. (Northerners could see that many of their schools would be affected, too.) There was a high potentiality of massive disobedience of the Court's decision—and of violence.

Vice President Spiro T. Agnew planned a speech in Atlanta in which he intended to indicate the Administration's "disfavor with the apparent consequences of recent court decisions." Conservative White House staffer Pat Buchanan punched out a draft for Agnew that would, in Buchanan's description, "tear the scab off the issue of race in this country." The draft included a reference to another attack on Fort Sumter.

Senior White House adviser Leonard Garment sensed that this was a political catastrophe in the making. Nixon concurred, canceled the Agnew speech, seized the issue himself, and ordered that a probing examination be made to have all sides of the question explored thoroughly. Nixon determined to bring closure in the executive branch by issuing a personal Presidential policy statement.

Who would manage the enormous amount of preparatory staff work required—researching the law, the conflicting decisions of lower courts, and the pros and cons of busing? Who could consult behind the scenes with advocacy groups, with the divided civil rights community, with educators, and with constitutional scholars? Who would keep political realities in mind—the fall 1970 elections, Nixon's "southern strategy," the "big referendum of 1972?" Who could thread his way among contending internal White House staff factions? Nixon knew that none of his Cabinet officers could handle this daunting series of tasks. He instructed Garment to "drop everything else for two months" and lead the entire enterprise behind what were, in effect, leakproof White House doors.

Developing a Plan

Keeping total control, Garment reached out to tap intellectual and program resources that could offer positive aid in the inflammatorily negative environment. He met with black leaders. (Some of them were more interested in political control of the school boards than in busing the students.) He met with civil rights statesman Clarence Mitchell, with Yale constitutional scholar Alexander Bickel, with famed educator James Coleman. He heard about a citizens committee in Greenville, South Carolina, that was organizing a citywide effort of reconciliation to build "a model community that leads the region and the nation in education, in economic progress, in spirit." Garment hosted the committee at a private evening dinner in the White House, quizzing them about how to initiate a successful, positive, community-wide endeavor—and how the federal government could aid such efforts. The Office of Education had been conducting an established technical assistance program for local school districts; Garment saw that one could expand and build upon that authority.

The General Counsel of the Department of Health, Education, and Welfare and the Assistant Attorney General for Civil Rights were invited in for discussion (but took no papers out of the White House). The White House conservatives—Buchanan, Harry Dent, and Bryce Harlow—were consulted as well, and picked away at Garment's ideas. Colleague, policy soulmate, and brilliant White House writer Ray Price put Garment's conclusions into the first draft of a Presidential statement.

A 200-page briefing book went to the President in early March, and after two and a half weeks of minute Nixon attention, closely supervised by domestic policy chief John Ehrlichman, the 8,000-word policy statement—eloquent, orderly, almost scholarly—was sprung full-blown upon the Cabinet, the public, the Executive branch, and the Congress.

Commitment to a Democracy

In the message, Nixon emphasized that his objective was "to place the question of school desegregation in its larger context, part of America's historic commitment to the achievement of a free and open society." He studiously avoided labeling the fearful southerners as "morally wrong"—indeed Nixon evidenced his recognition of parents' apprehensions, acknowledging:

- ▶ It is natural that whatever affects the schools stirs deep feelings among parents and in the community at large.

- ▶ Whatever threatens the schools, parents perceive—rightly—as a threat to their children.

- ▶ Whatever makes the schools more distant from the family undermines one of the important supports of learning.

- ▶ Quite understandably, the prospect of any change in the schools is seen as a threat.

Observing that "Communities desegregating their schools face special needs—for classrooms, facilities, teachers, teacher-training—and the Nation should help meet those needs," the President asked Congress for $1.5 billion to assist the affected school districts. The Congress appropriated an initial $75 million.

There was still further follow up. Garment persuaded the Reverend Billy Graham, a hero to many southerners, to make a series of films exhorting peaceful compliance. These films were arranged to be shown in donated TV time just before the schools opened in the fall of

1970. Taking an unusual initiative, in each of the seven deep southern states most affected by the Court's decision, Garment and White House Counselor George Shultz organized biracial committees—"blacks, whites, integrationists, segregationists, businessmen, union organizers, decades-long adversaries." President Nixon met with each biracial state commission in the Oval Office, and on August 14 in New Orleans, personally hosted a session with the chairmen and co-chairmen of all seven, telling them:

> This is one country, this is one people, and we are going to carry out the law in that way, not in a punitive way....I know of no time in our Nation's history when this country needs to hear of those many, many successes, where men and women of good will worked out the problem, rather than hearing only of those few instances that might be failures....As a result of these advisory committees being set up, we are going to find that in many districts the transition will be orderly and peaceful...and the credit will go to these outstanding southern leaders...

School desegregation controversies continue even to this day. The fall of 1970, though, was an anxious, contentious, but peaceful period. It could have been frightfully different.

Lessons Learned

First: when the Supreme Court issues an opinion that is terribly unpopular with much of the citizenry, the leadership task of the President is:

- ▶ To call upon executive branch resources to carry out the decision, *Fortiter in re*—as President Dwight Eisenhower did at Little Rock (recalling his famous desktop motto)—but *Suaviter in modo* as Nixon did in the instant case;

- ▶ Not to countenance Executive branch criticism of the Supreme Court;

- ▶ To explore, point to—and propose to help finance—ways of constructing compromises which, over time, will achieve the requirements of the law.

Second: when not only outside protagonists but the Administration's own Cabinet officers and inside staff disagree about the substance of an upcoming policy initiative, the President must take personal control of the issue, and will likely designate an especially trusted senior White House official to be fully in charge of collecting, analyzing, and presenting the disparate views. (In very rare instances, for example, aiding President Lyndon Johnson on Selective Service reform, a public advisory commission may be helpful. Recent Presidents have found the First Lady, the Vice President, and the spouse of the Vice President to be exceptionally adept advisers—but the preceding observation still stands.)

President Ford's Pardon
of Richard M. Nixon

By Mark J. Rozell

Article II, Section 2 of the Constitution grants to the President a nearly unlimited power to pardon. The only pardon a President may not grant involves "Cases of Impeachment." The constitutional framers had sound reasons for giving the President this unchecked authority. In the *Federalist Papers,* Publius expressed that reasons of state might necessitate the exercise of the pardon power and that such circumstances would justify unilateral Presidential action to protect the national interest. Nonetheless, pardons occasionally are controversial and Presidents need to use discretion in the manner in which they exercise this power. Congress and the American people may lack constitutional recourse against an unpopular pardon, but they may exact a political price against the President.

President Gerald R. Ford's pardon of former President Richard M. Nixon stands as such an example. On a Sunday morning, September 8, 1974, Ford issued his pardon proclamation. The President contended that Nixon could not obtain a fair trial because of the enormous publicity surrounding Nixon's actions in the Watergate scandal. Ford furthermore justified the pardon on the basis of the national interest. President Ford maintained that he had devoted too much of his time in office to Nixon-related matters and that a pardon was the only means available to enable him to focus on public policies rather than on the legal fate of one man. Ford also stated that the national "tranquility" would be disrupted by "bringing to trial a former President of the United States."

Some opponents of the Nixon pardon challenged the legality of Ford's action. These opponents included some respected constitutional law professors. Their arguments centered on the following:

First, that the timing of the pardon was improper. Opponents of the pardon argued that a President may not issue a pardon in anticipation that criminal charges may be brought at some point in the future. Nixon had not been convicted of anything, therefore there was nothing for which he could be pardoned. This argument presupposes that the legal process must be fully exercised all the way through the conviction stage before a President may issue a pardon.

Second, some opponents said that Ford's pardon proclamation was too vague in that it never specified the crimes for which Nixon deserved the pardon. Indeed, Ford pardoned Nixon "for all offenses against the United States which he, Richard Nixon, has committed or may have committed or taken part in during the period from January 20, 1969, through August 9, 1974." Some scholars cited the English common law practice that required the King, under certain circumstances, to specify the crimes for which he was issuing a pardon.

Third, some of those against the Nixon pardon argued that Ford's action violated the impeachment exception in the Constitution. According to this reading of Article II, Section 2, the President cannot issue a pardon in the case of someone who has committed impeachable offenses.

Fourth, opponents of the pardon said that Ford's action had violated the Special Prosecutor law. The Charter stated that the President could not use his constitutional powers to interfere with the independence of the Special Prosecutor. From this vantage, Ford's pardon had denied the Special Prosecutor the opportunity to further investigate Nixon's abuses of power.

Defense of the Pardon

None of these arguments against the pardon stood up to serious scrutiny. That many observers weighed in with arguments against the legality of Ford's action was in part a measure of the strong feelings running against pardoning Nixon. Nonetheless, sound constitutional analysis had to override any emotions or partisan views that characterized the immediate aftermath of the pardon.

Ford's pardon did not lack legitimacy because of its timing. There is no statement in the Constitution that the pardon power is restricted to the post-conviction stage. Indeed, the language of Article II, Section 2 leaves the President with total latitude in determining when to issue a pardon. Several key court decisions validate the President's authority to issue pardons prior to legal proceedings. Special Prosecutor Leon Jaworski wrote after Ford's action that the President's authority to issue pardons at any time was without any constitutional doubt.

The Constitution nowhere states that the President must specify the crimes for which a pardon has been issued. Constitutional law recognizes a distinction between full and unconditional pardons for offenses that are stated in the pardon statement preamble, and general pardons. Ford issued a general pardon to Nixon. There also were practical reasons for the general pardon in this case. If Ford had cited specific offenses (for which Nixon had not been convicted), some may have assumed that any actions by Nixon not specified were unprotected by the pardon. Therefore, anything short of a general pardon would have undermined Ford's stated purpose in issuing the Nixon pardon in the first place—to spare the nation of a trial of a former President and to put the matter to rest immediately.

There is no valid argument that Ford's pardon violated the impeachment exception in the Constitution. The Constitution clearly says "in Cases of Impeachment" and not "impeachable offenses." Furthermore, Nixon's resignation, not Ford's pardon of him, undermined the impeachment proceedings. The major potential outcome of impeachment proceedings—removal from office—already had been achieved by Nixon's resignation.

Finally, it is true that the pardon prohibited the Special Prosecutor from continuing his investigation of Nixon's alleged crimes. However, the Prosecutor's mandate cannot override the President's constitutional authority. Ford's power to pardon in this case was absolute, a fact recognized by Special Prosecutor Jaworski who wrote that this would have made any further effort on his part to investigate Nixon a "spurious proceeding" and "tantamount to unprofessional conduct."

President Ford was undoubtedly correct that given the emotions of the time and the enormous publicity surrounding Watergate, Nixon could not have received an impartial trial. The constitutional power to pardon clearly exists to serve individual justice as well as the national interest.

Ford did make mistakes in his action, however. He explained that personal sympathy for Nixon due to the former President's poor health was one justification for the pardon. That reason had no currency in constitutional, individual justice, or national interest terms. Ford publicly announced the pardon on a Sunday morning, giving the appearance that he was trying to minimize the public outcry by this unusual timing. Ford failed to exact from Nixon a meaningful statement of contrition as a condition for issuing the pardon. The weak statement that Nixon eventually agreed to issue only served to make critics angrier than they had been. Many said that Ford should have insisted on a stronger statement from Nixon before issuing the pardon.

In light of the enormous public and Congressional outcry at the Nixon pardon, Ford made the extraordinary move of agreeing to testify before a Congressional committee to explain his decision. He did not have to do so. The Constitution granted to him the unlimited power to pardon Nixon and there was nothing that Congress could do other than to complain or perhaps punish Ford's agenda. But Ford believed that he had to be as forthcoming as possible, especially in response to allegations that there had been an unseemly deal between Nixon and Ford—the Presidency in return for a future pardon. Despite some harsh questioning from a few Members of Congress, Ford gave a compelling presentation and convincingly made the case that there was no unseemly deal between him and Nixon. Ford's testimony did much to alleviate Congressional anger and to restore his reputation for integrity.

Lessons Learned

The Presidential power to pardon is largely unlimited and with good reason. Under certain circumstances Presidents must have the ability to act on behalf of the public interest and justice without regard to the partisan views and emotions of the day. President Ford acted primarily in the national interest and his action also served individual justice. Nonetheless, many critics remained unconvinced that either justice or the national interest had been served and much of this harsh reaction was due to the manner in which Ford issued the pardon and announced it to the public.

A President should exercise the pardon power as the constitutional framers anticipated, even if such action harms the President's agenda in Congress or popularity with the public. The judgment of history is whether the President acted in the broader national interest and not whether he protected his immediate public and political standing. None of this mitigates the importance of a President being forthcoming in his reasons for the pardon and taking care to issue the pardon in a manner that will enhance its legitimacy in the minds of Members of Congress and the public.

The Superconducting Supercollider

By Genene M. Fisher

In June 1987, President Ronald Reagan announced that the United States was committed to the design and construction of the world's largest and most powerful high-energy particle accelerator called the Superconducting Supercollider (SSC). Accelerators are the engines driving research in elementary particle physics, which is the study of the basic nature of matter, energy, space, and time.

The first step toward making the SSC a reality was to encourage Congressional support. Many Congress members were eager to have the SSC in their home states and to receive the billions of federal dollars that the program would generate. Twenty-six states competed for the SSC site. In 1988, Ellis County, Texas, was declared the winner. It was an advantage to Texas that from 1987 to 1989 James Wright was the Speaker of the House.

Before Reagan's announcement, the Department of Energy (DOE) had already spent $60 million in research on the SSC. The SSC budget rose annually—from $130 million in fiscal year 1988 to $650 million in fiscal year 1993. The SSC program office in Dallas grew to 100 administrators, 60 permanent staffers, and 40 more on temporary assignment from elsewhere in DOE. In 1992, President George H.W. Bush made personal appeals to Members of Congress to support the SSC budget and the project continued. By 1993, during the Clinton Administration, the SSC projected cost totaled $11 billion. Although $2 billion had already been spent, Congress voted to cancel the program.

With 20 percent of the SSC finished, $2 billion spent, 14.7 of the 54 miles of tunneling completed, and thousands of workers unemployed, it is obvious that the political support for the SSC failed. More importantly, after a huge investment in human and national resources, the SSC was a science program failure, and the Europeans took the lead in high-energy physics.

Lessons Learned

Presidential leadership is essential at all stages for large-scale science and technology projects. President Reagan announced the SSC as a national priority and fully supported the project. The continuation of the SSC throughout the Bush Administration was largely due to the President fighting to keep the project alive. Presidential leadership was definitely a reason for its successful beginning, but it is not clear if the lack of leadership can be blamed for its failure.

International support should have been incorporated into the project from the beginning. SSC supporters originally anticipated $1.7 billion in foreign contributions. There was some opposition to international involvement since it was argued that the technologies involved in the SSC should not be given away to others, and instead benefit American citizens. The United States did not approach other countries until Congress was debating whether to continue funding the high costs of the SSC. Although Japan was expected to be a contributor, it resisted pressures by President Bush to be a major partner. The European community was already planning its own supercollider. For a successful project there needed to be international cooperation from the beginning, with the other partners having a stake in the pursuit of its progress. Foreign investments and relationships can ensure that projects will continue between Presidential Administrations and Congressional election cycles.

The government needed a way to ensure support for large-scale projects during non-crisis periods. The end of the Cold War also was a reason for lack of support for the SSC. One of the rationales for building the SSC was to keep the United States preeminent in high-energy physics during competition with the Soviet Union. After 1991, America had been going through a period of pragmatic or strategic science aimed at short-range goals that led to well-defined benefits to health, the environment, or the economy. Esoteric curiosity-driven science with ill-defined long-range benefits was not a top priority.

Better oversight methods were needed for the escalating costs of this project. Another reason that the SSC failed was that it had unrealistic expected costs and expensive major design changes. Supporters of the SSC consistently understated its costs. Many improvements had to be made that were not originally in the budget given to Congress. The 1990 budget request for the SSC was based on a total project cost estimate of $5.9 billion. By the time the project was killed in 1993, the unofficial estimated cost was $11 billion. Better oversight, not increased oversight, is the lesson learned. DOE claimed to have massive oversight that increased the administrative and paperwork costs associated with the SSC.

In sum, better long-term planning is needed for large-scale science and technology projects. The failure of the SSC took place during a time of change in Administrations and Congress. The government needs a way to ensure funding of long-term projects insulated from the two-year

Congressional election cycle and the eight-year Presidential Administration. Originally, Congress strongly endorsed the SSC, as many members were eager to have the huge federal project housed in their states. Texas was declared the winner, and the large Congressional delegation from Texas guarded the SSC from being cut. James Wright, the former Speaker of the House, was a strong SSC supporter—backing that was lost when he had to leave Congress. Incoming Presidents and Congress members may feel little responsibility for the expensive costs and commitments of their predecessors, particularly if there has been a change of party. However, if there is a broad base of support, the loss of a few people in government will not put an entire project at risk.

The International Space Station

By Genene M. Fisher

In his 1984 State of the Union address, President Ronald Reagan authorized the National Aeronautics and Space Administration (NASA) to develop a permanently occupied space station within a decade and to invite other countries to participate in the project. The space station had the support of George H.W. Bush when he became President, although the project had undergone modifications several times since 1984. At one point in 1993 Congress canceled the space station due to budget constraints.

The Clinton Administration demonstrated strong support for the space program and dramatically changed its character. President Bill Clinton directed NASA to redesign the space station in 1993 because of cost overruns and high expected operating expenses. After a three-month redesign process, Clinton chose to build a modular space station and agreed to spend $10.5 billion over five years on what eventually was named the International Space Station (ISS). The multinational partnership, which included Japan, Canada, and nations in Europe, was expanded to include Russia.

The American goals in developing the ISS included: (1) maintaining U.S. leadership in space and in global competitiveness; (2) serving as a driving force for emerging technologies, which would sustain and strengthen one of America's strongest export sectors—aerospace technology; (3) serving as a symbol of the ability of nations to cooperate on a peaceful initiative; and (4) allowing the United States to focus the aerospace industries of Russia and other countries on non-military pursuits to reduce the risk of nuclear proliferation and slow the traffic of high-technology weapons to developing nations.

It was decided to merge the U.S.-led international space station with Russia's program. The first phase in the cooperative project involved joint flights of Russians on the U.S. space shuttle and Americans on the Russian space station Mir (scheduled for 1994-1998). Next, the ISS would be built with scientific contributions from all of the international partners (1997-1998). The ISS would then evolve into a multinational facility (1998-2002), which would operate for 10 years (2002-2012).

This restructuring of the program evoked concern in the scientific community about the amount of science that could be conducted on the scaled-down space station. The White House Office of Science and Technology Policy and the Space Studies Board of the National Research Council (NRC) reviewed the plan. They both asserted that materials science research could not justify building the space station, and questioned how much life sciences research could be supported. However, some scientists considered life sciences research on the effects of long stretches of weightlessness on human physiology as a prerequisite to sending people to Mars. Other supporters believed that the materials research conducted on the space station would lead to new profitable industries.

The NRC's Space Studies Board released a report stating that there was no need for a space station to support high-priority science missions for the next two decades. Although they were against using a space station for astronomy or earth sciences, it was acknowledged that there could be exciting benefits for biology and materials science. Eventually, the NRC Board agreed not to oppose the space station.

Lessons Learned

The ISS survived more than a decade of negotiations, studies, and budget battles in Congress. However, the scientific usefulness of the space station is unclear. The building of the ISS has advanced technological development, but the downsizing of the program has constrained many of the original scientific objectives. In addition, the United States has dealt with many Russian delays but still continues to fund the program and provide aid for the Russian component. Many consider the ISS a scientific failure—a science program in search of a mission.

Presidential leadership is essential for continuing support at all stages for large-scale science and technology projects. The Clinton Administration demonstrated leadership by ordering the redesign of the space station and by bringing Russia into the partnership. Since then, it appears that there has not been the necessary leadership to deal with Russian delays. The completion of the ISS has been postponed many times, and is now scheduled for complete assembly in 2005.

The risks and benefits of cooperating with economically unstable nations need to be assessed in long science projects. The ISS is the largest scientific cooperative program in history, drawing on the resources and scientific expertise of 16 nations. However, it is not clear if backup plans were made for countries that could not fulfill their commitments. Forming an alliance with Russia in the early 1990s was a political decision and it made the space station a part of U.S foreign policy. Ironically, it is that partnership that has kept the ISS program alive in Congress during difficult times. Helping Russia pay its portion of the ISS during its economic struggles is a means of providing foreign aid. Originally the space station had to be downscaled due to high costs, yet the United States is paying the Russian contribution.

The United States needs to consider its commitment to other countries in large-scale projects. The original non-U.S. partners have dealt with American budget battles over the program for more than 10 years. In 1993, the partners were disturbed about the redesign options because each change made would require modifications to their space station elements. Following several meetings of all the partners, however, they agreed to include Russia in the program. Since then, there have been numerous Russian delays, and this is not establishing a good reputation with the other partners. There are questions about the credibility of NASA's current program plan and the degree to which it is dependent on Russian participation.

Downsizing can result in a misguided research agenda. Scientists question if a downscaled space station can provide useful scientific results. When a science program is reduced, a new set of objectives needs to be set to determine the usefulness of the project. Many feel that the ISS is lacking a mission. The focus has been on foreign policy, rather than science objectives. There are questions regarding why a space station is needed, why it is needed now, and what scientific research can be conducted there.

The Genesis of the Human Genome Project

By Anne G. K. Solomon

The U.S. Human Genome Project (HGP) is a major scientific research effort coordinated by the National Institutes of Health (NIH) and the Department of Energy (DOE). The project is designed to map and sequence the entire human genome. It evolved in the mid-1980s from consensus among a number of leading U.S. molecular biologists that such an undertaking would be a powerful tool to understand disease and biology. In the years following its formal launch in 1990, the Human Genome Project became a central enterprise in human genetics and the largest centrally coordinated biology research project ever undertaken. Yet its genesis was one of the most politically contentious episodes in the recent history of science policy.

The Science

The human genome—contained within the nucleus of each of the 100 trillion cells in the human body (except the red blood cells)—provides all of the hereditary genetic information necessary to build a human being. It is composed of deoxyribonucleic acid (DNA) arrayed in a double-stranded, helicoid sequence of four chemical bases: adenine (A), thymine (T), guanine (G), and cytosine (C). The genome's structure is made up of 23 pairs of chromosomes for a total of 46—with each pair consisting of one chromosome from each parent. (An exception is the egg and sperm cells that have only 23 chromosomes each.) Each chromosome in turn carries thousands of genes that provide instructions to the cell on how to make a particular molecule, usually a protein. Proteins are the essential components of all organs and chemical activities in the body.

The entire genome has been likened to a set of cookbooks—the chromosomes to individual cookbooks; the genes to recipes—all written in the DNA language of As, Ts, Gs, and Cs—and the proteins to ingredients. The simplicity of this image, however, belies the enormity and complexity of the structure and functioning of the human genome. It is of vast size consisting of three billion chemical bases that, if printed out, would fill 1,000 1,000-page "cookbooks." The genes, however, are estimated to represent only about three percent of the entire genome. Individual genes of—to extend the cookbook metaphor—"recipes" are buried within an immense number of DNA sequences sometimes called "junk DNA" because their function is unknown.[1] Yet despite the genes' very small representation in the genome, the genes' import in determining the way we look, how we behave, and the state of our health is substantial.

If a gene's DNA language becomes garbled or a word is misspelled, the cell may make the wrong protein, or too much or too little of the right one—mistakes that often result in disease. Errors in genes are responsible for thousands of clearly hereditary diseases, including Huntington's disease, cystic fibrosis, neurofibromatosis, Duchenne muscular dystrophy, and many others. In addition, altered genes play a part in cancer, heart disease, diabetes, and many other common diseases. In these more common and complex disorders, genetic alterations increase a person's risk of developing that disorder. The disease itself results from the interaction of such genetic predisposition with other genes, biological development, and environmental factors, including diet and lifestyle.[2]

The Project Objectives

From the outset, the goals of the Human Genome Project have been to increase our scientific knowledge and technological capabilities associated with the structure and functions of the human genome. This has been done by improving existing genetic maps, constructing physical maps of entire chromosomes, and ultimately determining the complete sequence, or order, of the DNA base pairs.[3]

Broad objectives include furthering our understanding of the fundamental causes of disease, developing rapid and specific diagnostic tests for illness, and identifying and validating targets for drug development and prevention (e.g., by avoiding environmental conditions that trigger disease). In some cases, augmentation or even replacement of defective genes through gene therapy may eventually be possible.

The Human Genome Project's aims were consistent both with improving the public's health and well-being and with supporting advancement in basic scientific knowledge—traditionally two widely supported public policy concerns. Controversy nevertheless dogged the project's beginning and has continued to the present. An outline of the issues of contention and discussion of how those issues were managed give insight into science policy instruments and methods and provide lessons for the future.

The Issues, The Players, The Power

Issues debated throughout the early development of the Human Genome Project ranged from questions regarding the scientific merits and technical methods of genome mapping and sequencing, to issues of "big" science projects versus "small" investigator-initiated science, to issues of bureaucratic power and authority. The evolution of views in the scientific community and the process of institution-building that culminated in the Human Genome Project involved players and institutions that continue to shape U.S. research and innovation capabilities in molecular biology and other areas of science and technology.

New technologies often provide the capabilities for new directions in basic scientific research. The seminal technology that led to the genome project was a group of techniques developed in the mid-1970s for determining the sequence of base pairs in DNA. As the use of these techniques spread and a flood of new DNAsequence information became available, scientists needed ways to catalogue it systematically. New databases to contain this information were established just as the power of computers to analyze the data was becoming evident.

The idea to marry new scientific knowledge and technological capabilities in the bond of a major organized scientific project came from several different sources at about the same time. In 1985, Robert Sinsheimer, then Chancellor of the University of California at Santa Cruz conceived of a project to sequence the human genome. He was motivated in part by the desire to shape a project that would be attractive to private philanthropists. Later that year, Renato Dulbecco of the Salk Institute introduced the idea of sequencing the human genome as a tool to understand the genetic origins of cancer at a talk organized by the Italian Embassy in Washington, DC. But it was Charles DeLisi, the Director of the Department of Energy's Office of Health and

Environmental Research—working on genetic damage from atomic bomb radiation—who successfully launched the project by linking personal inspiration with the power and budgets of the federal government.

The proposal was controversial from the outset. Members of the scientific community heatedly debated the project's scientific merits as well as organizational and funding issues. Scientists were especially concerned that a large government-managed project would elbow out funding for work proposed by individual bench scientists. Informal discussions in university departments and also structured meetings involving members of the scientific elite (James Watson, Walter Gilbert, Paul Berg) that were convened at prestigious research entities (Cold Springs Harbor Laboratory and the Howard Hughes Medical Institute) pointed up sharp differences in opinions and helped define the issues. Ultimately, however, studies by two national science policy entities—the National Research Council (NRC) and the Office of Technology Assessment (OTA)—provided the foundation for consensus on research and institution-building strategies that enabled the project's launch.

Policy Making: the "Illuminators"

The National Research Council is the research arm of both the National Academy of Sciences and the National Academy of Engineering. Together with the Institute of Medicine, these elite professional societies provide advice to the federal government on a range of matters related to the health of the nation's research and innovation capabilities. National policy issues emanating from advances in scientific knowledge and technological capabilities also are examined. Most NRC studies are requested and funded by federal government mission agencies, in some cases directed to do so by the Congress. Studies are carried out by committees made up of scientists, engineers, economists, and scholars from different disciplines who consider extant knowledge relevant to the study charge. The committees issue overview reports with consensus conclusions and recommendations. The work of "The National Academies," as this group is now called, is generally regarded as balanced, credible, and intellectually sound. It carries significant weight in government decision making.

Moving the debate on the wisdom of mounting the genome project from freewheeling, unstructured discussions in the scientific community to a formal NRC study process helped catalyze decision making. Chaired by Bruce Alberts, then a professor of biochemistry at the University of California at San Francisco, an NRC committee set the scientific agenda for the Human Genome Project in a report, *Mapping and Sequencing the Human Genome,* issued in 1988. It neglected, however, to settle organizational and bureaucratic disputes. Committee members lacked sophistication regarding the highly complex federal bureaucracy and political process. Accordingly, their work failed to address adequately project organization and administration.[4]

The Office of Technology Assessment[5] report, *Mapping Our Genes:*

Genome Projects—How Big? How Fast? was released a few months after the NRC study and focused on bureaucratic structure and process, including the most contentious bureaucratic issue—whether the National Institutes of Health or the Department of Energy should be the project's "lead" agency with control of funding. The OTA report and its Congressional testimony were influential in a resolution of the issue in favor of an NIH/DOE collaborative effort. The process was far from straightforward, however, and involved classic Washington maneuvering.

Policy Making: Instruments of Power

NIH and DOE fought a very public battle for control over the Human Genome Project. Although both were under the authority of the President, the Reagan White House exhibited little interest in the controversy and exercised no authority in providing coordination.[6] Accordingly, agency strategies and Congressional actions were the deciding forces in shaping the project's bureaucratic structure. An account by Robert Cook-Deegan, who served as Director of the OTA study, is instructive.

The first move toward a genome bureaucracy came in the fiscal year 1987 DOE budget. DeLisi set aside $5.5 million of discretionary funds already appropriated, reprogramming them for his newly conceived genome research program. The first Congressional action came with the fiscal year 1988 budgets, during hearings in the spring and summer of 1987. DeLisi cleared a several-year program of genome research funding through the Department and then with the White House Office of Management and Budget. This was incorporated into the President's budget and duly appropriated, with earmarked spending authority beginning in October 1987.

On the NIH side, no request for genome research funding went into the President's budget request, but in response to questions from the House Appropriation's Subcommittee, James B. Wyngaarden, Director of NIH, indicated that it could use $30 million for gene mapping if Congress chose to appropriate $500 million or more than the President had requested. Nobel laureates James D. Watson and David Baltimore met with Members and staff from both House and Senate Appropriations Committees in May 1987, primarily to seek additional funding for AIDS research, but Watson also asked for $30 million in genome research funds. The House earmarked $30 million, but the Senate only earmarked $6 million, and a compromise between the houses split the difference. The genome project was thus established by congressional action at both NIH and DOE, beginning with the 1988 budget.

Lessons Learned

In June 1988 NIH and DOE, under pressure from the Congress, signed a Memorandum of Understanding agreeing to cooperate on the Human Genome Project. In September of that year, NIH Director James Wyngaarden appointed James Watson as the NIH Associate Director of Genome Research.

At the outset of assuming responsibilities for the genome project at NIH, James Watson set about mastering the intricacies of the federal bureaucracy and the policy process with passion and energy similar to that he devoted decades earlier to understanding the intricacies of the structure of DNA. Watson proceeded to set a course for the Human Genome Project that influences policy to this day. Norton Zinder of Rockefeller University described Watson as "standing like a colossus over the whole program."

Watson may have been instructed by the faltering steps, intrigue, and outright bureaucratic battles that preceded his appointment. The lessons were there. Marry the expertise and insights of the scientific community with the expertise and insights of those who know the federal science policy process. Learn the intricacies of the budget process and work closely with those who influence it at all stages. Master the workings of the government bureaucracy with special attention to the jurisdictional responsibilities in Congress. And in managing bureaucratic battles—seek the elegant solution, but settle for the attainable.

---

[1] *The Human Genome Project: From Maps to Medicine,* National Human Genome Research Institute, National Institutes of Health, NIH Publication No. 98-3897.

[2] Ibid.

[3] *Human Genome Program Report, Part I, Overview and Progress,* U.S. Department of Energy, 1997.

[4] Cook-Deegan, Robert, *The Gene Wars: Science, Politics, and the Human Genome,* W.W. Norton, 1994, p. 133.

[5] The Office of Technology Assessment, a highly respected Congressional science and technology policy analytical instrument, was abolished in 1995 during a budget reduction effort.

[6] Op. cit., Cook-Deegan, p. 149.

★ ★ ★ ★ ★

The Global Positioning System

By Anne G. K. Solomon

On March 29, 1996, President Bill Clinton issued PDD NSTC-6, shorthand for *Global Positioning System, Presidential Decision Directive, National Science and Technology Council #6.* This directive outlined a national policy on the management and use of the Global Positioning System (GPS). At the White House public announcement, or "roll out," the new policy was described as "opening the door for rapid growth in a burgeoning civil and commercial GPS market." First conceived in the 1970s as a navigational means to enhance the effectiveness of U.S. and allied military forces, by the mid-1990s GPS had become an integral component of the emerging global information infrastructure. GPS applications range from mapping and surveying, to international air traffic management, to global climate change research. Accordingly, PDD NSTC-6 was intended to ensure that U.S. economic and other civilian aims for GPS were well served, while protecting the nation's national security interests.

In initiating the GPS interagency policy review that culminated in PDD NSTC-6, the President designated the Office of Science and Technology Policy (OSTP) to coordinate with the National Science and Technology Council (NSTC) and the National Security Council (NSC). The President's charge to OSTP and NSC was to review GPS policy issues and to provide "a strategic vision" for GPS management and use. The working group's final conclusions and recommendations on GPS policy goals and policy guidelines, and agency roles and responsibilities, reflected the complexities of managing a powerful dual-use technological system, as well as the intricacies of brokering competing interagency interests.

The Technology, Its Origins, and Development

The Global Positioning System is arranged in three distinct segments that together provide users with highly accurate position, time, and velocity information:

1. The space segment with a constellation of 24 orbiting satellites that broadcast precise time signals;

2. The ground-based control segment that includes a control center and access to overseas command stations; and

3. The user segment that consists of GPS receivers and associated equipment.

Simply explained, the satellites transmit radio signals giving each satellite's position and the time it transmitted the signal. A user's receiver calculates the distance between the receiver and the satellite by subtracting the time the signal left the satellite from the time that it arrived at the receiver. The user's exact location—a three-dimensional position with longitude, latitude, and altitude—is determined by coordinating the distance from the user's receiver to four or more satellites. Additional calculations can provide the velocity at which the user may be moving.

The GPS is regarded as a science and engineering triumph integrating knowledge and capabilities in areas including the fundamental infrastructure of rockets, atomic clocks, integrated circuits, and bandwidth compression.[1] The Department of Defense (DOD) developed the system to increase the precision of weapons delivery and to guide strategic aircraft more accurately. The cost to U.S. taxpayers was more than $10 billion.

From the start, DOD considered GPS to be inherently dual-use with potential civilian applications for navigation, surveying, and time transfer. DOD recognized, however, that potential adversaries could use this powerful satellite-based system as well. To mitigate the danger of hostile use, DOD provided positioning capability at two levels of accuracy—the highly accurate Precise Positioning Service (PPS), encrypted and restricted for use only by the U.S. military and its allies, and the less accurate Standard Positioning System (SPS), provided at no cost to civilian and commercial users worldwide. The DOD additionally degraded the accuracy of the civilian SPS through a technical means called "selective availability."

Two events were pivotal in shaping the perceptions of the value and potential of GPS that led up to the 1996 PDD NSTC-6 policy review. The first was the September 1983 Soviet shoot down of the Korean airliner, KAL-007, which had ventured into Soviet airspace. In response, President Ronald Reagan committed the United States to making GPS internationally available to improve civilian aviation safety. The second event a decade later was Operation Desert Storm—where in a featureless, sand-blown desert, GPS guided U.S. and allied assaults on Iraqi forces, and thus dramatically demonstrated the system's military value. By the mid-1990s GPS was considered to be a vital element in the basic infrastructure of the world's economy—for air, sea, and land transportation systems; and for the Internet, scientific research, and a range of other activities requiring precise positioning and timing data. Simultaneously, GPS was a key instrument serving the U.S. armed forces.

Policy Challenges

The fundamental policy challenge posed by GPS was similar to those posed by many dual-use technologies. That is, the government needed to determine which U.S. policy strategies would achieve the desirable balance among national objectives (1) to enhance U.S. economic competitiveness and productivity, (2) to protect national security and foreign policy interests, and (3) to ensure continued progress in scientific and technological research and innovation.

To help illuminate specific issues relevant to GPS, Congress asked two public policy research entities, the National Academy of Public Administration (NAPA) and the National Research Council (NRC), to conduct independent studies of future GPS management and funding. These studies, and an additional review that OSTP requested of the RAND Corporation's Critical Technologies Institute, provided research and analysis, policy conclusions, and recommendations that informed the subsequent White House policy review.[2] In addition, the GPS Industry Association worked constructively with the White House, Executive Branch agencies, and Congressional players to convey private sector views.

The complexities were many, as indicated by a NAPA/NRC list of "powerful forces" shaping the policy environment:[3]

- ▶ GPS as a potential weapon of war and terrorism. The United States, having developed GPS, must retain the technology's military advantages for its own and allied forces use and deny these advantages to enemies. As with other technologies, other nations will acquire GPS-like capabilities. How fast this happens depends, in part, on U.S. policies and actions.

- ▶ Rapidly growing commercial markets. Sales of GPS-related products and services are expected to grow to more than $30 billion annually after the year 2000.

- ▶ Use by much larger segments of the general public. As GPS becomes a key part of vehicular navigation systems and mobile communications, millions of people will come to know and depend on it.

- ▶ Further potential technological improvements. Technological improvements will be made to the basic GPS system to improve accuracy, integrity, and availability.

- ▶ International markets and influences. International markets are expanding and foreign firms and governments are pressing the United States for assurance of continued GPS signal availability, and for international participation in system governance and management. Foreign unease with reliance on a U.S. military-controlled system provides incentive for international development of competing global navigation systems.

Contending Players and Bureaucratic "Stove piping"

Responsibility for managing U.S. interests associated with these "powerful forces" was split among several federal departments. These contending players were confined and restricted by a "stove piped" federal bureaucratic organization. For example, the Department of Transportation focused on air, sea, and land navigation; the Department of Defense on military considerations; and the Department of Commerce on productivity and competitiveness. There were misunderstandings and mistrust within and among mission agencies that stymied decision making on important issues of GPS governance, management, and budgets. The OSTP/NSTC and NSC policy review process brought together all of the relevant players to identify and resolve issues and to set policy guidelines—and did so successfully.

The entire process that led up to PDD NSTC-6 worked well—commissioning outside entities to identify and analyze issues, working closely with industry to understand the private sector perspective, and establishing within the White House a policy review process that facilitated debate and resolved differences among players. PDD NSTC-6 outlined a useful policy framework for an extraordinary technology with great potential.

Policy Outcome

The key components of PDD NSTC-6 were intended to reassure all American and friendly foreign stakeholders that the United States was committed to supporting their respective interests. The central element was assurance that America would keep the constellation of 24 GPS satellites and other components up and running—and available to scientists, consumers, businesses, and others around the world for their use, free of charge. This commitment was designed to assure all users, including foreign governments and international organizations, that they could depend on civil GPS services for their navigation and positioning needs. Such a commitment was necessary to ensure international acceptance of GPS as a global standard. Providing free access eliminated the economic incentives for others to invest the large sums that would be required to develop their own systems—systems that the United States feared could pose security threats.

The Presidential Decision Directive also committed the U.S. government to improving the quality of the civilian Standard Positioning System signal by eliminating "selective availability" as soon as the DOD developed the technical capability to selectively deny GPS to hostile entities. These steps together cleared the way for a revolution in international transportation by allowing unrestricted broadcast of enhanced GPS signals worldwide. Finally, the PDD established a permanent GPS executive board, co-chaired by the Departments of Defense and Transportation and including representatives from all relevant agencies, to coordinate GPS management and use.

Continued Policy Management

PDD NSTC-6 was a first step in a policy process that continued in the international arena. It provided the basis for a broad, coordinated U.S. government approach in negotiations with foreign governments and international organizations. A range of tough technical, commercial, and security issues required international resolution to make GPS an enduring component of the global transportation and communications infrastructure. Subsequent U.S.-international negotiations both addressed these important issues and also encouraged other governments to match the American integrated policy approach to reflect GPS policy complexities.

Lessons Learned

PDD NSTC-6 brought together the senior levels of government responsible for policies on national security, the economy and trade, and research and innovation. Such integrated policy initiatives and structures increasingly are required to adequately manage the complexities of advanced technological systems.

---

1   For an excellent discussion of some of the science and engineering accomplishments that made development of the GPS possible see The Global Positioning System: The Role of Atomic Clocks, part of the National Academy of Sciences "Beyond Discovery Series," http://www.nas.edu.

2   The Global Positioning System: Charting the Future. A report by a Panel of the National Academy of Public Administration (NAPA) and a Committee of the National Research Council (NRC) for the Congress of the United States and the Department of Defense, May 1995.

The Global Positioning System: A Shared National Asset. A report of the National Research Council, May 1995.

Pace, Scott, et. al., The Global Positioning System: Assessing National Policies. The RAND Corporation, MR-614-OSTP, 1995.

3   The Global Positioning System: Charting the Future, pp. xxiii-xxiv.

V. FISCAL POLICY AND INTERNATIONAL ECONOMICS

The Bretton Woods Institution

By Henry Owen

As World War II neared its end, thinking in many Allied countries turned increasingly to the question of how to ensure that the postwar period would not again be shattered by world depression. The United States offered to host a meeting of these countries at Bretton Woods, New Hampshire in 1944, to consider measures to avert such a catastrophe. That meeting was marked by intelligent discussion, but it seemed at times as though the goal of creating institutions that would preserve postwar prosperity would get lost in the discourse. U.S. President Franklin D. Roosevelt strongly supported the efforts of the Secretary of the Treasury to ensure that this did not happen. Lord Key made a strong and useful contribution.

In the end, agreement was reached on creating both a World Bank and an International Monetary Fund (IMF). The Bank would be a lender of last resort, a function that would have been critically useful when the Depression struck in 1929. The Fund was designed to avert, or at least cushion, the wild swings of currency fluctuations that had contributed greatly to the Depression.

After agreement had been reached, the Bank and the Fund were set up in Washington under U.S. leadership. The first President of the World Bank was American John McCloy, and the United States had made the largest single contribution to both the Bank and the Fund.

A main problem that emerged after these institutions had been in existence for some years was the uncertain attitude of the Congress toward their work. There was a general objection on Capitol Hill to so-called "give aways," and a more specific argument that the Bank and the Fund were no longer needed, because the private sector could now provide the loans. These views are reflected in the 2000 report of the majority of the Meltzer Commission appointed by the Congress recently to review the future of the Bretton Woods institutions.

That report proposes changes in the World Bank—and to a lesser extent, the IMF—which would reduce their effectiveness, relying on the private sector to fill the gap. There is some validity to this view, but only in moderation. Much will depend on how far the next Administration exercises this moderation. It will be important to preserve the development lending functions of the World Bank in areas where the Western private sector does not intervene sufficiently to meet current needs. Lending by the IMF to meet short-term emergencies, particularly in poor countries that commit themselves to following sound policies, also will be needed. Where this commitment is lacking, as in Russia, that lending should cease. The House of Representatives feels strongly on this point, and rightly so.

The reason that these two institutions survive and prosper, despite their critics, is not only that they have generally done a good job, but that successive U.S. Presidents have taken a special interest in their work and have come quickly and effectively to their defense when they were attacked. My recommendation to the next President is twofold:

1. Keep up the tradition of direct Presidential interest and involvement. Otherwise these two institutions will lack an effective U.S. constituency.

2. Seek the views of not only the Secretary of the Treasury but also of the private sector. For example, the Bretton Woods Committee, which is made up of businesspeople with leading positions in the U.S. private economy, has worked closely with these institutions, and they know what they are talking about.

3. When it is needed, as it often is, the President should press for innovations that will meet the changes taking place in the world economy without gutting these two institutions.

Lessons Learned

One major reason that the Great Depression was long and deep was that there was no lender of last resort, as pointed out by Professor Charles Kindelberg. After the First World War, the British no longer had the resources to play this role, and U.S. banks lacked the experience and self-assurance that was needed to take their place. Now this gap has been filled by the International Bank of Reconstruction and Development (IBRD) and IMF, and by the great growth in the rich countries' private lending and investment in the developing countries.

Whether this situation will continue depends very much on if the World Bank and the IMF continue to play their roles. It also depends on whether the President continues to take the lead in defending and reforming these institutions—so that they can stimulate, rather than replace, the growing role of the private sector.

Leadership in Establishing the Office of the Special Trade Representative

By Sherman Katz

Sometimes Presidential leadership is enhanced by measures the President didn't want or welcome. The establishment of the Special Representative for Trade Negotiations (STR) during the Kennedy Administration, and its later elevation to Cabinet-level rank and enlargement of the Office of the U.S. Trade Representative (USTR) by Congress during the Nixon Administration are good examples. But even if

President Kennedy didn't welcome this initiative at first, he and his successors have appointed distinguished and highly qualified persons to the position of USTR, as it has come to be known, to conduct trade negotiations for the United States. The growing importance of trade to our economic well being, and the convenience of having someone around to "take the flak" from some of the inevitably competing domestic commercial interests at play in trade policy decisions, have combined to make this a highly successful innovation both for the country and for the President.

In the late 1950s and early 1960s, Congress increasingly took the view that the State Department, which then had the largest share of trade policy authority (apart from smaller portions in the Treasury and Commerce Departments) was sacrificing U.S. trade interests to foreign policy concerns.

President John F. Kennedy went to Congress in 1962 seeking broad new authority to reduce tariff rates across the board (not just item-by-item) to meet the challenge of the new European Economic Community. Wilbur Mills (D-AR), the House Ways and Means Committee Chairman, raised the question of whether the State Department could be trusted with this new authority. Representative Mills, supported by Harry Byrd, Sr. (D-VA), Chairman of the Senate Finance Committee, proposed that the President designate a Special Representative for Trade Negotiations. By placing this official in the Executive Office of the President, Mills and Byrd hoped to leave no doubt that the STR was the paramount authority on trade issues. They were distrustful that neither the State nor Commerce Departments would be sufficiently responsive to agricultural interests, including those important to their constituents.

This mandate from Congress became law on October 11, 1962 (Section 241 of the Trade Expansion Act of 1962). Three months later, January 15, 1963, President Kennedy issued an Executive Order implementing the law. Kennedy accepted the mandate reluctantly—like most Presidents, he resisted efforts to establish special-purpose offices in "his" Executive Office.

In 1974, when the Nixon Administration proposed to place the STR on its Council on International Economic Policy (CIEP) staff, the House Ways and Means Committee responded by voting to make the Office of the STR (not just the person) statutory, in an amendment to what became the Trade Act of 1974. By the time the Senate finished its work on the proposal, Finance Committee Chairman Russell B. Long (D-LA) had given the head of the Office of STR Cabinet rank. Indeed, Long underscored legislators' sense that they owned a piece of the White House trade operation several years later when he suggested, during the confirmation hearings of President Jimmy Carter's STR, Robert Strauss, that "it might be a good idea for us to ask [the Secretaries of State and Treasury to meet with his committee] so that there can be no misunderstanding" about which official was to have trade primacy.

GATT Negotiations

Bob Strauss, one of Washington's best known and most highly respected lawyers and political leaders, was appointed by President Carter to take up the difficult task of conducting and concluding the Tokyo Round of the General Agreement on Tariffs and Trade (GATT) negotiations. Those talks had begun in 1974 and were struggling under the weight of what seemed like an endless list of differences between the United States and Japan about commodities such as beef, oranges, and rice. Ambassador Strauss not only had the political savvy to broker a deal with the government of Japan, he was able to sell ratification of it to a skeptical Congress, which was concerned that he was giving away the store. The results of the Tokyo Round contributed enormously to U.S. market access and exports around the world.

In fact the success of that Round, concluded in 1979, played a large part in creating strong domestic interest in the U.S. government for another multilateral round of trade negotiations in the 1980s. William Brock, former Republican Senator from Tennessee and Chairman of the Republican Party, was appointed USTR by President Ronald Reagan and helped create consensus for an ambitious agenda for new negotiations. He proposed to bring "trade in services" under the umbrella of GATT (since its creation in 1947, GATT had been only concerned with trade in goods). The United States was well ahead of most of its competitors in this sector. Indeed, our lead on service exports contributed to the reluctance of our European trading partners to begin another round of trade negotiations in 1984. But Senator Brock's vision on services opened the door to an enormous opportunity for the American economy.

Clayton Yeutter, a former Governor of Nebraska, was appointed USTR by President Reagan in his second term. Yeutter, previously a Deputy U.S. Trade Representative in the Nixon and Ford Administrations, created the international consensus necessary to start the Uruguay Round in 1986 within one year of taking office. He and his negotiating team made substantial progress toward a landmark agreement on trade in services and much needed improvement of procedures for trade dispute settlement.

President George H.W. Bush's brilliant USTR appointee, Carla Hills, an international lawyer of the highest standing, succeeded during 1992, the final year of Uruguay Round trade talks to bring intellectual property within the ambit of trade rules—an economic home run for the technology-rich U.S. industry. She also conducted most of the successful campaign to bring some discipline to the European Union's highly disruptive agriculture export subsidies.

USTRs Mickey Kantor and Charlene Barshefsky played leading roles in helping the Clinton Administration finish up key parts of the Uruguay Round including multilateral trade agreements on telecommunications, financial services, and information technology that have together helped lay the foundation for the blossoming of the information technology revolution and the spectacular growth of the global economy in the past nine years.

In short, the USTR, an institution whose creation two Presidents neither sought nor received gladly, has been a highly effective instrument of U.S. international trade policy.

The 1971 China Shock

By John R. Malott

As President, Richard M. Nixon had a flair for the dramatic. He saw himself as a great maker of history. And perhaps no single action of his Presidency was more dramatic and historic than his opening to China.

Nixon also had a penchant for secrecy. He and his National Security Advisor, Henry Kissinger, enjoyed cutting out Secretary William Rogersand his State Department from the planning and implementation of foreign policy.

Secret envoys and discussions, surprise announcements, dramatic policy actions that sometimes were "overkill" for the task at hand, and flamboyant rhetoric were part and parcel of Nixon's approach to the Presidency. (The *Atlantic Monthly* magazine once published two pages of Nixon quotes, most of which began "This is the first time in history that a President has....")

President Nixon's surprise announcement in July 1971 that Henry Kissinger had made a secret trip to Beijing and that he would visit China the following year was the quintessential example of Nixon's approach to the Presidency and his desired place in history.

It surprised and shocked everyone to see this ardent anti-Communist reaching out to change two decades of American policy. But it had been clear for a number of months before Nixon's announcement that U.S. policy toward China was starting to change.

Coupled with his policy of détente toward the Soviet Union, Nixon was working to adjust America's relations with its Cold War enemies. In February 1971 the U.S. government eased some travel and trade restrictions with China. In addition to these public announcements, the Japanese government was aware that behind the scenes the U.S. State Department was conducting a number of China policy reviews. Working-level consultations between American and Japanese officials were taking place.

But no one—not even the officials involved in the State

Department's policy reviews—was prepared for the dramatic and very Nixonesque announcement of July 1971.

Asian Security

Japan was not the only ally left in the dark about this dramatic change in U.S. policy. And it was not the only American ally in Asia to be affected—Nixon's actions had far-reaching consequences for the security of South Korea and Taiwan. The whole world was surprised and shocked, not just Japan. The Soviets also had reason to be concerned, as it appeared that Nixon was trying to pit the Soviet Union and China against each other at a time when their troops were engaged in border clashes.

So why did the so-called "Nixon Shock" become such a special problem in U.S.-Japan relations? And why have most analyses of Nixon's announcement focused on its impact on Japan, and not on other countries in the region?

Style is often more important than substance in U.S.-Japan relations. Our failure to inform the Japanese until Secretary of State Rogers called his counterpart, just a few minutes before Nixon's announcement, became the focal point of Japanese discontent. It did not help the atmospherics of the relationship that in later defending their decision not to inform the Japanese, U.S. officials said that they feared the Japanese could not keep secrets and would leak the information.

In the public mind, therefore, Nixon Shock has become an issue of style and a reminder of the importance that Japan attaches to consultation. Even today, such questions as how we treat Japan, whether we consult before taking action, whether U.S. officials visit Japan when they are in the region, and whether American officials meet with their counterparts at international gatherings are still "live" issues in the U.S.-Japan relationship.

Substantive Issues in Japan

But in reality, this focus on style obscures the real substantive issues that were impacted by Nixon's decision to visit China.

First was the U.S.-Japan security relationship, and in particular the use of American bases in Japan to prosecute the war in Vietnam. It was only a decade before that the Japanese government, despite major public protests, revised its security treaty with the United States. Now American ships and aircraft were stopping in Japan on their way to and from Indochina. U.S. war casualties were evacuated to military hospitals in Japan, and American and South Vietnamese military equipment was repaired there. The Japanese government was taking a lot of heat from its citizens, the press, and opposition parties. Anti-Vietnam War sentiment and demonstrations were as common in Japan as they were in the United States. Japan's police were called out frequently to use force and protect U.S. military facilities from angry demonstrators.

The Japanese government could defend itself from some of this domestic criticism by citing the importance of opposing communism and the threat that China (and the Soviet Union) posed to Japan. Now, with one announcement, Nixon appeared to be reversing U.S. policy toward China and undercutting the rationale that the Japanese government had put forward for allowing the use of military facilities in Japan to support an unpopular war in Vietnam.The political heat on Japan's Liberal Democratic Party (LDP) government was only going to increase.

The second substantive issue was the internal struggle within the LDP over Japan's own policy toward China. The country's long-serving Prime Minister, Eisaku Sato, was a member of the pro-Taiwan faction of his party. His brother, former Prime Minister Nobusuke Kishi, also was strongly anti-communist and pro-Taiwan, and often was used by Japanese businessmen as a liaison with the Taiwanese government. Other members of the LDP, however, including Kakuei Tanaka (who was maneuvering to succeed Sato as Prime Minister), were keen to improve Japan's relationship with China and move deeply into Chinese markets.

Faced with these differences within his party, Sato could justify his own pro-Taiwan position by citing the need for U.S.-Japanese solidarity on China policy. It has been a time-honored tactic for many governments in postwar Japan to avoid difficult internal policy discussions by citing foreign, and in particular, American "pressure." But now Sato found both his foreign policy and his domestic political position undercut by Nixon's decision. With America moving ahead in its China policy, Sato could no longer justify his own desired policy by citing the need to keep in step with the United States.

But the internal policy discussion was temporarily deflected to another issue. The proper question should have been, will Japan's policy toward China change? But that was a question that Sato's government did not want to answer, and it shifted the focus to a secondary question that dealt with the past and not the future, and with style rather than substance—why didn't the Americans tell us? By harping on this point, the LDP could deflect public attention away from the hard policy choices that it did not want to make. But by focusing on this point of style, it ingrained in many minds that the "China Shock" issue in U.S.-Japan relations was all about the U.S. failure to consult.

In February 1972, Richard Nixon walked down the ramp from Air Force One and set foot on Chinese soil, a scene that was broadcast live in Japan. The NHK television network periodically would cut to shots of Prime Minister Sato and his aides, reacting derisively to what they were watching on television.

Five months later, Sato was out, replaced by Kakuei Tanaka. And two months after forming his government, it was Tanaka's turn to walk down an airplane staircase in China, putting an end to the debate within the LDP over China policy. Japan normalized relations with China in September 1972, seven years before the United States did.

The question still remains, should the United States have

informed Japan (and others) of this major shift in its China policy? Given the great impact that such a decision would have on both security relations and domestic politics in many countries of the region, the logical answer is yes. But given the reality of Richard Nixon's Presidential style, that never would have happened. After all, why spoil a great surprise and lessen the drama of a wonderful historic moment?

The 1971 Dollar Shock and the 1973 Smithsonian Agreement

By John R. Malott

Not even one month after delivering his "China Shock" to Japan and the world (announcing his rapprochement with China), Richard Nixon did it again.

With his usual flair for creating a dramatic moment, Nixon announced that the United States would deal with its deteriorating international economic position by imposing a 10 percent surcharge on all imports. Although the surcharge obviously would affect all countries exporting to the United States, the Japanese once again saw it as directed specifically against them. Perhaps the timing of Nixon's announcement helped convince Japan—he delivered his speech on the 36th anniversary of V-J Day (the celebration date of Allied victory over Japan in World War II), August 15, 1971.

And because it was Nixon, there was the grand historical moment. In addition to the surcharge (which later was overturned in a legal challenge as a violation of America's international trade commitments), Nixon undid almost 40 years of history by announcing that the U.S. dollar no longer would be convertible to gold. Now the dollar's value would be free to float, within limits, and the value of other currencies, including the yen, would have to adjust accordingly.

It was hoped that this would make U.S. exports cheaper and Japanese and other imports more expensive.

In addition, Nixon said that he would remove the 7.5 percent federal excise (luxury) tax on automobiles. Although this tax break would apply equally to Japanese imports, in the end there would be a slight price advantage to U.S. carmakers, given the new 10 percent surcharge on Japanese imports.

In contrast to the China announcement, this time there was plenty of warning that the United States was growing concerned with its international economic position vis-à-vis Japan. And it wasn't a secret, either. American companies and labor unions both were increasingly critical of Japan's growing exports to the United States. American businessmen complained as well about restrictions on trade and investment in the Japanese market. With European markets still protected and Asian market opportunities still years in the future, it was the United States that felt the brunt of Japan's burgeoning exports.

On August 6, 1971, about a week before Nixon's announcement of the surcharge on imports, the Treasury Department announced that the United States had sustained a loss of gold reserves of more than a billion dollars. This led Congressman Henry S. Reuss, Chairman of the House Banking Committee at the time, to declare publicly his "inescapable conclusion" that the dollar must be devalued, or else gold sales must be suspended. Were the Japanese listening?

Senior officials within Nixon's Cabinet—Treasury Secretary John Connally, Commerce Secretary Maurice Stans, and Special Trade Representative (STR) William D. Eberle—also had been expressing their concern about the value of the dollar and gold both publicly and privately.

Japan: Full Speed Ahead

But with the Japanese political-economic system on "cruise control," the signs were not heeded. A decade of effort to strengthen Japan's international competitiveness was finally starting to pay off, so who in Japan would dare to take any actions that would hurt business and exports? Within Japan it was "full speed ahead." The government's effort focused single-mindedly on maintaining the status quo, which included keeping a fixed exchange rate at the same level it had been throughout the postwar era—360 Yen to a dollar.

With no movement in Japan, it was left to the United States, as the "affected" or "impacted" country, to do what was necessary. The actions that were taken—raising duties, lowering excise taxes, and abandoning the peg to the gold standard—were within the sovereign authority of any government to take. But because the government in this case was the United States—the world's largest economy and the destination of more than one-third of Japan's exports—the impact on Japan's companies would be immediate and serious.

After the China announcement, the press in Japan took the English word "shock" and converted it into the Japanese "shokku." Although Nixon's August 15 economic speech was not as surprising or "shocking" as his China announcement of the previous month, the Japanese press applied the same word to it. Even though it had an impact on the whole world, the "Dollar Shock" now joined the "Nixon (or China) Shock" as a bilateral event, recorded in the history of U.S.-Japan relations. (As the years went by, the Japanese press would attach shokku to all kinds of events, just as U.S. reporters add "____gate" to every political scandal. Shokku still is widely used in Japan, but it has evolved into a synonym for "surprised," a much softer meaning than the events of 1971 that provoked its first use.)

The point here is that there are shocks—and then there are shocks. There were many indications that the United States was dissatisfied with the current state of affairs, but Japan's government did not or could not act on them. It was left to Nixon, with his penchant for the dramatic, to change the situation.

In hindsight, it is clear that the August 15 speech was only the first in a series of events that would have a profound effect over the next few years on the world's financial system, the U.S.-Japan economic relationship, and Japan's own economic structure. Within two years, the Bretton Woods system of fixed exchange rates had ended. Japan entered a new era in which there would be a tension in U.S. policy between our security ties, which would continue to be cooperative, and our economic relations, which would be characterized by rivalry and contentiousness. And the Dollar Shock, when combined with the oil crisis of 1973, and the inflation and wage increases that followed from this, started a structural transformation in Japan that in the end made it an even more formidable competitor of the United States. In 1971, before the Dollar Shock, Japan was producing cheap, labor-intensive goods for stores such as Sears and K-Mart. A decade later it had achieved world-class quality and competitiveness in a full range of high value, high technology products. Thank you, Richard Nixon.

The Dollar Shock of 1971 also was the first time when the inadequacies in both governments' economic bureaucracies came to the forefront. Before 1971, few people spoke of international economic policy. Foreign policy meant political and defense relations. Economic problems, at least in the case of U.S.-Japan relations, meant disputes over specific products, such as textiles or typewriter ribbons (the latter being one of the first postwar disputes in U.S.-Japan economic policies). But seldom did issues between nations include the larger macroeconomic relations of trade and financial policies.

Impact of August 15, 1971, Speech

In retrospect, it is clear that all of this changed on August 15, 1971.

For two weeks after Nixon's speech, the Japanese government struggled to maintain the yen's exchange rate at 360. But it was a lost cause. As the Japanese proverb goes, it was like "spitting into the wind." In the end, the Bank of Japan suspended trading. And then Japan's banks and businesses entered a "brave new world." Now the markets—whoever they were—would determine everyday at 9 a.m. what the dollar and the yen were worth, not the Tokyo University alums at the Bank of Japan and the Finance Ministry.

Over the next two years, the world's economic system continued to evolve. The next time a major decision was made about the world's financial system and its exchange rates, Richard Nixon did not make it in seclusion at Camp David. Japan's Finance Minister joined his counterparts from the United States and the other developed economies at the Smithsonian Institution in Washington in May 1973. Now Japan was a full participant in determining its own economic future, as it would be once again at the Plaza Hotel in New York in September 1985. Japan may not have liked the results in either case—at the Smithsonian or at the Plaza—but the argument that Japan was caught unaware, that it was not consulted, and that it was dealt a "shock" by the United States could no longer be made. The Japanese were in the room.

Again in hindsight, 1971 also marked the beginning of a different "track" in U.S.-Japan relations. In 1972 for the first time, the United States began to train Foreign Service Officers to be specialists on the Japanese economy. The Commerce and Treasury Departments and Special Trade Representative began to be major players in U.S. policy toward Japan. In Japan, both MITI and the Finance Ministry started to become more assertive in their country's policy toward the United States. No longer would U.S.-Japan relations be the privileged domain of the State and Defense Departments and the Foreign Ministry in Japan.

Formation of National Economic Council

The tensions in U.S.-Japan economic relations—and among the bureaucratic institutions that dealt with them—would continue into the 1990s. In 1993 President Bill Clinton established the National Economic Council to parallel the National Security Council structure, and its members prided themselves on their ability to close ranks and speak with one voice to their Japanese counterparts. And by the 1990s it was widely accepted that with respect to international economic policy, it was in America's own interest to consult closely with the world's second largest economy, Japan. Economic tensions between the two countries also dissipated because American business no longer saw the Japanese as a threat.

Indeed, the worst affront to economic consultation in recent years came not from the United States but from Japan. Following the Asian financial crisis in July 1997, Japan's Ministry of Finance failed to consult with the United States and the International Monetary Fund when it proposed a $100 billion bailout fund for the region's economies with weak conditionality. American opposition killed the idea. But there was a certain joyfulness among U.S. officials—for once, they could chastise the Japanese for failing to consult.

Economic "Shocks" in U.S.-Japan Relations

By William Piez

On a number of occasions the United States has taken actions that were so unexpected by Japan that the Japanese press labeled them as "shocks." These actions have ranged across the board over political, security, and economic issues. This case study will focus on three "shocks" in the realm of economic relations—and consider what was done, what the consequences were, and how undesirable consequences could have been avoided.

Surcharge Shocks

During 1971, Richard M. Nixon's Administration undertook an intense review of the international payments situation in the United States, with particular attention given to the value of the dollar and Japan's rising trade surplus with the United States and the world. Over a weekend in August, and well out of the public eye, an interagency group fashioned a new economic plan. In a speech late on Sunday, August 15, President Nixon announced the plan that, among other decisions, included a 10 percent surcharge on all dutiable imports. The news hit Tokyo on Monday morning, Tokyo time. Because 90 percent of its exports to the United States were dutiable this action hit Japan hard, as the United States had intended. The surcharge immediately became the subject of strong Japanese protests and dominated every American official contact with Japan. Although Canada was a larger exporter to the United States, 75 percent of those exports were duty free and unaffected. The announcement was designed to force a revaluation of the Japanese yen and of European currencies, and eventually it did so. In this case study, however, the focus will be on Japan's reaction to the surcharge, even though the surcharge itself was of much less significance over the long term than yen revaluation.

Up until this time, U.S. efforts to deal with Japan's strong export push in American markets had been marked by two strategies. The first approach was to take up individual export products and negotiate limits on the quantities shipped by Japan, which resulted in voluntary quotas on some Japanese exports such as stainless flatware, steel, and textiles. The second approach was to tackle the many problems of access for U.S. exports to Japanese markets by requiring that the Japanese reduce tariffs, speed up procedures for processing shipments of imports, and adopt less restrictive import regulations. These methods were generally successful in managing U.S. complaints. Although talks on individual topics could seem quite acrimonious, especially as depicted in the Japanese press, they dealt with real problems and did not threaten to damage the fabric of the overall relationship. U.S. representatives in fact often went out of their way to state that trade problems relating, for example, to steel were not going to harm our otherwise good relations.

The surcharge shock thus came as a truly unexpected escalation. The United States was just seeking to solve trade problems by taking a macroeconomic approach covering all trade. Most individual products were not to be discussed separately in trade negotiations. The Japanese felt particularly aggrieved by this, and saw the Nixon measures as heavily tilted against them.

The surcharge crisis was finally resolved at the end of the year as part of general negotiations at the Smithsonian Institution on U.S. international payments. (This agreement is described in a separate case study in this series.) Not discussed at the time was the result of a lawsuit against the surcharge brought by U.S. importers who, after all, had to pay this tax. They won their suit, and surcharge payments were refunded to them.

This was not an accidental shock. It was intended to "get Japan's attention," and it worked. A strong argument can be made, however, that it was overkill, and that it had longer-term costs in the form of damaged confidence and trust. In retrospect it is probable that the Nixon plan would have been equally successful if the international payments package had not included the 10 percent import surcharge.

Since 1971 much has been done to strengthen the rules of international trade, especially through the efforts of the World Trade Organization and other international financial reforms. Exchange rate fluctuations are now available as a trade adjustment mechanism, in contrast to the fixed rate system of the Bretton Woods Agreement of 1944. Lessons have been learned. It is to be hoped that they stay learned.

Soybean Shock

In the summer of 1973 the Nixon Administration was deeply engaged in managing what the President described as our most important problem—price inflation. Against this background the price of soybeans on U.S. commodity markets rose sharply for reasons not easily understood since there had been no crop failures or other evident causes.

After deliberations (kept confidential in order not to influence markets), Secretary of Agriculture Earl Butz announced a full study of the supply and demand for soybeans and, almost incidentally, an embargo on soybean exports pending results from the study. This announcement appeared late on a Friday after commodity markets were closed. Japan was in immediate shock, pointing out that it was a major importer of American soybeans. Further, it was hard for Japan to reconcile such an embargo given the longstanding U.S. concern about its trade deficit with Japan. Japan was dependent on soybeans as an essential part of the traditional Japanese diet. Finally, Japan argued that there could be no good rationale for American government interference in a free market. U.S. soybean exporters also joined in, pointing out that Japanese demand, far from upsetting markets, was highly stable. Japanese demand, furthermore, was welcome to farmers as well as exporters. The initial U.S. government reaction was, on the following Monday, to amend the decree so that up to 50 percent of export orders could be filled, thus postponing any immediate shortages overseas.

Secretary Butz made a trip to Japan to heal the wounds as much as he could, and he was successful at least in hearing the Japanese out and assuring them that any consequences would be short lived. Japan's government treated Butz to a formal Japanese dinner of many courses, all of which consisted of soybeans prepared in different ways such as tofu made from soybeans, and an appetizer of soybeans served like peanuts in the shell. The dinner illustrated plainly how important soybeans were in Japan as basic food.

The study was duly completed. It revealed that much of the demand for soybeans was coming from traders who planned to resell, and that the demand from actual users of soybeans was not in excess of supply. Prices settled down and the embargo was lifted. Later examination of Japanese import data showed that Japan's imports had not changed much, the partial lifting of the embargo having been sufficient to permit normal shipments to proceed.

The soybean shock was accidental. No U.S. official had thought through the implications for Japan of the export suspension. The United States quickly backed off in a manner designed to preserve some face, but the damage was done. Food security became an even greater Japanese policy concern. Thereafter the issue came up repeatedly in international negotiations on agricultural trade, especially trade in sensitive commodities such as rice. Japanese negotiators could say with justification that Japan had to subsidize, preserve, and protect domestic grain production capacity because foreign supplies, however competitive, were not reliable.

The soybean embargo was an error, and fully conceded as such. In a speech given to the Japan Society in New York then-Secretary of State Henry Kissinger apologized for the embargo, an action in which he had been involved as National Security Advisor. It would have been better if the Secretary of Agriculture had announced a study of market demand and supply without adding the export embargo. That would likely have calmed markets, and relations with Japan would not have been harmed.

Auto Shock

Unlike the surcharge and soybean shocks, the auto shock was long in coming, and was the subject of prolonged and intense consultations with Japan. The shock related to how far the United States was prepared to go in forcing a "voluntary" solution.

In 1979 rising Japanese auto imports were stirring a firestorm of protest in America. Since the 1973 energy crisis, smaller fuel-efficient Japanese cars had been selling well, while U.S.-made autos were big gas-guzzlers. By 1980 Japan was building one out of every six cars sold in the United States, compared to one out of 16 in 1973. The U.S. auto industry and labor unions were demanding action to curb imports. Their combined influence, and the case they made in defense of U.S. jobs, were compelling arguments.

U.S. Trade Representative (USTR) Reuben Askew responded to these demands in 1979 and 1980 by urging Japanese auto builders to put factories in the United States and to use U.S. parts in their cars. Japanese auto builders, as well or better organized as their U.S. counterparts, were reluctant. Knowing that American auto companies were investing in smaller car capacity, they hesitated to invest in new plants in the United States—plants that would come on line just as U.S. factories would be ready to build small cars.

In March 1980 Representative Charles A. Vanik opened hearings on the plight of the U.S. auto industry. Stating that he had not prejudged the issue of legislated import quotas on cars, the threat of just that was implicit. He noted that American autos had long been essentially shut out of Japan's market, but he also faulted the U.S. industry for not initiating construction of smaller cars in 1973 when oil price increases first impacted auto demand. At the hearings United Auto Workers President Douglas Fraser supported import quotas, and also supported Japanese auto investment in the United States, expecting that any new plants would be organized by his union.

Faced with Japanese reluctance to build cars in the United States, USTR Askew was left with few options. Early in 1980 Representative Vanik again stated that Japanese auto exports had to be curbed, suggesting quotas of about 1.6 million cars, compared to 2.5 million imported in 1979. Vanik met with Japan's top auto negotiator, Naohiro Amaya, Vice Minister at the Ministry of International Trade and Industry (MITI). Amaya carried that message back to Tokyo, and serious negotiations followed.

A voluntary restraint agreement was concluded on the eve of a visit to Washington by Japanese Prime Minister Suzuki on May 5, 1981. Initially for three years, the agreement was later extended. MITI included voluntary restraint agreements in its own negotiations with Japanese auto companies over the "export plans." These voluntary, informal limits continued into 1992. In the latter period, however, export levels were close to what a free market would have allowed, and would have had an effect only in the case of an export surge.

The auto shock came when Representative Vanik announced his intention of imposing quotas through legislation, not by negotiating with Japan. This was a complete shift on the part of the United States, which had always negotiated import limits with Japan. Japan felt threatened by the possibility of unilateral legislative action in place of bilateral negotiated agreements. The Japanese have been obliged ever since to give much more consideration to opinions in Congress as well as in the Executive Branch.

After agreeing to limit its shipment numbers, Japan steadily shifted its production into higher value cars. As the energy crisis eased and gas prices declined, Japan started to compete with U.S. automakers not only in smaller cars, but also in high priced luxury models with much higher profit margins. Prices for American consumers rose, as forecast, but so did the profits of U.S. car companies. Thus both Japanese and American auto companies were the winners, and U.S. car buyers were the losers.

The Greenspan Commission and the Social Security Reforms of 1983

By Rudolph G. Penner

It was evident by the mid-1970s that the Social Security system was in trouble. Benefit costs exceeded income and the assets of the Social Security trust fund were rapidly declining. On May 12, 1981, the Reagan Administration proposed a series of benefit cuts, the most important of which would dramatically reduce benefits for early retirees. The benefit cut for someone retiring at age 62 was to be more than 30 percent.

Prior to submitting the proposals, the Administration made no attempt to get the advice of key Congressional leaders or to educate the public. In the political firestorm that ensued, President Ronald Reagan had no allies in the Congress and was, of course, opposed vigorously by the American Association of Retired People, the AFL-CIO, and numerous other interest groups.

The President responded by creating the bipartisan 15-member National Commission on Social Security Reform in September 1981. It was to report by the end of 1982—conveniently after the Congressional elections. The Commission was chaired by Alan Greenspan, who had served throughout the Ford Administration as Chairman of the Council of Economic Advisors, and who was known to be fair minded and politically skillful. Members were appointed by Thomas P. (Tip) O'Neill, Speaker of the Democrat-controlled House; by Howard Baker, Majority Leader of the Republican Senate; and by President Reagan. Each of the three chose both Democrats and Republicans. It proved important to the future success of the Commission that nine of the members were professional politicians who either were or who had recently been Representatives or Senators. All had played key roles in the oversight of the Social Security system.

It appeared initially as though the Commission would fail miserably, as so many other Commissions appointed to resolve controversial national problems had. The Democratic members were adamantly against benefit cuts while the Republicans opposed tax increases just as vigorously. Administration and Congressional leaders kept hands off at first and did not help to break the deadlock. The Commission asked to extend its deadline by one month. It was given two extra weeks.

Break in the Log Jam

In early January 1983, Senator Robert Dole, a Commission member and Chairman of the Senate Finance Committee, wrote an opinion piece suggesting that tax increases might play a role in solving the problem. Commissioner and Senator Daniel P. Moynihan detected a break in the log jam and seized the opportunity. He initiated discussions that included Greenspan, Dole, Commissioner Robert Ball, and Barber Conable (the ranking minority member on the House Ways and Means Committee). This "gang of five" began intensive discussions with White House Chief of Staff James Baker, his aides Richard Darman and Kenneth Duberstein, and OMB Director David Stockman.

The most important elements of the compromise that emerged were structured to be precisely balanced between benefit cuts and tax increases. A six-month delay in the cost-of-living-adjustment to Social Security benefits saved $40 billion during the 1980s, and an acceleration of a previously scheduled tax increase raised $40 billion. An additional $30 billion would be raised by making 50 percent of benefits taxable for middle-class and richer taxpayers. That provision could be comfortably characterized as either a tax increase or a net benefit cut. Other provisions expanded coverage by bringing in new federal civil servants and preventing the withdrawal of the state and local employees who were already in the system. Taxes were raised on the self-employed and there was a general revenue transfer to help pay the benefits of former military personnel.

The compromise, with some qualifications, was supported within the Commission by a 12 to 3 margin—the three dissenters were conservatives who objected to the tax increases. The Congress debated the recommendations quickly. The debate was expedited in the Senate by an informal rule promulgated by Senator Dole. It stated that anyone opposing the Commission recommendations was obliged to provide an alternative solution.

Although the Commission recommendations completely solved the immediate financing problem, they only closed about two-thirds of the deficit for the entire 75-year time period traditionally used in assessing Social Security's financial condition. Remarkably, the Congress was willing to be more courageous than the Commission and to solve the long-run problem as it was then perceived. They adopted the Commission recommendations and added an initiative by Representative J.J. Pickle to gradually increase the normal retirement age (NRA) to 67 by 2027.

Pickle had the support of Chairman Dan Rostenkowski of the House Ways and Means Committee, and in the House-Senate conference overcame a somewhat more timid Senate proposal that had increased the NRA to 66. The added provision reduced the long-run actuarial deficit of the trust fund more than any single proposal made by the Commission.

During the Congressional debate, the reforms were attacked vigorously by the left and the right, but President Reagan and Speaker O'Neill remained steadfast in their support of the compromise. When signing the bill, President Reagan said, "[T]he essence of bipartisanship is to give up a little to get a lot....I think we've got a great deal."

Viewed from the vantage point of a much more partisan era, the compromise appears as an extraordinary bipartisan achievement. It would not have been possible were it not for the coincidence of a very special set of conditions and personalities.

First and foremost, something had to be done. The trust fund would have been emptied and full benefits could not have been paid after mid-1983. At the time, the law did not allow the trust fund to borrow or otherwise draw on general revenues. Although legal authority might have been provided in order to postpone painful decisions, the public's confidence in Social Security was already badly shaken and would not have been helped by such an action.

Second, the Commission played a crucial role in facilitating the decision making process and developing an acceptable, rational compromise. This could only happen because the Commission had an effective and flexible chairman and politicians skilled at the art of compromise. It also required people like Robert Ball, defender of the system par excellence, and Alexander Trowbridge, representative of the business community, who were willing to yield on numerous issues in order to get something accomplished.

Third, the ball had to be carried in the Congress and it was extremely helpful that the Commission contained Congressional leaders like Dole and Moynihan. But it also took non-Commissioners showing great courage, such as Chairman Rostenkowski, to score the ultimate touchdown.

Last, but certainly not least, it could not have happened without President Reagan and Speaker O'Neill being willing to set aside ideological differences in pursuit of a pragmatic solution.

The U.S.-Japan Framework for a New Economic Partnership

By William Piez

Every American President coming into office has the option of dealing with trade and economic questions with Japan under a formal structure of contacts. The alternative is to avoid such formality and adopt a less structured style by dealing with individual issues as they arise. The Ronald Reagan Administration did not initially have a general agreement to talk about issues. Instead there was a series of negotiations and agreements with Japan, ranging from routine renewals of the Agreement on Nippon Telephone (NTT) Procurement to the extensive talks on Yen-Dollar Exchange Rate Issues concluded in May 1984. In January 1986, that case-by-case approach changed when Secretary of State George Shultz and Japanese Foreign Minister Shintaro Abe together received and confirmed reports on a series of issues, thus bringing individual subjects under a wider bilateral structure. The Administration of President George H.W. Bush made the structure even more formal with the Structural Impediments Initiative (SII) and, in January 1992, the Global Economic Partnership Agreements.

The Administration of President Bill Clinton decided early on to adopt the second option and engage Japan in broad trade and economic contacts under a written agreement. At a meeting between President Clinton and Prime Minister Kiichi Miyazawa in April 1993, three months after Clinton's inauguration, it was agreed that the two countries would establish a Framework for a New Economic Partnership. This Framework was strongly reminiscent of the SII, which set up a structure of Deputy Minister and lower-level meetings, a schedule for completing reports, and a list of topics to be considered.

Framework Provisions

The Clinton-era *Joint Statement on the United States-Japan Framework for a New Economic Partnership* was concluded on July 10, 1993. It fulfilled an understanding between President Clinton and Prime Minister Miyazawa that they had reached at their meeting the preceding April. The text opened with a statement of basic objectives. These were to establish a new economic relationship that would be "balanced and mutually beneficial." The goals of the Framework were to "deal with structural and economic issues in order substantially to increase access and sales of foreign goods and services through market-oriented and macroeconomic measures; to increase investment; to promote international competitiveness; and to enhance bilateral economic cooperation. . . ." Japan was to pursue strong and sustainable domestic demand-led growth and increase market access for foreign goods. The United States was to pursue a substantially reduced fiscal deficit, promote domestic savings, and encourage stronger international competitiveness.[1] Together these measures were expected to reduce the external payments imbalances of both countries. Steps taken under the Framework also were to apply to other countries on a Most Favored Nation basis.

The Japanese got American agreement to a provision that consultations would be limited to matters within the "scope and responsibility" of government. Japan had long believed that the United States often expected that its government administrative guidance should be used to influence the trading and practices of individual Japanese businesses, and that Japan should use such guidance even when it was not supported by law or regulation. Japanese representatives wanted to curb such tendencies from the start.

The two sides also decided to resolve differences in the context of the Framework or, where appropriate, under multilateral agreements. In addition, they agreed to achieve "tangible progress," a provision that led to much bickering later.

After this general statement of objectives and limitations the two countries decided on a list of issues of interest to both. These were:

▶ **Government Procurement:** Japan was to increase government procurement of competitive foreign goods, and the United States was to encourage its firms to take advantage of these opportunities. The United States gave assurances of nondiscriminatory, fair and open competitive opportunities under the General Agreement on Tariffs and Trade (GATT) Government Procurement Agreement for sales to U.S. government agencies.

▶ **Regulatory Reform and Competitiveness:** Essentially Japan was to deregulate its economy by reducing or repealing laws, regulations, and restrictive standards. Sectors mentioned for this treatment were financial services, insurance, competition policy, and distribution.

▶ **Other Major Sectors:** This catchall category included autos and auto parts, and the United States was to promote their export. Problems in market access were to be removed.

▶ **Economic Harmonization:** This title was to cover foreign direct investment in Japan and the United States, intellectual property rights, technology, and long-term buyer-supplier relationships.

▶ **Implementation of Existing Arrangements and Measures:** By reference, past commitments were to be met, including commitments made under SII that were to be absorbed into this forum as appropriate.

Structure

Each of the above-listed issues, or baskets, was to be the subject of a working group chaired at the sub-Cabinet level. Agreements were to be concluded on government procurement, insurance, autos and auto parts, and other priority areas by the time of the next Heads of Government meeting in 1994, or within six months. On other topics, agreements were called for at a second Heads of Government meeting in July 1994.

Common Agenda

The two countries agreed to pursue jointly common objectives in both global and bilateral contexts. These objectives included developing technology, the economy, and environmental protection. The text then listed the following common topics—the environment, technology, human resources development, populations, and the AIDS crisis. Progress reports to the Heads of Government were to be prepared.

High-level Consultations

As part of high-level consultations the two governments were to assess progress in each sectoral or structural area using objective criteria, either quantitative or qualitative, and drawing upon relevant information and data. Deputy Minister-level meetings were to be held twice a year to prepare reports to the Heads of Government. Working-level meetings of bureau chiefs or their deputies were to be held as appropriate. The Framework consultations were to run for two years, after which they were to be evaluated and possibly extended.

Attached Letters

U.S. Trade Representative Michael Kantor and Ambassador Takakazu Kuriyama exchanged letters dated July 12,1993 providing that Japan could withdraw from the Framework if the United States took action to restrict Japanese market access. The action referenced in this provision was trade retaliation under Section 301 of American trade law. The U.S. letter in reply agreed to utilize the Framework to address bilateral issues, but reserved its rights under American laws and regulations.

Clarification Agreement

By an agreement of May 23, 1994 the two countries reaffirmed and clarified the original Framework. The goals included revised statements regarding medical technology/communications, insurance, and autos/auto parts. This agreement was the only follow up to the Framework, which was never formally renewed as it might have been after two years.

A separate paragraph on measuring results called for the use of "objective criteria," which were described as "quantitative and quali-tative criteria considered as a set, with no one criterion determinative." It stated that the criteria were not numerical targets, and were to be used only for evaluating progress toward the goals set for the Framework and the relevant sector.

Results

Not counting the Framework and its later clarification, 41 agreements, renewals, and other action announcements were concluded between America and Japan. Although some Japanese have said publicly that bilateral economic talks with the United States would be replaced by contacts through multilateral forums, especially the World Trade Organization (WTO), the intensity of bilateral contacts and resulting documents have not receded.

Most of those 41 agreements related in one way or another to the goals of the Framework, and they have fulfilled those goals to varying degrees. Results sorted out by Framework baskets (or objectives) are:

Reduce Payments Imbalances of Both Countries

Payments imbalances, meaning the American global trade deficit and Japan's global trade surplus, did not move toward balance. In 1992, the U.S. trade deficit with Japan was $49.65 billion, and $84.5 billion with the world. Japan's trade surplus with the world was $106.6 billion. In 1999, the U.S. deficit with Japan was $73.4 billion, and $328.8 billion with the world. Japan's trade surplus with the world had risen to $122.9 billion. Many reasons can be cited for the increases. In 1992 America was in recession and imports were relatively low. Strong U.S. prosperity since has contributed to rising deficits. Japan has been in recession since 1991 and has relied on exports to support production while imports have been stable. The goal of reduced imbalances remains out of reach.

Government Procurement

Two agreements were concluded on November 1, 1994, on public sector procurement of telecommunications and medical technology products and services. These agreements did not result in much change, although some U.S. companies found that procurement of medical equipment and technology had been favorable. Procurement agreements with NTT and its successor companies were renewed, but there was no notable change in NTT procurement.

Regulatory Reform and Competitiveness (Insurance)

Deregulation and competition policy were the subject of four identified agreements, one of which was procedural. Certainly Japan has made progress in deregulation, but there has been little improvement in the way that trade results have occurred.

Competition policy change remains elusive. The Japanese preference for established suppliers, mostly Japanese, is strong—and the Japanese government has limited authority to do much about it. Framework agreement terms providing that only actions within the "scope and responsibility" of government could be interpreted to mean that Japan would do little in dealing with monopolies and quasi-monopolies. Most countries, including Japan, do not act as aggressively as the United States in opposing activities in restraint of trade.

Insurance was the subject of important agreements in 1994 and 1996. Essentially the Japanese agreed that U.S. insurance companies could operate in Japan in both traditional areas (life and fire insurance are examples), as well as in non-traditional areas (such as cancer and other more exotic kinds of insurance). The deal provided that Japanese and American companies would be treated equally in both traditional and nontraditional types of insurance, but with a time delay for admitting Japanese companies into nontraditional areas. The rationale for the delay was that large Japanese companies could quickly dominate that nontraditional so-called "third sector," while U.S. companies would have great difficulty entering the traditional fields where Japanese companies were so long dominant.

Problems arose when it appeared that Japanese companies were jumping the gun in entering the third sector, and the problems became even more complicated when a letter signed by the U.S. Trade Representative seemed to sanction such action by a Japanese company that had bought control of a U.S. company in the third sector.

Nevertheless, U.S. companies did gain much broader access to the Japanese market for insurance of all kinds. As a result of agreed upon deregulation, and despite conflicts in agreement interpretation, foreign companies have a significant place in the Japanese insurance market.

Other Major Sectors (Autos and Auto Parts)

This basket came down mostly to dealing only with autos and auto parts. It was the subject of an extensive agreement concluded in January 1994 during the Clinton Administration. Japanese companies met most of their "planning objectives" under that agreement, although the hoped-for number of new foreign auto dealerships was not achieved. The August 1995 auto agreement was hard fought. Japanese negotiators insisted that there be no targets or other suggestions that trade would be "managed." Subsequently Japan did successfully improve opportunities for auto exports, but Japan did not deal with anti-competitive and related practices that made auto sales increases so difficult. Furthermore, Japan's growing recession overshadowed prospects for actual export increases. Under the circumstances, which were not favorable, sales of U.S. autos declined.

Economic Harmonization (FDI and Intellectual Property)

Financial services was the subject of agreement in 1995, and foreign direct investment (FDI) was covered in separate agreements on deregulation. In 1996 Japan put through a major reform of regulations controlling financial services that became known as the "big bang." The reform created significant opportunities for U.S. financial and investment managers whose presence in Japan increased substantially. This was an important success for a process that began before the Clinton Administration and came to fruition during it.

In 1997 Japan agreed to expand its copyright protection of sound recordings dated before 1971. This followed a decision against Japan in a WTO case. Full compliance by Japan was a significant gain for sound copyright owners in the United States.

Implementation of Existing Agreements and Measures (SII)

This basket only carried over measures covered in the extensive Structural Impediments Initiative documents of 1992, if they were not covered in other talks subsequently.

Measuring Results

The May 1994 Clarification to the Framework went into considerable detail about measuring results. The representatives of the Clinton Administration believed that previous Administrations had been too willing to accept concessions that provided expanded market opportunities, but did not assign critical importance to quantitative results. The language in the Framework about qualitative and quantitative results was a compromise, as was language that there would be no numerical targets, or any reliance on only one criterion. Perhaps the Japanese had in mind the semiconductor agreements that called for a stated market share, not as a "target," but as a desired event. This question about measuring success was never fully settled, but it is clear that changes in the value and quantity of American exports was of primary importance to the United States, and that Japan did not choose to be bound by that standard.

Conclusion

The Clinton Administration followed a traditional pattern of dealing with Japan on economic and trade issues under a written umbrella agreement that provided for both general and detailed negotiations on specific issues, and reporting to the Heads of Government on progress. Results were mixed. Much was achieved following Japan's independent decision to deregulate in important sectors such as finance and insurance. The negotiation process, although not the primary reason for that, did no harm, and helped by providing Japan with greater incentives to change and by giving Japan a measure of credit for doing so.

---

[1] This U.S. commitment to increase domestic saving and reduce the fiscal deficit is based on the idea that a savings-investment gap will cause a trade deficit, with the excess of imports covering the gap. Japanese negotiators have traditionally argued this theory, and the United States has generally accepted it as at least a factor in trade deficits.

The Mexican Financial Crisis and U.S. Financial Rescue

By Sidney Weintraub

When the Mexican government made the decision on December 20, 1994, to raise the upper limit of the band within which the peso was allowed to fluctuate by 15 percent (in effect, to depreciate the peso with respect to the dollar by that amount or less), there was no premonition that this would be the onset of a serious economic crisis. In a speculative pool among insiders in the U.S. Treasury Department, the betting was that the peso would fall by about 9 percent, that is, not even the full 15 percent allowed by the Mexican action. A U.S. swap line of $6 billion designed to help Mexico deal with temporary currency problems already was in place and it was anticipated that this amount, plus some additional Canadian support, would be sufficient to deal with the temporary shock from the devaluation.

It became evident just two days later, on December 22, that the original calculation was wrong. A run on the peso reduced Mexican foreign reserves to less than $6 billion—a loss of $4 billion in two days—and the peso was allowed to float. The foreign support package was increased on January 2, 1995, to $18 billion, $9 billion from the United States and the rest from the Canadian and other central banks. Even this underestimated the extent of the crisis. Just 10 days later, on January 12, 1995, U.S. President Bill Clinton proposed legislation for a $40 billion loan guarantee package for Mexico.

What was not fully grasped in the original assessments was the utter lack of confidence, within and outside of Mexico, that the country could meet its short-term obligations. At the end of December 1994, when foreign reserves had fallen to $6 billion, outstanding tesobonos held by private parties, including foreigners, were more than $106 billion. Tesobonos were peso debt instruments indexed to the dollar, in effect dollar obligations. These bonds were floated by the Mexican authorities to raise dollars to avoid an abrupt devaluation of the peso in 1994. In addition, they could be marketed at a lower interest rate than pure peso instruments. The Mexican authorities did not contemplate that the tesobonos, almost all short-term in duration, could not be refinanced under the circumstances that prevailed. The Mexican government was faced at the end of 1994 with sovereign default—unless there was a U.S. rescue.

President Clinton Opts for Rescue

President Clinton opted for rescue and he was supported in this position by the Secretary and Undersecretary of the Treasury (Robert Rubin and Lawrence Summers), and the Chairman of the Federal Reserve Board (Alan Greenspan). Greenspan's support carried much weight in the Congress because he was seen as politically independent.

The fear of the Treasury Department and the Fed was that a Mexican financial collapse would lead to financial contagion in the United States itself. The concern of the State Department was that allowing the Mexican drama to play itself out would lead to internal social instability, and that this would result in increased illegal immigration into the United States.

President Clinton first secured the support of the Republican leaders in the House and the Senate, Speaker Newt Gingrich and Senator Robert Dole, before he submitted his proposal for a $40 billion loan to support Mexico. The backing of the two leaders did not do the job—and when it was clear that the legislation would not succeed, it was withdrawn. It was replaced on January 31,1995, by a support package that exceeded $52 billion, although not all of the money was drawn by Mexico. Of this, $20 billion came from the Exchange Stabilization Fund (ESF) controlled by the U.S. Treasury, $17.8 billion from the International Monetary Fund, and the remainder from many central banks, mostly operating through the Bank for International Settlements.

The ESF had not been used before for such a large and potentially durable bailout, and questions were raised about the legality of the action. The General Accounting Office, in its report on the rescue package, speculated about the justification in using the ESF in this way, but conceded that it was legal. The ESF option was not chosen first for two reasons: concern that the criticism would reduce future Treasury Department flexibility in using the fund; and the desire to build the total package to at least $40 billion. It was deemed that the funds in the ESF were insufficient for such large usage.

Two other objections were raised to the rescue. The most basic was that it would not work and that the U.S. government would be the loser, notwithstanding an escrow account in the New York Federal Reserve Bank based on Mexican oil sales in the United States. The second objection was the issue of moral hazard—that investors who made risky investments in order to obtain higher returns should not be bailed out. The first objection disappeared when the loan, made at a penalty interest rate, was repaid in full by Mexico before the due date. The moral hazard issue remained and became a major issue later in the unfolding of the Asian financial crises in 1997.

Mexican President Zedillo chose to use shock treatment to correct Mexico's internal economic and balance-of-payments problems. Consequently, Mexico's gross domestic product plunged by almost seven percent in 1995, but recovered sharply in 1996 and subsequently. Almost all of the tesobonos were retired in 1995 and Mexico's external debt has been lengthened. Mexico had suffered currency shocks on a regular pattern every six years starting in 1976, generally coinciding with Presidential elections. Thanks to the post-bailout economic policy, there is no expectation that this will recur in 2000.

Sentiment in the Congress opposed the bailout, as did public opinion. Yet the rescue worked and Mexico has been stronger economically ever since. There are many reasons why the Institutional Revolutionary Party (PRI) was ousted peacefully from the Presidency after 71 years in the 2000 election, but public memory of the hardships in 1995 surely contributed to dissatisfaction with the PRI. What is evident is that President Clinton, with the support of his key economic advisors and the Chairman of the Fed, took courageous action in the face of substantial opposition to carry out a rescue package, the largest of its kind as of that date. The rescue clearly accomplished its central objectives of leading to economic stabilization in Mexico, and of preventing whatever financial contagion there might have been in the United States in the aftermath of a Mexican default.

★　★　★　★　★

The National Economic Council and The Economic Policy Board

By Rudolph G. Penner

On January 23, 1993, President Bill Clinton established the National Economic Council (NEC) to manage his economic policy making process. The Council was to be chaired by the President and the membership included the Vice President; the Secretaries of State, Treasury, Agriculture, Commerce, Labor, Housing and Urban Development, Transportation, and Energy; the head of the Environmental Protection Agency; the Chair of the Council of Economic Advisers; the Director of the Office of Management and Budget (OMB); the U.S. Trade Representative; the Assistants to the President for Economic, Domestic, and Science and Technology Policy; and the National Security Advisor. The Secretary of the Treasury remained the main economic spokesman for the Administration while the Director of OMB was the primary spokesman for budget policy.

The establishment of such a group had been recommended by two committees, one headed by New York Governor Mario Cuomo and the other established by the Carnegie Endowment for International Peace and the Institute for International Economics. The staff of the NEC was to be headed by the President's Assistant for Economic Policy. He was to serve as an honest broker. That meant ensuring that economic policy decisions were consistent with the President's overall goals, and that the views of all members of the Council were fairly represented to the President, along with the views of other departments and agencies, where relevant. The first Assistant to the President for Economic Affairs was Robert Rubin, who was subsequently appointed as Secretary of the Treasury.

Ford and Clinton Model

In many ways, the National Economic Council was similar to the Economic Policy Board (EPB) established by President Gerald R. Ford. Both are examples of what Roger Porter calls the "multiple advocacy model" of decision making, where an effort is made to represent the views of all important interest groups before policy decisions are finalized. Porter contrasts this with (1) the "centralized model," in which policies are analyzed within the White House and by the sizeable staff of the Executive Office of the President, and (2) the "ad hoc model," in which the President puts together special committees to resolve individual policy problems. The ad hoc committees consist of the leaders of those departments and agencies most affected by the policy issue.

Most Presidents mix the various approaches to decision making, but the Ford and Clinton Administrations relied most heavily on the multiple advocacy model. Although decision making may be simpler and more consistent philosophically under the other two models, the other models are also more likely to produce major errors. They often lack the input of experts from within departments and they can fail to take account of the views of important interest groups.

The EPB began with a membership list similar to that of the later NEC, but a small executive committee did much of the work. That executive committee was eventually expanded to include a large portion of the entire membership of the Board. The addition of the State Department was particularly important because early in the Ford Administration tensions were created by several of Secretary of State Henry Kissinger's international economic initiatives that EPB members felt paid too little attention to domestic budget constraints. After the addition of the State Department as a member of the Executive Committee, international and domestic policy coordination proceeded more smoothly, although it was not completely free of tensions.

Although the NEC and EPB were based on similar concepts, there are some important differences. Ford's EPB met more often than Clinton's NEC (sometimes daily for long stretches of time), partly because there was a perceived economic crisis in 1974 and 1975 as the economy first descended into and then recovered from the largest peak-to-trough recession since the Great Depression. More important, the EPB had essentially no professional staff and was run on a day-to-day basis almost entirely by William Seidman, President Ford's Assistant for Economic Affairs, and his deputy Roger Porter. The EPB was chaired by William Simon, the Secretary of the Treasury, who was the President's main spokesman on economic policy—but he remained aloof from the mechanics of running the EPB.

Seidman and Porter did not see themselves primarily as being originators of policy ideas, and left that largely to other members of the EPB. For staff support, the EPB drew extensively on the professional personnel of the Executive Office of the President and on experts from various departments. This may have made it easier for Seidman to play the role of an honest broker. It certainly raised the morale of staffs in the departments who felt like they were an integral part of the decision process, and it may have added to the camaraderie among EPB members. The EPB consisted of an especially congenial group of officials, despite occasional tensions over particularly contentious issues.

The NEC does have a significant professional staff of about 30 people, and from time to time they do make policy proposals. These are sometimes opposed by more expert technicians in the departments and that can create tensions. Nevertheless, some who have examined the NEC argue that it is important for such a group to have a professional staff, and they maintain that it is possible for the leader of the group to be both a strong advocate for particular policies and an honest broker.[1] Others disagree and argue that the lack of a sizeable staff actually made the EPB a more effective mechanism.

Lessons Learned

Nevertheless, it is clear that most of the time both the NEC and EPB served well the interests of their Presidents. When policy fiascoes occurred, they often involved decisions formulated outside of the NEC and EPB mechanisms. One official described the decisions leading up to President Clinton's failed health care reform proposals as being developed "in a broom closet." The decisions were not reviewed intensely by a broad interagency group such as the NEC. President Ford once allowed Secretary of Labor John Dunlop to independently develop a legislative initiative involving a contentious labor-management issue. The initiative drew fierce opposition from a business group, the Associated General Contractors of America, and Secretary Simon threatened to resign unless President Ford changed his position. The President reversed course, but Secretary Dunlop then resigned.

The role of the NEC was grievously weakened when it took 11 weeks to choose Laura Tyson as a successor when Robert Rubin moved to the Treasury Department in late 1994. A lot of hard work had to be done to restore its role. The NEC also was criticized for its overly informal style, especially early in its history. It operated with an erratic list of invitees to meetings and did not formally record its decisions or analyses in memoranda.

Both the NEC and EPB have been criticized for being too insulated from political considerations.[2] But most observers agree that Presidents should get political advice on decisions independently from technical advice. As one Ford White House staff member put it, a President should not want "political advice from economists nor economic advice from his expert in Congressional relations."

---

[1] Kenneth I. Juster and Simon Lazarus, *Making Economic Policy: An Assessment of the National Economic Council,* Brookings Institution, 1997.

[2] Most agree that Eugene Sperling, the current head of the NEC, has increased its political sensitivity.

The International Financial Crisis of 1997-1998

By Roy C. Smith

Between May and December 1997, a financial firestorm spread throughout Southeast Asia and caused serious economic damage to the region. The area encompassed the much-praised Asian "Tigers"—Korea, Hong Kong, Singapore, and Taiwan—and the most promising developing economies of Indonesia, Malaysia, Thailand, and the Philippines. Currency values plunged relative to the dollar, with the Thai baht, the Indonesian rupiah, the Malaysian ringgit, and the Korean won each losing more than 40 percent of its value. Stock markets collapsed, interest rates soared, and credit markets dried up. The impact transferred quickly to the real economy, forcing severe contractions in gross domestic product (GDP) in all but the strongest of the developing economies in the region. The newly industrialized economies, including Korea, would decline by an average of 3 percent, but the developing economies such as Indonesia would contract by an average of 10 percent of GDP. The events shattered the confidence of foreign investors in all of the developing (or emerging market) economies, triggering sales of securities in Latin America and Eastern Europe.

The International Monetary Fund (IMF) intervened at the request of several affected countries, and by December 1997 it had organized unprecedented "rescue packages" totaling approximately $100 billion for South Korea, Indonesia, and Thailand in exchange for promised reforms. The total amount of rescue funds was vastly more than any previous IMF-led rescue, and more than half of the money was going to just one country, South Korea (the world's 11th largest economy). Despite the intervention, the countries in the region had to suffer the consequences of economic contraction and tightened credit. Bankruptcies increased sharply and included failures of important enterprises, and these exposed the many nearly fatal weaknesses of their banking systems. Calling in the IMF to administer draconian reforms was an admission of failure, and many of the governments in the region fell or were replaced at the next election. It was a very difficult time for all of the affected countries, yet by September 2000 signs of recovery were visible and the contagion that had been expected had not spread significantly beyond Southeast Asia.

Reason for Crisis

There were good reasons for the crisis. From the early 1990s on, huge investment flows were making their way from institutional investors in the industrialized world into high-growth Pacific Rim economies. Capital controls no longer impeded these flows, and early gains in market values on the investments attracted further investments. But the bull markets were not to last as economic realities caught up with the euphoria. In most of the developing economies macroeconomic conditions had worsened appreciably, forcing fragile economic management systems to cope with problems beyond their capabilities. As bankruptcies increased, concerns grew about inappropriate government policy responses. The investors decided to get out before things got worse. As panic took over in one market, they abandoned the next—and conditions resembling a "run on the bank" took over. Concerns grew that the failures in the region could spread to Japan, where the underlying banking system was in terrible shape, then perhaps move on to the large industrial countries, threatening like dominoes the safety of the entire world financial system. Forecasts for world economic growth were lowered, and when the Russian government defaulted on its foreign debt in June 1998, the fears were immediately rekindled. This sharply affected financial prices and liquidity in markets for securities and commodities in all world financial markets, including the United States.

International financial "crises" are becoming common. Generally, they are of two types: those that are short lasting and those that may have significant long-term effects on the global economy. The short-lasting crises, like the 1992 devaluation of the pound that was forced on the British government by "speculators" such as George Soros, have only nominal effects on the world economy, even though government officials may be embarrassed and individual investors betting the wrong way may be wiped out. Longer-term crises, however, such as the Third World debt crisis of the 1980s (which resulted in a decade of economic contraction in regions such as Latin America) can also denigrate banks and other credit institutions in industrial countries and thereby weaken the world financial system.

After nearly two decades of deregulation, the effects of technology, and increased competition in financial markets, private sector financial flows in markets around the world vastly exceed the resources of the IMF or of individual governments seeking to stabilize them. The market value of all securities traded in the world exceeded $50 trillion in December 1999, and the daily average trading volume in foreign exchange markets now exceeds $1.5 trillion. These funds are capable of moving very quickly, far faster than the best prepared IMF-led interventionist effort could.

The IMF was established in 1944 to be the official international lender of last resort. The fixed exchange rate financial system has long since been abolished but the IMF has continued to be involved in many individual country rescue efforts in the floating-rate financial system. Nearly 70 of these efforts were still on the books in September 2000. The IMF did not intervene in a large, unified way in the case of the Third World debt crisis, which took nearly 10 years to develop and another 10 years to resolve. In view of the seriousness of that crisis, perhaps it should have taken action. The Fund intervened in the Asian crisis, however, not to prevent the devaluation of individual currencies—market forces had moved too quickly and powerfully to do so. Instead, the IMF hoped to shorten the economic response and recovery time, to force its preferred institutional reforms into political systems that previously had opposed them, and to protect the world banking system from another round of serial country defaults.

Criticisms of IMF

These were worthy objectives and on many levels the intervention appears to have been successful. But nonetheless, the Fund has been strongly criticized by academics, journalists, and political commentators as: (1) being too late or otherwise unnecessary, (2) imposing wrong-headed, out-of-date policies that made problems worse, and (3) giving a free ride to speculators who were "bailed out" by loans made to governments to repay private sector debts. Some also point out that good money was used to support regimes that applied bad policies, and market forces alone could be relied upon these days to apply the necessary discipline to straighten things out at no cost to taxpayers. Michel Camdessus, the IMF Director at the time of the Asian crisis, was personally criticized as being out of date and out of touch. Under pressure Camdessus announced his resignation unexpectedly nearly three years before the end of his term, and so was out of office as well.

When international financial crises arise, they pose three essential questions for the President of the United States and his economic team: (1) knowing when a set of events are truly a crisis deserving intervention (most probably they are not), (2) knowing what sort of plan to follow that can achieve the desired results, and (3) knowing how to execute the plan selected to achieve maximum results as quickly as possible. In the 1994-1996 Mexican case, the U.S. Secretary of the Treasury was able to lead the effort that was undertaken, and to act quickly and forcefully (despite significant opposition by Congress) to manage the intervention successfully. The intervention was effective, and the crisis was resolved (and the United States was paid back) almost before anyone knew it. In the Asia crisis, the case for intervention was much less clear. It was a region, not a country, and intervention after the collapse of foreign exchange rates would affect financial but not macroeconomic factors. The price tag was huge, exceeding the resources available to the IMF. The crisis forced the Fund to forge a large, unwieldy consortium, consisting of the World Bank, the Asian Development Bank (such loans were not within their mandates, however), and 12 industrial countries including America. There were a lot of side issues involved also, such as whether the United States and other countries would support a Japanese plan for Asian recovery. The overall project was difficult to coordinate, its intended results were vague, and the time by which the goals could be achieved was unclear. The consensus was that it would take at least several years to get the IMF's money back.

An intervention of the Asian variety is vastly more complicated (and difficult to justify) than one involving a nearby neighbor that has asked for help. In general, the IMF is the only entity capable of handing such an intervention, but the Fund is often highly unpopular among client governments and political parties that do not wish to take the medicine prescribed. Direct American interests in failing Third World economies are remote to U.S. voters, although concerns about world economic growth and financial solvency are important. It cannot be in America's interest to aspire to the role of the IMF, especially that of international lender of last resort. Yet if the Fund is ineffective, that role may be presented to the United States despite its wishes. It is therefore in the interest of the United States for the IMF to be strong, effective, and respected. America, of course, as the largest shareholder of the IMF, has considerable influence—but only when it is persuasive among the other G-7 countries. The U.S. government is most likely to be persuasive in periods between crises when open discussion of the changing IMF role and *modus operandi* can be conducted unthreateningly and out of the public eye. The change of U.S. Administrations can present uncommon opportunities for accelerated rethinking of the missions and roles to be supported.

Lessons Learned

International financial crises can be expected to appear periodically, and their potential size, cost, and complexity make them important to the United States. Indeed, a large crisis could become hugely important to world economic and political stability, equaling perhaps the order of magnitude of the threat posed by the Cold War. The next President is likely to face one or more of these international financial events, and when he does he will be expected to provide effective leadership. The President will need to know when not to condone intervention, as well as when to do so. It may then be necessary to support or oppose the IMF in its effort to control the situation. The future global financial influence of the United States depends upon its being able to manage this interaction with the IMF, and other world economic institutions, effectively through the President's appointed representatives. To be effective, the representatives need to understand the issues well (including the nature and massive power of market forces), and to be on good (but independent) terms with the IMF. Although the Clinton Administration was able to do this, it did not do much to resolve the important question of the future role of the Fund—and how and when it should intervene in crises. Left entirely to its own devices, the IMF may envision a larger role and mission for itself than many in the United States might like. It will be important and necessary for the new President to participate in the debate, and influence its outcome. This will be an early test of the President's international financial leadership, one that is likely to have consequences throughout his Administration.

TRIUMPHS AND TRAGEDIES OF THE MODERN PRESIDENCY

U.S.-Japan Relations During the Asian Financial Crisis

By William Piez

Since the collapse of the "bubble economy" in early 1991, Japan has been in an enduring recession. The problem is inherently difficult since its solution calls upon the leaders of Japan's powerful economy to take measures, which are both politically and economically difficult. This has been a continuing challenge for the United States and its President. For the U.S. leadership, it also presents the problem of how to encourage Japan to move in the right direction without overplaying the hand and appearing to be a bully.

With quarterly fluctuations above and below the line, real growth has been at or close to zero. Because banking institutions have a heavy burden of non-performing loans the Japanese government has put in place aggressive programs to reform the economy, restore growth, resolve the bad loan problems, and recapitalize or liquidate banks. However, the recession persists.

Excessive regulation and inefficient economic structures make recovery especially difficult for Japan. The government has done much to correct the problems, but not enough. Many proposals have been developed for actions that Japan should pursue more aggressively. These include:

1. Focusing on restoring confidence in the strength and productivity of Japan's economy. This requires fundamental change, not just first aid (as important as it may be) for immediate problems.

2. Restructuring and deregulating Japan's financial institutions. To that end Japan has set aside Yen 25 trillion to rebuild 17 leading banks. Yet many financial enterprises are under-capitalized and threatened with insolvency. Japan has established the Financial Stabilization Agency (FSA) to deal with these problems. The FSA has authority to inspect banks, disclose their financial situations, and supervise the rebuilding of banking institutions.

3. Instituting regulatory reform for all business. Strong measures that assure real competition are a proven means to build stable growth. Much has been done to deregulate financial enterprises, which opens up new opportunities for insurance companies, pension fund managers, and investment companies. New inward foreign investment has strengthened this sector, but more restructuring is needed.

4. Continuing to take both fiscal and monetary actions. Fiscal measures include heavy additional spending on public works. This has created much needed new demand for goods and services. The Bank of Japan maintained a zero interest rate policy for nearly a year to encourage growth. In August 2000 the bank raised its overnight dis-

count rate to 0.25 percent, a controversial move that, although possibly premature, may be interpreted as a sign that steady recovery has really started. Some economists, notably Paul Krugman of the Massachusetts Institute of Technology, argue that Japan should adopt an inflationary monetary policy. This would have an effect equivalent to negative interest rates, and would stimulate spending and recovery. Although such a deliberate policy of inflation is highly controversial, there is general agreement that deflation would cause further damage and is to be avoided.

5. Following the example of the United States and other countries by imposing lower and moderately progressive marginal tax rates on income. This would ensure a reliable tax structure that advances the interests of both producers and consumers. Faced with rising budget deficits, Japan increased its national sales tax shortly after the recession began, probably worsening the decline. In 1999 Japan enacted tax reductions amounting to Yen 9 trillion, a welcome stimulus that, however, is only for one year.

In each of the five areas above Japan has already taken many steps in the right direction. There is a major global interest in the country's return to stable growth. As East Asia's financial crisis abates, Japan clearly does not want to be a dampening factor (which it would be if its recovery were delayed). Japan is the world's second largest economy, twice as large as all other East Asian economies put together. Its economic leadership role can hardly be exaggerated. The United States and its President must inevitably be deeply engaged and concerned about Japan's economic prosperity. Anything we can do to improve the situation deserves high priority.

Contrary to popular opinion, Japan is often responsive to foreign views and has, in fact, one of the most open cultures to foreign ideas. Like other countries, however, it is sensitive to criticism from outside, and too much assertiveness will always be counterproductive. Several factors should be kept in mind as outsiders approach this problem:

1. No one has a greater interest in Japan's economic prosperity than Japan itself. Measures to restore growth will always be Japanese measures—developed, defined, and implemented by the Japanese.

2. Japan thinks of itself as part of a global community. Putting prospective recovery measures into the context of what is good for the world, as well as Japan, is helpful. In a speech given in Tokyo in February 1999, then U.S. Deputy Treasury Secretary Lawrence Summers discussed frankly the need for Japan's recovery, and wisely put that question in a global context. He included remarks about maintaining U.S. growth and increased growth in Europe and Asia. His speech confirmed that Japan is a key member of a global community with shared problems.

3. The Group of Seven system is a good place to engage Japan in discussion. The G-7 Finance Ministers and Central Bank Governors

have usefully considered Japanese topics—and their deliberations have undoubtedly stimulated Japan to make progress.

4. U.S. representatives have from time to time held talks with Japanese counterparts on deregulation, competition policy, and financial reform. Usually held at the Subcabinet level, these are good opportunities to go into details and planning, and to recognize progress. Such talks should be held whenever the two sides have issues or ideas that can be acted upon in a bilateral context.

In spite of seemingly intractable difficulties, Japan still has a very productive, efficient, and modern economy. Living standards are high, many opportunities for productive investment exist, and Japan plays an important role in the world economy both as a producer and consumer. In time Japan will rejuvenate its economy, although undoubtedly not fast enough to satisfy many. Rejuvenation will benefit Asia and the world, and Japan most of all.

VI. NATIONAL SECURITY INSTITUTIONS AND DECISION MAKING

President Eisenhower Establishes His National Security Process

By Robert R. Bowie

Dwight D. Eisenhower came to the Presidency in 1953 profoundly convinced that an orderly system for strategic planning and policy making was essential for the Cold War, and that a suitable organization was necessary for that purpose. Indeed, the National Security Council (NSC) had been created in 1947 to meet that need. But Eisenhower's service with the Truman Administration had convinced him that it had not developed such an organized system or coherent strategy. In the 1952 election campaign he had vigorously criticized this deficiency and had promised that rectifying it would be a top priority.

Accordingly, even before taking office, Eisenhower named Robert Cutler to be his Special Assistant for National Security Affairs. Cutler was a Boston banker who had served on General George C. Marshall's staff in World War II, as an assistant to Secretary of Defense James V. Forrestal, on President Harry S. Truman's NSC staff, and in Eisenhower's campaign. Cutler was not to be an advisor on substantive policy. His job was to reorganize the NSC system and then manage its operation for it to become the central instrument in the making of foreign and national security policy. The aim was to ensure that in reaching important decisions, the President would have the benefit of full information, thorough analysis, and candid advice—enhanced by vigorous debate among his top advisors in his presence and with his active participation.

In preparing his reorganization report, Cutler consulted extensively with Truman Administration veterans—who were surprisingly forthright in their criticisms of the Truman process and suggestions for reform, which in many respects paralleled the views of Eisenhower. By mid-March, Cutler's plan for a reformed NSC had been completed, approved by the President, and was being put into effect.

In the new NSC system, two elements were central to its effective operation: the role of the President and that of a Planning Board. The President was to chair the NSC meetings and to lead the discussion to assure full participation by the Council members. To facilitate discussion, their number would be limited—beside the President and Vice President, members included the Secretaries of State, Defense, and Treasury, the Directors of the Mutual Security Agency and the Office of Defense Mobilization, with the Director of the CIA and Chairman of the Joint Chiefs of Staff (and later the Director of the Budget Bureau) as advisors. Other officials might be invited when appropriate.

Throughout his tenure, President Eisenhower assiduously fulfilled his role: he regularly presided at the weekly two-hour Council sessions (missing only six of the first 179), and stimulated discussion by comments and questions. Eisenhower alone made the decisions—the

Council was only advisory. To remove any ambiguity, after each meeting he distributed a written record of what he had decided.

A New NSC

The NSC Planning Board was the engine of the system. Its policy reports provided the agenda for the Council. Eisenhower considered the work of the Planning Board to be indispensable for the proper functioning of the policy process. He told the Council that they did not have time to do the essential in-depth analysis, and that the Board must do it for them to provide the basis for their deliberations. The Board was made up of the senior planning official from each of the NSC agencies, nominated by its head, and appointed by the President.

The Board's reports for the Council were not intended to be detailed blueprints for operations. Decisions regarding day-to-day implementation, handling crises, or negotiating tactics were made by the President more informally in the Oval Office. The NSC reports were to provide strategic analysis and guidelines as the framework for such decisions. They sought to clarify and anticipate premises, trends, and threats; and to define U.S. interests, objectives, and priorities in light of risks, benefits, and feasibility. In addition, the reports were to balance ends and means in respect to the overall basic national strategy, and in particular states, regions, and issues.

In preparing its reports, the Board met in extended and lively sessions two or three times each week. It marshaled and analyzed data and drew on expertise from the members, agencies, and other sources, and sought to integrate and reconcile the various perspectives on interests, threats, objectives, and means. But Eisenhower explicitly directed the Board not to water down or paper-over serious divergences (or "splits"). These were to be highlighted by clearly stating the conflicting positions in parallel columns in the draft report so that the Council could understand and debate the issue.

To ensure that Council members came to the meetings adequately prepared for fruitful discussion, Eisenhower directed that each NSC member be briefed on the reports beforehand by his designated Planning Board member. The briefing also enabled other relevant agency officials to present their comments or criticisms on the draft reports.

As indicated above, the President made important operational decisions in the Oval Office at meetings attended by the officials concerned. Eisenhower was convinced that such decisions benefited greatly from the NSC process. In general, the strategic framework and guidelines developed in the NSC gave coherence and consistency to operational decisions, which made them more effective. And in crises or emergencies, as he told President Kennedy, the earlier NSC deliberations assured a "depth of understanding and perspective—that is a clear comprehension of the issues involved, the risks, the advantages to be gained, and the effects" of possible actions. Moreover, the existence of a well-understood strategy enabled Eisenhower to delegate decision making and execution on less critical issues to subordinates with the confidence that they would know his intentions.

In Practice

The first major task of the reformed NSC system was to develop Eisenhower's basic national security strategy. The death of Soviet leader Joseph Stalin shortly after he took office in 1953 led Eisenhower to initiate a unique exercise (known as "solarium") as input to the work of the Planning Board in developing the post-Stalin strategy to confront what was to become the Cold War. To analyze alternatives to meet the Soviet threat, he set up three small teams of well-qualified foreign policy, military, and intelligence experts to develop the best case for each of these strategies: containment, "drawing a line" on Soviet expansion, and coercive "roll-back" of Soviet power. In July, the teams presented their results to the President and top national security officials. After the initial discussion, the NSC referred these reports to the Planning Board for its consideration, along with other materials, in preparing a draft Basic National Security Policy. This process required three months of intensive work by the Planning Board and review of the NSC before approval by the President in late October. In its appraisal of the Soviet threat, U.S. objectives, and the military means required, the Eisenhower strategy differed radically from NSC68 (which Truman had approved in 1950 after the Soviet nuclear test and the Korean attack). Instead of seeking to coerce the early "roll-back" of the Soviet threat by a predominant power, the strategy sought to prevent nuclear war by deterrence and arms control. This would contain Soviet expansion until the eventual decline or decay of the threat, by means that would be economically and politically sustainable by the United States and its essential allies for the "long haul" of the Cold War.

Despite subsequent variations (often mainly verbal), the core elements of this strategy guided the Western pursuit of the Cold War until the Soviet collapse.

Public Diplomacy: How America Communicates With Others

By Barry Zorthian and Stanton H. Burnett

President Dwight D. Eisenhower believed that providing accurate information was as important in closed societies as in free ones. Communication was a means of sustaining the hopes and aspirations of people under oppressive governments, and Eisenhower placed particular stress on communicating with the people under Soviet domination. Thus in the early 1950s the U.S. Information Agency (USIA) was born.

Also established were Radio Free Europe and Radio Liberty (RFE/RL) to complement the work of USIA's Voice of America.

The process of communicating to foreign peoples can take many forms, and RFE/RL provide examples of the extraordinary resourcefulness of U.S. public diplomacy. In contrast to the national "voice" of the official radio broadcasts of many governments, RFE/RL were set up as surrogate radio stations (referred to as radios) to provide the independent broadcasts that the people in Eastern Europe might have had if they were free. These radios were staffed mostly by compatriots living primarily in the United States as exiles, and were funded by the U.S. government at relatively modest cost. Broadcasting in 23 languages of the Soviet empire, the radios provided accurate news, commentary, and information to millions of individuals behind the Iron Curtain. The broadcasts countered internal Soviet distortions and misinformation about the West, and provided hope and encouragement that contributed to the resistance of the general public against communism.

President Eisenhower believed that as democracy spreads in this modern age, the opinions of citizens—and certainly of their authentic leadership—would have an impact on the policies and conduct of their governments. This could be true only if the people received accurate and unvarnished information, and were encouraged in dialogue aimed at mutual understanding. Eisenhower's "People-to-People" program was indicative of this deeper intent.

In the mid-1980s, however, American public diplomacy faced a great challenge that gave the measure of our real capabilities. The Soviets elevated tensions by the provocative deployment of a new fleet of missiles called the SS-20s, which were unprecedented in their accuracy. With the missiles aimed at Western Europe, Moscow expected to watch the disintegration of the "tired" North Atlantic Treaty Organization (NATO) alliance. A well-orchestrated Soviet disinformation campaign accompanied the deployment of the SS-20s.

Instead of folding under the pressure, the governments of five European countries—Great Britain, West Germany, Italy, the Netherlands, and Belgium—agreed to counter-deploy Western mid-range missiles on their soil, while offering negotiations to wind down the confrontation. In all five countries, massive opposition appeared in both the streets and in Parliaments. Commentators considered it doubtful that all five would counter-deploy (especially the Netherlands and Italy, who were never known for their toughness against domestic peace movements). Public opinion polls confirmed the tide of opposition. Maintaining a common front was crucial. West Germany, for example, would not counter-deploy unless "another large continental ally" (such as Italy) went a pace ahead.

America's public diplomacy apparatus was put to the task of devising and executing a coherent strategy of persuasion. The International Information Committee, a quiet group in the White House led by USIA, worked on the orchestration of a total information counter-campaign.

This issue was so important that U.S. President Ronald Reagan, British Prime Minister Margaret Thatcher, and other European leaders gave the Committee a free hand in organizing their schedules to maximize the impact of the campaign.

In some instances, the necessary persuasive resources were those of "megaphone diplomacy," the ability to help the five countries opposed to SS-20 deployment to stage press events to counter domestic opposition media and street demonstrations. In others, the crucial resources were American Foreign Service Officers on the ground who possessed all of the necessary language skills, cultural sophistication, and personal access to opinion leaders and politicians. In a careful but fast-paced campaign of civilized persuasion, small victories started piling up. The President of the lower house of the Italian Parliament, a Communist, after six one-on-one meetings with USIA officers concerning issues such as the negotiations and the weapons technology involved, announced that she was breaking away from the party line to support counter-deployment. In another example, quiet arrangements were made to be sure that the famed "Greenham Common women" and an army of English protesters had protection (and even fresh water). This was done to ensure that their sit-ins and construction blockades produced no martyrs.

RFE/RL carried information in spite of the extensive and costly Soviet measures aimed at jamming their signals. Historians; analysts; and the words of the post-Soviet leaders such as Lech Walesa, Vasclav Havel, and others leave no doubt of the impact of RFE/RL. Providing accurate information was critical—it was an indispensable factor in the eventual breakup of the "evil empire." These tools fulfilled President Eisenhower's faith in the importance of providing accurate information to foreign people—and particularly accurate information about the United States, its policies, and intentions.

As a consequence of the public diplomacy campaign, all five allies stood firm and counter-deployed the missiles. The Soviets backed down and announced a phased withdrawal of the SS-20s. Many journalists and historians directly connect this "last great battle of the Cold War" to the changes that soon came in Moscow.

This victory reveals an important truth about America's public diplomacy: What ultimately helped us win was not the superiority of our military means—however important that is—but the content of our message. Through our message, we projected America's "soft" power—the ideals of democracy and free market economics—in contrast to the "hard" impact of our military Indeed, public diplomacy was America's most effective means of achieving our national interests.

The end of the Cold War also revealed an ugly political truth. American public diplomacy was about our achievements in education, art, culture, social issues, and the finding of common political ground between diverse traditions. However, political support for public diplomacy, at least in the Congress, stopped at the end of the Cold War. With some exceptions, there was no more support in Congress for the kind of civilized persuasion at which the U.S. government had become a master. Perhaps there was a decline of interest in the ideas that define America. Perhaps there was a belief that the America portrayed by commercial media abroad was, however coarse, satisfactory. Perhaps it was a simple failure to imagine the possibilities—which used to be everyday occurrences—of that lunch with an editor abroad that later translates into his or her newspaper's sympathetic understanding of our policies. What should have been the golden era of global understanding of American culture and ideals—because they were no longer geared so closely to Cold War strategies—became the era of dismantling. What should have been an increased challenge to our sophistication saw the best and the brightest look for other lines of work.

When the bipolar world broke up and democracy and market economies developed, public diplomacy should have become more central in the conduct of foreign affairs. However, this task of communicating with foreign peoples, the impact of foreign public opinion on the conduct of their governments, and the importance of dialogue and contact with both foreign groups and American non-government institutions lost its priority status. USIA—in the interest of cohesion, funding priorities, and efficiency—was merged in 1999 into the State Department as the agency primarily responsible for conducting U.S. foreign policy.

To merge them is not necessarily wrong. But the danger of this lies in the atrophy of the public diplomacy function in the face of budget constraints, short-term crisis diplomacy, and the traditional State Department culture of government-to-government relations. The loss of national assets in public diplomacy developed in the 46 years since President Eisenhower may lead to a dangerous failure to recognize the potential and the needs of diplomacy in the 21st century.

A new Administration through its policies, selection of senior officials, and agency structure, should seriously question the wisdom of losing this effective public diplomacy tool.

Reconciling Defense and Détente in NATO: The 1967 Harmel Report

By John G. McGinn

"Military security and a policy of détente are not contradictory but complementary." That statement from the December 1967 *Report on the Future Tasks of the Alliance,* better known as the *Harmel Report,* gave the North Atlantic Treaty Organization (NATO) a formula to reconcile two seemingly irreconcilable principles, defense and détente. This formulation helped NATO maintain its cohesion in the face of centrifugal forces in the late 1960s and remained as an important guiding principle for the Atlantic Alliance throughout the remainder of the Cold War.

Defense and détente pushed and pulled at the fabric of the Atlantic Alliance during the 1960s. By the mid-1960s, most NATO allies were eager to increase their political and economic connections with the Soviet bloc. In his famous October 1966 New York speech, for example, U.S. President Lyndon Johnson spoke of "building bridges" between the East and the West. NATO's European allies were similarly eager for potential increased cooperation with the East. At the same time, however, there were significant differences among the member states on the Alliance's military strategy. There was pressure from the United States, for example, to increase the NATO conventional force capability through the adoption of a strategy of flexible response. There also were heated debates over the control of Alliance nuclear weapons.

These internal NATO debates came to a head in 1966-1967. President Charles de Gaulle withdrew France from the NATO integrated military command in March 1966, necessitating the move of the Alliance headquarters from Paris to Brussels in the subsequent 12 months. In addition to this dislocation, NATO discussions about the proposed flexible response strategy and a formula for enhanced nuclear planning consultations were reaching a decision point. Finally, looming in the background was the end of the original 20-year term of the Washington Treaty in 1969. There was some question about whether NATO would continue at all beyond that year.

A Flexible Solution

Looking for a way to revitalize the Alliance and strengthen its cohesion, Belgian Foreign Minister Pierre Harmel proposed a study in late 1966 to take stock and define the future tasks of NATO. This approach had the energetic support of the Alliance's smaller nations, who wanted to find a way to maintain Alliance cohesion and ensure its continued longevity, but not necessarily on American or French terms. The United States supported Harmel's proposed study because it foresaw NATO as a coordinating body for détente, thereby keeping the United States involved in the process. The French were not as optimistic or enthusiastic about the proposed study, but went along because its results would not be binding on NATO members.

The Harmel process had a surprisingly positive impact on the Alliance during the tumultuous debates over flexible response and nuclear weapons. This was largely because the study was conducted at a high political level to avoid the fate of previously unsuccessful studies, and because it focused on issues—East-West relations, arms control, intra-Alliance relations, etc.—that were of significant interest to member states. The final report of the study was completed in November 1967 and published as an appendix to the final communiqué of the December 1967 National Atlantic Council Ministerial. It codified the desire of NATO members to pursue détente while still maintaining the territorial defense of Western Europe. The report stated:

The Atlantic Alliance has two main functions. Its first function is to maintain adequate military strength and political solidarity to deter aggression and other forms of pressure and to defend the territory of member countries if aggression should occur....[Its second function is] to pursue the search for progress towards a more stable relationship in which the underlying political issues can be solved.

The Impact

The Harmel Report codified détente as a formal Atlantic Alliance task for the first time, thereby reinforcing the existing Western trend of outreach toward the states of Eastern Europe. Individual countries, for example, had already begun increasing scientific, cultural, and financial contacts with the Eastern bloc. Still, détente was difficult for a military alliance to define and articulate because it focused on influencing perceptions and did not necessarily deal with concrete military capabilities. Nonetheless, NATO leaders wanted a relaxation of tensions with the Soviet bloc, and the Harmel formulation gave the Alliance a way to achieve those goals.

The impact of the Harmel framework on the Alliance was significant in the short and long run. In June 1968, for example, NATO issued the "Reykjavik Signal." Reflecting members' desires for détente, this proclamation explicitly stated NATO's willingness to enter into conventional force reduction talks with the Warsaw Pact at some point in the immediate future. When the Soviet-led invasion of Czechoslovakia in August 1968 dampened NATO's enthusiasm for détente, the Harmel framework allowed the Alliance to leave the door open for conventional force reduction talks—at the same time as member states took measures to strengthen NATO's defense posture.

In later decades, the Harmel framework was still very much at the heart of NATO and Western policies toward the Eastern bloc. The 1979 dual-track decision, for example, embodied the Harmel approach. This NAC decision to deploy intermediate-range nuclear forces (INF) in five NATO countries in response to the Soviet deployment of SS-20 missiles was coupled with, as the decision states, a "wide range of initiatives particularly in the fields of confidence-building and arms control designed to improve mutual security and cooperation in Europe." These initiatives helped lay the groundwork for the first major arms control agreement of the 1980s, the 1987 INF Treaty. Thus, the dual-track Harmel framework had allowed NATO to respond to the Soviet missile deployment, but it also had laid the groundwork for the peaceful elimination of all INF missiles. The INF Treaty and other advances that led to the end of the Cold War demonstrated the ultimate brilliance of the *Harmel Report's* reconciliation of defense and détente.

The Scowcroft Commission

By Charles A. Sorrels

On January 3, 1983, President Ronald Reagan established the President's Commission on Strategic Forces, which came to be known I as the Scowcroft Commission. The Commission was named after its widely respected Chairman, Brent Scowcroft, who had served as National Security Adviser to President Gerald Ford and was a retired Air Force Lieutenant General.

Origin

The impetus for the establishment of the Scowcroft Commission was a major legislative defeat for the Reagan Administration.On December 7, 1982, the House of Representatives, by a 69-vote margin (245-176), had denied nearly $1 billion in funding requested for initial production of five MX intercontinental ballistic missiles (ICBMs). Fifty Republicans joined 195 Democrats to reject the funding measure. Because of the size of the majority in the House, its position prevailed in the House-Senate conference on the bill. This setback was "the first time Congress ever had denied production of a major nuclear weapon requested by a President."[1] In the view of many Members of Congress, the Reagan Administration had failed to come up with a convincing mode for basing the 100 MX ICBMs envisioned in the President's strategic modernization plan announced in October 1981. Simply placing MXs in existing Minuteman silos, or in the new deployment scheme for silos, was seen as no improvement over the existing vulnerability of nearly the entire 1,000 silo-based Minuteman ICBMs. In fact, it was seen as only making the MX with 10 MIRVs (multiple, independently targetable re-entry vehicles) a more inviting target for the Soviets than the Minuteman III with 3 MIRVs. This was announced by the Administration—without consulting and briefing key members of the House and Senate in advance—on November 22, 1982.

Congress was the impetus in another way to the creation of the Commission on Strategic Forces. Seeking to rescue the MX, Robert C. (Bud) McFarlane, Deputy National Security Adviser to President Reagan, consulted with Senators Sam Nunn (D-GA) and William S. Cohen (R-ME), key members of the Senate Committee on Armed Services. Cohen urged McFarlane "to find outside experts who had credibility with Congress that [Secretary of Defense Caspar W.] Weinberger lacked."[2] McFarlane took the Senators' recommendation to William P. Clark, the National Security Adviser and close friend of the President. Clark approved the recommendation and at McFarlane's urging, President Reagan chose Scowcroft as the Chairman of the Commission. Initially it was to submit its report to the President by February 8, 1983, but this schedule was later extended until April.

Membership

The Scowcroft Commission was bipartisan and prestigious. It consisted of 11 members, several with directly relevant experience at or near Cabinet-level from four previous Administrations. One member was William J. Perry, former Undersecretary of Defense, and another was R. James Woolsey, Undersecretary of the Navy, both in the Carter Administration, who wrote the Commission's trenchant final report of 26 pages. Two other members were Reagan's first Secretary of State, Alexander M. Haig, Jr., and Richard Helms, Director of Central Intelligence under Presidents Johnson and Nixon. There were also seven "Senior Counselors to the Commission," which included four former Secretaries of Defense (Harold Brown under Carter, Melvin R. Laird under Nixon, Donald Rumsfeld under Ford, and James R. Schlesinger under Nixon and Ford) and one former Secretary of State, Henry A. Kissinger under Nixon and Ford.

The Scope of the Task and Depth of the Inquiry

President Reagan directed the Scowcroft Commission "to review the purpose, character, size, and composition of the strategic forces of the United States....In particular," the Commission was asked "to examine the future of our ICBM forces and to recommend basing alternatives." Over a three-month period, the Commission held "28 full meetings and numerous smaller conferences," and "talked to over 200 technical experts."[3]

Close Consultation with Members of the House and Senate

At McFarlane's urging, the Scowcroft Commission, from the beginning of its deliberations in January 1983, "consulted closely" with some Members of Congress, seeking a bipartisan consensus. For example, Chairman Scowcroft and Commission member Woolsey met "regularly" with Congressman Les Aspin (D-WI), sometimes at his home. Aspin was a key member (and future Chairman) of the House Committee on Armed Services. The Commission also consulted closely with Congressmen Norm Dicks (D-WA), Albert Gore, Jr. (D-TN), David McCurdy (D-OK), and John M. Spratt (D-SC). In the Senate, the Commission consulted with Senators William S. Cohen (R-ME) and Sam Nunn (D-GA), members of the Senate Armed Services Committee, and with Charles Percy (R-IL), Chairman of the Senate Committee on Foreign Relations.[4]

The Commission's Integrated Package of Recommendations

The Scowcroft Commission forwarded its unanimous report to President Reagan on April 6, 1983, and it was publicly released on April 11. The Commission made three basic recommendations, which it declared were an integrally related package. They were:

1. Deploy 100 MX missiles in existing Minuteman ICBM silos.
   The Commission argued that the vulnerability of ICBMs in the U.S.

strategic nuclear force structure should not be viewed in isolation but instead in the broader context of the overall survivability of strategic bombers on alert and submarine-launched ballistic missiles (SLBNs) deployed at sea. The Commission propounded several reasons for the MX. First, an ongoing MX program would be an incentive to the Soviets for reaching a "stabilizing and equitable" strategic arms reduction agreement. Second, "effective deterrence is in no small measure a question of the Soviet's perception of our will and cohesion." (The Commission was also mindful that a failure to proceed with the MX would critically weaken allied governments' support in NATO for deploying U.S. Pershing II ballistic missiles and ground-launched cruise missiles in Western Europe in late 1983.) Third, without the MX the United States would lack a counterpart to the Soviet capability for promptly destroying "hardened land-based military targets" in a limited attack. Such an imbalance would reduce the U.S. ability to deter "a massive conventional, chemical, biological, or limited nuclear attack" on its NATO allies in Western Europe. "Fourth, our current [1960s era] ICBM force is aging significantly."

2. Initiate development of a small, single warhead ICBM for initial deployment in the "early 1990s." Such a system would "reduce target value and permit flexibility in basing [including hardened mobile launchers] for long-term survivability."

3. Modify the U.S. negotiating position in Strategic Arms Reduction Talks (START). Specifically, in the interest of stability, reconsider (raise) the subceiling of 820 ballistic missile launchers. Such a change would encourage deployment of a small, single warhead ICBM, enhancing "survivability by moving both sides in the long term, toward strategic deployments in which individual targets are of lower value."

Response to and Impact of the Scowcroft Commission Report

President Reagan adopted the three recommendations and extended the duration of the Commission through 1983. However, there was substantial skepticism in both the House and the Senate as to whether the President was sincerely committed to the entire Scowcroft package, and not just the MX proposal. Congressman Dicks and others required a written commitment by the President to the whole package. A similar commitment was demanded by Senators Cohen, Nunn, and Percy, along with a pledge to adopt a specific proposal of theirs in START. President Reagan did make a written commitment to the whole package of Scowcroft Commission recommendations. The President thereby garnered the conditional but crucial support in both the House and Senate by "several dozen liberals and moderates" on successful (albeit by declining margins in the House) votes in 1983 on flight testing and procurement of the MX.[5]

For example, on May 24, 1983, the House approved by a 53-vote margin (239-186) the basing mode for the MX recommended by the Scowcroft Commission and funds for flight testing of the missile. "A crucial component in the 53-vote majority was a group of moderates and liberals led by Democrats Aspin, Dicks, and Gore"[6] who had worked closely with members of the Scowcroft Commission in lobbying for that result.

Without the Scowcroft Commission's unanimous "package" of recommendations, those voting reversals on Capitol Hill in 1983 probably would have been impossible. Congress, by denying MX funding in December 1982, prompted the Executive branch to be more deliberative, more credible in its "homework" on a controversial defense program. The Administration also benefited by consulting in advance (rather than simply informing after a decision had been made) with key Members of Congress for their perspectives and expertise, and for a bipartisan consensus.

Lessons Learned

If an Administration intends to present to Congress a proposal on what it knows will be a controversial defense program (such as a plan for basing the MX intercontinental ballistic missile), then it should consult in advance with key members of Congress, especially on the Armed Services and Appropriations Committees. An Administration needs to develop a consensus rather than surprise such members, who themselves have expertise to contribute. Alternatively, in order to avoid legislative defeat on such a controversial program, the appointment of a highly respected, bipartisan Commission, with a mandate that includes consulting closely with Congress, can build a consensus to save or sustain a program. If an Administration knows it lacks credibility in Congress on the subject, then the option of a bipartisan Commission is the prudent choice.

---

[1] *Congressional Quarterly Almanac,* 1982, (1993), p. 277.

[2] Lou Cannon, *Ronald Reagan: The Role of the Lifetime* (1991), p. 324.

[3] Cover letter by Chairman Brent Scowcroft to the President on the *Report of the President's Commission on Strategic Forces,* April 6, 1983.

[4] *Congressional Quarterly Almanac,* 1983 (1984), pp. 195-197.

[5] Ibid., p. 199.

[6] Ibid., p. 199.

The National Bipartisan (Kissinger) Commission On Central America, 1983-1984

By Howard J. Wiarda

Presidential Commissions can be used for many purposes. In times when the President is uncertain about a future policy course, he (or she) may appoint a Commission to study the matter and make recommendations. A President can use the commission strategy to stall for time while giving the appearance of being vigorous. Presidential Commissions may also be used to express a consensus on an issue when it is too risky for elected politicians to do so, thus providing "cover" for the elected officials. In the cases of both the Greenspan Commission on Social Security reform and the Scowcroft Commission on MX Missile Deployments in the early 1980s, that was precisely the purpose: to issue a consensus report supporting a policy that almost everyone realized was necessary but that was too politically sensitive for elected officials to state publicly.

The 1983-1984 National Bipartisan (Kissinger) Commission on Central America was appointed by President Ronald Reagan on the heels of the earlier successful Greenspan and Scowcroft Commissions. But its task was more complex than either of these other two Presidential Commissions. First, the facts were not as clear or the issues as clear-cut as on the other Commissions. Second, the Kissinger Commission had to forge a national consensus where none existed before—and indeed where the issue was partisan and highly divisive. And third, the Commission would have to convince a sometimes reluctant White House that it should support the findings of the Commission that might not always be in full accord with Administration policy. This would be a tricky undertaking.

Former Secretary of State Henry Kissinger chaired the Commission. By agreement between the White House and Congress, it was to consist of six Republicans and six Democrats, and there were considerable negotiations over the precise makeup of the Commission. Commission members (besides Kissinger) included Ambassador and Attorney Robert Strauss, former San Antonio Mayor Henry Cisneros, Boston University President John Silber, former Texas Governor William P. Clements Jr., AFL-CIO President Lane Kirkland, Yale Professor Carlos Diaz-Alejandro, Political Scientist Richard Scammon, Project Hope Director William B. Walsh, former Treasury Secretary Nicholas Brady, National Federation of Independent Business President William Johnson, and retired Supreme Court Justice Potter Stewart. Senior Councilors to the Commission were UN Ambassador Jeane Kirkpatrick; Council on Foreign Relations President Winston Lord; Attorney William D. Rogers; Senators Daniel K. Inouye, Pete Domenici, Lloyd Bentsen, and Charles Mathias; and Congressmen William Bloomfield, Jack Kemp, James Wright, and Michael Barnes. The staff was recruited principally from the Department of State and the leading think tanks; Ambassador Harry W. Shlaudeman served as Executive Director.

Reaching Consensus

Initially the staff prepared background papers for the Commissioners and recruited well-known university and think tank scholars to write additional papers. For each topic covered by the Commission (political, economic, strategic, and diplomatic), the staff was instructed to solicit one position paper from a Democratic scholar or think tank and one from a Republican. This way the partisan nature of the public, Congress, and White House—Congressional debate was perpetuated in the early papers and discussions of the Commission. At the same time, several members of the professional staff strove to reduce these differences and reach consensus.

A key turning point was the Commission's fact-finding mission to Central America. Before the trip some of the Republican members of the Commission might have been willing to accept some degree of human rights abuses in El Salvador as an unfortunate byproduct of the civil war. At the same time some of the Democratic members might have been inclined to accept the Marxism-Leninism in Nicaragua as the naive, if misguided, option of a newly revolutionary regime. But the degree and extent of human rights abuses in El Salvador shocked the Republicans on the Commission, while the arrogance and dismissiveness of Sandinista President Daniel Ortega in Nicaragua stunned the Democrats. Thereafter the two partisan sides began moving closer together.

The Commission issued its report in January 1984. The report was a consensus document. It called for democracy and human rights in Central America; sought to balance military assistance to the area with social and economic assistance; recommended that pressure (including military pressure as well as sanctions) continue to be applied in Central America, even while the door remained open to diplomacy; and it called for the long-term development of the region while insisting that immediate and short-term problems also had to be dealt with. In brief, the report presented a sophisticated and balanced argument. It was immediately published in both English and Spanish by a commercial publisher, as well as the Government Printing Office, and the report attracted widespread discussion throughout the country and in Washington.

The Commission report began the process of forging the consensus that had been lacking before. Of course, those on the extreme left and extreme right would never be happy with it. But by standing strongly for democracy, fair elections, human rights, socioeconomic development, and U.S. security interests, the Commission succeeded in getting most of the press, the public, Congress, business, labor, and other groups to support the policy.

A particularly sensitive issue was relations with the White House. After all, this was a basically centrist, moderate, and carefully balanced report in the context of a quite conservative Administration. But if the White House did not support the report, the Commission's work would have been wasted. As a result, the Commission Chair, its members, and top staff spent much of a weekend over at, and on the phone to, the White House convincing the senior staff that it should support the report. The White House eventually agreed and, more than that, gave its enthusiastic backing to the legislation as called for in the report— much of which subsequently was enacted by Congress.

On some particulars and in some policy disputes, Central America remained a controversial issue. Eventually the sticking points were resolved through a combination of pressure and diplomacy. But the Commission and its report represented a first and major step in reaching a solution to the problems. It broke the partisan and policy logjam, issued a consensus report on which most policy makers could agree, and made a series of balanced recommendations that not only led us out of the Central American quagmire, but also provided a model and framework for the organization of the National Endowment for Democracy (NED) and the National Republican and Democratic Institutes (NRI and NDI). In addition, the emphasis on elections, democracy, human rights, and diplomacy combined with pressure, provided a strategy for the pursuit of similar pro-democracy policies in Eastern Europe, Russia, East Asia, and Africa. Established in a divided and highly partisan political environment, the Kissinger Commission succeeded in building both the consensus that was lacking before *and* providing the framework and recommendations on which future successful policy could go forward.

Re-Opening Agreements: The FSX Controversy

By John R. Malott

During the eight years of Ronald Reagan's Presidency, there was a consistent tension in Japan policy between balancing the U.S. government's national security and economic interests. The economic agencies wanted Reagan to take a harder line on Japan, pushing it to open its markets faster or face retaliation. The Congress generally supported this position. The U.S. national security apparatus, however, was seeking a build up in Japanese military strength and political cooperation in order to counter the Soviet Union's growing influence in the Far East. When faced with a choice between taking a hard line on either economic or security issues in dealing with Japan, Reagan—who was determined to win the Cold War—consistently came down on the side of America's political-military interests.

By the time George H.W. Bush became President in 1989, anger with Japan's economic policies was at an all-time high. Several well-publicized Japanese investments in the United States, including Rockefeller Center and Columbia Pictures, only added to the emotions. Public opinion polls indicated that the American people thought Japan was "winning the economic war" and that their own government was doing nothing about it.

Meanwhile, Reagan's strategy toward the Soviet Union had succeeded. The Soviet empire was on its last legs and soon would disappear from the face of the earth. With the Soviet Union on the verge of collapse, the American economy in trouble, and anti-Japan emotions running high in the United States, the stage was set for a shift in the balance of power in Washington over whose views would dominate policy toward Japan.

The test case came barely a month into George Bush's Presidency. Bush said he would re-open an economic agreement that already had been negotiated with the Japanese about co-development and co-production of an advanced Japanese military fighter, code-named the FSX. The President wanted U.S. manufacturers to have an increased role in the project.

This was not simply a decision to side with the economic agencies in a disagreement about Japan. It was the first time that America's commercial and technological concerns were inserted directly into "military decisions" that previously had been the exclusive domain of the Defense and State Departments.

The irony for Japan was that it had not wanted to co-develop the FSX with the United States in the first place. Originally the plane was to be Japan's own 100 percent indigenous aircraft. It was to be a source of technological and national pride. America's European allies produced their own military systems, so why shouldn't Japan?

But to the Defense Department and the U.S. aircraft manufacturers who had been selling and licensing their products to the Japanese for years, this was unthinkable. They did not want the Japanese to go it alone. The American manufacturers saw a business loss, and they also had an interest in acquiring whatever technology the Japanese might develop from the FSX. The Departments of State and Defense were concerned about the reaction in Asia if Japan started developing weapons systems independently of the United States.

In addition, in the 1980s one of the Defense Department's goals vis-à-vis Japan's military was its compatibility and co-operability with U.S. forces. If Japan started to make its own decisions about what weapons it would acquire, and if they were not co-operable with U.S. systems, this would be a step backwards.

Finally, there were economic considerations. At a time when the United States wanted Japan to step up defense spending, a purely indigenous fighter would be expensive—perhaps twice as expensive as importing F-16s directly from the United States. So a co-production arrangement offered more "bang for the buck."

The pressure was applied to the Japanese. For the sake of our security relationship, the argument went, let us develop and produce this airplane together. In the end, Japan relented.

Enter the "economic nationalists" in both countries. To many Japanese, starting with the vocal right-winger Shintaro Ishihara (today the Governor of Tokyo), the agreement was a direct strike at Japan's sovereignty and right to independent action. Worse yet, it was racism— the United States had never told its European allies what they could produce.

In the United States, people (and industries) that were concerned about Japan's growing economic and technological prowess saw the deployment of America's best technologies as an unbelievable "give-away." Haven't we learned our lesson yet, they asked? First cars, then computers, and now aircraft. Fearful that Japan would be moving into aviation, the opposition sprang into action to stop the agreement. (Overlooked in their argument was Japan's well-entrenched policy banning weapons exports, which meant that the FSX would never compete with U.S. companies in other markets. The American critics never were able to produce convincing arguments about how military jet fighter technology would pose any risk to Boeing's domination of the commercial aircraft market.)

1988 Presidential Election

Japan policy was a major issue in the American Presidential election of 1988. By the time George Bush took office, Congressional and media interest in the FSX issue was high, and something had to be done. Many of Bush's nominees were not even in place in February 1989 when Commerce Secretary Malcolm Baldrige, supported by Secretary of State James Baker, moved to re-open the agreement.

As the Secretary of Commerce, Baldrige's reasons for intervening were clear. Baker's reasons were more complex and reflected the approach that he and subsequent Secretaries of State often would take. "Good" foreign policy increasingly had become whatever would defuse Congressional pressures and get the press and special interest groups "off our backs." So Baker worked the issue closely with his Congressional and media advisors. Those with expertise on the issue were shut out—after all, they were the ones who had produced the "bad agreement" in the first place.

Baker and company succeeded in renegotiating the terms of the work-share agreement so that American companies would be responsible for 40 percent of the project. (They also would have greater access to whatever new technologies were developed by their Japanese partners.) On April 28, 1989, President Bush personally announced one of the first foreign policy "victories" of his Administration. The language he used shows clearly what his intentions were in re-opening the agreement:

> The United States is the world's leader in aircraft manufacturing. I believe this aircraft will improve the defense of the United States and Japan, and this agreement also helps preserve our commitment that U.S. aerospace products of the future will continue to dominate the world markets.

A decade later, what have the results been? The FSX flew for the first time in 1995, but with the end of the Cold War and budget cutbacks, Japan's Self-Defense Agency has reduced the number of planes it will buy.

Japan has not been able to challenge America's lead in aviation and aerospace—if indeed it ever could—just as many other dire predictions of the Japan "revisionists" never came true.

How successful was the revised work-share and technology transfer agreement that Bush's new team negotiated? Despite the Administration's self-satisfaction, Mark Lorell of the RAND Corporation concluded that Japan came out ahead on the FSX arrangement. The Japanese got a far better assessment of U.S. technological strengths and a closer linkage in policy between technological and security objectives. A 1995 General Accounting Office report said of the FSX program, "no one currently knows what benefits, if any, Japanese technologies will provide to the United States. In addition, U.S. evaluation has been incomplete and ineffective."

The Japanese government also seems to have learned how to avoid co-development and co-production arrangements with the United States, and how to avoid putting itself in a position where it becomes subject to the whims of the American political process. Japan has decided to build and launch two photo-reconnaissance satellites without U.S. help, even though this approach will take longer and cost more.

In 1973, President Richard Nixon banned the export of soybeans because the Japanese allegedly were trying to corner the market. Although the ban lasted for only a few days, it convinced the Japanese to diversify sources of supply away from America. Japan moved to help develop the soybean industry in Brazil, which today is a competitor of U.S. farmers. Japan, like any other country, has options, and American policy actions that produce short-term "victories" also can produce unintended and undesired consequences for the United States over the longer term.

The Enlargement of NATO, 1994-1999

By Lawrence S. Kaplan

The inclusion of Poland, Hungary, and the Czech Republic was to have been the centerpiece of the 50-year anniversary of the signing of the North Atlantic Treaty. The allies took considerable care to celebrate the inclusion of these three former Warsaw Pact nations as a fitting tribute to the vitality of the alliance as it entered its second half-century on April 4, 1999. Regrettably, the anniversary, along with the addition of three new members the month before, was overshadowed when the military campaign against Serbia in Kosovo began on March 24.

In retrospect, it appears that the emphasis on enlarging the alliance rather than concentrating on the continuing crises in the Balkans may have been misplaced. And yet the impulse to tie the former Communist nations to the West was understandable. The three new members—and others in Central Europe as well—identified themselves with the West and looked upon membership in the North Atlantic Treaty Organization (NATO) as a guarantee of security in the event of future aggression from a revived Russia. The question in the mid-1990s was whether enlarging the alliance was the appropriate way of managing "out-of-area" issues in the East. The NATO partners were well aware of the dangers an imploded Russian empire posed to Europe and the alliance. A wounded Russia seeking revenge, ethnic conflicts within such countries as Hungary and Romania, and potential economic upheavals everywhere in the former Communist East could all produce the kind of disasters that befell the Balkans in this period.

To mitigate these problems NATO had established a North Atlantic Cooperation Council (NACC), which was to form an "interlocking network" with the NATO allies that would help these "liaison partners" deal not only with defense issues but also with civil-military relations, conversion of defense production to civilian purposes, and the development of scientific and environmental programs. Through these activities the smaller nations would feel the warmth of NATO's protection and the larger benefits of NATO's political and economic support.

Few of these objectives were reached, as the development of viable free economies and stable democracies was uneven and often uncertain. Russian resentment at its inferior status and continuing East European apprehension about the ultimate intentions of their restive neighbor rendered the Council meaningless. Russia would not accept NATO's repeated assurances that the organization was a friend and supporter, and the East Europeans would not accept membership in the Council as a substitute for membership in the organization.

Pressure from the Central European countries to join the alliance, abetted by Germany's wish both for a secure eastern border and economic opportunities in a traditional area of influence, elicited a NATO response in the form of the "Partnership for Peace" (PfP), unveiled at the summit meeting of the North Atlantic Council in January 1994. The Partnership proposal superficially replicated the NACC arrangement, as the partners would engage in a variety of confidence-building activities, such as joint military exercises and access to NATO technical data. What was distinctive about this plan was the possibility of some of the new partners becoming full members of NATO after meeting the requirements of civilian control of the military, the development of the nation's military capability to the level of interoperability with other members, and proof of an irreversible commitment to democracy.

It was likely that NATO planners thought that the PfP would be a means of relieving pressures for immediate membership while reinvigorating the functions of NACC. This expectation did not materialize. Within the year the Clinton Administration had accepted the principle of early admission for Poland, Hungary, and the Czech Republic, the three countries that were putatively able to meet the foregoing qualifications. The issue entered American politics. Both Republican and Democratic friends of the former Warsaw Pact nations pressed for expanding membership without reference to the impact on Russia. The new Republican majority in Congress in 1995 made an issue of the Clinton Administration's putatively excessive concern about Russian sensibilities at the expense of its fearful neighbors. Within a week of each other in December 1994, two influential statesmen, Zbigniew Brzezinski and Henry Kissinger, writing op-ed columns for the *New York Times* and the *Washington Post,* respectively, urged the President to bring the three nations into the organization as quickly as possible.

A Complex Objective

For American skeptics, there were many objections to enlarging the alliance. They included three major caveats. First would be the impact on relations with the Russian Federation. President Boris Yeltsin had been suspicious of the PfP from the outset, although he agreed for a time to join the partnership if a special status were accorded the nation as a major power distinct from its neighbors. But the admission of Poland into the Western alliance revived the Russian belief that NATO remained a hostile entity, moving as it would into Russia's traditional sphere of influence. There was a legitimate worry that admission of the former Warsaw Pact countries would endanger Russian democracy, and result in a neo-Communist restoration or a military dictatorship that would revive the Cold War.

Second, less frightening but still a matter that contained problems in the future was the precedent that the admission of the three new members raised. There was a precedent for enlargement; indeed, major milestones in the alliance's history centered on the admission of such nations as Greece and Germany. But Greece and Germany reflected specific exigencies of the Cold War, while the admission of the three former Soviet bloc powers opened the way for others to join regardless of the alliance's needs. In August 1997 France proposed Romania, and in the wings were such candidates as Slovenia and Slovakia. Would the Baltic countries also be appropriate candidates for NATO membership? Lithuania was clamoring for membership. Where would enlargement stop? Little thought was given to the problems inherent in decision making by consensus when the enlargement process goes beyond 19 countries.

A third issue involved the cost of enlargement and the appropriate use of funds. Should the new allies spend their financial resources on meeting the requirements set in 1994 to bring their military establishments up to the level of other members of the organization? And if this goal could not be met, would the United States be held responsible for bearing what might become an enormous financial burden as new countries came into the alliance?

These questions received little serious consideration as the Clinton Administration prepared to seek Senate approval of enlargement. And there was not much consideration of the potential unintended consequences of enlargement as the 50th anniversary of the signing approached. A major lobbying effort was launched by the State Department as it established a special office to promote support of the cause for enlargement. No "Great Debate"—similar to the Senate deliberations on NATO in 1949 and 1951—took place after invitations to the three applicants were extended in 1997. The President was able to take advantage of the effort of the bipartisan U.S. Committee to Expand NATO, which effectively supplemented the bipartisan Congressional pressures. The mobilization of public sentiment in favor of enlargement was reminiscent of the lobbying done by a combination of public officials and private organizations in the service of the Marshall Plan and the North Atlantic Treaty 50 years before. And success in 1999 was achieved more easily than in 1949.

A Nascent Outcome

The problem of Russia predictably was high on the agenda, and it was seemingly solved by the semantic device of substituting "enlargement" for "expansion" in presenting the case, as "expansion" held too many negative implications. A special relationship was established with the Russian Federation in the form of the Founding Act in 1997 that created a Permanent Joint Council to provide a mechanism for consultation and coordination with respect to the security concerns of both parties. Whether this arrangement put to rest Russian objections remained open in 1999.

Since the cost of enlargement could not be settled until after the accession of the new members, wildly conflicting figures were circulated depending upon who was doing the calculating. The watchdog Congressional Budget Office estimated a cost of $125 billion, while the RAND Corporation projected figures between $42 billion and $110 billion. The President understandably promoted a State Department version that had the United States bearing a share of only $2 billion over a 12-year period.

If the Senate accepted these justifications, it was not because of its faith in the accuracy of financial projections, or its conviction that the problems with Russia were resolved, or that the decision-making apparatus would not be affected. Rather it was because of a national disposition in favor of undoing the stain of Yalta by reuniting the nations of the East with the West, as Vaclav Havel of the Czech Republic and Lech Walesa of Poland so eloquently pleaded in their visits to the United States. Whatever doubts legislators—or Administration officials—may have harbored were subsumed under a bipartisan consensus that judged welcoming new members as a fitting symbol of NATO's viability in its anniversary year.

NATO enlargement must be counted as a major achievement of the Clinton Administration's foreign policy. But its success was in the short run. Further expansion of the alliance in light of the potential consequences would not be in the interest of the next President. It is ironic, and yet fitting, that the Kosovo crisis that put a damper on the anniversary celebrations in 1999, also identified the kind of "out-of-area" issues that should be of primary concern to the next President. NATO enlargement is not one of them. The relative silence on the subject as the Presidential election approaches suggests appropriate bipartisan doubts about further enlargement in the immediate future.

Presidential Leadership:
Bill Clinton and "NATO Enlargement"

By Robert E. Hunter

The reform and restructuring of the North Atlantic Treaty Organization (NATO) during the 1990s often has been called President Bill Clinton's most important achievement in foreign policy. This is not just because of the significance of the result—that the alliance that was most consequential to American power and purpose during the Cold War has become vital to the future of security for the 21st century Europe. It is also because, in the process, Clinton demonstrated what can be done with the proper application of Presidential insight and leadership.

The recreation of NATO was not, of course, about the organization itself. Rather, it was about finding an instrument, and shaping it appropriately, to meet the new demands for security that emerged in Europe following the end of the Cold War. History did not come to an end. Indeed, the application of American power—as well as of American values shared with its European partners—rapidly proved to be as critical for the new era as it had been for the old. The demands on NATO ranged from trying to stop conflicts in the former Yugoslavia, which saw the first serious fighting in Europe since hostilities ceased in 1945—to dealing with the future of Russia, a nation bereft of power, empire, pride, and ideology. There were hundreds of millions of people, for so long shut off from the world and from their aspirations to live free lives, who were now unfettered by communism and Soviet power. They wanted only to fulfill their dreams and destiny of being secure and firmly embedded in the West.

Clinton's leadership began by creating continuity. President George H.W. Bush had the original insight to treat Russia like Germany after 1945 rather than like Germany after 1918—the earlier actions leading to economic collapse and Adolf Hitler, the later actions producing democracy and the extraordinary success of the Federal Republic. Clinton followed suit, starting his venture in European diplomacy with a solid bipartisan base, a hallmark of great Presidential politics. He also accepted the need to preserve NATO as the central mechanism for keeping the United States rooted to the continent as a European power. But Clinton went further, and he did so in two decisive ways. First, by accepting the need for the North Atlantic allies to take responsibility for halting the conflict in Bosnia, a small place in a remote corner of Europe. Second, Clinton saw that the renaissance of NATO was needed both to help Central European states fulfill their destinies and to try drawing Russia out of its 70-year self-imposed isolation. And these twin efforts—from halting the conflict to devising and implementing the grand concept—were to be pursued in parallel.

It was no accident that the United States, in the summer of 1993, tried to gain allied support for using NATO military power in Bosnia. The Clinton Administration developed a policy called "lift and strike"— that is, to lift controls on shipments of arms (which affected Bosnia's Moslems the most), and to use NATO air power to protect so-called United Nations safe areas. Washington also was working toward a defining summit of NATO leaders for the start of 1994. In August 1993, the United States twice negotiated allied agreements to employ air power in Bosnia in support of UN efforts—only to be thwarted (then and later) by other allies who were prepared to follow the U.S. lead at the NATO table but then undercut allied decisions either at the UN or in the field. And thus, in parallel, in October 1993 President Clinton decided on a package of proposals for the alliance that recognized that advancing European security, in its broadest sense, had to be done as a totality— beginning with NATO reform. The President hoped that it would be complemented by steps taken by the European Union, where the United States had no formal say.

Farsighted Leadership

Simultaneously, the Clinton Administration proposed the creation of a new Partnership for Peace (PfP), perhaps NATO's most important development in a generation. From the outset, it had two purposes. First, PfP was to help countries in Central Europe prepare to meet the military challenges of becoming NATO allies. And second, the organization would enable the countries that did not join the alliance to work closely with NATO—so closely that they would have no sense of somehow being left out, consigned to a gray area or buffer zone.

The PfP proposal foreshadowed Clinton's bold step at the January 1994 NATO summit in Brussels in calling formally for NATO to start taking in new members from Central Europe. This initiative stemmed in part from Clinton's sense that full engagement in Western institutions was critical to the future well being—and hence the security—of Central European states. He had been impressed by the appeals made by regional leaders at the April 1993 dedication of the Washington Holocaust Museum. At that time, Clinton championed a "coming together of Western Europe and Central Europe and Eastern Europe...the first coming together of those regions ever as democratic states."

Clinton supported the inclusion of Central European states in NATO even though none faced a threat of invasion. Rather, they faced a compelling need for confidence that such a threat would not again emerge, that they would not again be plunged into circumstances like those that had twice led to continent-spanning conflicts in the 20th century, followed by the extinction of independence under Soviet domination. Some of our allies at the Brussels summit were not yet convinced that enlargement would take place. So to underscore his own commitment—and that of the United States (whose willingness to extend strategic guarantees was far and away the most important in the alliance)—President Clinton afterward toured Central Europe. During his tour the President stated flatly that NATO enlargement was not a matter of "whether, but when and how."

At the Brussels summit, Clinton had recognized again that this new venture in building a broader, modernized alliance could not succeed unless the conflict in Bosnia were dealt with successfully. Prompted by NATO Secretary General Manfred Worner, Clinton argued that NATO should either be willing to honor its pledge to use air power in support of UN peacekeepers, or it should vacate that pledge—there was no middle ground. The pledge was thus sustained, although it took another year and a half and the slaughter at Srebrenica before the most reluctant of the allies finally accepted the need to act militarily, thereby bringing the Bosnia conflict to an end and to the Dayton Peace Accords.

The timing of this final willingness of all 16 allies to use air power in Bosnia was significant; it came only after the rebuilding process of NATO was firmly established under U.S. leadership—when the "architecture" was clearly completed. Agreement came only when there was something in NATO's future, as the most critical European security institution, that had to be protected. In this case, NATO had to be protected against charges that it had failed in the simple act of stopping a minor conflict in Bosnia.

Success in the Making

"NATO enlargement," a shorthand term for so much of what the alliance did in the 1990s, was in fact a collection of interlocking policies, each designed to reinforce the others and all designed to make possible a radical transformation of European security. NATO enlargement was attempting to validate what George Bush had called—in a term readily embraced by Bill Clinton—the creation of a Europe "whole and free." Inviting three countries to join at the 1997 Madrid summit showed that NATO was sensitive to Central European needs, while it enabled Germany to "surround itself" with NATO (as it also sought to do with the European Union). The policy of the "open door," proposed by the United States in 1996—which said that any European country was eligible to join the alliance if it "were ready and willing to undertake the responsibilities of NATO membership"—made sure that no country desiring to join the organization would see itself shut out. And this principle even extended to Russia, should it one day seek to join and prove itself able to meet NATO requirements. This underscored that enlargement was not about creating new lines of division in Europe. The Partnership for Peace was open to all (and all of the countries that emerged from the wreckage of the Warsaw Pact and Soviet Union joined it). PfP pursued its work of democratizing and reforming militaries; and it teamed with a new Euro-Atlantic Partnership Council, the direct descendent of the North Atlantic Cooperation Council that had been created during the Bush Administration.

Equally important, before the decisive 1997 Madrid summit, when Poland, Hungary, and the Czech Republic were formally invited to join NATO, the allies negotiated and signed a NATO-Russia Founding Act, following an historic meeting between President Clinton and Russian President Boris Yeltsin. The Founding Act created a Permanent Joint Council, gave Russia a "voice but not a veto" in some NATO deliberations, and even opened up the possibility, in the future, of a NATO-Russian strategic partnership. Meanwhile, the United States had negotiated for the participation of Russian troops in the Implementation/Stabilization Force (IFOR/SFOR) in Bosnia, on the same basis as NATO troops. At the same time, NATO negotiated a charter with Ukraine and developed a special partnership. The alliance reformed its integrated command structure—focusing more on the potential military challenges of the 21st century—with devices like the new Combined Joint Task Force headquarters. It also negotiated a new relationship with the Western European Union, under which the so-called European Security and Defense Identity could be created within NATO, "separable but not separate from it."

This was a formidable list of undertakings. It was by doing them all together that the United States, under President Clinton's leadership, was able to give concrete expression to George Bush's aspiration for a Europe whole and free. NATO enlargement was thus one aspect of a comprehensive policy that could give each European state—at least all of those willing to share in the benefits of a new approach to European security—a sense that it had gained something positive and lost nothing in terms of its own security.

Presidential leadership—and through it, the leadership of the United States at NATO headquarters in Brussels—was not just important in dealing with the allies, the Russians, and others. Clinton also had to lead in the United States. Some American military leaders were skeptical of NATO enlargement and saw the Partnership for Peace as a substitute. But PfP became an instrument in reducing fears that enlargement would weaken the alliance. At the State Department, the European Bureau tried to rush NATO enlargement, in time and scope— and nearly scared off the allies—while the "Russia hands" tried to block any increase in NATO's size. In both cases, the larger perspective prevailed, through efforts engineered at the White House and at the U.S. Mission to NATO. And thus the President's ambitions were fulfilled for a comprehensive, successful approach to a renovated, inclusive European security.

Clinton's final task was to ensure that NATO enlargement could command the support of the American people and, more immediately, the U.S. Congress. This required sustaining support for U.S. troop deployments on the ground in Bosnia (in IFOR/SFOR), and it required garnering formal acceptance in the Senate of the three new candidates for NATO membership. Following sustained Presidential efforts, the 80-19 favorable vote in April 1998 for NATO enlargement was not just a simple act of ratifying this one step. The vote was in fact a referendum on all that President Clinton—building on the work of President Bush— had tried to achieve over a five-year period in terms of confirming U.S. power and purpose on the European continent.

Thus "NATO enlargement," the short-hand term for so much that was achieved, has proved to be one of those very rare events in U.S. foreign policy—where the goal was decided first, a strategy crafted around it, and the tactics designed to bring the larger purpose to fruition. This is an excellent example of where Presidential leadership—at home and abroad—can make the difference in achieving the nation's larger purposes.

Miscalculations Leading to Conflict

By Samuel R. Williamson

Every President and every Presidential Administration in the last five decades has made serious miscalculations that have caused international crises, contributed to their aggravation, or possibly, in rare instances, helped to resolve the crisis.

Presidents have miscalculated because of the pressures of time, because they failed to consider all of the options, because they depended too heavily on their staffs and/or the governmental bureaucracy, because of significant intelligence failures, or in some instances, because they relied too heavily on their own perceptions, ideology, and past experience. A surprising number of the miscalculations have come during periods of transition, either as an Administration came into office or was on the way out. Issues of Presidential election politics have contributed to conditions that have made miscalculations more likely.

Korea 1950

On June 25, 1950, North Korean forces surged across the 38th parallel, surprising Washington and Seoul. This attack resulted directly from a set of miscalculations by the Administration of President Harry S. Truman. Early in the year Secretary of State Dean Acheson had given a speech that suggested that the Korean peninsula was not in the American security zone. Moscow and Beijing concluded that they could attack without the risk of an American response. In this instance an American miscalculation led to their miscalculation, since Truman did respond and successfully so over the next three years.

The Truman-Acheson miscalculation came in part from their preoccupation with the Soviet threat in Europe and their focus on the creation of the North Atlantic Treaty Organization (NATO), and in part from their inability to assess the full strategic significance of the fall of China in the autumn of 1949. They also failed to grasp that a policy statement by Acheson could be interpreted by their Cold War adversaries as a statement of future American intentions, when it was an attempt to assure Europe of the American commitment to its defense. Or put another way, a fixation on one set of issues led to miscalculations in a geographical arena of almost equal importance. The lesson learned from this miscalculation, or the alleged lesson learned, had much to do with the subsequent American entanglement in Indochina.

The Gulf War 1990

On August 2, 1990, Iraqi troops moved into Kuwait, meeting almost no resistance and quickly seizing the country. This "surprise attack" should in fact have been no surprise. That it was unexpected reflected a series of miscalculations. Some dated from the late 1980s when the United States supported any Iraqi effort to blunt the Iranian challenge. Some came from the summer of 1990 when the American Ambassador, on instructions from Washington, essentially made an Acheson-type statement on July 25th that the United States was indifferent to border issues. Even when intelligence reports suggested an Iraqi build up, these were not given more than passing attention. Instead the Bush Administration, believing in the efficacy of the President's personal contacts with Arab leaders and in particular, with President Hosni Mubarak of Egypt—who assured Washington that Saddam Hussein did not intend to attack Kuwait—remained unprepared for the Iraqi incursion.

The miscalculations stemmed from a willingness to tolerate Saddam Hussein, despite his own past record and his own efforts to create weapons of mass destruction, because he was useful against Iran. They also came in part from the Administration's preoccupation with the rapidly changing situation in the former Soviet Union, almost to the exclusion over all other issues—including, for example, the equally dangerous situation in Yugoslavia. The role played by misunderstanding the intelligence reports remains unclear, given the continued classified nature of most of the electronic intelligence. But it should be noted that the CIA was more aggressive in warning of the possibility of an attack than the military intelligence apparatus, and that gross overestimates of the ability of the Iraqi forces may also have played a part in the miscalculation. In this instance a series of incremental miscalculations led to the "surprise" situation in early August 1990.

Kosovo 1998-1999

The 1999 Kosovo crisis reflected less dramatic miscalculations by Washington than the other two cases. In this instance the Clinton Administration's clear preference not to be drawn further into the alleged Balkan morass sent an ambiguous signal to Belgrade and to Slobodan Milosevic. He could interpret Washington's hesitance to get further involved—an interpretation that was strengthened by Republican Congressional attacks on Clinton's Bosnian policy and then on the impeachment issue—as a signal that he could move to regain effective Serbian dominance of the mythic Serb homeland of Kosovo. Thus Milosevic began the ethnic cleansing of the majority Albanian population from Kosovo in late 1998 and early 1999.

The subsequent decision by NATO and by the European community to use force to coerce Belgrade also had a pair of miscalculations: that air power alone and quickly would force Milosevic to change his position and that Russia would play a helpful role in the settlement. The sustained bombing campaign achieved but modest success; arguably only the increasing talk of the use of ground forces stationed in Bosnia swayed Milosevic to accept a settlement. But his resistance to the bombing and its length allowed the Russians to intrude into the diplomatic process, a fact that made the peace arrangements a European and not a

NATO operation, and thus gave Russia a place in the peace settlement. In this instance the calculation by the Clinton Administration to exclude, and publicly so, the use of ground troops for so long prolonged the crisis.

Miscalculations will always be a feature of national security policy. The complexity of the issues, the differing perspectives of the security bureaucracy, the personalities of the key actors including the President, and a frequent inclination to go with solutions that pose the least momentary domestic political risk all contribute to miscalculations. A degree of humility, a certain skepticism (especially about military plans), an ability to think through the problem from the point of view of the other government or governments, and an imaginative ability to see beyond one crisis to the larger context all may help to reduce miscalculations.

In this set of uncertainties, the admonition, recently cited by Professor Ernest May in his study of the French defeat of 1940 is most appropriate. Oliver Cromwell, in the midst of the English Civil War, told the General Assembly of the Church of Scotland in 1650, "I beseech you in the bowels of Christ think it possible you may be mistaken." No President should ever forget this injunction.

VII. FOREIGN INTERVENTIONS AND INTERACTIONS

The Bay of Pigs Invasion, 1961

By James P. Pfiffner and John M. Goshko

Fidel Castro led a revolution in Cuba in 1959 that overthrew the Batista regime and drew Cuba into the communist camp. President Dwight D. Eisenhower's Administration decided that Castro had to be replaced by whatever means necessary. On March 17, 1960, Eisenhower authorized a secret CIA plan entitled, A Program of Covert Action Against the Castro Regime. The plan centered on creating a force of about 1,400 anti-Castro Cuban exiles to stage what would appear to be an independent invasion to liberate Cuba. In reality, this force would be trained and equipped secretly by the CIA, which provided other aid, including a propaganda campaign to incite the Cuban populace against Castro. The training of the force took place largely at a secret base in Guatemala, and the program was designed to provide deniability about any involvement by the U.S. government.

As John Kennedy was taking office as President, he was briefed by the CIA on the plans, and he gave his approval for further planning. In March 1961 the fully developed CIA plan was presented to the President. It called for an invasion of the island at Trinidad, with the invading brigade of Cuban exiles being supported by U.S. air cover. The CIA argued that the invasion would precipitate a popular uprising against Castro and lead to his overthrow. If the invasion did not immediately succeed, the invaders were to retreat into the Escambray Mountains and organize guerrilla resistance against the Castro regime.

Decision Making

Kennedy was reluctant to provoke a confrontation with the Soviet Union and did not want the United States to be seen as attacking the small island, so his condition for approval was that no American forces would be directly involved. He insisted on complete secrecy; imposed strict limits on direct American involvement in the actual invasion; and labored to create elaborate cover stories to maintain the fiction that once the invasion actually began, the exiles were acting on their own and were not employed by the United States. In an attempt to decrease the immediate visibility of the invasion, the site of the attack was shifted away from Trinidad to the Bay of Pigs.

Despite his misgivings about the viability of the CIA plans, Kennedy was reluctant to call off the invasion. In the 1960 campaign he had criticized the Eisenhower Administration and called for a harder line against Castro. He also did not want to seem afraid to use force, nor did he want to overrule the professionals in the CIA who had been planning the operation. In addition, if there was to be a move against Castro, any delay would have given Castro more time to improve his defenses and train his troops to use the Soviet equipment, including jet planes, that was pouring into the country daily. On the American side, any delay would have aggravated the exiled Cuban troops, there would have been grumbling that they were ready to go, and complaints that Kennedy was passing up an opportunity to get rid of Castro.

So the invasion was allowed to proceed, and on April 17, 1961, about 1,400 exiled Cubans attacked Cuba at the Bay of Pigs. Kennedy did relent in allowing one U.S. supporting air mission to provide cover for Cuban-piloted planes attacking Castro's air force, but the timing was wrong and Castro's air force survived. The CIA then urged Kennedy to reverse his decision not to allow further direct U.S. support to the exiles, but Kennedy refused, fearing Soviet retaliation and the opprobrium of the international community. Thus Castro's air force was effective in attacking the invaders—who were facing Castro ground forces of 20,000 men. The whole operation was a fiasco from the United States and Cuban exile perspective, with 114 men killed and 1,189 captured.

The immediate effects were to rally the Cuban people behind Castro and strengthen his hold on power. The CIA's reputation for infallibility was shattered, and there was a tendency in international circles to view the Kennedy Administration as a group of inept and amateurish bunglers. That was particularly the view of the Soviet leader, Nikita Khrushchev, who was emboldened by the American misadventure and convinced that the United States would again attack Cuba. He thus set in motion plans to place the Soviet nuclear missiles in Cuba that would provoke the Cuban Missile Crisis in October 1962.

Lessons Learned

Kennedy assumed full responsibility for the attack—and was criticized from the right for not providing sufficient support to assure a U.S. victory, and from the left for backing an invasion of a small country. His private reaction was, "How could we have been so stupid?" The answer to his question provides some lessons for future Presidents.

1. The CIA was both the planner and the advocate for the operation, and secrecy was kept so tight that there was no full-scale evaluation of the plan by anyone other than its advocates. Kennedy had asked the Joint Chiefs of Staff for an analysis of the CIA invasion plans, but they did not staff it out fully. Their assessment was that the chance for success of the operation was "fair," which Kennedy took to mean reasonably good. But the military assessment meant fair as opposed to good or excellent (Neustadt and May, *Thinking in Time,* p. 142).

2. The CIA made several miscalculations. Most importantly, the Agency assumed that once the invading force arrived in Cuba that the Cuban people would rally to their support and rise up to overthrow Castro. But the assumption was based more on wishful thinking than on hard intelligence. As the internal CIA Inspector General's review of the operation concluded in its report: "...we can confidently assert that the agency had no intelligence evidence that Cubans in significant numbers could or would join the invaders or that there was any kind of an effective and cohesive resistance movement under anybody's control, let alone the agency's, that could have furnished internal leadership for an uprising in support of the invasion" (Tim Weiner, "CIABares Its

Bungling in Report on Bay of Pigs Invasion," *New York Times,* February 22, 1998). The CIA also miscalculated in that they (and the Cuban exiles) thought that Kennedy, despite his statements, would provide U.S. military support rather than let the invasion fail.

3. Part of the failure was due to the pressure of transition. The Administration was a new team of people who did not yet know each other fully. Kennedy's advisers were involved with so many other pressing actions in taking control of the government that they were unable to devote sustained attention to the CIA plans. They were reluctant to challenge the expertise of the CIA, which had been working on the plans for a year. The President's advisers did not want to seem weak by being afraid to take strong military action, and they did not want to be accused of blowing a chance to dethrone Castro. They were also affected by the hubris that often comes when a new Administration takes over the government and thinks that they can do no wrong.

4. The decision making process was marked by a number of flaws. Experts who should have been consulted were not aware of the plans, and few of the CIA officers planning the operation could speak Spanish. Even Theodore Sorensen, Kennedy's top aide, was not informed of the operation until it was over (Sorensen, *Kennedy*, p. 295). Military experts did not do a full analysis. The same people who developed the plan were entrusted to evaluate it objectively. The assumptions upon which success depended were never fully explored. The CIA Inspector General's report criticized the "…failure to reduce successive project plans to formal papers and to leave copies of them with the President and his advisers and to request specific written approval and confirmation thereof" (*New York Times*).

In sum, the lessons of the Bay of Pigs invasion were that Presidents need their personal staffs to perform full, independent analyses before undertaking risky operations, and that plans need to be subjected to formal and rigorous criticism from informed participants before they are approved.

The Cuban Missile Crisis: Decision Making Under Pressure

By James P. Pfiffner and John M. Goshko

Perhaps the greatest pressure any President can face is the possibility of nuclear war. The closest the world has come to a nuclear exchange occurred during the Cuban Missile Crisis of 1962 when President John F. Kennedy and Soviet Premier Nikita Khrushchev faced each other over Cuba. In May 1962, Premier Khrushchev, seeking both to deter a U.S. invasion of Cuba and to counter American superiority in nuclear missile strength, secretly began placing intermediate-range missiles in Cuba. By

October 16, U.S. reconnaissance photos revealed the Soviet move to the Kennedy Administration. On October 22, President Kennedy announced on television that a nuclear attack on the United States from Cuba would be responded to as an attack from the Soviet Union.

The first nuclear warheads arrived in Cuba on October 4, 1962, and on October 14 a U-2 spy plane flew over Cuba and revealed that several missile sites were under construction. National Security Adviser McGeorge Bundy gave Kennedy the news early in the morning on October 16. From the beginning, Kennedy and his advisers felt that the presence of nuclear missiles in Cuba was an unacceptable threat to U.S. national security interests, even though Secretary of Defense Robert S. McNamara and Bundy judged that they did not affect American strategic military superiority. But Kennedy felt that he could not afford to appear weak to the international community, particularly after the failed Bay of Pigs invasion and a less than successful summit meeting in Vienna, Austria. Any sign of weakness could encourage Khrushchev to be more aggressive in Berlin and elsewhere in the world. Domestically, Kennedy had criticized the Eisenhower Administration for inaction on Cuba, and he did not want to seem "soft" on national security issues.

Decision Making

Kennedy formed a team of special national security advisors known as the National Security Council Executive Committee (ExCom). It negotiated publicly and, more importantly, through back channels with Khrushchev, and made decisions outside of the scrutiny of the public. The initial consensus among Kennedy's military advisers (with the exception of General Maxwell Taylor) and some of his civilian aides was for immediate military action, specifically an airstrike to destroy the missiles. But Kennedy led the group through a series of high-tension meetings over the next 13 days to decide what to do. The debate covered a range of options, from ignoring the missiles to a full-scale invasion. In contrast to the Bay of Pigs deliberations, Kennedy and his civilian advisers did not hesitate to challenge the military on recommended options. They determined that a "surgical airstrike" could not guarantee the destruction of all of the missiles and that a full-scale air attack would probably kill many Cubans and Soviets, and thus provoke Soviet retaliation.

Kennedy finally decided that a naval quarantine would be the best way to confront Khrushchev as an initial step that would not close off options (as an air attack would). It would give Khrushchev time to reconsider his actions and possibly withdraw the missiles. Kennedy was careful to allow free debate over all of the options, and deliberately did not attend some sessions of the ExCom so that his presence would not inhibit some of the junior members from presenting their candid opinions or disagreeing with their superiors in the presence of the President. Attorney General Robert Kennedy played the role of inquisitor by carefully questioning the assumptions behind each proposal.

The key was that each leader felt that nuclear war was an unacceptable option, but Kennedy felt that it was possible if Khrushchev were backed into a corner with no face-saving alternative. So the American President did his best to present Khrushchev with options that did not humiliate him. Kennedy tried to see the situation from the Soviet Premier's position by psychologically putting himself in Khrushchev's shoes. Although the President thought that Khrushchev was duplicitous, Kennedy did not think that Khrushchev was stupid. The President was sensitive to the Soviet leader's domestic and international need to save face and to not appear to be humiliated in the exchange. Communications were carefully worded, and Kennedy deliberately refrained from attacking Khrushchev personally. Kennedy tried not to back Khrushchev into any corner that would make him feel so trapped that his only option would be to launch a nuclear strike against the United States.

Despite the need for secrecy in the beginning, outside experts on the Soviet Union were brought into meetings to give their best advice. Weaknesses of each proposed course of action were carefully plumbed and contingency plans were formulated. The group was not forced into an early and false consensus, which was sometimes frustrating, but instead kept open minds. The top members of the group changed their minds about options several times during the course of the deliberations.

Kennedy's ability over the duration of the crisis to craft a solution that achieved U.S. goals—yet did not provoke retaliation by Khrushchev—was based on his willingness to listen carefully to the broad range of advice that he was given and to evaluate it with a cool head. His strength and acumen were demonstrated when he rejected the more precipitous and bellicose options in favor of less threatening actions. Despite Kennedy's perceived political need to appear strong and unyielding to domestic and foreign audiences, he rejected a full-scale invasion, a limited airstrike, and a full blockage in favor of a limited quarantine. The quarantine would be restricted to nuclear weapons, and there would be plenty of warning to the Soviets about its implementation. Kennedy moved the naval quarantine line closer to Cuba to give Khrushchev more time to deliberate. He did not react with hostile action when an American U-2 spy plane was shot down over Cuba on October 27. Kennedy had his brother negotiate the secret removal of Jupiter missiles from Turkey in exchange for the removal of the Soviet missiles, and he pledged that the United States would not invade Cuba. At each turning point Kennedy decided on the moderate option, despite criticism from some of his military and civilian advisers.

Lessons Learned

Aside from the possibility that some of Kennedy's actions may have encouraged or allowed Khrushchev to come to the decision to place nuclear missiles in Cuba in the first place, his conduct of decision making during the missile crisis was exemplary. Kennedy emphasized flexibility in the negotiations through such means as controlling the escalation of the crisis so that both sides had several options. He was careful not to act precipitously—despite the advice to attack immediately, Kennedy resisted the temptation to strike out at Castro and Khrushchev. His Executive

Committee was designed to prevent one or two strong-willed individuals from dominating the discussion and formulation of recommendations to the President. Kennedy ensured that all options, favored and unfavored, were thoughtfully scrutinized. He was careful not to back Khrushchev into a corner with no face-saving options. He insisted on negotiation rather than unilateral action. Kennedy was not cowed by older and more experienced military leaders.

The crisis demonstrated that rapid and reliable communications between world leaders, especially those with nuclear weapons at their disposal, is crucial. Following the Cuban missile crisis, Washington and Moscow gave top priority to establishing such links.

As the editors of *The Kennedy Tapes,* Ernest May and Philip Zelikow concluded: "It seems fortunate that, given the circumstances that he had helped create, Kennedy was the President charged with managing the crisis."

The Vietnam War

By Fredrik Logevall

The Vietnam War stands as the longest military conflict in U.S. history. It cost the lives of more than 58,000 Americans, and between two and three million Vietnamese. Only the Civil War and the two World Wars were deadlier for Americans. During the 10 years of the heaviest U.S. military involvement, beginning in 1964, the federal government spent more than $140 billion on the war, enough money to fund urban renewal projects in every major American city. Yet victory did not come. Despite repeated promises by top American military leaders that the war effort was succeeding and that ultimate victory was assured, the United States in the end failed in its aim of preserving a separate, independent, non-Communist South Vietnam. After April 1975, the Communist-led Democratic Republic of Vietnam ruled in both the North and the South.

Today, a quarter of a century later, Americans are still coming to grips with the war and its legacy. Beginning in the late 1970s, examination of the Vietnam experience became something of a national obsession, as Americans fought the war again in feature-length films, novels, and military-oriented magazines. Strategists began warning of a "Vietnam syndrome," by which they meant a general unwillingness on the part of both decision makers and the public to intervene militarily in unstable parts of the developing world. And indeed, the ghosts of Vietnam have come up whenever the United States has faced a military adventure. Nicaragua, Grenada, Panama, the Persian Gulf, Somalia, Haiti, Bosnia, Serbia, and Kosovo all have been seen through the lens of Vietnam.

The initial reasons for U.S. involvement in Indochina seemed compelling and logical to Washington officials. During World War II

President Franklin D. Roosevelt had expressed support for Indochina's independence from what he regarded as France's exploitative and repressive colonial rule. But FDR was ambivalent about how independence should happen. His successor, Harry S. Truman, was less troubled by France's record in the region. More important, President Truman and his advisors increasingly came to see Indochina not as a colonial issue but as part of the global anti-Communist struggle. Drawing an analogy with the failed appeasement of Adolf Hitler before World War II, the Truman Administration believed that any sign of Communist aggression must be met quickly and forcefully by the United States and its allies. This policy became known as containment.

In Vietnam the target of containment was Ho Chi Minh and the Vietminh front he had created in 1941. Ho and his lieutenants were Marxists, with longstanding ties to the Soviet Union. But they were also ardent nationalists who had fought the Japanese occupiers during World War II and were determined to prevent a restoration of French rule in its aftermath. When war broke out between France and the Vietminh in late 1946, Washington sided with the French. In the seven-plus years that followed, the United States would steadily increase its support of the French war effort—until by 1953 it was paying three-fourths of the cost. Washington's aim was two-fold-to prevent a Vietminh victory in Vietnam, and to ensure Paris's cooperation on the European Cold War front.

By the middle of 1954, France had essentially lost the war. Following a disastrous French defeat at the remote outpost of Dien Bien Phu, an international conference in Geneva, Switzerland provided for a temporary North-South partition of the country, to be followed in 1956 by elections for reunification. The United States was not a signatory to the Geneva Agreement and began to foster the idea of the creation of a non-Communist bastion in the territory of what was now South Vietnam. The Administration of Dwight D. Eisenhower accordingly threw its support to Ngo Dinh Diem, an exiled Catholic with strong anti-Communist credentials and influential admirers in the United States. Diem would stay in power for eight years, but despite massive American financial and military assistance he would fail to solidify control of South Vietnam. By November 1963, when first Diem and then U.S. President John F. Kennedy were assassinated, more than 16,000 American military advisors were in South Vietnam, some of them authorized to take part in combat.

Vietnam Becomes an American War

In the year and a half that followed, Vietnam would become a major American war. In early 1965, President Lyndon B. Johnson initiated sustained bombing of North Vietnam and enemy-held areas of South Vietnam, and deployed the first American ground troops. By the end of that year, some 180,000 U.S. troops were on the ground in Vietnam, and the number would grow to more than half a million by 1968. In that same 1965-1968 period, U.S. and South Vietnamese air forces dropped more than one million tons of bombs in the South, and approximately 643,000 tons in the North.

In 1968, negotiations for peace began in Paris, but failed to yield results. Not until January 1973 would a deal be reached. The Paris Peace Agreement provided for the withdrawal of all U.S. forces from Vietnam, the return of American prisoners of war (POWs), and a cease-fire, but it did not require that North Vietnam withdraw its troops from the South. The American troops and POWs came home, but the fighting did not end. Only in April 1975, when North Vietnamese tanks rolled into Saigon, was the war at last over.

Vietnam was not one crisis but a string of crises that plagued American Presidents for close to three decades. Step by step North Vietnam's President Ho Chi Minh and his colleagues closed off easy choices for U.S. leaders, who were torn between a strong desire to avoid fighting another land war in Asia and an equally strong aversion to suffering what they assumed would be a humiliating retreat. It would be humiliating not only in national terms but also in partisan and even personal terms. (For Presidents Kennedy, Johnson, and certainly Nixon, Vietnam's importance derived in large measure from the potential harm it could cause to their domestic political positions and their historical reputations.)

Which leads us to the lessons of the Vietnam War for today's leaders. Probably a dozen or more such lessons have been put forth over the years, but six stand out in importance. *The first is that in foreign policy, practice the democratic principles you preach by considering the opinions of Congressional leaders and sentiment of the public in the decision making process. Kennedy, Johnson, and Nixon deceived the Legislative Branch and the public about their intentions and planning at key junctures, in large part because they knew that popular support for the war effort, although in some respects quite broad, was also thin. When these deceptions were revealed, the credibility of each President took a heavy hit, as the populace came to distrust its leaders.*

Second, maintain a relatively open decision making environment to avoid being isolated from competing ideas. Presidents Johnson and Nixon relied heavily on small and cloistered groups of advisors on Vietnam. Each had an advisory system that effectively excluded contrarian voices from the deliberations and discouraged the in-depth reexamination of the fundamentals among those who remained. Johnson, for example, neglected to convene even one meeting of the National Security Council from October 1964 to the eve of the Pleiku attack in February 1965—a crucial period in his Vietnam policy making.

Third, seek to apply American military power in the context of multilateral decision making (except in the case of territorial self-defense of the United States). In the months prior to the Americanization of the war in 1965, the Johnson Administration worked hard to get allied backing for the escalation, with virtually no success. Although some aides warned Johnson against proceeding without broad international support, the President ignored this advice.

Fourth, in wartime, be sure to understand the mind-set of your adversary. This is a vitally important admonition for today's leaders, but its applicability to the Vietnam case should not be exaggerated. No doubt there was much about North Vietnam and the southern Vietcong that senior U.S. officials did not know, but they understood much more than they later claimed. Contrary to the recent statements of former Secretary of Defense Robert McNamara, for example, he and his colleagues did not fail completely to anticipate the commitment to ultimate victory of the North Vietnamese, or the corresponding lack of commitment in the South. They knew they faced long odds against success, even as they Americanized the war. Vietnam was no quagmire—or if it was, American leaders entered it with eyes wide open.

What the U.S. government was not willing to do, however, until well after the start of full-scale fighting, was to maintain serious and high-level diplomatic contacts with their opponent. *Hence the fifth lesson—communicate with your adversary at a high level. In the key months prior to the 1965 escalation of the war, and in the early years thereafter, Washington refused to give serious consideration to early negotiations for a diplomatic settlement.* Even preliminary talks were out of the question on the grounds that the American bargaining position was too poor. As a result, Washington officials did not know that there was flexibility in Hanoi's negotiating position, and that the United States had real cards to play.

Sixth and finally, acknowledge that American military power, no matter how great in relative terms, is ultimately limited, and that some problems in international affairs have no solution, particularly no military solution. Although most senior American officials in fact were far less optimistic about the prospects in the war than is often suggested—even with the introduction of major American fighting forces—they always framed the Vietnam problem as primarily a military one, requiring a military solution. They never fully grasped (or if they did, never admitted) that success in the war effort depended ultimately on gaining a stable South Vietnamese government that possessed broad popular backing—something that was never close to materializing.

Some postwar analysts, continuing to frame the issue in military terms, blamed the defeat on what they saw as undue limitations on the military's operations placed on them by civilian politicians, but this argument fails on two counts. Hundreds of thousands of ground troops and the most massive aerial bombardment in human history (some eight million tons of bombs from 1962 to 1973) can hardly be considered a limited use of force. More important, the war was fundamentally never about the military strength of the United States—it was about the political strength and legitimacy of the government of South Vietnam.

TRIUMPHS AND TRAGEDIES OF THE MODERN PRESIDENCY

Okinawa Reversion in the Nixon Administration

by Michael Schaller

Okinawa, the main island in the Ryukyu chain, is both the site of the last great Japanese-American land battle of the Pacific War and the final piece of occupied territory returned to Japan by the United States. From 1945 to 1972, this small island chain (with a population of about one million in 1969), remained under American military administration and played a key role in the Korean and Vietnam Wars. Although the U.S. military considered Okinawa to be a critical link in the security chain in the Pacific, most Japanese on and off of the island bitterly resented the prolonged refusal by a series of American Presidents to restore sovereignty to this tiny, but symbolically important, part of their homeland.

In 1969, newly elected President Richard M. Nixon acted decisively to break the deadlock over Okinawa. Nixon's keen appreciation of how important the island's return was to Japan, along with his determination to reduce America's conventional military role in East Asia, prompted him to push a settlement through a contentious bureaucracy. Unfortunately, the President's effort to tie a secret trade deal to the reversion decision undermined much of the good will he had cultivated among the Japanese. On balance, however, Nixon's motives and methods defused Japanese anger over the prolonged occupation of their territory and forged a consensus that permitted the American military to retain most of its bases on Okinawa.

The San Francisco Peace Treaty of 1951 (effective 1952) ended the occupation of Japan. Negotiator John Foster Dulles (later to become Secretary of State) bowed to pressure from the Pentagon to retain control over several small islands, including Iwo Jima and Okinawa. The United States acknowledged Japan's "residual sovereignty" over these islands, but insisted on the right to administer and develop military bases on the islands as long as it saw fit. Okinawa's network of land, sea, and naval facilities resulted in it playing a key role in both the Korean and Vietnam Wars.

From the middle-1950s on, Japanese political leaders pressed unsuccessfully for return of the occupied territory. In the early-1960s, President John F. Kennedy responded to protests by Japanese farmers whose lands had been taken for military bases, and to pleas by Ambassador Edwin O. Reischauer and Undersecretary of State George Ball (who criticized the military's "colonial" rule), by appointing a commission that recommended several reforms. Despite objections by the Defense Department, Kennedy agreed that American civilians should play a larger role in administration, Japanese residents should be given a greater say in local affairs, and Tokyo should be allowed to sponsor economic development projects on the island. However, rapid escalation of the Vietnam War after 1964 overshadowed these reforms.

Air, naval, and ground storage facilities on Okinawa played a critical role in the Vietnam conflict. One million transport and combat flights originated in the Ryukyus during the war. KC-135 tanker planes refueled B-52 bombers flying from Guam to Indochina, and the giant warplanes sometimes carried out their missions directly from Okinawa. Unrestricted by the terms of the 1960 mutual security treaty that governed U.S. bases in Japan proper, American forces stored chemical and nuclear weapons on the island. Nearly three-fourths of the 400,000 tons of supplies required each month by American troops in Vietnam passed through the ports and warehouses of Okinawa. Small wonder that beginning in 1965 the Defense Department referred to Okinawa as the "keystone of the Pacific" and placed this logo on local license plates.

Most Japanese harbored misgivings about the Vietnam War and their nation's supporting role in it. Although U.S. military orders accelerated Japanese economic growth during the 1960s, and even helped raise the standard of living on Okinawa, first Japanese leftists then peace activists, and finally many conservatives, questioned the wisdom of the war and their indirect participation. The bases on Okinawa, which played such an important role in Vietnam operations, became a focal point of anti-American sentiment. By the time Richard Nixon took the oath of office in January 1969, even the strongly pro-U.S. governing Liberal Democratic Party (LDP) and its leader, Prime Minister Eisaku Sato, considered the return of Okinawa to be a prerequisite for continuing to enforce the U.S.-Japan mutual security treaty after 1970, when either side was free to abrogate it. Early in 1969, Sato announced he would make reversion of Okinawa, without the presence of U.S. nuclear weapons, his first order of business with the new Administration. Nixon had to balance the competing claims of the Pentagon, which objected to any loosening of American control, with that of his conservative allies in Japan, who pledged to finally end the continued "occupation" of Japanese soil.

Added Pressure

As Vice President in the 1950s and as a private business consultant in the 1960s, Nixon had visited Japan on several occasions and had developed personal ties to conservative stalwarts such as former Prime Minister Kishi Nobusuke and current leader Eisaku Sato. Nixon told his new National Security Council (NSC) staff, headed by Henry Kissinger, that Okinawa was a powder keg. Even a small, violent incident involving U.S. military personnel there could endanger the larger framework of military cooperation with Japan. He sympathized with the LDP's pledge to seek the reversion of Okinawa, and saw this as a way to deprive the Japanese left of a popular issue that they might otherwise use to build an anti-American coalition. The trick would be to arrange the island's reversion under terms that granted the United States liberal enough base rights to placate the Pentagon without alienating the Japanese. To achieve one without the other was useless.

Because Nixon considered Okinawa a key issue, National Security Adviser Henry Kissinger made it a priority. Both the NSC staff and State Department Japan specialists supported Nixon's approach. The only serious opposition to change came from the Joint Chiefs of Staff (JCS) who "considered our Okinawa bases to be of inestimable value," not just for ongoing operations in Indochina "but for our whole strategic position in the Pacific." Yet, even the Joint Chiefs recognized that without the cooperation of the Japanese, the Okinawa base network could not be effective. They resolved to talk tough, hoping to get Nixon and Sato to agree on a plan that interfered as little as possible with base rights after reversion. The JCS wanted an agreement that permitted American use of the Okinawa bases for combat operations in Vietnam, a right to reintroduce nuclear weapons in an emergency, and an acknowledgement by Japan that under the mutual security treaty Tokyo had a stake in the defense of Taiwan and South Korea. They even hoped to get Japan to permit unrestricted use of Okinawa bases to mount operations in defense of Taiwan and South Korea.

Nixon accepted the logic of the argument made by the Joint Chiefs and worked to incorporate several of these points into an agreement. By March 1969, the NSC staff cautioned Kissinger and Nixon that domestic "pressures on Japan for reversion of Okinawa were now unstoppable." The risk of trying to retain the status quo far "outweigh the military cost of having somewhat less flexibility in operating the Okinawa bases under Japanese sovereignty." A refusal to accept Japanese demands for the island's return without nuclear weapons might result, the NSC warned, in "losing the bases altogether"—not only in the Ryukyus, but in Japan as well.

On April 30, 1969, as embodied in NSDM-13, Nixon settled on a formula that combined the approaches advocated by the Pentagon, the NSC, and the Japan desk officers in the State Department. The United States would return Okinawa in the near term if Japan granted general approval for American forces based there and on the home islands to carry out regional defense operations. The President was "prepared to consider, at the final stages of the negotiations, the withdrawal of [nuclear] weapons while maintaining emergency storage and transit rights, if other elements of the agreement were satisfactory."

A Complex Agreement

In a deft move, once Kissinger and Nixon set out the formal goal in April 1969, they allowed skilled career diplomats in the Tokyo embassy and the Department of State to negotiate details with their Japanese counterparts. By the time Nixon and Prime Minister Sato met in November, their subordinates had crafted a well-balanced agreement that only needed final blessing. Essentially, Washington wanted a broad measure of operational control over the bases on Okinawa, but would accept specific limits to secure this. Tokyo desired the restoration of sovereignty and the right to impose certain rules on the use of American bases. The most critical point was the withdrawal of nuclear weapons. In return, Japan would grant the United States wide latitude to use the bases for operations in Vietnam, Korea, or Taiwan.

In Washington, Undersecretary of State U. Alexis Johnson, a Japan-hand since the 1930s, developed the public scenario that Nixon and Sato eventually followed. When the two leaders met in Washington in November 1969, Johnson proposed, they should conclude their summit with a joint communiqué announcing the return of Okinawa by 1972. American bases remaining on the island would then fall under the terms of the U.S.-Japan mutual security treaty that barred storage (but not "transit") of U.S. nuclear weapons on Japanese soil without prior approval. To placate the Joint Chiefs, Sato would announce that the security of South Korea was "essential" to Japan and that of Taiwan was "important." If, by 1972, the Vietnam War continued, Tokyo would agree that "reversion would be accomplished without affecting the United States' efforts to assure the South Vietnamese people the opportunity to determine their own political future without outside interference." This would permit combat operations.

In addition to the joint statement, Sato would deliver a speech, written in consultation with Johnson, declaring that if the United States required bases in Japan proper to meet an attack on South Korea, the Japanese government would "decide its position positively and promptly." A similar "positive attitude" would apply to Taiwan. These assurances, while not legally binding, went well beyond previous Japanese commitments to regional security.

Sato hesitated to meet Nixon without prior assurance on the issue of nuclear weapons. Nixon insisted on holding back a promise to withdraw them until the Japanese agreed to all other terms. To give the Prime Minister political cover at home, Kissinger arranged a "leak" to a journalist who then wrote a story confirming that President Nixon would almost certainly agree to a "non-nuclear" return. Nevertheless, Nixon was reluctant to conclude an agreement without some assurance from Sato that Japan would "voluntarily" agree to restrain the export of synthetic fibers to the United States. This was an especially sensitive issue among southern textile producers who had contributed generously to Nixon's 1968 campaign. Not surprisingly, Japanese textile exporters saw this as an unfair restraint and pressed Sato to resist the American demands. To finesse the trade impasse, Kissinger and a "private" emissary representing Sato, Professor Wakaizumi Kei, met in advance of the summit and agreed that the Prime Minister would impose export restraints after he returned to Tokyo, rather than during the summit. This would insulate Sato from the charge that he sold out Japanese industry to regain Okinawa. But the Americans insisted on one further side agreement: Sato must sign a "secret" pledge to permit the reintroduction of nuclear weapons to Okinawa under emergency conditions.

A Complex Outcome

The Nixon-Sato summit proved to be one of the most harmonious meetings between a postwar President and Prime Minister. Sato promised to extend the mutual security treaty beyond 1970 and agreed on the installation of a "hot line" between Tokyo and Washington. Nixon offered to return Okinawa, without nuclear weapons, by 1972. Technical negotiations on legal, financial, and military base issues for implementing the return would begin immediately. (A technical agreement was signed on June 17, 1971; the Senate confirmed a treaty of return that November; and reversion took place on May 15, 1972.) U.S. military bases on the island would function "without detriment to the security of the Far East." Nixon pledged to honor the "particular sentiment of the Japanese people regarding nuclear weapons," but reserved the right to request their introduction in an emergency. No public mention was made of the secret pledge guaranteeing that right.

According to NSC staff member Roger Morris, as the formal talks ended, "Nixon asked Sato to join him and Kissinger alone in an anteroom of the Oval Office." The President then insisted on a "necessary private agreement." Nixon explained that the Pentagon, Congress, and American business interests considered his return of Okinawa to be a "give-away." As compensation, he wanted Sato to impose stringent limits on future textile exports. Although an American translator characterized Sato's response as vague, something like "I will do my best to solve the problem," Nixon and Kissinger took this as a firm commitment.

In fact, despite two years of growing American frustration, Sato could not convince his own Cabinet or Japanese manufacturers to accept U.S. limits. Nor would he publicly admit the connection between the Okinawa reversion and promised textile deals. Nixon interpreted this as a betrayal of trust and justification for his refusal to give Sato any hint of his secret opening to China. In fact, not until the fall of 1971, when the President threatened to impose the terms of the World War I-era Trading with the Enemy Act did the Sato government finally agreed to a pact on textile exports.

Despite this problem, Nixon's firm and fast handling of the Okinawa question virtually removed it as bilateral flashpoint after 1969. While awaiting reversion from 1970 to 1972, the Japanese government and public were cautious about criticizing Nixon's policy in Vietnam or taking any foreign policy stand that might antagonize the President or Senate before ratification and implementation of the treaty returning Okinawa.

In retrospect, Nixon's decisive setting of a policy goal at the inception of his Administration maximized cooperation among often contentious bureaucracies. The President made clear what he wanted and why, limiting opportunities for stalling. After setting the goal and timetable, Nixon deferred in most cases to career Japan specialists in the Department of State who negotiated the details of the reversion. Only when the President tried to use Okinawa as leverage to solve an extraneous foreign trade problem did his strategy and tactics falter. Ultimately, however, Nixon's determination to solve the Okinawa impasse in order to preserve the more important U.S.-Japan security relationship proved to be a highly successful policy.

Nixon's Opening to China

By Peter W. Rodman

"Only Nixon could go to China." That cliché contains much truth, but it was never as easy for President Richard M. Nixon as it may seem in retrospect. The "policy management" challenges included the following:

- ▶ Convincing the Chinese that Nixon, the notorious anti-Communist, was serious about a rapprochement—and for reasons relevant to Chinese concerns about the Soviet threat;
- ▶ Soothing U.S. allies in Asia who were bound to be shaken by the initiative (a problem compounded by the secrecy of the preparatory moves); and

► Reassuring his domestic political base—those American conservatives who remained deeply suspicious of Beijing and concerned about the survival and security of Taiwan.

Approaching China

The idea of an opening to China was not brand new—the Kennedy and Johnson Administrations had flirted with the idea. Yet they were stymied by various factors. One was the Democrats' fear of being denounced by Republicans for "softness on Communism." Another was the geopolitical confusion in their own minds. The Johnson Administration had settled on an anti-Chinese rationale for the U.S. involvement in Vietnam, and was aspiring to a détente with the Soviets. One can visualize President Hubert Humphrey in 1969 or 1970 unveiling an initiative toward Beijing in his characteristically enthusiastic way—and falling flat.

Nixon approached China in a quiet and deliberate way, beginning with small steps, which hinted at a new American attitude but did not require Chinese reciprocity. The Chinese in 1969 were still mired in the Cultural Revolution and were not in a position to respond. Nixon started using the official name "People's Republic of China" and quietly dropped the anti-China rationale for our Vietnam policy. He took small unilateral steps such as easing trade and travel restrictions. Nixon sent back-channel messages of a general nature through friendly heads of state who were trusted by both sides. He began a gradual unilateral withdrawal from Vietnam while pursuing negotiations with Hanoi.

It was the Soviet Union that provided the real impetus, however. Military clashes in 1969 along the Sino-Soviet border—where the Soviets had massed a million troops armed with nuclear weapons—shook the Chinese and prompted their interest in having other diplomatic options. The United States sent a crucial public signal in the fall of 1969—without communicating with Beijing—that it would oppose any Soviet military attack on China. This was a controversial move in the United States, where many still perceived the Soviets as the good guys. But the Chinese saw that Nixon's geopolitical calculation coincided with their vital interest. Diplomatic contacts resumed in 1970, first through Ambassadors in Warsaw and later through head-of-state intermediaries (Romania and most importantly, Pakistan).

Soothing Allies

Nixon paid a price for keeping the early contacts secret. The dramatic announcement of July 15, 1971—that Henry Kissinger had just been to Beijing and that Nixon was set to visit early the following year—was the first "Nixon shock" to hit Japan. (The second was unlinking the dollar from gold, one month later.) Allies such as Japan, South Korea, Taiwan, Indonesia, and Australia got no advance notice at all, and their leaders were publicly embarrassed.

Probably some method should have been devised to give key allied leaders some, even if brief, advance notice. But beyond that, it was not clear that there was a better option. The Japanese had every incentive and inclination to fear overtures to China; Taipei (and Moscow) had every incentive to sabotage it. Even Armin Meyer, U.S. Ambassador in Tokyo, who first learned the news over the radio while in a barber chair getting a haircut, conceded in his memoirs that Nixon was on-balance right to keep the Kissinger trip totally secret. The explosive nature of the breakthrough argued for maintaining maximum control over the way it was disclosed, so that the proper perspective and reassurance would be a part of the world's initial reaction. When the trip was disclosed, the United States both benefited from the display of diplomatic mastery and could emphasize that the interval between July and the President's trip the following year would be consumed with maximum consultations and concrete reassurances that allied interests would not be jeopardized.

The breakthrough should not have come as a complete surprise, moreover, given the expanding pattern of public signaling that had accompanied the behind-the-scenes evolution. When the back-channel contacts approached fruition in the spring of 1971, for example, the Chinese offered a dramatic public signal of their own—the famous invitation to the U.S. Ping-Pong team in April 1971. American liberals were delighted by the opening to China, having long had a (perhaps overly) favorable view of Chairman Mao Tse-tung's regime. But conservatives were shocked.

Nixon sought to manage this problem, first of all, by reassuring Taiwan (or the (Nationalist) Republic of China, as we knew it then) that he had no intention of jeopardizing its survival. This was borne out by the hedged language of the Nixon-Zhou Enlai Shanghai Communiqué of February 1972, as well as by Taiwan's continued flourishing to this day. Nixon made a point to brief key conservative American leaders like Arizona Senator Barry Goldwater and California Governor Ronald Reagan on a continuing basis. He persuaded them that Taiwan's interests would be preserved and that the initiative to Beijing had significant geopolitical value vis-à-vis both Moscow and Hanoi. Nixon also brought William F. Buckley, Jr., along as part of the press corps on his visit (although Buckley was never entirely won over).

More steps that Nixon took to shore up a bipartisan consensus included promoting visits to China by House Majority Leader Hale Boggs and Minority Leader Gerald Ford in June 1972, and later by Senate Majority Leader Mike Mansfield and Minority Leader Hugh Scott. China soon became a mecca for Congressional delegations of all stripes.

Lessons From Carter's Camp David Summit

By William B. Quandt

President Jimmy Carter invited President Anwar Sadat of Egypt and Prime Minister Menacham Begin of Israel to Camp David in the summer of 1978 for two main reasons. He was worried that the chance for Arab-Israeli peace was slipping away, and he was convinced that it was a waste of time to talk to anyone other than the top leaders who could make the decisions. Carter's was an act of frustration as much as one of statesmanship.

Carter had initially thought that the Camp David Summit could be concluded within a few days. He seemed to feel that the sense of historical drama, the isolation, the press blackout, and his own personal involvement would cause Sadat and Begin to rise to the occasion and make peace. It did not work out that way. Instead, each came to the Summit with deep suspicions of the other party and a determination to sway the American mediator to his side. After the first few days, Sadat and Begin did not meet.

Carter, who had expected to be little more than a facilitator, ended up being a draftsman and a forceful persuader. He personally wrote the first version of the Egyptian-Israeli treaty. And on at least one occasion he resorted to quite blunt pressure on each of the leaders.

The most innovative technique that was used by the American side was "the single negotiating text." The Americans would produce a draft, show it to one side, get their reactions, and undertake to produce another draft that would take the expressed concerns into account. The new draft would be shown to the other side, with the same rules—they could comment on it, but not dictate changes. The understanding was that the Americans would keep on producing drafts as long as it took to narrow the differences. Some 27 drafts later, all but two major issues had been resolved, at which point Carter met with Sadat and then with Begin to try to forge the final agreement.

On the whole, the outcome of the negotiations was a success for Carter and for the parties. Within months, an Egyptian-Israeli peace treaty was signed and has been in effect ever since. But the Americans and Egyptians had hoped that a serious step toward Israeli-Palestinian peace could also be made, and that hope was not fulfilled. In fact, the one serious error at Camp David on the American side was the careless handling of a commitment by Begin to stop building settlements in the West Bank. Carter thought that Begin has promised a prolonged freeze; Begin said he had only agreed to a three-month pause. The dispute generated much ill will and distrust—and left both Carter and Sadat intensely frustrated, to say nothing of the Palestinians who had little reason to welcome Camp David without the settlement freeze.

Personal Presidential Leadership

During the lengthy talks that preceded Camp David, and at Camp David itself, U.S. policy constantly had to adjust to two realities: (1) that events in the Middle East could not be easily controlled or influenced, so developments there frequently caught the Americans by surprise and obliged them to revise their strategies; and (2) that domestic American political realities intruded with particular force on the decision-making process regarding the Middle East. A President must simultaneously adjust his plans to the unpredictable twists and turns of Middle East politics and keep an eye on his domestic political base.

What seems possible and desirable in the first year of a President's term is likely to be seen as hopelessly ambitious by the third year. The result of these Middle East and domestic pressures is to move American policy away from grand designs with strong ideological content toward a less controversial, and less ambitious, middle ground that can win bipartisan public support, as well as acceptance by Arabs and Israelis. To do so, of course, is not always possible, as much as it might be politically desirable—so American policy toward the Middle East rarely manages to satisfy everyone that has an interest in shaping it. Presidents seem to tire of all the controversy generated by Middle East problems, and the seeming intractability of the issues is a source of much frustration.

The Camp David Accords demonstrate the limits of what in fact can be achieved by American-led diplomacy, even with a massive commitment of Presidential effort. But the Accords are also a reminder that diplomacy can produce results—if the will, the energy, and the creativity are there. The historical verdict on Camp David cannot be fully rendered, although with each passing year it seems to be more widely accepted as part of the new reality of the Middle East. By any standard, however, this remarkable adventure in summit diplomacy achieved more than most of its detractors have been willing to acknowledge, and less than its most ardent proponents have claimed.

★ ★ ★ ★ ★

Lessons for the Next Administration on the "Consequences of Japan Passing"

By Michael J. Green

For the last five years American policy makers have demonstrated a bipartisan commitment to the U.S.-Japan alliance. It is noteworthy that both the Republican and Democratic policy platforms list "strengthening the security relationship with Japan" as one of their planks. Almost everyone in diplomatic life in Washington agrees—the alliance with Japan is critical. And almost everyone has lost sight of one fundamental truth about our alliance with Japan—when it comes to security, the Japanese are increasingly thinking for themselves. That is not to say that Japan is looking for ways to break from the alliance. Just the opposite, Japan is looking for ways to hedge against inconsistent and incomplete American attention as Tokyo wakes up to what has turned out to be a less than benign post-Cold War neighborhood.

Several specific examples in recent years demonstrate the consequences of what journalists in Tokyo call American "Japan passing."

Ancient history offers the crux of the lesson, however. In the 5th century B.C., Thucydides noticed that Athens' smaller allies in the Pelopennesian War faced a dilemma. On the one hand, they feared entrapment in Athens' confrontation with rival Sparta. On the other hand, they feared that abandonment by Athens would expose them to Spartan expansion. These allies were therefore consumed with the business of winning security commitments from Athens in a way that did not pull them into Athens' fights.

The same dynamic dominated U.S.-Japan alliance politics throughout the Cold War. Japan secured an American defense commitment in the U.S.-Japan Mutual Security Treaty and sought continual reassurances from Washington of that commitment, but resisted any participation in NATO-style regional collective defense arrangements. Japanese political leaders from Yoshida Shigeru forward made full use of Article Nine of the post-World War II Constitution as their conscientious objector card. Although often frustrated with the ambiguity of Japan's security role in the Cold War, U.S. officials grew comfortable that Tokyo was squarely in the Western camp. When it came to pressing Tokyo to expand support for American bases or to acknowledge even an implicit role in the security of the region, U.S. officials expected to expend lots of "gaiatsu" (external pressure) for very incremental results. Japan's reticence to send even noncombatants to the Persian Gulf in 1990-1991 only reinforced this view of Japan as a passive security actor.

The striking thing about Japan's security culture today, however, is how quickly this passive cocoon-like existence is fading. Today the Japanese public and politicians are debating Constitutional revision; confronting the Chinese over missiles and contested territorial islands; warning South Korea and the United States to stay vigilant to the missile threat from North Korea; and otherwise standing up for "national interests" even if they put at some risk traditional economic interests. This new security realism derives from the immediacy of post-Cold War threats to Japan, in particular episodes such as the 1996 Taiwan Straits crisis and the August 1998 North Korean Taepodong missile launch over Japanese airspace. The Japanese people also are more sensitive to security threats because they are so much less secure about their traditional cocoon—the economy—which has been essentially flat for a decade. Finally, generational and political changes matter. The end of the Cold War eviscerated the old pacifist left and opened the door for a new generation of centrist politicians who are less encumbered by war guilt and are hungrier to establish Japan's status as a "normal" nation.

This change has meant opportunities for strengthening the U.S.-Japan alliance. In 1997 Washington and Tokyo successfully negotiated a revision of the bilateral Defense Guidelines to clarify Japanese rear-area support for U.S. operations in regional contingencies beyond the immediate defense of Japanese home islands. In 1998 the United States and Japan agreed to joint research on Theater Missile Defense. Throughout the late 1990s, the two allies have been strengthening intelligence cooperation as the new Japan Defense Intelligence

Headquarters has come into its own. These important incremental steps forward in the defense relationship required very little of the gaiatsu that accompanied similar consolidation of the alliance in the 1980s.

At the same time, however, U.S. officials working with Japan also have noted that gaiatsu is less effective on issues such as Host Nation Support (financial backing) than it used to be. If anything, gaiatsu seems to cause more of a backlash against the U.S. position. The most striking example of this was the Japanese Diet's decision to go ahead with autonomous spy satellite development after press reports of American opposition. In fact, this occurred in large part because of the U.S. opposition. The United States no longer has to push for Japan to strengthen its defense capabilities, and just saying "no" to certain capabilities, does not work the way it once did.

This trend is not all bad, of course, and may be long overdue. But the next Administration must now pay close attention to how its defense commitment to Japan is being perceived in Tokyo. Or looked at another way, the next Administration must recognize that Japan is far more serious about its own defense than it used to be—and Japan is increasingly more serious than the United States appears to be.

Several specific examples in recent history bear this out:

▶ In 1997 tensions between Japan and China rose over the contested Senkaku/Diaoyutai Islands. China was sending semi-official "research vessels" around the islands, and Japanese right-wing activists were building small light houses and planting Japanese flags. Sensitive to domestic nationalism over the issue and reluctant to concede the legal issues of administrative control over the islands, neither side backed down. The Japanese media and conservative politicians pressed Washington for a clarification that Article V of the Mutual Security Treaty (covering the defense of Japan) would "apply" to the Senkaku/Diaoyutai Islands. The U.S. State Department appropriately chose to remain neutral in the territorial dispute, but mistakenly argued that Article V did not apply. This was clearly wrong since earlier U.S. policy had acknowledged the Senkaku chain as being under the "administrative" control of Japan and therefore covered. The State Department would not budge, however, and eventually the Pentagon declared that Article V did, in fact, apply.

▶ In June 1998 President Bill Clinton embarked on an extended visit to China designed to repair bilateral relations with Beijing after the difficult Taiwan Straits confrontations of 1996. To demonstrate his Administration's commitment to the relationship, the President agreed to Chinese requests that he not visit any other Asian countries, including Japan, which traditionally figures into any significant summitry in the region. Moreover, in Beijing the President used the occasion of a press conference with his host, President Jiang Zemin, to criticize Japan for its failure to stimulate economic growth. Whether or not this gesture was deliberate is a matter for future historians to determine, but in terms of "loss of face" it was devastating for Prime Minister Hashimoto in Tokyo. The Japanese Prime Minister later told Secretary of State Madeleine Albright that he did not mind, but the damage to his credibility in the region and at home eventually proved fatal. The press in Japan coined a new phrase that has recurred continually since—"Japan passing."

▶ In August 1998 North Korea launched a long-range ballistic missile over Japan in a failed attempt to put a satellite in orbit. The launch galvanized Japan's growing insecurity about North Korea and led Tokyo to unilaterally suspend funding for the Korean Peninsula Energy Development Organization (KEDO). Eager to prevent the launch from undermining the 1994 Agreed Framework, in which North Korea exchanged its Yongbyon nuclear capability for a proliferation-proof set of two light water reactors, Washington pressed Tokyo to maintain its commitment to KEDO. The U.S. side knew well that Tokyo had every interest in the Agreed Framework and KEDO, and pressured Tokyo to abandon its position. Meanwhile, the Clinton Administration reached an agreement with Pyongyang to "accelerate" KEDO construction to satisfy North Korean complaints about delays. News of the "acceleration" infuriated Tokyo, which was supposed to foot $1 billion of the cost. Moreover, the U.S. and Japanese intelligence agencies engaged in a ridiculous and costly debate about whether the North Korean launch was a "missile test" or a less nefarious "satellite launch." The threat to Japan was the same either way, of course, but Washington's unwillingness to acknowledge that threat did great damage to the credibility of the alliance, and established the political environment for Japan's first indigenous spy satellite system.

There are other examples that could also be used, but the pattern should be clear. To put things in the proper perspective, it must be restated that U.S. officials have not abandoned the defense commitment to Japan. For most, it is a sine qua non for U.S. engagement and forward presence in Asia. In addition, these incidents did not present immediate threats of war against Japan. Tokyo's own response to the three mini-crises was hardly strategic or in Japan's own long-term interests. Finally, the United States did eventually recover from each incident. In the Senkaku confrontation, the Pentagon reasserted the original U.S. position. In the case of the macroeconomic criticism, the Clinton Administration moved to tone down its rhetoric in 1999—it recognized the counterproductive nature of "shaming" Japan. And in the case of the Taepodong, the Administration agreed to Congressional demands to establish a review of policy and a trilateral coordinating mechanism with Japan and South Korea.

It should be equally clear, however, that there are consequences for the U.S.-Japan alliance from excessive complacency about—or contempt of—Japan's own emerging views of its security. Japan is not about to break from the alliance. There simply are no better options than alliance for either partner. However, America has little interest in seeing Japan develop redundant capabilities or maverick diplomacy because of doubts about the U.S. commitment to Japanese security. An expanded political and even security role for Japan in Asia is in U.S. interest, but the expanded role should be based on confidence in the alliance, not hedging against a fickle Washington.

To be sure, the political terrain in Tokyo for reasserting the U.S. commitment to the alliance is not ideal. Japanese political leadership is weak. Coalition politics are proving to be highly fluid and unpredictable. Japan's sense of insecurity is only reinforcing risk aversion about operations like East Timor. Nobody in Tokyo is putting new attitudes about security into a clear national strategy (except perhaps Ozawa Ichiro, whose political future is not clear at all). And the prevailing mood in Tokyo is that Japan should demonstrate a more independent identity, not rely more on the alliance—even as the U.S. view of the alliance remains a critical determinant of Japan's own security policies.

The policy tasks for the next Administration related to the alliance require a rethinking of both fundamentals and process:

Fundamentals: The next Administration should push for a U.S. government consensus on the proper role for Japan and then articulate that clearly to Tokyo. This should include long-term access to U.S. bases and a continuation of current roles and missions within the alliance. A long-term U.S. position of supporting Constitutional revision in Japan and an incrementally expanding Japanese role in areas such as peacekeeping, humanitarian relief, and support for U.S. operations throughout the region should be pursued.

Process: Senior U.S. officials must establish working relationships with their counterparts in Japan that make certain neither side is surprised by the actions of the other and that in most cases they can expect the other's support. This means clearly explaining U.S. objectives on key security problems such as Taiwan to the Japanese side, and then taking into full account Japanese objectives and concerns. The working relationship also means a fuller strategic dialogue on possible contingencies and responses. In short, it will require the next Administration to demonstrate a commitment to Japan on security issues that are not high priorities for the United States, so that Japanese support can be counted on when there are crises that are critical to U.S. interests.

Reagan and Lebanon

By Peter W. Rodman

President Ronald Reagan sent U.S. forces to Lebanon as peace-keepers in the summer of 1982, and withdrew them under humiliating circumstances in early 1984. This debacle occurred because of a policy failure in two dimensions: a miscalculation of the evolving political circumstances on the ground in Lebanon, and a bureaucratic stalemate in Washington that Reagan was unwilling to break.

The Pitfalls of Peacekeeping

U.S. troops were sent to Lebanon in benign circumstances as neutral peacekeepers. Israel had invaded Lebanon in June 1982 to crush the Palestine Liberation Organization (PLO). In August a multinational force (MNF) was created, with U.S. participation, to shield the controlled withdrawal of PLO fighters from Lebanon. (The United States contributed about 800 Marines, who accompanied British, French, and Italian forces.) Israel, Syria, all factions in Lebanon, and most Arab governments endorsed the exercise. Reagan emphasized, with justification, that there was "no intention or expectation that U.S. Armed Forces [would] become involved in hostilities." As the MNF was completing this mission in mid-September, 700 to 800 Palestinian civilians were massacred by Lebanese Christian militias in the refugee camps at Sabra and Shatila near Beirut. A second MNF deployment was immediately organized, this time with the goal of bolstering Lebanese government authority in the Beirut area. The United States contributed 1,200 Marines to this effort, with the same—legitimate—expectation that this was a neutral humanitarian mission with broad support and minimal risk of involvement in hostilities.

Subsequently the political ground shifted dramatically, yet the U.S. government did not draw appropriate conclusions about the role and vulnerability of its forces in Lebanon.

Secretary of State George Shultz helped Israel and Lebanon negotiate a peace treaty, signed on May 17, 1983, under which all Israeli forces were to withdraw from Lebanon in exchange for peace. But this treaty was immediately denounced by Syria, which egged on its radical allies in Lebanon to seek the forcible overthrow of the government of President Amin Gemayel. Syria, rearmed by the Soviets, had recovered its bearings after its humiliation at Israel's hands during Israel's initial 1982 invasion. By this time, moreover, the Israeli public was tiring of the Lebanon adventure. Thus, the balance of forces in Lebanon had tilted badly, and the peace agreement did not reflect the new geopolitical reality. The U.S. Marines and their MNF allies found themselves in the middle of an escalating war around Beirut.

Bureaucratic Stalemate

At this point, the United States faced a choice. If the Israeli-Lebanese peace treaty was strategically important to us, then there was a case for using our military leverage to support the Lebanese government. Secretary of State Shultz made this case, arguing that to allow Syria and its radical allies to topple a U.S.-brokered peace agreement would set an ominous precedent for the Arab-Israeli peace process and embolden radical forces throughout the Middle East.

Secretary of Defense Caspar Weinberger and the Joint Chiefs of Staff, in contrast, wanted U.S. forces in no such role. Perhaps with an eye toward their productive and growing military relations with Persian Gulf Arabs, Weinberger and the Chiefs did not want U.S. forces to seem to be fighting a war on Israel's side against Syria. They wanted the MNF and the Marines to pull out.

Either Shultz's policy or Weinberger's policy would have been a coherent choice. What Reagan did, however, was evade the choice and try to split the difference. Every time a specific decision was presented, the President agreed to an incremental increase in U.S. military pressures but never a decisive one. The battleship *New Jersey*, for example, joined the naval task force off of the Lebanese coast, but it used its 16-inch guns only sporadically—never in a sustained, systematic fashion to affect the battle. The Pentagon interpreted the rules of engagement restrictively because it opposed continued involvement.

The result was that the United States was engaged enough to be clearly taking sides and staking its prestige, but was not enough to win. The Marines on the ground started taking casualties, and Congressional support began eroding. Bloody terrorist attacks on the U.S. embassy (in April 1983) and on the Marine barracks (in October) finally shattered domestic support. Reagan withdrew the U.S. forces in February 1994 as the Gemayel government was engulfed.

Assessment

Peacekeeping is sometimes a form of war, as Eliot A. Cohen has observed. Just as in Somalia in 1993, what started as a relatively riskless humanitarian involvement turned into something else as the political context changed on the ground. The policy requirement is to draw the proper conclusions: Do we still want to be there? If not, we should get out. If yes, we need to ensure that our military exertion is adequate to the goal that we have decided is important.

President Reagan, however, was reluctant to order the U.S. military to fight a war that their leaders did not want to fight. Yet he also was persuaded by Shultz's argument that the United States had a strategic stake in the outcome of this Lebanese struggle; thus he was reluctant to "cut and run" until the very end when defeat was imposed. In other words, Reagan did not in this case step up to his responsibility to make a clear-cut choice between two distinct — and incompatible — policies.

★   ★   ★   ★   ★

Strategic Partners: Reagan and Nakasone

By Lou Cannon

Few modern leaders from different cultures have bonded as successfully as Ronald Reagan and Yasuhiro Nakasone. The U.S. President and the Japanese Prime Minister met in January 1983 in Washington and Reagan paid a reciprocal visit to Japan in November of the same year. At Reagan's initiative the two leaders were soon on a first-name basis, addressing each other as "Ron" and "Yasu." Reagan and Nakasone exchanged so many one-liners that reporters called their joint appearances the "Ron and Yasu Show."

The cordiality between Reagan and Nakasone contributed to constructive discussions during a tense time in U.S.-Japanese relationships. Early in 1983, the United States was emerging from a severe recession that had fueled protectionist sentiments, directed largely at Japan. The U.S. trade deficit with Japan then stood at $20 billion, roughly a fifth of the current deficit, and American unemployment was 10 percent, more than twice the present rate. Despite Reagan's free-trade leanings, he had yielded in 1981 to pressure from the auto industry and accepted import quotas on Japanese cars—disguised with the fig leaf of "voluntary" restraints. By 1983, other embattled industries were clamoring for protection and urging the Administration to demand that Japan open its markets more widely to U.S. exports.

For its part, Japan resented being the scapegoat for the U.S. trade deficit. Guided by the useful counsel of Mike Mansfield, whom Reagan had kept as U.S. Ambassador to Japan, Secretary of State George Shultz was sympathetic to the Japanese view. Shultz noted that the U.S. trade deficit had soared to new highs during a decade when Japan had opened its markets more than ever before. At the time, Japan was importing $7 billion annually in U.S. agricultural products and was the leading importer of American meat. Japanese agricultural interests were as protectionist (and politically influential) as American automakers and didn't want further lowering of barriers. Japan's leaders saw large trade surpluses as the means of maintaining a high employment rate. And Japanese consumers were the mirror images of their American counterparts—they saved more than they spent and resisted buying foreign goods. Beyond economic concerns, Nakasone was trying to build up Japan's air and sea defenses in the face of heavy pressure from the Soviet Union.

As a result, it was widely believed that the United States and Japan faced obstacles that could not be bridged merely by friendly feelings between the nations' leaders. In a sense that was certainly true—extensive negotiating would be required between Shultz, Japanese Foreign Minister Shintaro Abe, and the trade and military experts on both sides before agreements could be reached. But the good will between Reagan and Nakasone gave the negotiators the necessary running room. It helped that Nakasone had made an exceptional impression in Washington—an editorial on January 23, 1983, in *The Washington Post* called him "that unusual leader with a coherent vision and considerable political courage."

Reciprocal Friendship

By the time Reagan made his 1983 reciprocal visit to Tokyo, Nakasone was in political trouble. Taking advantage of the President's visit to draw attention to his own world status, Nakasone compared Reagan to a baseball pitcher and himself to a catcher who together formed "a formidable battery over the Pacific" and were "excellent team-mates of the free world." The President obligingly played straight man by replying that he sometimes didn't know "who is pitching and who is catching," a line that was a hit with the Japanese. The Reagan visit was extensively televised—a long segment was devoted to an interlude at Nakasone's rustic retreat outside Tokyo where, after a tea ceremony, the Nakasones and the Reagans were served a six-course lunch. On November 11, 1983, Reagan became the first U.S. President to address the Japanese Diet. He hit all the right notes. After denouncing the "folly" of protectionism, Reagan declared that "Japanese-American friendship is forever." He was applauded loudly when he said, "Anuclear war can never be won and must never be fought."

Useful developments flowed from these 1983 reciprocal visits and a subsequent meeting in Los Angeles 2, 1985, after both leaders had weathered the elections of 1984. A first step was the lowering of trade barriers on additional agricultural products in 1983; a bigger step was taken in 1986 (after protracted and difficult negotiations) that improved U.S. access to Japan's telecommunications and pharmaceutical markets. Nakasone meanwhile joined with Reagan in advocating a "strategic partnership" with the United States, which was more preferable to Asian nations with enduring memories of World War II than a unilateral Japanese buildup. But it was Japan that needed reassuring on nuclear issues, especially after the "walk in the woods" formula discussed by U.S. and Soviet negotiators in 1982 that proposed reducing Soviet intermediate-range nuclear missiles in Europe but not in Asia. Reagan assured Nakasone that he would not ignore Japan's needs, and the 1987 Intermediate-Range Nuclear Forces agreement between the United States and the Soviet Union accounted for Japanese concerns.

Much has happened since the Reagan Presidency to change the U.S.-Japan relationship. The intervening years have been unkind to Japan, once overestimated as the global menace of "Japan, Inc." and now too often dismissed as an economic relic. Leaders have come and gone on both sides, the U.S. trade deficit with Japan has persisted, and China has become the region's dominant power. Nonetheless, the United States and Japan remain strategic partners, and the relationship between the two nations remains crucial to Asian security. This relationship reached its apex in the Reagan-Nakasone years. In his memoirs Secretary Shultz said that it heralded the beginning of the great "global intertwining" that would become the salient feature of the new century.

Summary

Although there are limits to the power of personal diplomacy, a constructive relationship between national leaders can create a climate of good will and encourage technical negotiators to find solutions. The bond between President Reagan and Prime Minister Nakasone was a catalyst for improved relations between the United States and Japan during the critical decade of the 1990s.

The New Era: Reagan and Gorbachev

By Lou Cannon

Of all the associations forged between world leaders in the second half of the 20th century, the most fateful was the symbiotic relationship of American President Ronald Reagan and Soviet leader Mikhail Gorbachev. Born of adversity and nourished by necessity, this unlikely relationship overcame ideological suspicions and flourished in the twilight of the Cold War it helped to end.

What happened seems inevitable now; it didn't then. In the words of British historian C.V. Wedgwood, "History is written backward but lived forward. Those who know the end of the story can never know what it was like at the time." Don Oberdorfer began *The Turn*, his seminal book on the end of the Cold War, with this quotation. He then traced the declining course of U.S.-Soviet relations during Reagan's first term, when the President and a series of Soviet leaders traded insults and took their nations to the brink. The low point came on September 1, 1983, when a Korean Air Lines jumbo jet with 269 people aboard, including 61 Americans, wandered into Soviet airspace and was shot down by a fighter jet. This "crime against humanity," as Reagan described it, set off a war scare that reached its height two months later when the United States and its allies conducted Exercise Able Archer. This secret military exercise was a routine test of communications and command procedures for using nuclear weapons in case of war, but the Soviets interpreted it as a rehearsal for a U.S. nuclear attack. Although nothing came of this scare, it is a reminder that the Cold War could have ended in a nuclear conflict in which, in a famous phrase, the survivors would have envied the dead. That it instead ended peaceably was the result of a determination by Reagan and Gorbachev to prevent a cataclysmic outcome.

Ostensibly, Reagan and Gorbachev—products of different generations, experiences, and political systems—had little in common. Reagan had taken a unique path to the Presidency, advancing from humble small-town beginnings in Illinois to successful careers as a radio sports announcer, movie actor, and television host before he entered politics. Fervently anti-Communist, he had as President described the Soviet Union as an "evil empire" and "the focus of evil in the modern world." Gorbachev was born to peasant stock in the northern Caucasus. His grandfathers were arrested and tortured during Stalin's collectivization of private farms. Later, the region was overrun by German invaders during World War II, and his brother was drafted and killed in the war. Gorbachev nonetheless prospered—first as an award-winning farm worker, then as a law student, and later as a member of the legal faculty at Moscow State University. As he advanced up the Communist ranks, Gorbachev became a protege of Yuri Andropov, former head of the KGB and Soviet leader during the period of heightened U.S.-Soviet tensions in 1983. Gorbachev was well read, reform minded, and keenly aware of Soviet deficiencies. During a visit to London in 1984, he had impressed British Prime Minister Margaret Thatcher, who conveyed her opinion to Reagan.

The New Era Arrives

On the evening of March 10, 1985, ailing Soviet leader Konstantin Chernenko died and was replaced the next day by Gorbachev, the fourth Soviet leader in the four years President Reagan had been in office. Reagan had never met any of them, although he had reached out to Leonid Brezhnev early in his Presidency by writing him a conciliatory letter. According to Alexander Haig, then Reagan's Secretary of State, the hand-written draft "talked about a world without nuclear weapons [and about] disarmament." This alarmed Haig, who persuaded the President to soften the passage, but the excised words were a vital clue to Reagan's thinking. Reagan, although not strong on technological detail, knew what he wanted to accomplish. He viewed the military buildup he had advocated to confront Soviet expansionism as a means, not an end. The President was convinced that the Soviet Union could not compete with the United States and that the buildup would lead the Soviets to the bargaining table.

Brezhnev died in November 1982. His successor, Andropov, died in February 1984. He was followed by Chernenko, who was in power just more than a year. With the U.S. military buildup a reality, Reagan anticipated meeting a Soviet leader but complained that "they kept dying on me." Within days after Gorbachev's ascension to power, U.S. and Soviet negotiators began planning what would become the first of four productive summits—in Geneva, Reykjavik, Washington, and Moscow. According to Nancy Reagan, an expert witness on the behavior of her husband, Ronald Reagan was impressed with Gorbachev and sensed his "moral dimension" when they first met at Geneva in November 1985. Gorbachev was also impressed. Pavel Palazchenko, his trusted interpreter, recalled at the 1993 Princeton Conference on the end of the Cold War that he was with Gorbachev and other Soviet officials at Geneva when one of them launched into a harsh criticism of Reagan and his policies. Gorbachev interrupted, saying, "This is the President of the United States, elected by the American people." Palazchenko went on to say that Gorbachev's respect for Reagan had a significant effect at Geneva and subsequent summits.

Oberdorfer and many others (I among them) have written extensively about the summits and the evolving Reagan-Gorbachev relationship. This relationship led to the 1987 Intermediate Nuclear Force (INF) treaty, the first agreement to reduce U.S. and Soviet nuclear arsenals, and in time to the end of the Cold War and the collapse of the Soviet Union. Particularly notable are the accounts of George Schultz, Kenneth Adelman, and Jack Matlock, all of whom played significant roles in what transpired. These participants emphasized various factors: the U.S. military buildup; the shaky economic condition of the Soviet Union; Reagan's imaginative Strategic Defense Initiative (or "Star Wars"), which threatened the Soviets with expensive technological competition; and the shared commitment to freedom expressed by Reagan, Thatcher, and West German Chancellor Helmut Kohl, among others. Gorbachev realized that the Soviet Union could not survive without altering course—he had the courage to launch reforms that he could not control and the decency (the "moral dimension" seen by Reagan) to refuse to preserve communism by force of arms.

Idealism at the Center

No comprehensive assessment is possible in this short space. My assertion here is that the personal relationship between Reagan and Gorbachev, and their mutual conviction that the superpowers were on a path to nuclear conflict, had much to do with the Cold War ending in peace. It is notable that both leaders downplayed ideology to achieve results. This did not mean that they abandoned their positions. Gorbachev remained committed to socialism and never accepted Reagan's view that the Strategic Defense Initiative, even if shared, would make the world safer. Reagan discarded his harsh rhetoric about the Soviet Union without abandoning his conviction. He expressed in a memorable speech at the Palace of Westminster on June 8, 1981, that "the march of freedom and democracy...will leave Marxism-Leninism on the ash heap of history." I was a few feet away from the two leaders as they strolled through Red Square at the Moscow summit in 1988 when Reagan was asked (in a probably planted question) if he still considered the Soviet Union to be an evil empire. Reagan replied that he had been talking about a different time and that this was a "new era." And so it was.

As to nuclear weapons, both Reagan and Gorbachev acknowledged that the doctrine of mutual assured destruction (or MAD) had preserved the peace but that it was improbable that this could continue in perpetuity with thousands of nuclear missiles on hair-trigger alert. Sooner or later, one side or the other would launch its weapons through accident or miscalculation, leaving the other side with a decision of whether to engage in mutual annihilation. Because they feared the status quo, Reagan and Gorbachev were willing to take risks to change it, as they did most notably at the 1986 Reykjavik summit, where the two leaders galloped ahead of subordinates in discussions about banning all nuclear weapons. They didn't quite succeed, but a summit that was seen as a failure led to the INF treaty and subsequent nuclear arms reductions.

Alexander Bessmertnykh, first deputy to Soviet Foreign Minister Eduard Shevardnadze at Reykjavik, observed at the Princeton Conference that the Cold War was ended by human beings, not impersonal forces. Reagan and Gorbachev, he said, "each had their own ideals which they tried to follow all through their lives. The ideals were not similar, but the dedication to those ideals was similar. They both believed in something. They were not just men who could trim their sails and go any way the wind blows....This is what they immediately sensed in each other, and this is why they made good partners." Expressing his admiration of Reagan, Bessmertnykh said, "I was across the table at all the summits and followed this President for all those years, and I personally admired the man very much. He was a good politician. He was a good diplomat. He was very dedicated. And if it were not for Reagan, I don't think we would have been able to reach the agreements in arms control that we reached later, because of his idealism, because he thought that we should really do away with nuclear weapons. Gorbachev believed in that. Reagan believed in that. The experts didn't believe, but the leaders did."

Summary

In an age when nuclear superpowers have the capacity to destroy civilization, the self-interests of nations are also the self-interests of mankind. The idealism and courage of leaders, and their willingness to take risks for peace, can be decisive. The Cold War could have turned out differently than it did. That it ended peaceably is due in large measure to the ideals, determination, and far-sightedness of Ronald Reagan and Mikhail Gorbachev.

The U.S.-Panama Crisis: Lessons in Effectiveness of Coercive Diplomatic Measures

By Gina Marie L. Hatheway

Introduction and Background

On December 20, 1989, the U.S. launched a military intervention targeted at General Manuel Noriega and the Panamanian Defense Forces (PDF) to: protect American lives, defend democracy in Panama, apprehend Noriega and bring him to trial on drug-related charges, and ensure the integrity of the Panama Canal Treaties. In citing these reasons for intervention, President Bush claimed that Operation Just Cause was the last resort in U.S. efforts to remove Noriega and his regime from power. An analysis of this operation provides valuable insights into the difficulties of a superpower to effectively respond to the actions of a small dictatorship, and the failure of coercive measures short of intervention to achieve our foreign policy goals.

U.S.-Panama relations date back to 1903, when the U.S. became involved in Panama's independence from Colombia because of U.S. strategic interests in building a trans-oceanic canal. During the course of the century, the U.S. regularly engaged in Panamanian politics, and at times resolved Panama's internal political problems through diplomacy and/or the use of limited military force. Until the 1990s (the Panama Canal Treaties called for the U.S. to withdraw all military personnel and bases from Panama by December 31, 1999), the U.S. military had maintained over a dozen military installations and over 12,000 troops in Panama. While the U.S. was willing to negotiate the Panama Canal Treaties in 1977 with then dictator General Omar Torrijos, relations with Panama deteriorated when his successor, Noriega, further began to restrict democratic practices. In 1987, when a high-ranking PDF officer broke ranks with Noriega and publicly accused him of human rights abuses, election fraud, and drug trafficking, relations between the countries began to degenerate into a full-blown crisis.

U.S.-Panama Crisis and U.S. Coercive Measures

During the 1987-89 crisis, the U.S. Government pursued a series of different coercive measures against Noriega and his regime: (1) The U.S. Congress cut off economic and military assistance in late 1987; (2) The effects of President Reagan's orders to freeze Panamanian assets in U.S. banks and to implement U.S. economic sanctions in March 1988; (3) The effects of the Executive Order issued in April 1988 through the International Emergency Economic Powers Act (IEEPA) which prohibited, among other things, all direct and indirect payments by all people and organizations in the U.S. to the Noriega regime; (4) A handful of U.S. emissary missions by the Defense Department and State Department demanded that Noriega change his behavior and/or step down; (5) The Miami and in Tampa federal grand juries' drug indictments in February 1988; (6) A series of negotiations with the State Department in the spring of 1988 which further urged Noriega to resign; (7) The U.S. attempt in 1988 to pursue covert operations; and (8) U.S. military build-up and the execution of psychological operations in the summer of 1989 intended to send a signal to Noriega and his supporters that the U.S. was losing its patience and would not tolerate his continued intransigence. All of these measures fell short of changing Noriega's behavior and ultimately removing him from power.

Noriega also withstood internal Panamanian pressures including two military coup attempts, an attempt to oust him by the civilian Panamanian President, and efforts by the Organization of American States to negotiate his voluntary withdrawal from power.

Why Coercive Measures Fell Short of the Objective

Four key issues undermined the U.S. strategy to oust Noriega: (1) U.S. demands shifted during the course of the crisis from urging him to change his anti-democratic practices to demanding that he give up power; (2) the timing of the crisis during a Presidential election year delayed efforts by the Administration to develop a well-thought-out and coordinated strategy to preserve democracy and protect U.S. military and canal interests in Panama; (3) U.S. Government inter-agency differences, particularly between the more aggressive, hawkish State Department and the more restrained Defense Department, weakened overall policy; and (4) Noriega's determination to stay in power increased as the crisis escalated.

First, with the denunciation of the Noriega regime by a high-ranking PDF member in June 1987, the U.S. Government initially demanded that Noriega restore basic democratic principles. The crisis was considered by most U.S. Government agencies involved to be a Panamanian crisis that warranted a solution by the Panamanian people. When the federal grand juries in Miami and Tampa Bay issued federal drug indictments against Noriega in February 1988, the State Department specifically demanded that Noriega voluntarily resign. The indictments came as a surprise not only to the American public and Noriega but also to U.S. Government agencies including the Central Intelligence Agency (CIA) and certain Drug Enforcement Administration (DEA) offices that still pursued relations with him. The political situation was now a U.S.-Panama crisis. After a failed attempt by the State Department to negotiate Noriega's voluntary departure from power in May 1988, it became clear to some U.S. Government agencies that Noriega's removal from power—either voluntarily or involuntarily—was the only solution to the crisis. However, not until after Noriega committed election fraud in the May 1989 Presidential elections in Panama and ordered his Dignity Battalion to beat the opposition candidates in the streets did the U.S. Government unite behind the demand for Noriega's removal. The publication of pictures of Vice Presidential candidate Guillermo Ford, covered in blood, was a defining moment; the world had seen the real face of the bankrupt Noriega regime.

Second, the timing of the political crisis during a Presidential election year in the U.S. complicated and delayed the execution of the coercive diplomatic strategy. As is often the case every four years, the political focus in the U.S. was more on the Presidential elections than on foreign policy crises. Efforts by the Democratic Party to elevate the Administration's handling of the crisis to a campaign issue did not resonate with the electorate. Noriega took full advantage of the opportunity to raise the morale of the PDF by harassing U.S. military personnel and civilians in Panama without engendering any reaction by the U.S. Government. This harassment continued until the May 1989 Panamanian elections, after which President Bush ordered additional military personnel to Panama and ordered the Defense Department to execute a series of psychological operations to demonstrate U.S. military force and capabilities.

Third, different U.S. agencies had different interests with regard to the Noriega regime. The State Department and Members of the U.S. Congress wanted to cut all ties and communication with the regime, and were willing to use military force. The Defense Department, certain DEA offices, and intelligence community agencies took a less aggressive approach, claiming that the U.S. could still work with Noriega to achieve regional objectives in fighting communism and apprehending drug traffickers. They also felt they could convince Noriega to change his anti-democratic practices. In fact, the latter agencies continued to engage Noriega during the crisis, sending mixed signals to him that while certain arms of the U.S. Government were pressing him to step down or face serious consequences, other agencies were willing to excuse his reprehensible actions.

Finally, Noriega's determination to stay in power strengthened as the crisis escalated. Noriega had been successful in undermining the U.S. coercive diplomatic strategy for over two and a half years by seeking outside help from other countries including Nicaragua, Cuba, and Libya, and by raising charges of Yankee imperialism through propaganda against the U.S. For example, banners portraying a picture of the U.S. Ambassador to Panama dressed as a cowboy shooting Santa Claus served as Noriega's metaphor for how he saw the U.S. role in Panama. The drug indictments also complicated the situation by effectively leaving Noriega no desirable choice other than to stay in power. The U.S. Congress was on record against the 1988 negotiations have him step down in exchange for the dropping of the drug indictments; several Cabinet officials and the Vice President shared this view. Noriega was aware of the disagreement and concluded it was safer for him to remain in power.

Decision to Intervene—The Last Option

The Reagan Administration had been divided on U.S. objectives regarding the situation in Panama, and it never came to the conclusion that Noriega had to be removed from power. According to senior Reagan Administration officials, one weakness of the Administration was that Reagan preferred to forestall decisions of importance when his senior advisors and departments disagreed. Interagency differences coupled with a lack of specific leadership from the President resulted in policy paralysis. Conversely, President Bush and his Cabinet were interested from the outset in ending the crisis. The decision was made that Noriega had to be removed from power, and a strategy was created to realize this objective.

Mindful that the crisis was intensifying, President Bush agreed to an escalating "step by step" effort to get rid of Noriega by sending additional U.S. troops to Panama, bringing military families back to the U.S., and executing a series of psychological warfare operations. By the time a new Commander-in-Chief of the U.S. Southern Command arrived in Panama in October 1989, the Bush Administration already had a clear vision of what they wanted him to do: protect American lives and property, and defend the Panama Canal.

While there were a few specific missions that were not successfully executed, including one that resulted in the loss of Navy Seals, the U.S. military intervention achieved all four objectives outlined by President Bush. This success was demonstrated by a well-planned and coordinated operation that resulted in a low number of casualties (23 U.S. military, 3 U.S. civilian, and approximately 300 Panamanian deaths). Within the first hours of the operation, the military dictatorship was toppled and a democratic government installed. Within two weeks, General Noriega was arrested and sent to the U.S., where he would later be tried and convicted of drug trafficking charges. Dubbed unofficially the "Ma Bell" offensive, senior U.S. military officials prevented a major loss of life by phoning PDF commanders at various garrisons and convincing them to surrender. This telephone campaign led to the surrender of approximately 75% of Panamanian forces. Just ten days into the intervention, the Administration began to rapidly withdraw forces, and by mid-February, when the operation ended, U.S. forces in Panama were below the pre-invasion level.

Despite the fact that Noriega's fate was already determined, the fate of the PDF remained undecided until late 1989. The U.S. Government had encouraged the PDF—originally seen as part of the solution to ending the crisis—to remove Noriega from power. However, after the October 1989 failed military coup attempt and later the killing of an American soldier by PDF forces, the PDF was seen as part of the problem as well. U.S. Government officials concluded that the PDF as an institution had to be destroyed.

Lessons Learned

First, concerted efforts by the U.S. Government showed clearly that the necessary resources can be marshaled to apprehend a dictator and bring him to justice. But the initial lack of a clear objective resulted in an overall weakened strategy which enabled Noriega to face up to a superpower and prolong the crisis. Before May 1989, U.S. pressure was inconsistent, and there was a lack of real political will to end the crisis.

Second, U.S. coercive threats lacked credibility. During 1987-88, the U.S. government pursued each policy action as part of a broader try/see approach. It is probable that had a series of massive pressures been applied against Noriega during early 1988, when he was weak, they may have worked to convince him to step down. During a six-week period in the spring of 1988, Noriega survived a military coup attempt, an ouster attempt by President Eric Arturo DelValle, the announcement of U.S. economic sanctions, and the announcement of drug indictments. A sense of urgency followed by an ultimatum at this time may have had a more profound effect. Instead, U.S. strategy lacked a specific, time-limited demand and a threat of punishment for non-compliance.

Third, high expectations of a Panamanian solution to the crisis were overly optimistic; senior Defense officials in 1988 could not understand why Panamanians were not willing to use violence to remove Noriega from power, as has been the case in neighboring countries. Historically, Panama has not been a violent country. During the crisis, many Panamanians, accustomed to external solutions to internal strife, wondered what the Americans were going to do to get rid of Noriega. Panamanian passivity was further illustrated when the U.S. intervened military and the PDF put up at most token resistance. Thus, the U.S. Government must fully understand the will and realistic capabilities of a nation's people in resolving a crisis.

Fourth, negotiations were not compelling enough to convince Noriega that he had no better alternative than a negotiated settlement. While the negotiators were skilled professionals, their negotiations lacked the backing of a credible force, resulting in an unsatisfactory outcome. As long as certain U.S. Government agencies were still willing to work with Noriega, he was convinced that it was safer to stay in power than to step down and possibly be sent to the U.S. to be prosecuted for drug trafficking charges or be vulnerable to threats from his former drug trafficking partners.

Fifth, the introduction of domestic U.S. legal actions against Noriega dramatically altered coercive diplomatic efforts. The federal drug indictments proved to be a point of no return in dealing with Noriega, limiting options for resolving the crisis. State Department officials questioned how federal attorneys, who normally do not play a role in foreign policy, were able to follow through with the indictments and not take into consideration the consequences of indicting a de facto head of state. State and Defense officials claimed that they never took seriously the possibility of indictments until the U.S. Attorney General actually approved the indictments. A lesson drawn from this crisis is that there should be better coordination between Justice Department and State Department officials when considering extra-territorial actions.

Sixth, the strategy for the military intervention lacked a plan to maintain law and order in the streets. The result was millions of dollars worth of property damage in Panama that could have been averted and that also reflected poorly on the U.S. and its decision to intervene.

Seventh, when considering intervention to resolve a crisis brought about by corruption, it is important to analyze the nature of the corruptive influence. It may be primarily the result of the influence of a single, charismatic actor, or, as is more often the case—and was the case in Panama—institutional factors support and encourage corruption and require correction and/or dismantling of whole institutions (e.g., the PDF) to bring about a resolution.

Finally, the U.S. Government underestimated Noriega's understanding of U.S. policy and his belief that the U.S. would never intervene. Even when Noriega was informed by loyalists and intelligence sources that U.S. Air Force C-141's with paratroops, etc., were en route to Panama, Noriega was still not convinced that the Americans would intervene militarily. Noriega believed that his past relations with various agencies—providing intelligence information on different Latin American regimes and assisting with U.S. law enforcement in counter-drugs—would make it difficult for the U.S. Government to turn against him. The deeper and more complex Noriega's conflicts grew, the more Noriega sought to assist the U.S. agencies with their foreign policy efforts. U.S. tolerance for Noriega was quite high, and it had always been easier for U.S. officials to look the other way when Noriega was accused of doing something than to reprimand him. He was fully aware of the disagreement among U.S. agencies and was convinced that his importance to various agencies would prevent a direct military intervention.

★ ★ ★ ★ ★

Presidential Leadership: The Case of German Unification, 1989-1990

By Philip Zelikow

Since the story was so complex and rushed, the events of the unification of Germany and the transformation of Europe in 1989 and 1990 are not widely understood. Witnessing the wave of popular unrest and seeing the result, many observers still assume that Western leaders were just carried along by the rushing current. Or, being generous, they credit leaders with being good river rafters, steering the craft well enough to dodge the rocks—but with the underlying forces still providing all of the propulsion.

Neither view is correct. When young, I wondered how television worked. It was, and is, a bit hard to understand. So I eventually reasoned that television came from electricity. After all, when the power was turned on the television started. If the TV was unplugged no programs could be seen. This view did, however, overlook the intricate engineering that converts energy into a particular configuration of sound and pictures. So although electricity is necessary to television, it is not sufficient to explain it.

The upheavals in Central Europe that began in 1989 were not bound to produce German unification, as opposed to the continued existence of two Germanies as separate states or linked in some form of confederation. They were not bound to produce unification in 1990 (and the timing was crucial). They were not bound to produce a new Germany that absorbed East Germany into the political structures of the Bonn Republic rather than fashioning an entirely new political form. And those upheavals were not bound to have produced a Germany that remained a full member of NATO, including its integrated military command, with Western troops remaining and all Soviet troops out. These and many other details shape the life of Germany and Europe today. These particular outcomes rippled outward to restructure NATO, add political union to the European Union enterprise, and help push the Soviet Union toward its own internal collapse.

The United States played a leading part in these developments. President George H.W. Bush and Secretary of State James Baker deserve great credit and they have increasingly received it, especially from the Germans—who, after all, know the story best. So there are some lessons here for Presidential leadership. For this short paper, three will serve.

1. Principles Can Set Priorities

George Bush supported the unification of Germany. He began saying so any time the subject came up—in May, September, and October of 1989 for instance—times when his National Security Advisor Brent Scowcroft, and even his German allies, thought it was inconvenient or impolitic for him to be so forthright. For reasons of his own that are still somewhat murky, perhaps reinforced by some things he heard and read from a couple of friends and advisors in early 1989, Bush had arrived at a pronounced conviction that the Germans had dealt with their historical legacy and were entitled to choose their own destiny, and free unification was a natural choice.

Contrary to some popular opinion, it is not remarkable for Presidents to have convictions. More often the problem is that they have too many. In the German case, for instance, most American officials had some sympathy for German national aspirations. But many of them tempered that sympathy with other legitimate concerns, like the common belief that Europe's stability depended on the continued division of Germany. So it was especially important that Bush not only had a conviction, but made it clear that, to the extent possible, this belief would take precedence over other concerns. In other words, he applied his principle to the predictable tradeoffs and indicated his priority. The U.S. government thus had guidance on a central question, a question that would come up in a hundred different ways, large and small. And foreign governments could see that.

2. Operational Strategies Can Push History, Rather Than Follow It

At several points the U.S. government, working closely with Bonn, developed specific strategies to push history in its preferred direction. Operational objectives were set, diplomatic strategies were articulated, and policies were designed to put those strategies into action. For example, Washington:

▶ Developed a framework and a timetable for getting a treaty reducing conventional military forces in Europe, a framework that later was a key way to handle the security issues connected to German unification;

▶ Decided that Germany's internal unification had to go as fast as possible and have the form of a Western takeover, not a merger;

▶ Designed a diplomatic process, the "Two Plus Four," to manage the international aspects of unification—but did so in a way that made unification seem inevitable, lifting the expectations of East German voters as they prepared to choose their future;

▶ Delayed the onset and narrowed the scope of the Two Plus Four negotiations in order to reduce outside interference with German choices, current and future, and give Washington more time to cement common allied positions into place; and

▶ Then coordinated the Two Plus Four with other diplomatic initiatives, including NATO and G-7 summits, to present a persuasive message to Soviet Premier Mikhail Gorbachev (as in the "nine point package" Baker presented to Gorbachev in May 1990).

Bush did not devise these strategies. He empowered others, starting with Baker and Scowcroft—carefully monitoring their work, making sure the process was running well, and deploying himself or his authority whenever he was needed on the frontlines. In turn, Scowcroft's and Baker's subcabinet officials worked effectively with each other and with other agencies to fashion the detailed strategies that were needed.

3. Presidents Need a Rigorous Process for
Analyzing Choices and Defining Decisions

President Dwight D. Eisenhower had a highly structured National Security Council (NSC) process in the 1950s. A Planning Board coordinated the work as analysts took an idea "up Policy Hill." Then an Operations Coordinating Board made sure the journey down Policy Hill was equally orderly, translating decisions into implemented actions. Naturally such an elaborate process can lapse into stale, mediocre habits, as happened more and more during Eisenhower's second term in office. In an ill-considered overreaction, President John F. Kennedy threw it all out. A planning process was reconstituted in ad hoc ways, but the function of the Operations Coordinating Board—which Kennedy and his officials did not fully understand to begin with—has never really been brought back.

However, from time to time, and during German unification, the U.S. government has put together processes that forced up real written analysis of genuine choices and insisted on quality work. The European Strategy Steering Group, chaired by Deputy National Security Advisor Robert Gates, was an example. Informed by these efforts, reasonably concrete decisions could be made.

Just as important as the analysis that went into the decisions was the follow up that came after. Meetings would produce detailed summaries of what had been decided. These too would be circulated among the participants, so that gaps or misperceptions could rapidly be discovered and addressed. Thus the component organizations, and bureaucrats, had reasonably clear operational guidance for putting a policy into practice. In other words, if the President is willing to pour his concern and authority into the boiler, the White House-led structure below him should and can convert that energy into useful motion in an efficient process that does not dissipate too much of the original heat.

The U.S. and Iraq, 1990-1991

By James Kitfield

As is so often the case throughout history, the Persian Gulf War began out of strategic and diplomatic miscalculation. After the 1979 revolution that toppled the U.S.-supported Shah of Iran and led to the taking of American embassy personnel hostage in Teheran, U.S. strategy in the Persian Gulf shifted toward support of Iraq as a counter-balance to the possible destabilizing spread of Iran's Islamic revolution. During the eight years of the Iran-Iraq War (1980-1988), the

American government thus gave trade credits to Iraq and supplied the Iraqi armed forces with valuable intelligence information through Saudi Arabia. Despite the fact that Iraq started the war and that Saddam Hussein's forces repeatedly resorted to poison gas attacks to thwart Iran's Revolutionary Guard troops, the United States also dropped its objections to the efforts of allies such as France to give weapons and other supplies to Iraq.

The end of the bloody Iran-Iraq War left Iraq with a massive, well-equipped army of more than one million troops, and a crushing debt burden of more than $90 billion. Saddam especially blamed his smaller neighbors Kuwait and the United Arab Emirates for his debt troubles, since they had declined to offer Iraq debt relief and had broken oil quotas set by OPEC, driving oil prices down. Saddam also accused Kuwait of siphoning off $2.5 billion in Iraqi oil from the Rumaila oil field, which the two countries shared.

U.S. strategy failed to adjust to the fact that Iraq had become the most dangerous and aggressive country in the Persian Gulf. Thus when Saddam Hussein began massing troops near its border with Kuwait in July 1990, American Ambassador to Iraq April Glaspie told him that "...we have no opinion on the Arab-Arab conflicts like your border disagreement with Kuwait." Essentially, the Ambassador was signaling that if Iraq moved against Kuwait, it was not the concern of the United States.

No one will ever know whether a sterner diplomatic posture by the American government would have deterred Saddam. On August 2nd, more than 80,000 of Iraq's elite Republican Guard troops poured across the Kuwaiti border. Rather than seize the Rumaila oil field in a limited land-grab, as U.S. intelligence had predicted, the Republican Guard rolled rapidly on to Kuwait City and further south toward the border with Saudi Arabia.

U.S. Interests

After the energy crises of the 1970s and the Soviet invasion of Afghanistan in 1979, President Jimmy Carter issued in 1980 what became known as the "Carter Doctrine." The President declared that any attempt by an outside or aggressive force to control the Persian Gulf would be regarded as a direct assault on the vital interests of the United States.

After Iraqi forces had solidified their hold on Kuwait, it was certainly not difficult to understand the vital strategic interests in jeopardy. Already Saddam had control over 20 percent of the world's oil reserves. A 30-mile push into Saudi Arabia would quickly bring him another 20 percent. If Saddam could solidify his hold on Kuwait, U.S. officials feared his domineering position would lead other Arab states to start cutting deals and paying extortion, making him the preeminent power broker in the Persian Gulf.

In confronting the Iraqi crisis a year after the fall of the Berlin

Wall and at the end of the Cold War, President George H.W. Bush and some of his key advisers came to believe that an important strategic principle was at stake. Early in the crisis, for instance, the United Nations Security Council had voted 14-0 to condemn the invasion and demand an immediate and unconditional Iraqi withdrawal from Kuwait. For the first time in the history of the United Nations, the Soviet Union sent signals that it would stand with the United States and approve UN-backed military action to repel an act of aggression.

At the uncertain dawn of the post-Cold War era, Bush and confidants such as National Security Adviser Brent Scowcroft came to believe that a concerted international response to turn back the Iraqi invasion would strike a principled blow against nation-state aggression toward other states, which had been the great scourge of the 20th century. That was the "New World Order" that Bush had talked about, and the strength of the vision was evident when only days into the crisis the President was asked if he was contemplating military action.

"This will not stand," said a grim-faced President Bush, jabbing the air with his finger for emphasis. "This will not stand, this aggression against Kuwait."

Objective

The initial objective was to deploy sufficient military forces to the Persian Gulf to deter an Iraqi invasion of Saudi Arabia. As early as October 1990, however, it became clear to insiders that the ultimate objective would be to either compel Iraq to withdraw its troops from Kuwait, or else to liberate Kuwait by military force.

Options

Saddam Hussein revealed an almost uncanny penchant for poor timing when he chose 1990 as the moment to provoke a confrontation with the United States and its allies. Freed from Cold War constraints, the Bush Administration was able to isolate Iraq diplomatically, leading to a unanimous vote in the UN Security Council condemning Iraq and the invasion of Kuwait. That, in turn, facilitated the imposition of crippling economic and trade sanctions on Iraq. The UN Security Council later voted overwhelmingly to approve "any means necessary" to turn back the Iraqi aggression.

That year also represented a high-water mark for the U.S. military, which was riding a 1980s wave of Cold War military spending yet was free of many Cold War concerns. Thus the Pentagon was able to deploy to Saudi Arabia the three heavy divisions of VII Corps in Germany that had been responsible for anchoring the NATO defense against the former Warsaw Pact countries. With two full Army corps, two Marine Corp divisions, assorted allied units, six aircraft carriers, and Air Force fighters and bombers filling every airfield in the region, the military options available to the United States were abundant and overwhelming.

The major limiting factor was one of time. Defense Department officials did not believe they could adequately support such a large force in the barren Saudi desert through one of the region's brutally hot summers. That meant that the diplomatic isolation and economic sanctions would have to work by spring 1991 at the latest, or U.S. and allied forces would have to choose the military option.

Decision Making

The ultimate success of the Persian Gulf War can be traced in large measure to the experience and competence of U.S. decision makers in the national command authority, beginning at the top with President Bush. As a World War II veteran and former head of the Central Intelligence Agency, Bush drew on his deep experience to reach an early decision that Iraq's aggression in Kuwait "would not stand." His steady resolve that Iraq's aggression must be reversed charted a clear course for his national security team to follow through many months of crisis.

As a former Ambassador to China and two-term Vice President, Bush also used his numerous personal relationships with international leaders not only to help isolate Iraq diplomatically, but to help finance the deployment of the nearly one-half million U.S. troops in the allied coalition, aided ably by Secretary of State James Baker. In National Security Adviser Brent Scowcroft, a retired Air Force general, Bush had an equally experienced national security alter ego. While making the strategic decisions on when and if to go to war, and on what terms, Bush and his White House team studiously avoided the micro-management of tactical decisions that characterized the White House of President Lyndon Johnson, who used to boast during the Vietnam War that, "I won't let those Air Force generals bomb an outhouse without checking with me first."

As a former Congressional leader and White House Chief of Staff, Defense Secretary Dick Cheney also revealed a penchant for careful deliberation and decisiveness during Desert Shield/Desert Storm, the names given to first the planning operation and then the implementation phase of the war. Early on in the crisis Cheney took the controversial step of firing the Air Force Chief of Staff for what he considered imprudent remarks to a newspaper reporter, thus firmly establishing civilian authority in managing the crisis. In Chairman of the Joint Chiefs of Staff General Colin Powell, a former National Security Adviser in the Reagan White House, Cheney also had a military adviser who was equally steeped in the military and political aspects of the crisis. Finally, as the commander in the field the mercurial General H. Norman Schwarzkopf proved himself an able tactical leader. Schwarzkopf also benefited greatly from the 1986 Goldwater-Nichols reforms that made his subordinate commanders from the other services answerable to him instead of to their service chiefs. Thus the sniping among the services that had characterized earlier crises such as Grenada and Desert One in Iran was largely absent.

Strategy

With Iraq almost totally isolated diplomatically and economically—and with Iraq's static forces outmatched by a U.S. military totaling nearly 500,000 troops and another 200,000 coalition troops— the strategy was to compel Saddam to blink and withdraw from Kuwait. Failing that, the strategy was to evict Iraqi forces from Kuwait forcefully by, as General Colin Powell famously said, cutting off the Iraqi army in Kuwait and killing it.

Outcome

After a 40-day air campaign that saw allied air forces launch 41,309 strikes against Baghdad and the Republican Guard and regular Iraqi troops, destroying roughly half of Iraq's armor and artillery forces in Kuwait, U.S. and allied ground forces defeated the Iraqi army in a 100-hour ground war and liberated Kuwait. This was one of the most lopsided military victories in history in terms of damage and casualties inflicted upon Iraqi forces versus those suffered by U.S. and allied forces.

Lessons Learned

It has often been said that military forces learn far more from their defeats than from their victories, and the axiom probably applies to Desert Storm. In many ways, the Persian Gulf War was more the last Cold War confrontation than a preamble to the challenges the American military would confront in the post-Cold War era. The conflict was a classic clash of heavy tank forces, for which the United States had spent decades in Europe preparing. It was fought in an environment that maximized U.S. advantages in standoff weaponry and training (the desert environment, for instance, virtually duplicated conditions at the Army's National Training Center in the Mojave Desert). That is not to denigrate the superb performance of the U.S. military in Desert Storm. Rather, it is simply to note that the United States is unlikely to face future foes foolhardy enough to want to challenge the American military with conventional forces on a battlefield where it enjoys virtually every advantage.

Even so, the Persian Gulf War suggests a number of important lessons. Although in some ways such naked state-on-state aggression presents an easier choice for leaders than the failed state model so common in the post-Cold War era, President Bush's early and unwavering determination that vital U.S. interests were at stake—and that the Iraqi aggression "would not stand"—provided a clear strategic reference point and infused the national command authority with a sense of common purpose.

The Bush Administration has been criticized for stopping the war too early and leaving Saddam Hussein in power, and the Persian Gulf War does suggest that U.S. leaders need to focus more on their strategy for after the fighting has stopped. Bush rhetorically encouraged the

Shite and Kurd minorities to rise up in opposition to Saddam, for instance, and then did nothing to help avert their slaughter by Iraqi Republican Guards. Schwarzkopf mistakenly allowed Iraqi forces to continue flying helicopters as part of the surrender agreement, not anticipating that they would be used as gunships to suppress the uprising. In terms of whether Bush should have sent allied forces to Baghdad to unseat Saddam when he had the chance, however, this was never part of the strategy. Such a move would almost certainly have splintered the alliance and angered the Arab members. The United States was also still concerned that a fragmented Iraq would not be able to serve as a counterweight in the region to Iran.

Although it was regarded as too risky by some of his closest advisers, Bush's decision to finally seek Congressional approval for military action seems wise in retrospect. The Senate debate on the issue was one of most eloquent in memory, and it largely dispelled the specter of the 1964 Gulf of Tonkin Resolution, when after only perfunctory debate Congress essentially ceded its war powers to the Johnson Administration concerning Vietnam. After the close but successful Senate vote endorsing military action against Iraq, no U.S. service member in the Persian Gulf could seriously doubt that the country was united behind the effort.

In many ways, the Persian Gulf War also revealed the wisdom of the 1986 Goldwater-Nichols reforms. No longer were the component commanders in the field taking back-channel orders from their service chiefs in the Pentagon that tangled chains of command. Schwarkopf enjoyed near total authority in the region, and his chain of command to Cheney seemed streamlined and concise.

Although the Goldwater-Nichols reforms envisioned the empowered Chairman of the Joint Chiefs of Staff serving as the Secretary of Defense's primary adviser, it did not view him as being directly in the chain of command in a crisis. However, by de facto serving as the link in terms of orders and instructions between the Secretary of Defense and the commander in chief in the field, first in Panama and then in the Persian Gulf War, General Colin Powell put himself directly in the chain of command, elevating the role of the Chairman of the Joint Chiefs beyond even what the Goldwater-Nichols reformers imagined. Subsequent Chairmen have adopted that expanded model of their role.

Finally, the ability of U.S. air and space assets to pinpoint targets and effectively strike them with precision-guided weapons during Desert Storm represented a paradigm shift in the importance of air power. The information dominance that Schwarzkopf and his commanders enjoyed in the Persian Gulf—allowing them to see the enemy while at the same time keeping him largely blind to their movements—whetted the U.S. military's appetite for what some have called a "revolution in military affairs."

Bush, Clinton and Somalia

By John M. Goshko

On March 25, 1994, President Bill Clinton ordered the last American soldiers to leave Somalia, thereby ending the operation started by his predecessor, George H.W. Bush, in December 1992. The mission in Somalia was to safeguard the delivery of desperately needed food and supplies to that war-torn and famine-stricken East African nation. The originally limited U.S. intervention grew to include involvement in the civil and political warfare between feuding Somali factions. The intervention had led to the killing in October 1993 of 19 U.S. soldiers in Mogadishu during an abortive attempt to capture the local war lord, Mohammed Farrah Aidid. By halting American involvement in the Somalia operation, President Clinton committed what, in retrospect, was arguably the most far-reaching and significant foreign policy move of his eight years in office.

The Somalia operation set the tone and parameters for most of what the Clinton Administration would do in the foreign affairs arena from that point on. Ending the operation had profound effects on U.S. relations with the United Nations and damaged the American reputation for using its position as the world's preeminent superpower for leadership in the international arena. It gave the U.S. military establishment, which had been forced into a cautionary mode by its unhappy experiences in the Vietnam War, a de facto veto over future politico-military decision making. The withdrawal revealed a strong streak of post-Cold War isolationism in the American public that became fodder for partisan political purposes. The isolationism since Somalia has acted as a strongly inhibiting force on how active and forceful the White House is willing to be in dealing with foreign policy problems.

All of these factors remain part of the foreign policy-national security equation as a new President prepares to take office in January—and faces the void created by the trauma that Somalia inflicted on the thinking of American policy makers. At some point, the new President almost certainly will be confronted by some unfolding, as yet unknown, crisis and will have to consider whether to deal with it within the constraints imposed by post-Somalia thinking, or whether to break free of those fetters and move U.S. policy in a new direction.

Origins of the Problem

When Bill Clinton was elected President in 1992, the Somalia operation seemed to fit closely into the relatively sketchy foreign policy ideas that he had articulated during the campaign. Drawing heavily on the thinking of Richard Gardner, the Democratic Party's principal exponent of working more closely with the United Nations, Clinton advocated an approach of "assertive multilateralism." With this approach other countries, working through the United Nations or other formal and informal groupings, share with the United States responsibility for dealing with the regional crises popping up in various parts of the globe in the aftermath of the Cold War. Somalia seemed especially amenable to this approach. In its early stages, U.S. forces, working through a UN Security Council mandate that kept them under the command and control of American rather than UN officers, successfully helped to safeguard the delivery of supplies and humanitarian aid by separate UN peacekeeping forces—and Clinton enthusiastically endorsed U.S. participation. Later, however, the UN operation grew into a larger, more intrusive mission aimed at pacification that drew the American forces into an irregular urban war and culminated in the tragic deaths in Mogadishu and Clinton's decision to cut his losses and get out.

The Broader Impact

The ripple effects of what had occurred went far beyond Somalia. Within the Clinton Administration, it literally caused a 180-degree turn in thinking about foreign policy. Prior to the Mogadishu disaster, Administration policy makers had been formulating the ambitious Presidential Decision Directive (PDD) 25, which was originally intended as a detailed blueprint of the President's ideas on burden-sharing multilateralism. However, the tragic result of the killings in Mogadishu caused the White House to abandon the original aim and to switch to a very different set of ideas. The final form of PDD 25, which emerged in May 1994 (and an amplifying document, PDD 56, of May 1997) set very restrictive rules and parameters dictated by what had happened in Somalia. The main points were these:

▶ U.S. decisions about whether to take part in multilateral operations should be guided by whether a clear and compelling U.S. interest is involved.

▶ A clear mandate is critical to preventing the kind of "mission creep" that turned the original Somalia operation into a highly personal manhunt for a recalcitrant warlord that led to the deaths of 18 Americans.

▶ To guard against such mission creep, clear entry and exit strategies are needed.

▶ In becoming involved in multinational operations, it is necessary to recognize that there might be conflict among the participating countries and the U.S. government should be aware that these might impose limits on what the operation can realistically accomplish.

▶ Rules of engagement must be simple, direct, and unclassified. (In Somalia, these rules frequently were amended and vaguely worded, leading to several incidents where U.S. forces interpreted the rules differently than troops of other countries.)

▶ When and if the United States agrees to take part in a multinational operation, it should reserve the right to determine what form this participation will take. (In that respect, the document displayed a clear aversion to committing U.S. personnel to situations where they might encounter violence and PDD 25 expressed a preference for limiting the U.S. contribution to providing communications, intelligence, and air and sealift assistance to transport soldiers from other countries to the crisis zone.

The emergence of PDD 25 as the guiding policy for U.S. approaches to multilateral operations has been a matter of sharp controversy in the international community. American officials contend that it is simply a road map for avoiding problems in the future by paring back earlier overly idealistic and unrealistic thinking about the ability of the United Nations to apply its peacekeeping doctrines to contemporary regional disputes. They argue that the rules it sets for American involvement are simply good sense. However, among foreign diplomats, there is a clear feeling that the aim of PDD 25 is to raise the bar for U.S. involvement in peacekeeping and peace enforcement so high that it effectively rules out American participation in most instances. According to this argument, PDD 25 essentially is an excuse for the United States to avoid involvement in situations where its position as the world's only true superpower gives it the leadership role necessary for effective action to be taken. The critics point to the 1994 massacres in Rwanda and the current inability of UN efforts to halt the violence in Sierra Leone as situations that might have been mitigated by more vigorous U.S. leadership.

What Drives the U.S. Approach?

There is no black and white answer to whether U.S. officials or foreign diplomats are right in their assessments of PDD 25 and its consequences. But there is no question that PDD 25 was formed by a confluence of powerful forces that the Clinton Administration was unwilling or unable to resist. Moreover, the Republican Party not only was subject to the same pressures but was strongly complicit in the events that motivated Clinton's retreat from Somalia and his subsequent policy approaches. In addition, there so far is no sign that either Al Gore or George W. Bush is willing to confront these forces and try to effect changes that might ease some of the restrictions weighing on U.S. freedom of action. For example, three years ago, when Vice President Gore was asked by a New York audience why the United States was not taking a more active role to end the killing in Bosnia, he replied: "I'll give you a one word answer—Somalia." And, last January, when Texas Governor Bush was asked in an interview what he would do "if God forbid, another Rwanda should take place," he answered, "We should not send troops to stop ethnic cleansing and genocide outside our strategic interest. I would not send U.S. troops into Rwanda." Chief among the factors motivating these positions are:

Hostility of the U.S. armed forces to operations such as peacekeeping that do not meet the criteria of traditional warfare and its doctrines. This attitude, sometimes labeled the Weinberger-Powell Doctrine (for former Defense Secretary Caspar Weinberger and former Joint Chiefs of Staff Chairman Colin Powell), sets forth many of the basic tenets later formalized in PDD 25. These ideas, engrained in U.S. military thinking by the Vietnam experience, include ensuring:

1. That there is dominant force powerful enough to guarantee victory;

2. That there are clearly defined political and military objectives in advance;

3. That there is a clear end point for terminating the operation; and

4. That there is strong support from American public opinion.

Added to this are additional factors such as the strong hostility of the American military to placing U.S. troops under foreign commanders, and the feeling that if American soldiers were exposed to combat as part of a multinational operation, they would be singled out by the opposing forces as prime targets.

The result, particularly in the wake of Somalia, has been to make protection of U.S. troops the top priority in any commitment to multilateral operations. That is why PDD 25 stresses providing logistical or transportation support rather than troops who might be exposed to fighting and become casualties. This policy has been a major, at times decisive, factor in subsequent U.S. military activities. A few days after the Mogadishu killings, U.S. and Canadian troops on a ship about to dock in Port-au-Prince, Haiti, hastily turned back when an anti-American mob appeared on the docks, even though most observers felt that the protesters would have been dispersed by a minimal U.S. show of force. Also in the immediate aftermath of Mogidishu, the United States refused to use its troops and balked at approving a UN peacekeeping force to combat the Rwanda genocide. The Weinberger-Powell Doctrine is why the U.S.-led campaign against Serbian forces in Kosovo relied exclusively on high-altitude bombing that would keep American flyers relatively safe from Serbian anti-aircraft fire, even though it gave Serbian forces on the ground more time and opportunity to kill and expel Albanian civilians. Among U. S. allies, this has led to a belief that the American military wants to be involved only in sure-thing operations that are guaranteed in advance to succeed with no, or at least minimal, casualties. As Robert Oakley, who served as Clinton's special envoy in Somalia, observes, "It has encouraged our enemies to think there is a weak U.S. link: cause a few casualties and the U.S. will fold." It is not a reputation designed to inspire confidence in America as a world leader. But it was an attitude that Clinton was unwilling to challenge. And the indications are that neither Bush nor Gore will be willing to do so.

Hostility toward the United Nations. For all of its many shortcomings, the United Nations remains the best available instrument and framework for mounting multinational operations. As Secretary General Kofi Anan has noted, the traditional UN approach to peacekeeping—interposing lightly armed troops as referees between feuding factions to oversee cease-fires or elections—no longer fits the kind of crises confronting the world today. Now most involve disputes between opposing groups within a single country who are divided by intense hatreds and who cannot be relied on to respect the authority and neutrality of the peacekeepers. For the United Nations to be effective in such situations, there must be a major restructuring of the peacekeeping operation and its rules of engagement to allow some degree of movement from passive peacekeeping to a peace enforcement capability. Given the faction-ridden politics of the United Nations, winning agreement of the membership on such changes is a daunting task. Many experts on the world body believe that it cannot be done without strong support and leadership from the United States.

Yet, U.S. relations with the United Nations, which were never that good, were dealt a blow so severe by the Somalia situation that it is likely to require years to repair the damage. As noted above, the U.S. involvement in Somalia was crafted from start to finish to keep American forces under the command and control of U.S. officers, and independent of the parallel UN peacekeeping operation. This was true of the ill-fated venture where 18 Americans were killed in Mogadishu. The operation was planned and carried out by order of U.S. officers, and two senior American generals subsequently testified to that fact before Congress.

Nevertheless, immediately after the killings, the Clinton Administration mounted a deliberate and sustained campaign to create the impression that responsibility for the operation rested with the United Nations. Clinton himself loudly proclaimed that U.S. troops never again would be under UN command (even though they had not been), and his Administration ever since has refused to retract the false accusations that made the United Nations the scapegoat in the eyes of Congress and the American public.

The performance of Clinton's Republican opposition was even worse. In plain contradiction of the facts, Republican Congressional leaders charged that Clinton had turned control of U.S. forces in Somalia over to then-Secretary General Boutros Boutros Ghali. The Republican campaign reached its apogee at the party's 1996 Presidential nominating convention when former Senator Robert Dole, in his acceptance speech, devoted most of the foreign policy portion to heaping scorn on Boutros Ghali and vowing that no UN leader would ever give orders to American soldiers. This scapegoating of the United Nations (much of it done with the cynical knowledge that it was erroneous) came at a time when efforts were underway to resolve the problem of more than $1 billion in U.S. arrearages owed to the United

Nations. Inflaming the situation through reckless charges about Somalia only served to undermine further Congressional support for the organization and make it even more unlikely that the United States could lead the way to improved UN peacekeeping.

Hostility of American public opinion. Following the deaths in Mogadishu, Clinton Administration officials found themselves the target of demonstrations from the families of American soldiers and others demanding that U.S. troops be withdrawn from Somalia and other places where they might face danger. What made the demonstrations especially notable was that they were staged on behalf of members of an all-volunteer army who had signed up with the understanding that military service might occasionally place them in harm's way. Nevertheless, the demonstrations were a sign of a post-Cold War fatigue within the American public that had distinctly neo-isolationist overtones. In effect, people seemed to be saying, "We won the big one, and we don't want to be bothered by these little brush-fire conflicts that we don't understand in places that we never heard of. They just aren't worth risking the lives of young Americans for any reason." This was an attitude that fit well with the new emphasis of both political parties on the economy and domestic issues. And realizing that foreign conflicts had fallen to a low position on the public's priority list, neither Clinton nor his Republican opposition seemed inclined to challenge it. Thus public sentiment clearly was opposed to sending U.S. forces into the cauldron of seething ethnic hatreds in the Balkans. Even when the Mogadishu tragedy was followed a few days later by the outbreak of massive genocide in Rwanda— one that saw from 600,000 to one million men, women, and children murdered—American public opinion did not criticize or challenge the contortions engaged in by the Clinton Administration to avoid intervening. Instead, the public seemed to agree with the assessment of a State Department official who privately summed up the feeling of the U.S. military: "What happened in Somalia has frankly made the American military gun-shy. I don't know how many times I've heard American officers say, 'These people are not worth one American life.'"

The United States could not totally avoid involvement in multinational ventures, however. Washington's credibility with its NATO allies did force it to join the operations in Bosnia and Kosovo. And, in the operation that American officials like to cite as proof that they are not afraid to take an activist role, the United States did intervene decisively in Haiti. Even there, it did so only after fleeing Haitian boat people were threatening to flood Florida—and the Clinton White House found itself increasingly unable to ignore pressures from the African American community. In the main though, the U.S. government has taken a decidedly reactive stance. America has reacted only when circumstances have forced it into a corner where inaction no longer was an option.

The Future

Whether the next President will be able to maintain this posture of reactive drift is unclear. In retrospect, Rwanda, in particular, has had a delayed reaction on the conscience of the world. What happened there could be repeated elsewhere. If so, will the world—and its leading super-power—stand by ineffectively once again? For the United States, in particular, a new Rwanda will raise questions about whether to cleave to the PDD 25 commandment about not getting involved where there are no vital U.S. interests at stake, or whether to decide that humanitarian considerations cannot be ignored. And, if the future President finds himself in circumstances where he feels compelled to act, will he be willing to do so even if all the other tidy prescripts of PDD 25 are not met? The post-Somalia experience has shown that events cannot be compartmentalized so neatly. The problems of Bosnia, Kosovo, and Haiti were not solved by outside intervention. Yet in each of these places, the situation is at least marginally better than it was before. When the new President takes office in January, he might well find it profitable to move away from a purely reactive stance and set his Administration to planning how interventions can be handled better in the future and used as the springboard for long-term solutions to at least some of the regional conflicts that are likely to keep troubling the world in the years ahead.

The "Japan By-Pass" and Clinton's 1998 Trip to China

By John R. Malott

President Bill Clinton visited China from June 25 to July 3, 1998. He was the first U.S. President to visit China since the Tienanmen massacre of 1989. Clearly a Presidential visit to China was long overdue and in America's strategic interests.

Clinton correctly said that it was in Japan's interests as well—"I think it is good for Japan if America has better relations with China. I think it is good for America if Japan has better relations with China."

But the length of the China trip was unprecedented for a Presidential visit anywhere—nine days in-country. If you could spend that much time away from Washington, then why could you not add on at least one day at the end to de-brief and consult with your most important ally in Asia—Japan?

So went the argument. Clinton's long visit to China and his decision not to stop in Japan (his critics called it his "failure" to visit Japan) became a major grievance in that country. In the United States, experts on Japan derided it as a mistake and another indication of the Administration's failure to properly tend to America's alliance relationships.

This was not the first time the Japanese took umbrage at the tendency of U.S. officials to by-pass Japan after visiting China. After President Richard M. Nixon's opening to China in 1972, National Security Advisor Henry Kissinger became a regular visitor to Beijing. But his plane would simply land at Yokota Air Base outside Tokyo for refueling and then head back home. This became a sore point in Japan. A senior American Embassy official said that he was trying to convince Kissinger why it was important to de-brief the Japanese on his China visits:

Let's imagine you're Henry Kissinger. You're a great intellectual. You love the grand sweep of history and the tectonic movement of geopolitics. You go to Beijing and you sit down with Mao Tse-tung and Chou En-lai—men who have changed the course of history—and you discuss where the world is going in the next hundred years. Then they ask you to come to Japan, where you'll meet with aging Japanese political leaders whose only real concern is whether they can get another bridge built in Kagoshima. Where would you like to go? Which discussion would you find more interesting?

In the end, Kissinger learned that it was in his interest to stop in Japan. But Japan experts in every Administration have faced the same problem—trying to convince their leadership why they should go through what often appears to be symbolic and substance-less meetings with their Japanese counterparts. Numerous Secretaries of State have expressed personal frustration that their opposite numbers are not well informed and that nothing happens in the meetings. With so many other demands on them, they often see their Japan meetings as a waste of time, a feeling that is compounded because of the need for consecutive interpretation.

In his eight years as President, Bill Clinton has sat across the table from seven Japanese Prime Ministers. And his two Secretaries of State have faced Foreign Ministers who usually were chosen not for their foreign policy expertise but for factional balance within the ruling party. With such frequent turnover, it is difficult for Japanese officials to learn the issues, and it is a problem for both sides to establish any personal rapport. In this situation, it is easy to understand why senior U.S. officials believe they simply are being asked to "go through the motions" of meeting with their Japanese counterparts.

Nine days after President Clinton left China, Japanese voters concerned about their faltering economy handed Prime Minister Hashimoto a major election defeat, and the next day he resigned. Even if Clinton had stopped in Japan to meet Hashimoto, the President soon would have had to meet yet another Prime Minister.

As long as U.S.-Japan summit meetings seem long on style and short on substance, Japan experts in any U.S. Administration will always have difficulty convincing senior officials to make the long journey over the Pacific to get together with their Japanese counterparts—but they must continue to do so. At the same time, however, those

Japanese government officials and reporters who are so quick to criticize the alleged indifference of U.S. Administration leaders need to consider their own country's responsibility to carry on a meaningful, mature, and substantive dialogue at the top levels of their government.

No one could accuse President Clinton of ignoring Japan. One of his first overseas trips after becoming President was to that country. Clinton's first state dinner was in honor of Japan's Emperor and Empress. During his Presidency, he continued to meet regularly with Japan's Prime Ministers in the United States and Japan, and at the Asia-Pacific Economic Cooperation (APEC) and G-8 summit meetings in third countries.

Furthermore, there is nothing that says a U.S. President or Secretary of State must stop in Japan anytime he or she travels to Asia. One does not hear complaints from the British, our most important ally in Europe, that they have been "by-passed" on Presidential visits to Germany or France. And the U.S. government does not express concern when a Japanese Prime Minister visits Canada or Mexico without stopping in Washington.

So What Was Really Bothering the Japanese?

Frankly stated, it was insecurity and a lack of confidence about their leadership position in Asia and their relationship with the United States.

Less than a decade before Clinton's 1998 trip, U.S. and Japanese leaders were speaking of a "Global Partnership." Deputy Secretary of State Lawrence Eagleburger raised European eyebrows in 1989 when he said that the center of American foreign policy gravity was shifting to the Pacific, and specifically to Japan. *The Economist* magazine had a cover story on "Uncle Sam's Roving Eye."

Now the Japanese, still mired in recession and adrift both politically and economically, wondered whether Uncle Sam's eye was roving again, and whether the center of American foreign policy gravity in Asia was shifting from Japan to China. A nine-day visit to China—the devotion of that much Presidential time—was unprecedented. What did it mean? Japan was looking for reassurance and it did not appear to be forthcoming.

Although Clinton's first Administration devoted a lot of attention to Japan—especially on the trade front—by the time the second Administration was underway it was common to hear complaints. Japan felt that it was being ignored and by-passed, and that with the Cold War over, the United States no longer considered Japan important to its interests, let alone as an economic threat. So what appeared to have been a question of style—the need to go through the motions of consultation and the Kabuki-like rituals of the U.S.-Japan relationship—actually had a deeper meaning.

This is not 1989, and we cannot turn back the foreign policy clock to the "good old days" of Global Partnership. Asia and the world are very different places today, and the United States and Japan have traded places economically. Talking about our respective views of Asia's and the world's future and how our two countries can work together in the years ahead is an urgent task for the next Administration and its counterparts in Japan.

China has a clear vision of its future role in Asia, and the United States is attaching great priority to its engagement with the Middle Kingdom. But what is Japan's view of its future? How does Japan see its leadership role in Asia and the world today, and how will it respond to China's newfound confidence?

America cannot make its Japan policy in a vacuum. It needs a clearer understanding of Japan's foreign policy future, and that is something only Japan can provide.

At the same time, U.S. leaders need to understand that the regular "care and feeding" of our critical alliances, from Europe to Asia, is not symbolism. Rather, it should be an essential part of their job descriptions—because by definition, our alliances are vital to our national interests.

Kosovo, March 1999-June 1999

By James Kitfield

The crisis over Kosovo and the North Atlantic Treaty Organization's (NATO's) war with Serbia conclusively proved the perils of "coercive diplomacy," and ultimately the drawbacks of coalition warfare waged with strict limitations. The conflict was vastly complicated by the fact that President Bill Clinton was in the midst of an impeachment battle with Congress, and thus did not effectively assume his typical leadership role in NATO during times of crisis. Murky strategic goals also contributed to a great sense of unease about the war in Washington, D.C. and in European capitals. For example, NATO waged war against Serbia on behalf of the Kosovar Albanians, yet rejected the Albanians' aspirations for independence from Serbia.

Serbian strongman Slobodan Milosevic had provoked nationalistic wars and ethnic cleansing in Slovenia, Croatia, and Bosnia-Herzegovnia in the early and mid-1990s. U.S. officials understood that he would likely turn his attention next to the Serbian province of Kosovo, whose ethnic majority of Muslim Albanians he had systematically repressed since taking office in 1989. After two diplomatic showdowns with Milosevic in 1995 and 1998, U.S. officials had also come to believe that the former Communist apparatchik responded only to the credible threat of military force.

Milosevic's forces began a punishing offensive against Albanian separatists in the summer of 1998—destroying 250 villages and forcing tens of thousands of ethnic Albanian civilians to flee as refugees. A U.S.-led NATO used the threat of imminent air strikes to coerce Milosevic into signing an 11th hour ceasefire. It was only the second time in the alliance's history (the first was in Bosnia in 1995) that NATO nations agreed to authorize military strikes. However, after Serb forces massacred 45 Kosovar civilians the following January, and expelled the U.S. diplomat in charge of the peace-monitoring mission in Kosovo, it was clear that Milosevic was intent on testing the limits of NATO's resolve.

At peace talks in Rambouillet, France in February 1999, mediators from the United States and the European Union once again resorted to coercive diplomacy. Either Milosevic would sign a treaty granting Kosovo limited autonomy, much as the province had enjoyed before Milosevic took power, or NATO would launch air strikes. For a number of reasons, it was a risky gambit on NATO's part. Unlike Bosnia or Croatia, Kosovo was a province of Serbia, and it resonated deeply in the Serbian psyche. Milosevic had propelled himself into power based on a nationalist appeal to bring the Albanians back under the Serbian yoke, and many observers doubted that he could survive in office after "losing" Kosovo. Compelling someone to sign a treaty was also considered by many in uniform as a questionable goal for the use of the military, since just by the act of not signing an adversary could claim victory.

When the Rambouillet talks broke down, NATO felt compelled for the sake of its own credibility to launch largely symbolic air strikes that did little real damage to Serbian forces. NATO leaders clearly believed that Milosevic would quickly back down when confronted with their overwhelmingly superior forces. When instead he launched a massive ethnic-cleansing campaign in Kosovo with his regular and irregular forces, eventually producing more than one million refugees, NATO was caught badly off guard and thrown into a major crisis. On its 50th anniversary, the world's most powerful alliance had stumbled into a war it could not afford to lose, but that it seemed to lack the political will to win.

U.S. Interests

In the early 1990s, when separatist wars erupted in the Balkans over the breakup of the former Yugoslavia, Secretary of State James Baker famously commented that the United States "had no dog in that fight," ceding the handling of the crisis to NATO allies in Europe. However, after the European Union and NATO seemed impotent to intervene through more than two years (1992-1995) of atrocities in Bosnia (committed primarily by Serbian forces loyal to Milosevic), many Western publics began to question the purpose of the NATO alliance in the post-Cold War world. The vast number of refugees created by the Balkan wars was also destabilizing to allied nations, especially in Southern Europe.

In 1995, the United States once again took the NATO lead and formulated a new hard-line approach, combining coercive diplomacy and air strikes against Serbian forces to bring the belligerents to the negotiating table, where they eventually signed the Dayton Peace Accords ending the conflict in Bosnia.

Even before the war in Bosnia, however, U.S. officials understood that Kosovo was a particularly volatile tinderbox and a potential threat to NATO cohesion. In late 1992, President George H.W. Bush thus issued a stern warning to Milosevic that ethnic violence against Kosovars would be met by U.S. force. The fear was that repression of the ethnic Albanians in Kosovo could lead to refugee displacements, potentially destabilizing neighboring Albania and Macedonia, which had their own large ethnic Albanian populations. Such a crisis would almost invariably lead to calls for a "greater Albania," which would provoke the Greeks. If the Greeks interceded, Turkey would almost certainly move on the other side. America's vital national interest, then, was to prevent a Kosovo crisis from destabilizing Southern Europe and potentially sparking a conflict between NATO allies Greece and Turkey.

Objectives

The initial objective of NATO air strikes was to coerce Milosevic into signing the treaty at Rambouillet granting limited autonomy to Kosovo, and to end his repression of its large ethnic majority of Albanians. That was a particularly nuanced objective for the blunt instrument of military force, and NATO's initial pinprick strikes had the opposite effect from what was intended. Milosevic responded by ethnically cleansing nearly the entire Kosovo province, sending more than one million refugees fleeing for their lives. At that point, the objective was to force Milosevic to capitulate and allow for the return of the refugees under international supervision before they could destabilize neighboring countries.

Options

With Serbia already economically isolated by international sanctions, and a recalcitrant Milosevic firmly entrenched in power, the diplomatic options were nearly exhausted. However, the most powerful military alliance in history should have had virtually unlimited military options in confronting a war-weary and isolated "poor man of Europe." Instead, the unexpectedly complex politics involved in the NATO alliance fighting its first "out of area" war negated many of the military options.

Because NATO's political and military leaders fully expected Milosevic to buckle after only symbolic strikes, the alliance failed to amass adequate air power in the region to conduct a serious air campaign. Thus when Milosevic reacted by lashing out in Kosovo, NATO officials were caught off-guard and unprepared, and they did not have the option of immediately ratcheting up the severity of the air campaign. In fact, NATO military leaders scrambled for weeks to amass a larger air armada in the region.

Equally damaging, NATO political leaders would not allow the military commanders to strike at strategic targets in Belgrade in the first stages of the war. This delayed the day of reckoning for Milosevic and gave his forces ample time to complete their ethnic cleansing, replete with mass executions and rapes.

Even after being confronted with the ethnic-cleansing campaign, NATO military commanders were so worried about the reaction to allied casualties that they forbade pilots from flying lower than 15,000 feet on their bombing runs. The restriction negated the potential for low-flying tank and infantry busters such as the U.S. Air Force A-10s and the Army Apache gunships that might have halted the Serbian ground offensive.

Perhaps the most damaging decision in the early stages of the war was to take the ground force option off of the table. U.S. and NATO officials insisted that it was simply not politically feasible to introduce a ground option early in the conflict given the objections of the United States, Germany, and others. But this decision essentially gave Serbian forces free reign inside of Kosovo, and greatly complicated the task of air planners. Ground troops in the theater, for instance, could have forced the Serbian fighters to mass into large formations, thus making them easier targets for air strikes. Only ground forces could have put a quick stop to the ethnic cleansing.

Decision Making

The fact that President Bill Clinton was in the midst of an impeachment crisis during the war deprived the alliance of its traditional leader in the midst of one of its greatest crises. Indeed, the war in Kosovo soon became a surrogate for the never-ending duel between Clinton and the Republican-controlled Congress, creating a spectacle that badly unnerved some NATO allies. Republican leaders called the conflict the "Clinton-Gore" war, for instance, seeming to forget the participation of other NATO nations. In a vote that could have had a negative impact on the ability of a future President to use force, or the threat of force, as an instrument of U.S. diplomacy, the House at one point voted to require Congressional approval for the use of ground troops, and deadlocked on a vote authorizing U.S. involvement in the ongoing operation.

The requirement of unanimity that governs NATO decisions revealed itself as cumbersome in the preamble to the Kosovo conflict. Even after the war began, the constant scrubbing of the air campaign target list by NATO politicians (in close consultation with allied capitals) also undermined the decisive use of military force. The unwillingness of political leaders to allow the military command to strike strategic targets in Belgrade produced a gradualism in the air campaign that very likely prolonged the conflict. Indeed, the entire war highlighted the limited effectiveness of a NATO command structure designed for a defensive Cold War, not an offensive hot one.

Strategy

Although crises in the future will undoubtedly dictate the use of coercive diplomacy, the Kosovo conflict clearly revealed the potential perils behind following such a strategy. Military force is generally most effective when applied in the furtherance of clear goals and objectives. Compelling a leader to sign a treaty or change his or her mind seems to fall well short of that criteria, since by not doing so the antagonist can claim a victory of sorts.

It is not clear that NATO had a viable strategy for what to do after the bombs stopped falling. By fighting on behalf of the Albanians while simultaneously denying them their aspirations of becoming independent of Serbia, NATO risked getting embroiled in a landscape where it had no natural allies, and where its presence would be required indefinitely to quell renewed violence.

Outcome

After NATO began striking strategic targets such as bridges, electric grids, and communications links in Belgrade, bringing the war home to the Serbian people (and on the eve of NATO's approving a ground force option), Milosevic capitulated in June 1999. With few options left, the Serbian strongman signed an agreement granting the limited autonomy for Kosovo that NATO officials had been seeking, and the refugees soon returned from neighboring countries to try and rebuild their lives. Since that time, however, NATO forces have been unable to deter constant attacks on the small Serbian minority left in Kosovo by vengeful ethnic Albanians.

Lessons Learned

If wars help define nations, the image of America mirrored in the war over Kosovo is of a country both preternaturally strong and deeply conflicted. There is little doubt that the United States and its NATO allies fought and won a just war. That they did it solely from the air without a single combat casualty marks a watershed in modern warfare. But the achievement also raises many questions and teaches multiple lessons.

Slobadan Milosevic's one hope for successfully weathering the war was that the NATO alliance would fracture under the extraordinary pressures of an 11-week bombing campaign that included several errant strikes, scores of unintended civilian casualties, and the accidental bombing of the Chinese Embassy. The fact that the alliance held together despite profound rumblings in a number of left-of-center coalition governments in Europe is NATO's greatest achievement of the war, and the strongest argument for the alliance's continued credibility and vitality.

To avoid a repeat of the tentative, war-making-by-committee approach that led to a gradualism in the air campaign that likely prolonged the conflict, NATO needs to reform its decision making and crisis management structures. In the view of NATO military experts such as General Wesley Clark, Supreme Allied Commander during the conflict, once NATO's political officials reach consensus that military action must be taken, military officers must then be given greater latitude and discretion in shaping the campaign. Perhaps most significantly, military leaders should be able to bring all of the elements of military power to bear. An opponent should never be relieved of having to worry about whether allied ground forces will be introduced.

The Balkan war also revealed the depths of the technology gap between American military forces and their NATO counterparts. U.S. commanders supplied roughly 70 percent of the air assets for the war. The Americans had to conduct the overwhelming majority of air strikes because the Europeans lacked the necessary electronic-jamming aircraft, advanced command-and-control systems, precision-guided weapons, stealth technology, advanced reconnaissance and surveillance systems, and even secure communications.

In terms of the U.S. military, the slowness of the deployment during the conflict of the Army's Task Force Hawk, with its two dozen Apache helicopters, raised serious questions about the Army's readiness to handle the kinds of challenges many experts believe it will face in future operations. The Army's claims that it would need two to three months to insert viable ground forces into the Balkans also ignited a debate about whether an Army largely built around heavy Cold War-era divisions is light or mobile enough for today's less predictable missions.

The fact that NATO won a conflict largely with air power, and without a single casualty, reinforces the idea that a new paradigm has been created in terms of the effectiveness of air power and the coming "revolution in military affairs." Certainly the future of precision-guided bombs seems more secure than ever. U.S. Air Force officials claimed a 99 percent accuracy rate in an air campaign that broke an enemy's will while killing an estimated 5,000 enemy troops, compared to zero NATO service members lost in combat. Military officials will have to address the morality, however, of a tactic of flying at an altitude of 15,000 feet that may have led to the killing of more innocent civilians through errant strikes.

By deciding to initiate military operations without the expressed approval of the United Nations, NATO also set an important precedent that the alliance will take its own counsel in crises impacting the stability and security of Europe. Likewise, NATO's intervention in what amounted to a civil war set the international precedent that in some cases concerns for human suffering and instability will trump national sovereignty.

Although much was made of the new "Clinton Doctrine" on humanitarian interventions after the conflict, Kosovo probably revealed once again that any grand strategic doctrine on the use of military force will collapse under the pressure of events and the unique character of any given contingency. Within days of the pronouncement of the "Clinton Doctrine," for instance, Administration officials hastened to add conditions. Besides a clear moral justification, they said, the United States must also have a strategic interest involved, and a reasonable assumption that the operation will not exact too heavy a price. That sounds a lot like the same selective and pragmatic approach that has governed U.S. actions for much of the 1990s—it led the United States to withdraw quickly from a humanitarian mission in Somalia when casualties began to mount, and avoided direct intervention in Rwanda despite mass genocide.

VIII. MANAGING THE EXECUTIVE BRANCH

The President's Managerial Leadership Responsibilities

By Dwight Ink

Background

The managerial leadership role of the President stems from the Constitution, and not from our political processes. It states "The executive Power shall be vested in a President of the United States" who is to "take care that the laws be faithfully executed." Despite this plain language, it is often assumed that the many roles that our President is expected to perform leaves little time for carrying out his constitutional management responsibilities. The current campaign debate never mentions the subject, and there is no organized constituency that pulls the lever for "good government."

Yet the success of Presidential programs and policy initiatives depends heavily on good management. Enormous political damage can result from mismanagement, which may lead to failed Presidential promises, scandal, and loss of public trust. The public is cheated by a government that administers laws wastefully or unfairly.

This case study describes a range of opportunities for a busy President to provide leadership in making government work. It is the result of a series of interviews with 20 former Presidential appointees, most with high-level White House or Office of Management and Budget (OMB) experience. Those interviewed include former Chiefs of Staff and other White House assistants having a close association with Presidents from Eisenhower to Clinton. The interviews were conducted by a working group of the Center for the Study of the Presidency established to identify how Presidential leadership can best contribute to an effective national government.

With the fast pace, the intrusive media, the clamor of special interest groups, and Congressional and foreign affairs demands on a President's time, the White House is an extraordinarily difficult environment within which he can think much about management. What can be done to help a President provide the necessary managerial leadership while avoiding unrealistic demands on his busy schedule? Suggestions from the interviews begin with utilizing the President's personal activities.

President's Personal Activities

Communication. The interviews underscored the view that only the President carries the weight to instruct his staff on the role that management must play in his Administration if his programs are to be successful. Edward DeSeve and others commented on how much Presidential leadership can be exercised in the course of his daily activities. How clearly he makes assignments and issues instructions, the type of questions he asks, and even the inflection of his voice, make a big difference.

Program Linkage. The President needs to make sure his staff members recognize that good management is the vehicle for policy implementation and program success, and must be integrated into policy development and program reviews. Several of the interviewees spoke of the lack of this linkage as greatly handicapping Bill Clinton's health care reform proposals.

Commitment. The President's commitment to a major initiative must be seen as genuine. Lyndon B. Johnson was often characterized by agencies as launching new management efforts so frequently that the changes were viewed as public relations gimmicks by many people and not taken seriously.

Transition. The interviews underscored the importance of using the Presidential transition period to require that "manageability" be built into the very first steps to translate campaign rhetoric into practical programs. Because a transition environment is not conducive to this, someone in the transition team needs to be assigned to watch for these opportunities.

President Ronald Reagan used the transition to put in place much of the staff and White House organization he would need, and in the process he began to develop teamwork among his prospective top political appointees. Because of workable operational plans developed during the transition, Richard M. Nixon was able to begin with a series of bold management reforms the first few weeks after inauguration.

Alice Rivlin thought that a central lesson to be conveyed during transition orientation sessions of incoming appointees is that the career service is the new appointee's most valuable asset and should not be regarded as an obstacle or an enemy, a stereotype that is too often embedded in campaign thinking.[1] Constance Newman noted the value that came from the very positive meeting President George H.W. Bush had with the top career people during his first week after inauguration.[2]

Sustained Leadership. Failure to stray the course has doomed some important Presidential efforts to improve government, as was demonstrated by Nixon's waning support for his departmental reorganization as political issues in the 1972 election took center stage.

Presidential Appointments

Alice Rivlin and Fred Fielding were among those who gave special emphasis to the appointment power of the President as a powerful tool for strengthening the operation of government, a tool not always well utilized.

White House Staff. Personal loyalty and compatibility with the President's philosophy are essential, but these traits have to be accompanied by competence and intelligence. Repeatedly, the Working Group was told that serving as campaign advance men and women is not a good qualification for governing, with the exception of public affairs work. Early transition assignments can provide a useful testing ground for some of those under serious consideration for appointment, both with respect to their performance and how they function as a team.

Department Heads. A President should make clear his expectation that a department or agency head understands his or her responsibility for managing the department effectively and avoiding scandal. There was strong agreement that either the Secretary or Deputy Secretary of each department must have previous experience in running large organizations, regardless of how much is delegated to lower levels. No Presidential or OMB role can substitute for departmental management leadership. Although the role of departmental leadership in major policy development is perceived as declining somewhat, the appointees who were interviewed all stressed the continued extent to which a President must rely on the departments for effective program management and policy implementation.

Lower-Level Appointments. Most of those interviewed had limited familiarity with lower-level political appointees, but there was concern about the adequacy of their oversight. Fred Fielding believes a President needs to instruct departmental leadership to monitor the actions of low-level political appointees more carefully.[3] This was mentioned as especially worrisome in the case of departments and agencies whose leadership lack a strong base of their own and are vulnerable to end runs by their political subordinates.

Charles Bowsher was one of several who thought that there are far too many low-level political appointees. Others did not see a problem with the numbers, but were concerned about whether low-level appointees are in a position to represent the thinking of the President with whom they have so little contact. On particular issues, some appointees were viewed as being more responsive to the interests of their political patron, which might be a special interest group, than to the Secretary or the President.

Vice President

Policy Leadership. A President can assign a management policy leadership role to a Vice President, just as Clinton has done. He can have considerable value as one with political credibility, as a vigorous advocate, as a public explainer, and as a motivator. But all agreed that the decision for the role of the Vice President must be left for each President. Management policy leadership should not be regarded as a continuing responsibility of the Vice President.

Government Manager. In contrast to the positive reaction to a possible role of policy leadership, the office of Vice President is not viewed by any of the interviewees as a good location for the institutional leadership needed to implement management policies among the departments and agencies. Several reasons were advanced for why the Vice President should not be involved in institutional leadership:

▶ There is no assurance that the apparatus will survive the next election,

▶ Attention may falter as the next election approaches,

▶ Vice Presidential institutional leadership confuses and weakens the statutory management role of OMB,

▶ There will probably be a late start while the Vice President becomes oriented and decides what to do,

▶ There is a danger of the management agenda being skewed or blunted by political considerations that might be given undue weight.

White House Organization

All agreed that a President must have great flexibility in organizing the White House, but how he exercises that flexibility matters.

President Dwight D. Eisenhower installed a structured approach that fit his military background and worked well for him. After rejecting the Eisenhower approach, however, John F. Kennedy experienced major setbacks from his unstructured arrangement in which he tried at first to be his own Chief of Staff. These setbacks were particularly visible in the national security arena as illustrated by the Bay of Pigs. Nixon strengthened the role of his White House staff and met disaster as he isolated himself behind this inner circle. The early Jimmy Carter and Gerald Ford "spokes in a wheel" approaches did not work. Reagan's passive approach to White House management was overly dependent on the quality and maturity of his staff, thereby contributing to the Iran-Contra crisis when the early high-level of quality declined.

Several interviewees commented that how a President-elect does, or does not, exercise managerial leadership during the transition often sets a pattern for his Presidency. Negative consequences of a late start in organizing his new team will haunt a President for some time. Additional comments:

Structure. The people interviewed by the Working Group had diverse ideas about the details of how a White House should be organized, pointing out that it depends heavily on a President's personal style of operation and changing times. However, several said that there has to be a degree of structure that is more formal than some Presidents prefer. It is difficult for an incoming President to understand the negative impact on government operations that grows out of a poorly organized White House—it quickly breeds confusion and uncertainty within the Executive Branch.

Serving the President. A President has to set up a staff that will help guard against one-sided advocacy, too hasty prescriptions, and other mistakes. The staff must also get him the information he needs when he needs it. Lee White and David Chu stated that Presidential assistants must be willing to serve as lightning rods for criticism when necessary and accept blame for events or policies not of their making. They need to help compensate for Presidential weaknesses rather than, as in the case of Nixon's staff, exploiting them to advance their own power.

Protecting the President. A President has to be protected from the deluge of people that threatens to engulf him, while at the same time avoiding both the Nixon type of isolation and the too loose arrangements of the early Kennedy and Clinton years. Jack Watson and others stressed the need for the quality of staff that will minimize missteps that embarrass a President and divert attention from his goals.

Chief of Staff. There was wide agreement that someone has to be in a position to regulate access to the President, control the paper flow, and ensure that recommended policies and actions are staffed out. Most felt this could best be done through a Chief of Staff, a position they believe has become a necessity rather than an option. Although agreeing with the need, Elmer Staats thought this position has taken on too great a public role. It was recognized that over-concentration of power in a Chief of Staff remains a potential danger, but those interviewed believed that the need for the position is too strong to hesitate because of this risk.

Managing the White House. Whatever organizational arrangement a President adopts, he has to manage it.[4] He, not the staff, sets the tone and the rules. The President is accountable for how the whole place works. But again, a President needs staff help to avoid getting drawn into time consuming details.

White House Staff

The roles of the White House staff have changed and become even more important as agencies have proliferated and the Executive Branch program structure has become more fragmented, thus forcing more issues to the White House. Selecting key staff, especially the Chief of Staff, early in the transition period is critical. Otherwise, confusion will grow rapidly and position jockeying by some will have a higher priority than helping the President translate his campaign promises into a workable agenda that he can present upon assuming office.

Basic Role of Staff. Frank Carlucci, in particular, cautioned that a President should instruct the Chief of Staff and other White House aides that they should function as coordinators, facilitators, and "quality control" people, not as operators. Ed Meese also warned that White House staff become too powerful when assuming an operational role. There are not effective checks and balances on such activities, and public accountability is undermined, as we learned from the Iran-Contra episode. Further, White House staff do not have the special expertise needed for operations that is found in the departments. Ed Meese and others said that a President has to delegate heavily to key staff, but needs some means of early warning when misuse of these delegations begins to develop.

Coordinating Role. Much of the more important policy development is said to have shifted from the departments to the White House. This change was lamented by some as shifting motivation too heavily from long-term public benefit to short-term political interest. Several interviewees also said that managerial workability of policies and new programs is ignored as a result of the more dominant White House role. However, most expected this trend to continue.[5] As a result, White House staff need to possess the increasingly high qualifications that are required to coordinate very complex policy development in a pressure environment.

Size of Staff. The larger the staff of policy advisors, the greater the risk of confusion. Channels of communication get clogged and responsibilities become unclear with a large staff. Relations between the White House and the departments suffer. Yet there was recognition that Presidential needs for staff vary substantially, and no one supported a formal ceiling.

Broad Perceptions. Most agreed with Charles Schultze in saying that staff should be knowledgeable in the broad fields in which they will be working, but should not be technical experts in narrow areas. Neither should they be ideologues wedded to certain positions or advocates for special interest groups. This is at times a difficult balance.

Arrogant Staff. Several spoke of the arrogance that characterizes some Presidential assistants. Such behavior alienates Cabinet members and infuriates Members of Congress, including those from the President's own party. A President-elect should establish a positive tone for his Administration during the transition period. General Goodpaster stated that White House staff and department heads must have, or quickly develop, an understanding of what government is and the values that are important in public service.

Representing the President. Too many lower-level White House staff cultivate the perception that they are speaking for the President when they often have almost no direct contact with him and lack a deep understanding of what the President is striving to accomplish. They should not invent interpretations of Presidential intent. David Chu also stressed that it is essential that White House staff at all levels dedicate themselves to the President's agenda, rather than their own agenda as, for example, occurred with OMB Director David Stockman and National Security Advisor Admiral John Poindexter under Reagan. The influence that goes with working in the White House must be exercised with care—a point the President needs to make very clear to each staff member.

Knowing the President. Having worked with the President prior to their appointments increases the access, trust, and attention of top White House staff. They are also more likely to provide the frankness the President needs. At the same time, the Presidential staff should include some diversity of backgrounds and perspectives.

Honest Broker. The role of "honest broker," rather than policy advocate, was stressed in some interviews, although several thought that the fragmentation of agencies is such that the President now has little choice but to turn to his staff for policy recommendations that are not dominated by special interest groups. Several believed that experienced and sensitive assistants could, and should, do both.

Personnel Office. This office tends to be undervalued, and probably understaffed in view of the large number of political appointees now in the government. For lower-level political appointees, the current system leaves this office with little opportunity to look beyond the investigative and disclosure procedures and consider qualifications in any depth.[6] Further, this office needs to function in high gear from the outset of the transition, meaning that considerable planning has to be done before the election. This is critical to Presidential leadership.

Congressional Relations. The President needs to make clear how he expects the Congressional Relations Office and other White House staff to relate to each other and to Congress. There are occasions in which staff other than those working for the Assistant for Congressional Relations will need to communicate with Members of Congress, but William Timmons and Robert Griffin stressed that these contacts should be within a framework developed with the Assistant for Congressional Relations, not independently as Bob Haldeman in the Nixon Administration and some others have done. Elmer Staats urged a restoration of the close communication with the Congressional committees that the Bureau of the Budget (BOB) (the precursor to OMB) management and legislative reference staffs had up through the first Nixon term. This worked because they acted in collaboration with the President's Congressional Relations Office, thereby mutually reinforcing each other.

Management Experience. It was suggested that a President include among his key White House staff someone who has management experience involving large and complex organizations. This should not be a management position, however, as that role would result in conflicts and confusion with the OMB management role. Rather, in the course of his or her principal policy work, this assistant would be also in a position to involve the OMB management staff and make sure that the management dimension of policies is involved at the earliest stage of their development.[7]

The Cabinet

No one interviewed regarded the Cabinet as an effective management or decision making body today. Yet it can be useful for a few purposes.

▶ The Cabinet can provide a forum for the President to launch government-wide management initiatives.

▶ It can provide a forum for motivation, information exchange, and addressing crosscutting management issues.

▶ John Koskinen and Edward DeSeve, while heading management in OMB, found the Cabinet Secretary to be very helpful in transmitting important messages to the departments as part of his conference calls to departmental Chiefs of Staff.

Cabinet Councils, each consisting of the relevant department Secretaries, for most purposes have greater utility than convening the whole Cabinet. Beginning with the Urban Affairs and Rural Affairs Councils under Nixon, they have since been reconfigured in several ways to serve different Presidents.

▶ Ed Meese and Jack Watson discussed in some depth how Cabinet Councils were useful for policy development in the Carter and Reagan Administrations. They take advantage of the White House coordinating role, but maintain a significant policy role for department heads.

▶ To the extent that the President chairs the Councils, he is able to provide strategic guidance as well as keep himself informed.

▶ Through departmental participation, Councils help guard against a President becoming isolated by the White House staff.

▶ No Council should be permitted to evolve into an executive committee for the Cabinet.

▶ Councils need to meet regularly in some form. Most agreed that decision making sessions should be chaired by the President, and that attendance should be limited to principals. Much of the work of a Council, however, has to be conducted in a less formal format. Under Reagan, there were many Council meetings chaired pro tem by one of the Cabinet members, but no major decisions were made except when chaired by the President. In most Presidencies, there are numerous Council meetings at the Deputy or Assistant Secretary level, chaired by White House staff, dealing with such things as developing options, setting agendas, and coordinating implementation actions. Jack Watson and Ed Meese found Council task forces and working groups to be useful in helping Councils address specific problems.

▶ Councils need to be supported by good White House staff who are facilitative and effective in moving the work forward without dominating or trying to control their outcomes.[8]

▶ Cabinet Councils should be at the discretion of a President, not in statutes that limit Presidential flexibility.

Presidential Commissions

Beginning with William Howard Taft's Commission on Efficiency and Economy, a number of Presidents have appointed special commissions to review government structure and operations. Some have been perceived as effective, others have not. Characteristics mentioned in the interviews and by several in the Working Group as important for successful commissions (by whatever title) included:

▶ A mandate to confront a significant social/economic/governance problem that the normal Legislative and Executive processes have not been able to handle.

▶ Visible support and genuine commitment from the President, and the development of support from a fair number of the affected groups and some of the media.

▶ Composing commissions with objective, highly respected people who do not have close ties to any of the affected groups. For example appointing postal union or postal industry leaders, or competitors, would be fatal to a commission looking at postal functions.

▶ Avoiding commissions made up of key figures currently in Congress and the Executive Branch. It is difficult for these officials to step back from their current high profile roles and look objectively at basic organization and management issues. They are also too busy.

▶ Highly qualified professional staff. The notion of a group of wise individuals brainstorming their way to a practical solution is illusory. In past years, most have also benefited from considerable Bureau of the Budget staff input, although Nixon's Ash Council relied primarily on its own staff

▶ Willingness to follow up their recommendations and convince decision makers to act.

Office Of Management And Budget

There was strong agreement that there should be an organization that constitutes a stable, continuing management arm of the President and provides government-wide leadership on management issues. Most believed OMB provides that arm, mentioning the following assets:

Government-wide. OMB is truly government-wide in its scope and it is in a position to provide the broad Presidential perspective on government operations.

Program Management. In addition to the more limited administrative management that is the principal focus of the General Services Administration, the Office of Personnel Management, and the Treasury Department, OMB is concerned with program management, which has a direct relationship to Presidential goals and priorities.

Professional Resource. OMB has the capacity to function as a high-quality professional resource serving the President and the Executive Branch. It should not be another instrument in the Executive Office focusing on partisan political objectives. At the same time, OMB has demonstrated the ability to be politically sensitive.

Independent Advice. Several of those interviewed thought OMB has developed a reputation for being quite objective in the field of management. They viewed it as a valuable source of independent judgment and advice to the President, countering some of the overzealousness or skewing that comes from the agencies or special advocates that are sometimes found on the White House staff.

Institutional Support. OMB has provided the institutional capacity to support a number of the most important Presidential initiatives and reforms of the past, although some interviewees had the impression that this capacity has declined over the years.

Budget Linkage. Several stressed the leverage for management leadership they believe results from the OMB role in budget and program evaluation for the President.

John Koskinen and Ed DeSeve described how important their use of the budget leverage was for their management initiatives. Further, most high profile issues involve both budget and management decisions that need some level of coordination. In fact, several of those interviewed could not conceive of ways of providing effective leverage other than through the budget, a point that triggered some disagreement. Otherwise, they see management as on the outside, looking in.

Coordinating Groups. By chairing such groups as the President's Management Council, the OMB Deputy for Management is in a position to coordinate work on government-wide management issues.

Early Warning. When properly staffed, OMB can provide the President with an effective early warning capacity regarding program problems. There was disagreement as to whether OMB should be concerned with field operations.[9]

Despite these positive attributes, there were words of caution from several who were familiar with OMB:

Poor Utilization. Most Presidents and their political leadership are not fully aware of the OMB management resource or use it wisely. Important opportunities are often missed and management initiatives tend to be started much too late.

Political Filtering. Several expressed concern that the political layering of OMB may be leading to a gradual diminution of its positive image as an objective, independent source of advice for the President.

Political Battles. In order for OMB management leadership to be trusted and succeed, it has to function as a dispassionate honest broker in addressing management issues. The current close linkage with the budget, however, at times clouds management relationships with the agencies because of the adversarial nature of the budget process and the bitter political battles that are involved. This linkage also reduces the insulation OMB management staff otherwise have from these divisive political issues as they deal with Members of Congress.[10]

Budget Overwhelms Management. To the extent that the budget dominates OMB, some thought that it is difficult for management considerations to compete.[11] Another concern was that the dominance of the annual budget process limits its independent judgment on important management problems that require drawing upon far more than budgeting skills. Jack Watson and Charles Bowsher also pointed out that there are a number of critical aspects of management that are not associated with the annual budget. In fact, decisions that are based solely on their impact on the budget are often viewed as harmful to management initiatives, particularly those requiring long-term investment of resources and analysis of the impact of federal actions on communities and families. Some of the highly visible IRS and air traffic control system problems were mentioned as examples.

Even among those who are familiar with OMB and oppose a separate Office of Management, most nonetheless believe there is need for some rebuilding of a capacity to address crosscutting management and organization issues that have Presidential significance. Koskinen, Bowsher, and Staats also pointed out the need for OMB staff to spend more time in the field, regardless of whether they are concerned with budget or management matters.

Program Management. There were suggestions for strengthening OMB program management attention, ranging from policy development to implementation and evaluation. The Government Performance and Results Act (GPRA) was mentioned by John Koskinen and Edward DeSeve as a useful instrument to help OMB and the President assure good program performance.

Working Group Observations

A surprising range of opportunities for Presidential managerial leadership emerged from these interviews of Presidential appointees, all but two of whom had occupied important positions in the White House or OMB. Most of these appointees had contributed significantly to positive management actions by the Presidents for whom they worked. But many key White House staff have a very limited view of management as a concern of theirs. Most think of management only in terms of managing policy development, giving little thought to the Presidential leadership needed for implementing those policies. Others think of management primarily in terms of administrative processes such as accounting and procurement, which are seen as OMB roles. Particularly significant, the interviews revealed a void of anyone at the beginning of a Presidency in a position to recognize the full range of opportunities for Presidential leadership in managing the government.

This leads the Working Group to urge that a person in the transition team of the President-elect be assigned the task of arranging orientations to acquaint the President's proposed top appointees with these opportunities and to develop plans whereby the new President can take advantage of them. These plans should direct close attention to how Presidential leadership can be exercised effectively while minimizing the amount of personal time required of the President.

The Working Group finds compelling evidence that the operation of our national government requires much stronger Presidential management leadership. It has to be woven into the daily functioning of a Presidency, and there are many opportunities to do so. To take advantage of these opportunities, however, a pressure-ridden President must have much more help in providing this leadership than he usually gets.

Integrating the workability dimension into policy, program development, and implementation should take place at the outset of a new Administration. It must begin during the transition and become ingrained as a normal practice.

---

[1] Transition funds for management orientation of key political appointees is authorized by H.R. 4931, which was passed by Congress in September, 2000.

[2] The Working Group stresses the importance of orientations or workshops that help new political appointees develop approaches for effective leadership of the career service. Failure to provide such leadership has frustrated and handicapped many well-intentioned new appointees in their efforts to hit the ground running.

[3] The Working Group believes that there are a series of problems with respect to the growth of lower-level political appointees that affect agency operations adversely and should be reviewed?

[4] This point is developed by James P. Pfiffner, "Can the President Manage The Government?" in *The Managerial Presidency*, James P. Pfiffner, ed., 2nd ed., (College Station, TX: Texas A & M University Press, 1999).

[5] The Working Group believes this shift in policy roles of moving broad issues from departments to the White House raises problems that have not been well analyzed concerning accountability and questions of access of the Congress and the public to White House staff. These issues were raised in the press and Congress by Nixon's reorganization proposals.

[6] In the opinion of the Working Group, under the last several Presidencies there has been a mismatch between the capacity of the Personnel Office and the large number of political applicants and appointees the office has to process.

[7] Carter looked to his Secretary to the Cabinet, Jack Watson, to perform much of this role, particularly that of coordinating the implementation of policies and actions resulting from meetings involving Cabinet members.

[8] There are some indications of a trend toward formal meetings of Council members that are chaired by White House staff rather than the President or a member of the Cabinet. Although such a development may have practical value, the Working Group is not aware that the long-term implications have been given careful thought.

[9] The Working Group sees no need to restore the OMB field capacity of the 1970s, but believes it needs some capacity to monitor field operations problems such as interagency coordination, difficulties in headquarters-field communications, and systemic intergovernmental problems.

[10] The Working Group notes that prior to establishing OMB, the management staff in both Republican and Democratic Administrations worked almost exclusively with Congress on a bipartisan basis while representing the President.

[11] Most of those who were interviewed assumed that the co-location of management and budget provided management with leverage that outweighed the drawbacks, although several of them disagreed with the recent combining of the examiners and management personnel. Two, however, believed management will never be effective in the budget-dominated OMB. Several had not given the issue any thought. The Working Group supports the transfer of the management leadership role from OMB to a separate Office of Management within the Executive Office of the President, a reorganization recommended by two panels of the National Academy of Public Administration and Mr. Horn, Chairman of the House Subcommittee on Government Management, Information, and Technology.

The Ash Council Recommendations

By Dwight Ink

Summary

Upon taking office, President Richard M. Nixon quickly initiated a number of government management reforms. Seeking advice on how to proceed with the most difficult of these reforms, the restructuring of government, he appointed six experienced men to the President's Council on Executive Organization, called the Ash Council after Roy L. Ash, its chair. Their recommendations persuaded Nixon to submit bold proposals to Congress to restructure the Executive Office of the President and the domestic departments and agencies.

After sharp debate, Congress permitted Nixon's Executive Office reorganization proposals to go into effect. The Bureau of the Budget (BOB) was restructured into the Office of Management and Budget (OMB) and the Domestic Council was established. Nixon also forwarded the Ash Council reorganization plan recommendations to Congress for the establishment of the Environmental Protection Agency (EPA) and the National Oceanic and Atmospheric Administration (NOAA). Most other recommendations were acted upon within the Executive Branch.

Based on Ash the Council recommendations, Nixon sent to Congress the most comprehensive structural reorganization of domestic agencies ever proposed by any President. By proposing to consolidate seven departments and several independent agencies into four departments, the President courageously challenged many of the most powerful special interest groups and Congressional committees. As the result of extensive lobbying work on Capitol Hill, major portions of the reorganization seemed to be nearing Congressional approval when the 1972 election and Watergate brought this impressive initiative to a halt.

After the 1972 election, the President and his aides, working in self-imposed isolation, attempted to circumvent Congress through Presidential restructuring actions that concentrated power in the White House and reduced the roles of the departments. Both this closed process and the centralized philosophy Nixon adopted in his second term were in sharp conflict with the Ash Council and OMB advice he had embraced in the first term, and this ill-advised effort failed. No restructuring concept of comparable scope has been advanced since.

Nixon's contrasting approaches to restructuring in his first and second terms demonstrate how important teamwork within the Executive Branch and cooperation with Congress are to the success or failure of Presidential reforms.

The Setting

Campaigning for office in 1968, Richard Nixon pledged to reform the federal government. Among other things, he promised a Commission on Government Reorganization "to set in motion a searching, fundamental reappraisal of our whole structure of government."[1] Upon taking office, it quickly became apparent that this new President was very serious, and was willing to battle hard on behalf of reform. (This was in sharp contrast to the public image left by Nixon during the Watergate disaster.) He believed that the government was not only too unwieldy, but that it had grown into a costly tangle of overlapping and conflicting activities.

Nixon's legislative office (headed by Bill Timmons) and the new Office of Executive Management (OEM) (headed by Dwight Ink) in the Bureau of the Budget quickly forged bipartisan relations with the key Congressional committees concerned with government operations.[2] Working relationships with the public interest groups were developed simultaneously. The President then moved into action.

Two months after inauguration, he issued the broadest directives concerning federal field structures and coordination in U.S. history. These directives included the establishment of 10 standard federal regions to be headquartered in the cities that administered the largest number of state and local grant programs.[3] Ten regional councils were established, made up of representatives from all major domestic grant-dispensing agencies. A massive streamlining effort by OEM started making drastic changes in how grants and contracts were administered throughout the domestic agencies. Government-wide decentralization of operations was launched and greater reliance on state and local governments began-actions that elicited strong bipartisan support from state and local governments across the nation.[4]

With the encouragement and close cooperation of Comptroller General Elmer Staats, a number of financial management reforms began, along with a comprehensive productivity enhancement program. With the support of former officials from the Lyndon B. Johnson Administration, the troubled Post Office Department was soon to be transformed into a de-politicized U.S. Postal Service with most of the attributes of a government corporation.[5]

Under OEM leadership (except for the Postal Service), these actions involved developing new interagency machinery and were unprecedented in scope. OEM did not have the stature, however, to address an even more far-reaching issue—that of the basic organizational structure of the non-defense departments and agencies of the federal government that Nixon thought were outmoded and dominated by special interests. Therefore, on April 5, 1969, Nixon appointed an independent Advisory Council on Executive Organization, commonly referred to as the Ash Council. The work of this Council led to far-reaching government reform proposals, indeed the most comprehensive legislative structural proposals of any U.S. President.

Ash Council Operations

Roy L. Ash, President of Litton Industries, chaired the Council and other members were Harvard Business School Dean George P. Baker; former Texas Governor John B. Connally; former CEO of AT&T Frederick R. Kappel; and Richard M. Paget, president of a management consulting firm. The Council's broad mandate from Nixon was "to undertake a thorough review of the organization of the Executive Branch of Government."[6] More specifically, it was directed to consider:

1. The organization of the Executive Branch as a whole in light of the changing requirements of government;

2. The solutions to organizational problems that had resulted among the plethora of departments, offices, agencies, and other separate Executive organizational units; and

3. The organizational relationships of the federal government to states and cities in carrying out the many domestic programs in which the U.S. government was involved.

At first, nothing happened. Ash was heavily involved with Litton's corporate problems, so on June 2, 1969 Nixon persuaded Walter N. Thayer, President of Whitney Communications Corporation, to become Special Consultant to the President (the only Council member so titled) and the sixth member of the Council. Reflecting the President's impatience, the White House stated that Thayer "will have the responsibility for securing and organizing the Council's staff and directing its activities."[7]

Murray Comarow, a Booz-Allen Hamilton partner with prior government experience, was appointed Executive Director in July,[8] and Andrew M. Rouse, a BOB Deputy Assistant Director became Deputy Executive Director. The Council directed the staff of 25 to prepare studies on a wide range of targeted subjects, beginning with the Executive Office of the President.[9]

Once organized with strong leadership at both the Council and staff levels, the Ash Council moved rapidly. The staff analyzed every government organization study back to the Brownlow Commission in 1937, and interviewed several hundred present and former officials, business executives, scholars, and individuals who had participated in past studies. Multiple options for every reorganization were developed, recognizing that no structural arrangement could possibly resolve all conflicts, or could be realistically regarded as a "solution." As a result, the Council concluded that:

▶ Departments should be organized around broad missions and should seek to integrate the professional skills and governmental functions necessary to accomplish those missions;

▶ The number of departments should be reduced;

▶ Within departments, similar or interdependent programs should be grouped together to avoid the need for excessive coordination and to permit decision making on all issues relevant to their missions; and

▶ Departments should not be perceived primarily as representing the interests of a profession or clientele group. Rather, the general public interest should be served and special interests subordinated to the broader mandate.

Thirteen memoranda were sent to the President between August 20, 1969 and November 17, 1970. Each presented major recommendations to reorganize the Executive Office of the President. Every recommendation of the Ash Council but one passed unanimously.[10]

The most ambitious recommendations led to Nixon's 1971 Cabinet reorganization plan in which he intended to restructure seven departments and four independent agencies into four departments.[11]

The Council warned, and President Nixon recognized, that such massive changes would be resisted and attacked by dozens, if not hundreds, of interest groups. Opposition did develop, but the largest obstacles turned out to be unrelated events both during and following the 1972 election.

The Fate Of Council Recommendations In The First Term
Executive Office of the President

On August 20, 1969, the Ash Council forwarded to Nixon two major recommendations on the Executive Office of the President. First, was a proposal for establishing a Domestic Council chaired by the President and made up of the Vice President and the Secretaries of nine Cabinet departments. The Domestic Council's staff was to be headed by an Executive Director who would also be an Assistant to the President, an arrangement that later drew considerable Congressional fire over the issue of Congressional accessibility to White House staff.

Second, building on President Dwight D. Eisenhower's reorganization plan, the Ash Council also recommended reconstituting BOB as an Office of Executive Management. Although its functions were not too different from those already in BOB, it was believed that the restructuring and renaming would help in achieving a greater emphasis on management and program coordination.[12] In fact, the Council saw management, not budget, as the overarching function of its proposed new OEM.

When Nixon approved these first recommendations, no one predicted that they would precipitate an intense confrontation with Capitol Hill. However, by the time they were both incorporated into Reorganization Plan No. 2 of 1970 and submitted to Congress by Nixon on March 12, 1970, extensive Hill briefings had revealed that several key congressmen had serious concerns.

Chief among the doubters was Representative Chet Holifield, a Democrat from California. He was the most influential member of the House Government Operations Committee, which had jurisdiction over reorganization proposals. There were grumbles about why the President would send up a plan that simply changed the name of the Bureau of the Budget unless there was some hidden motive involved. More importantly, Holifield and a majority of his colleagues charged that the plan placed all of the former BOB functions in the Executive Office of the

President. This would arguably leave Nixon with discretion as to which BOB functions he might wish to delegate to the new organization (now called the Office of Management and Budget) and which he might delegate elsewhere. They believed the that the plan would "give the President almost unlimited power to restructure the administration of those functions at any time, delegating them where he might at that moment desire, without any action or review by Congress."[13] Holifield was also convinced the plan would weaken the Civil Service.

Although considerable time was devoted to sharp questioning about the proposed OMB, the Committee's greatest anger was directed at the companion portion of the reorganization plan, the proposed Domestic Council. The committee saw the Domestic Council as weakening the department heads and providing a power base for White House staff who would not be accessible to Congress. This was a separation of powers issue of great sensitivity. Neither Chairman Ash nor OEM Director Ink provided counter-arguments that the Committee found persuasive, and on May 8 it forwarded a proposed House resolution to disapprove Reorganization Plan No. 2, with five of the Republicans dissenting.[14]

The unions opposed the reorganization plan, the General Accounting Office expressed concern, and the vote count looked very doubtful with only a few days left before action was to be taken by the full House. However, BOB embarked on a major last minute effort to generate support on the basis of a need for a domestic counter-weight to the foreign policy attention given the National Security Council and National Security Advisor Henry Kissinger. This argument proved effective with the OEM state and local networks, and was largely responsible for saving the plan.[15] For the only time in our history, on May 13 by a vote of 193-164, the House rejected a recommendation from the Committee on Government Operations to disapprove a Presidential reorganization plan, thereby permitting OMB and the Domestic Council to come into being.[16]

Environmental Protection Agency

As the result of other Ash Council recommendations, on July 9, 1970 President Nixon sent to Congress Reorganization Plan No. 3 to establish the Environmental Protection Agency and Reorganization Plan No. 4 to establish, within the Department of Commerce, a National Oceanic and Atmospheric Administration. EPA drew the most controversy.

Environmental responsibilities were lodged in more than a dozen Federal agencies, and there was no organizational focus for a concerted program to reverse environmental damage done over the years by pollution and neglect. Although reluctant to establish another government agency, Nixon accepted the Ash Council's view that setting and enforcing environmental standards must be performed outside of the affected agencies. There was widespread surprise that Nixon would propose an environmental agency-this is one example of why the most conservative elements of the Republican Party never embraced Nixon.

After OMB defined the specific components of the proposed agency, advance discussions with Congress revealed a surprising split between the two key House members, both liberal Democrats and close friends, whose support was required to offset opposition that would otherwise kill the plan. Holifield thought that transferring environmental protection responsibilities from existing agencies with huge programs in various fields would reduce the agencies' sense of responsibility for protecting the environment. On the other hand, Representative John Blatnik of Minnesota believed that only a Department of Environment encompassing most environment-related activities would possess the leverage and command enough attention to be effective. OEM finally negotiated an agreement, which Nixon forwarded in the form of a successful reorganization plan (similar to the Ash Council recommendations) for an agency, not a department.[17] Conservatives from both parties, and several committee chairmen guarding their turf, continued to be opposed, but public concern was sufficiently strong that the 60 days in which a resolution of disapproval could be filed passed without such an action, and the plan establishing the Environmental Protection Agency was permitted to go into effect.

OMB then established a task force to develop the arrangements for establishing the agency. It assisted the first agency head, William Ruckelshaus, who provided effective leadership in building the agency that was to face a myriad of controversial issues including air and water pollution, pesticides, and radiation hazards.[18] The task was made more difficult by the lack of an "organic act" to integrate the many different functions, and also the necessity of relating to dozens of Senate and House committees.[19] However, an organic act was thought to have had no chance of passage at that time. EPA has had its ups and downs, but its overall impact has been very substantial. In addition to EPA and NOAA, other Ash Council recommendations were submitted, dealing with such subjects as organized crime, narcotics trafficking, and drug abuse.

Departmental Reorganization

Nixon approved in principle the Ash Council's far-reaching reorganization of the domestic departments, as modified by the White House staff and OMB. The most significant change was to eliminate the new Department of Transportation and divide its functions between the proposed Departments of Community and Economic Affairs. That made the package more difficult to sell.[20]

Nixon believed that his reorganization objectives would fail if pursued in bits and pieces, since specific clientele and bureaucratic resistance could overpower small proposals. It was also felt that Congress and the public were entitled to see the whole picture of how the government would be changed. The best chance for action would result from a bold comprehensive package to be sent to Congress.

Nixon turned to the new Office of Management and Budget and its Assistant Director for Executive Management, Dwight Ink, to undertake the huge task of translating the Ash Council recommendations into legislative proposals. His Deputy Assistant Director, Alan L. Dean, was designated staff coordinator of the Department Reorganization Program (PDRP).[21] Four interagency task forces were organized, in which the budget examiners were also heavily involved, to address each proposed department. There was also a fifth task force, chaired by Charles Bingman, Director of the Government Organization Staff who was charged with assuring that each departmental plan had an effective organization and management structure.

The new OMB political leadership of George Shultz, Caspar Weinberger, and Arnold Weber, together with White House staff, assured cooperation of the disappearing departments and agencies in meeting rigorous deadlines, making it possible to submit the proposals to Congress by March 1971. During this process several significant internal organization concepts were developed that were well received by Congress, such as the need for providing department-wide management leadership through an Undersecretary for Management and the popular decentralized field program delivery systems utilizing regional offices. To help Congress and the public understand how the new structure was to work better, section-by-section analyses and analytical reports were prepared explaining in detail the structure, role, and program components of each department.[22]

Holifield, now chair of the Government Operations Committee, reacted to the PDRP with derision, and shock waves hit Congressional committees concerned about losing jurisdiction after the consolidation of functions into "superdepartments" as the four proposed organizations became known. Yet after intensive discussions with OMB staff, Timmons arranged a White House meeting with Nixon at which Holifield now said that he saw some merit in the proposals. He warned the President, however, that these proposals would arouse opposition from virtually every interest group in the country that sought narrowly based agencies or departments responsive to their constituencies. The political landscape would be covered in blood, Holifield said. Nixon replied that he had enough political experience to be well aware of that, but he thought special interests had too much power. He explained that too much decision making had gravitated to the White House, and that his reorganization would lead to many issues being settled before they reached the White House. He stressed his belief that this reorganization was the right thing to do, and he planned to do everything he could to gain Congressional support.

Holifield, who had never liked Nixon, was surprisingly touched by this response. He then held overview hearings on the overall PDRP, followed by hearings on the Department of Community Development (DCD) that was reported out of the committee favorably by the encouraging vote of 27-7. A Timmons vote count indicated a clear majority in both houses would support the DCD, and the Senate, with the strong approval of Democratic Senator Henry "Scoop" Jackson of Washington, would support the Department of Natural Resources (DNR), although the House was uncertain.[23] However, issues related to the 1972 Presidential campaign and election prevented moving the bills to the floor of either House before Congress adjourned.[24]

The Second Term Attempt To Establish
A "Supercabinet" Unilaterally

After the election, the OMB management staff prepared to resubmit the reorganization proposals with some changes to ease passage. It was not clear whether the scars from the 1972 election could be overcome, but there was some reason for hope as Holifield said he might be receptive to the department of community development and Democratic Senator Abraham Ribicoff of Connecticut said he was sympathetic to both the Department of Community Development and the Department of Natural Resources. However, it soon became clear that Nixon was impatient with the slow and uncertain legislative approach and wanted to accomplish by Presidential action much of what he had earlier hoped to gain through the legislation.

As a result, while taking pains to avoid the use of either legislation or reorganization plans that would involve Congress, Nixon and the White House staff developed an arrangement that became known as the "Supercabinet." At the top were five Assistants to the President who were to "integrate and unify policies and operations throughout the Executive Branch of the Government, and to oversee all of the activities for which the President is responsible."[25] Beneath them Nixon appointed three Cabinet members as counselors who were to coordinate the handling of interagency issues within broad functional areas.[26] On the bottom rung were the other Cabinet members such as the Secretary of the Interior and the Secretary of Labor. At the same time, a number of White House staff were placed in departments and agencies in an effort to make the bureaucracy more responsive to the White House, a step that began to politicize the career Civil Service.

Nixon did not reconvene the Ash Council to advise him as he developed this new White House-dominated approach that violated the Ash Council concept Nixon had earlier embraced, which was to relieve the White House of the less critical decision making and rely more on department heads.[27] This White House layering and centralization of control was opposed by Ink who was then surreptitiously taken out of the whole process.[28] Nixon's successful first term practice of careful advance consultation with Congress was abandoned. In fundamental ways, Nixon's second term approach to restructuring was the opposite of that which he had employed in his first term, in both process and content.

Although this second reorganization design did go into effect in 1973, it never worked. The top level of White House assistants were regarded as power hungry, and the Counselors never came close to achieving the leadership role Nixon envisioned. The arrangement was resented by both the political and career leaders in the subordinate departments and by Members of Congress who regarded it as a scheme to circumvent Congress and of questionable constitutionality.

When the pressures of Watergate forced the resignation of top White House aides Bob Haldeman and John Ehrlichman, the entire Supercabinet arrangement collapsed immediately, ending the last Nixon effort to improve the structure of government. No restructuring of comparable scope has been proposed since. So what were the results of the Ash Council's work?

The Council developed the most far reaching, integrated effort to rationalize our domestic departments ever proposed. The BOB, later OMB, staff developed a concept for internal department organization that was well received on the Hill. Nixon's Congressional Relations staff was respected and effective. And there were early successes resulting from the Ash Council's work, particularly establishing EPA and NOAA.

Yet few today believe that changing BOB to OMB achieved the objective of increasing the emphasis on management. Indeed, most observers (including Murray Comarow, the Council's Executive Director and the first OMB Assistant Director for Management, Dwight Ink) believe the management capacity has declined significantly during the existence of OMB. Many also believe the replacement of BOB has paved the way for too much political filtering of the independent views of the career staff on both budget and management issues that used to be available to the President. [29]

The Domestic Council facilitated domestic decision making at first, but as the 1972 election approached, it became more of a political instrument to reelect Nixon, including some of the unsavory activities of the Watergate period. It was later abolished, but then revived in different forms by successive Administrations. Finally, the ambitious departmental reorganization proposals approved by President Nixon failed completely. Why did the excellent work of a highly regarded Presidential advisory council not lead to better results?

Lessons Learned

▶ **Value of Commissions.** The advice the Ash Council gave Nixon was generally of very high quality and provided a needed vision and strategy for rationalizing the domestic departments. [30] The sweeping scope of their recommendations would not likely emerge from any internal review of organization. Hence, the Ash Council illustrates the value of convening an outside body for addressing broad issues, particularly those challenging the turf of large groups. However, many external factors are likely to determine the ultimate success or failure of such an instrument.

▶ **Need for a Fast Start.** It was not until early June that the Council was in a position to move forward, a handicap that diligent work by an able staff could not overcome. The time lost by the Ash Council in getting underway did not seem to be serious at the time. However, had Congressional hearings been completed two months sooner, the House and Senate would probably have passed two of the departmental consolidation proposals before getting sidetracked by 1972 election problems. A running start is an invaluable asset for an incoming President.

▶ **Commission Staff.** Once organized, the Ash Council moved quickly on a wide variety of very challenging issues (most of which carried highly charged political implications), demonstrating the value of utilizing the unusually high caliber of experienced staff that Walter N. Thayer and Murray Camarow had engaged.

▶ **Institutional Support.** The critical role of OMB demonstrated the need for an institutional capacity to provide technical and substantive leadership for translating recommendations of an outside body into action. These proposals required much more than collecting good management ideas; they were fraught with serious conflicts over shifts of authority, potential losses of budget, and disruptions of existing relationships among agencies, clients, and Congress. A trusted institutional staff of this type with an ability to speak for the President is invaluable to move Presidential reform forward.

▶ **Value of Reorganization Plan Authority.** The implementation of the Ash Council recommendations for EPA and NOAA through reorganization plan authority demonstrated the value of this as a Presidential instrument for structural reform. Many believe this authority should be reactivated in some form.

▶ **Price of Politics.** The fate of the Ash Council work illustrates how easily political actions can torpedo actions designed to improve the effectiveness of government. Had the Domestic Council continued to carry out the policy role envisioned by the Ash Council, Congress would not have abolished it. Political mistakes made during and after the 1972 election lost Nixon the political capital needed for any chance to move forward with the departmental restructuring in which he had invested so much effort. The more political character of the second term restructuring approach placed Nixon's efforts at reform in further jeopardy.

▶ **Need for Presidential Leadership.** Without the leadership of President Nixon, and the willingness he demonstrated during his first term to stand fast against special interests arrayed against his bold restructuring proposals, there would have been no serious consideration of the legislative proposals resulting from the Ash Council's work. When that leadership faltered as the 1972 election approached, there was no way the Council or OMB could save the program. Sustained Presidential leadership is required for major reform.

▶ **Complexity of Reform.** At the beginning of the Nixon Administration, an integrated organizational infrastructure was at work in the Executive Office of the President involving the Ash Council, the White House staff, BOB/OMB, the President's Assistant for Legislative Affairs, and the President himself. It also involved careful laying of groundwork with Congress and key public interest groups.

This teamwork disappeared in 1972 as Nixon and his immediate staff began to insulate themselves and ultimately ignore everyone else. The White House concentration of power after the 1972 election moved the President toward simplistic and indefensible approaches to restructuring that were doomed to failure.

True structural reform today is an extremely complex affair, which requires involvement by many stakeholders, an institutional support capacity beyond what exists today, and strong, sustained Presidential leadership. It will usually involve partnership roles for the private sector and with state and local governments. Global implications may emerge. Today, there is also much greater difficulty in engaging Congress to consider sweeping changes affecting the turf of various agencies and Congressional committees. Therefore, to have any chance of success, future structural reforms of magnitude, no matter how desirable, have to be designed with extreme care and managed with great professional and political skill, a combination that rarely exists.

---

[1]   A CBS Radio campaign statement by Nixon on June 27, 1968.

[2]   The OEM was established at the close of the Johnson Administration in an effort to strengthen management and program coordination within BOB. Dwight Ink was appointed Director in early 1969. The OEM was given strong support by BOB Director Robert Mayo and Deputy Director Phillip Hughes.

[3]   These actions caused an initial torrent of criticism from many Senators and Congressmen whose states or districts did not include the 10 headquarters cities. But within months this was replaced with broad support from state and local groups who applauded the sharp reduction in red tape and the increased accountability that resulted.

[4]   For a description of Nixon's early actions, see *The Nixon Presidency,* second chapter, "Nixon's Version of Reinventing Government," edited by Joan Hoff and Dwight Ink, Center for the Study of the Presidency, 1996.

[5]   This reorganization resulted from the work of President Johnson's Commission on Postal Reorganization whose chair, Frederick R. Kappel, became a member of the Ash Council.

[6]   White House press release, April 5, 1969.

[7]   White House press release, June 2, 1969.

[8]   Comarow's distinguished career included service as Executive Director of President Johnson's Commission on Postal Reorganization (the Kappel Commission) that proposed the transformation of the Post Office Department to the U.S. Postal Service.

[9]   Unlike most of the earlier commissions, the Bureau of the Budget staff was not drawn upon for support.

[10] See the President's Advisory Council on Executive Organization, *Memoranda for the President of the United States,* November 10, 1970, a compilation of the Council's memos to the President.

[11] Departments of Human Resources, Community Development, and Economic Affairs.

[12] This organization would supersede the more limited existing OEM, which had by then developed considerable momentum, but had no budget or evaluation responsibilities.

[13] House Committee on Government Operations, *Disapproving Reorganization Plan No. 2 of 1970, 91ˢᵗ Congress,* p. 3.

[14] Ink argued that Congressional accessibility would be provided by the Domestic Council members, and that to make the Executive Director available for hearings would give him "a much more central role than is deemed desirable" and "would detract from the influence of the Cabinet-level Council members."

[15] On July 13, 1970 the President received a letter of support for the reorganization and the OEM work, signed by the Council of State Governments, the National Governors Conference, the National League of Cities, the U.S. Conference of Mayors, the National Association of Counties, and the International City Management Association.

[16] Several days before the plan was to go into effect, H.R. "Bob" Haldeman and John Ehrlichman summoned BOB Director Robert Mayo and Ink to inform them that the OMB would report to the President through Ehrlichman. This was contrary to the intent of the Ash Council and the commitments Ash and Ink had made to Congress. Mayo and Ink protested vigorously with the result that Mayo, with whom Nixon had never felt comfortable, was fired and Ink was layered over by a political appointee in the new OMB. True to the Ash Council plan, however, all the OMB Directors have reported directly to the President, as had the Directors of BOB.

17 Establishing a department would have required legislation, whereas an agency could be established under the reorganization authority, which enabled a President to move ahead without legislation unless one of the two houses of Congress disapproved within 60 days—an approach more likely to be successful.

18 The OMB task force was headed by a career employee, Howard Messner, who became the first EPA Assistant Administrator for Administration.

19 Relying on a reorganization plan resulted in having to retain all 13 Presidentially appointed positions from the constituent organizations. By contrast, the National Aeronautics and Space Administration (NASA) and the Federal Aviation Administration, organized by legislation, had only two.

20 The Department of Transportation (DOT) was already viewed by many as a major purpose department, but local governments believed that federally assisted roads and highways needed to be more closely related to community planning, a primary reason for the change. Some believed that the White House animosity toward DOT Secretary John Volpe also played a role.

21 Mr. Dean had been the career Assistant Secretary for Administration of DOT, and had earlier worked on many reorganization proposals while in BOB. Mr. Bingman had served in NASA and the Atomic Energy Commission.

22 These documents, together with the President's message, were compiled by OMB in a bound volume *"Papers Relating to the President's Departmental Reorganization Program"* and accompanied the legislative proposals.

23 Timmon's two Deputy Assistants to the President for Congressional Relations, Tom Korologos (who covered the Senate) and Richard Cook (who covered the House), had very accurate vote counts on which the Hill often relied.

24 Another problem was the sudden White House decision to retain the Department of Agriculture, caused in large part by the difficulty in persuading Earl Butz to agree to appointment as Secretary of a disappearing Agriculture Department, thereby compromising the Ash Council concept. Learning of this unexpected change at a 7:30 a.m. White House meeting, for two hours Ink was unable to track down Holifield. At an early morning hearing Holifield had just expressed support for the President's plan to eliminate the Department and the Undersecretry of Agriculture had begun to testify in support of eliminating his department. Holifield was deeply offended by this failure to consult, or even inform him, and immediately suspended hearings on PDRP.

25 The five were Haldeman, Administration of the White House; Ehrlichman, Domestic Affairs; Dr. Kissinger, Foreign Affairs; Shultz, Economic Affairs (as well as continuing as Secretary of the Treasury); and Ash, Executive Management (as well as Director of OMB).

26 Butz, Secretary of Agriculture, became Counsellor for Natural Resources; Weinberger, Secretary-designate of HEW became Counsellor for Human Resources; and Lynn, Secretary-designate became Counsellor for Community Development.

27 The Ash Council has been unfairly criticized by some who have mistakenly assumed this second term "Supercabinet" approach was the product of the Ash Council rather than the very different "Superdepartment" concept of the first term that the Council did design.

28 Ehrlichman secretly assigned work directly to Ink's staff with instructions that the Assistant Director not be informed that such assignments had been made, an example of how the White House environment changed after the 1972 election with greater secrecy and White House staff control.

29 Prior to these changes, Presidents were assured of having the professional budget and management views of senior career staff to consider along with political advice in much the same way the Joint Chiefs of Staff provide independent professional advice on military issues.

30 An exception might be the proposed Department of Economic Affairs that was viewed as an indefensible " catch-all" by OMB staff.

Transforming FEMA

By Stephen Barr

When Presidents take office, they usually devote much of their policy and political energy toward filling the most important Cabinet posts—at the Departments of Defense, State, Treasury, and Justice—and setting up a White House staff operation. Few Presidents spend an equal amount of time worrying about their appointments to the agencies that directly touch the lives of Americans, such as the Social Security Administration, the Internal Revenue Service, the National Weather Service, and the Federal Emergency Management Agency (FEMA).

But there's little dispute that President Bill Clinton got it right when he named James Lee Witt as the FEMADirector in 1993. As amazing as it sounds, Witt was the first FEMAhead who came to the position with direct experience in emergency management, having previously served as the Director of the Arkansas Office of Emergency Services for four years.

Witt was among the many Arkansas friends and associates of Clinton who accompanied the President to Washington during his first term. At the start, however, Witt seemed among the least likely to become a major player in the Administration.

FEMA had been labeled a "political dumping ground" in one Congressional report, and Senator Ernest F. Hollings, a Democrat from South Carolina, had called the agency "the sorriest bunch of bureaucratic jackasses" he had ever known.

The public and press also held FEMA in low regard, primarily because of how the agency had handled two big hurricanes. In September 1989, Hurricane Hugo struck near Charleston, South Carolina, and quickly and violently moved through the center of the state. Thousands of people were left homeless, and disaster-stricken communities found FEMA to be slow and incompetent. Hugo was followed in 1992 by Hurricane Andrew, which flattened the region south of Miami, Florida. Again, FEMA seemed ineffective. In Washington, the common joke was that every storm brought two disasters: one when the hurricane arrived and the second when FEMA arrived.

Transforming Leadership

After his Senate confirmation, Witt began by paying attention to the morale of his employees. His first morning on the job, he stood in the lobby of FEMA headquarters greeting employees as they came to work. He asked senior career executives at FEMA to rotate jobs, providing fresh perspectives on what the agency did.

On Witt's recommendation, Clinton filled most of the FEMA jobs reserved for political appointees with persons who had previous experience in natural disasters and intergovernmental relations.

Just as importantly, Witt pulled together his staff and directed them to develop the agency's first new mission statement in a decade. For many employees, it was the first time they had seen FEMA clearly lay out its organizational goals.

Congressional and public criticism of FEMA's performance led Witt to recast the agency's strategies. He set out a series of goals, such as improving FEMA's partnership with other federal agencies, state and local governments, and nonprofit groups. In almost every area, Witt pushed to revitalize FEMA. He reorganized the agency and shifted its mobile communications vehicles that had long been held in reserve in case of nuclear war to the front-line response teams for natural disasters. He streamlined the disaster application process to get more relief to victims faster.

The restructured FEMA focused on coordinating a broad disaster relief strategy, with responsibilities shared by the partners. Another focus involved assisting communities to set up so-called mitigation programs that would help them to avoid becoming disaster victims.

Witt expanded the agency's interpretation of its statutory authority to allow for the advanced positioning of disaster crews and relief supplies when weather forecasters provided adequate warnings. He set up rapid response units so that FEMA could deploy teams to any event within four hours.

Many of these changes were made possible because FEMA won praise for its handling of two disasters in the months after Witt took charge. The "great flood" in the spring and summer of 1993 submerged millions of acres of farmland in nine states after 10 times the normal amount of rain fell in the nation's midsection, overwhelming the Mississippi and Missouri rivers. The flood response was handled in an orderly fashion, with FEMA supporting state emergency teams. The next crisis came in January 1994, when an earthquake snapped highways and buildings in the Los Angeles area, killing 61 people. FEMA responded quickly to help earthquake victims, and subsequent Congressional reviews offered little criticism.

FEMA now distributes checks to disaster victims within 7 days instead of 30 days. Temporary housing assistance reaches customers within 7 to 10 days instead of 20, according to agency officials.

In early 1996, Clinton added FEMA to the Cabinet, affirming his trust in Witt and sending that message to the White House staff and senior Administration officials.

From the start, Witt promoted FEMA efforts in the press and on Capitol Hill. Witt's first Public Affairs Director reached out to newspapers and television, providing them with information about disaster relief efforts in an attempt to improve the agency's image. Witt testified before numerous Congressional committees and met privately with key committee chairmen.

Although the Clinton Administration often cites FEMA as a "reinventing government" success story, the agency's reforms seem to be more about an Administration's need to get the right leaders into the right places.

Clinton's appointment of Witt underscores the importance of selecting agency heads with the right experience for their jobs, and then letting them go to work on bureaucratic inertia or reforms. An experienced agency head can save the White House from waking up one morning engulfed in criticism from ordinary Americans frustrated by how they have been treated by their government.

★　★　★　★　★

Mobilizing for Y2K

By Stephen Barr

John A. Koskinen was in Europe, touring with his wife, when White House officials called. President Bill Clinton and Vice President Al Gore wanted him back in government—as their Year 2000 (Y2K) czar.

Clinton and Gore followed up with separate telephone calls, outlining what they had in mind and appealing to Koskinen to return to the Administration. By March 1998, he was on the job as Chairman of the President's Council on Year 2000 Conversion.

"Things were a little grim," he recalled later in a National Press Club speech. "Some in Congress had just given the federal agencies a grade of D-minus for their efforts to prepare systems for the Year 2000....After three months of my leadership, the grade changed—to an F. The consensus was that the government wouldn't make it. The FAA, the IRS, the Health Care Financing Administration, which runs Medicare and Medicaid, the Department of Defense, were all thought to be lost causes. Some were predicting that there was a significant chance that these failures alone would send the economy into a deep recession, or worse."

The lights, as we know, stayed on during New Year's Eve. The government's computers not only made a successful transition from 1999 to 2000, but so did the incredibly complex networks operated by banks, telephone companies, and utilities. Police and fire systems continued to operate without a hitch. Overseas, the Y2K glitch also was a dud—even in Russia, China, and other nations believed to be at risk of computer breakdowns.

In the United States, the Y2K repair bill exceeded $100 billion. At times, the Y2K effort seemed engulfed in irony—sophisticated machines and systems were at risk of failure because of an old programming practice, the use of two digits to represent a four-digit year. That meant computers might interpret "00" as 1900 instead of 2000, leading them to spew out erroneous data or to crash.

Although fixing the machines was fairly simple, the scope of the work—checking and testing millions of lines of software code and countless "chips"—amounted to what Koskinen called "the greatest management challenge the world has faced in the last 50 years."

In selecting Koskinen, Clinton knew he would bring years of private-sector experience in crisis management to bear on the Y2K challenge. The President also trusted Koskinen—they had first met at a Renaissance Weekend—because he and other Presidential advisers saw Koskinen as a straightforward broker, easy to work with and not easily deflected from his goals.

Koskinen took charge of the government's Y2K project from a two-room office in the Old Executive Office Building with a permanent staff that ranged from three to 15, depending on the month.

A Yale law school graduate, Koskinen came to the government after working for 25 years as an executive at the Palmieri Co., which specialized in restructuring financially troubled businesses. He had learned how to make hard strategic decisions, and how to make them fast.

His introduction to vast computer networks came during Koskinen's first stint in the Clinton Administration, when he served as Deputy Director for Management Issues at the Office of Management and Budget (OMB). While there, he got a taste of political crises, helping to handle two partial shutdowns of the government during the 1995-1996 budget war between Clinton and Congressional Republicans.

As the OMB Deputy Director for Management Issues, Koskinen met with top agency officials from across the government who were responsible for technology, financial management, daily operations, and personnel. He learned where to pull the levers to get things done inside the bureaucracy.

Institutional Leadership

Koskinen resigned from OMB in 1997 for family reasons, but soon found himself being called back by Clinton and Gore, who said little about Y2K in public but were privately concerned that Cabinet departments were not on top of the problem. In some departments, Y2K program managers were quitting or retiring, and repair efforts lacked discipline. Few Cabinet chiefs and senior political appointees understood the dimensions of the problem.

Koskinen began by putting in long hours—from 8 a.m. until 11 p.m. on most days. He extended his personal reach through e-mail, sending out more than 100 messages on an average day—a substantial change in work habits for a person who five years earlier did not know how to use the word-processing programs on an office computer.

He soon started visiting troubled agencies, and later held monthly senior management meetings at the agencies that seemed to be lagging on Y2K repairs. With Gore at this side, Koskinen met with Cabinet officers to hammer out a consensus that Y2K repairs would be the highest priority in federal agencies.

Koskinen also spent time with the private sector, especially the critical infrastructure sectors—airlines, electric power, banks, retail, oil and gas, pharmaceuticals, and telecommunications. He organized more than 25 task forces to reach out to industry groups, corporations, the United Nations, and foreign trading partners.

He collected confidential industry information to assess potential Y2K risks and convened closed-door meetings to educate himself about the Y2K problems facing chemical plants and industrial plants dependent on embedded systems.

On January 1, 2000, the Y2K glitch caused no major inconveniences for Americans or their trading partners. The globe's largest cities celebrated the New Year with lights and phones and fireworks.

But there were some problems, providing a reminder that Y2K held the potential to disrupt everyday transactions. The Defense Department was embarrassed when an intelligence satellite system became totally inoperable for several hours during the rollover. Low-level windshear alert systems failed at the New York, Tampa, Denver, Atlanta, Orlando, Chicago O'Hare, and St. Louis airports. A Y2K glitch at a Chicago bank halted electronic Medicare payments to some hospitals and doctors. A few small retailers billed customers multiple times for a single purchase because of a credit card-related software defect.

The Y2K project provided some important lessons that future Administrations will likely want to study. In a global economy dependent on technology, future Presidents will need to look for leaders like Koskinen, who:

▶ Do not fear "what if" scenarios, know how to set priorities against a deadline, and can show top political appointees and career managers that they need to be more involved in operational issues that put at risk how their organizations conduct their business;

▶ Can form valuable partnerships across large bureaucracies to achieve a common goal;

▶ Can show industry that government can adjust quickly to events, serving as a catalyst for the sharing of information among business competitors;

▶ Can work across party lines, winning the confidence of partisan critics and ensuring that they do their part to pass needed legislation or appropriations; and

▶ Trust the public with more rather than less information. The Internet explosion makes it easy for misinformation and false assumptions to spread quickly. That can only be countered by a leader who feels comfortable in establishing relationships with the press and a willingness to answer large and small questions at almost any time, in public or in private.

With that kind of leader working on his behalf, a President can speak confidently to the nation.

On November 10, 1999, with 51 days to go until the New Year, Clinton issued the Administration's final Y2K status report and, standing on the South Lawn, assured the public that he expected "no major national breakdowns" because of the computer glitch.

"Y2K," he said, "will be remembered as the last headache of the 20th century, not the first crisis of the 21st."

Technology Policy in the First Clinton Administration[1]

By David M. Hart

During the Cold War, the United States laid great emphasis on staying ahead of the Soviet Union in military technology but the real challenge was in realigning related missions and advisory structures. The USSR was geographically proximate to American allies in Western Europe, and it possessed a substantial military advantage on the ground. The U.S. government did not want to station the enormous numbers of troops in Europe that would have been needed to counter the Soviet threat in conventional military terms. High technology was the answer. The country therefore made enormous investments in defense laboratories and procurement of advanced weaponry. The high-tech strategy required that the President have the knowledge to make informed choices about expensive and complicated systems. To do so, he increasingly drew on scientific and technical advice, a function that was institutionalized in the Office of Science and Technology Policy (OSTP) and personified by the Assistant to the President for Science and Technology (commonly referred to as the President's "science advisor") in the late 1950s and early 1960s.

As the years passed, OSTP and the science advisor got involved in a wide range of issues beyond military and space technology. Scientific and technological questions permeated an array of federal policy areas, inevitably drawing the White House in. Yet, not until Bill Clinton's election did a new overarching mission supplant that of the Cold War era. The new President's top priority was "the economy, stupid" (as the campaign slogan went). The new Administration proposed a fundamental overhaul of the science advisory structure to support this Presidential priority.

What concerned President Clinton was the slow growth of industrial productivity in the United States and the emergence of technological challengers in Europe and, especially, Asia. Unless productivity growth could be accelerated, real wages were consigned to grow slowly, and slow macroeconomic growth was likely. Where the new President parted company from his immediate predecessors, who also were aware of the problem, was in his belief that federal resources could make a substantial contribution to its solution. The President proposed, among other things, that new federal research and development (R&D) spending be focused on industrial technology, that the government join with industry in new partnerships to enhance the payoff from that spending, and that government laboratories build new linkages with the private sector to speed the transfer of know-how.

The Administration's commitment to this new vision of technology policy was reflected in the names that it gave to two of the organizations that were responsible for its oversight. Like the National Security Council (NSC), the preeminent policy making body of the Cold War era, they began with N and ended with C. The National Economic Council (NEC) was staffed by some 20 professionals and led by Robert Rubin, formerly of the investment firm Goldman Sachs, who was named the Assistant to the President for Economic Affairs. Key NEC personnel were drawn from Congressional staffs and the campaign, and they used their connections to aggressively advance the technology policy program put forward during the 1992 campaign.

The National Science and Technology Council (NSTC) was similar in its formal structure to the National Economic and Security Councils. However, it had no staff of its own, relying on Office of Science and Technology Policy personnel and on employees from federal agencies. The NSTC was quickly drawn into interagency combat over the federal R&D budget, and this important but tedious task absorbed the bulk of its energy. Moreover, this task lay quite squarely in the turf of the Office of Management and Budget (OMB), the largest and most powerful element of the Executive Office of the President. By and large, the National Science and Technology Council proved unable to make and enforce priorities without OMB's support; OMB too often found the NSTC's decision making process cumbersome and even counterproductive.

Institutionalizing a New Approach

One must be careful not to place too much stock in the formal organizations of any White House, and this is even truer of the Clinton White House. The President's style was freewheeling, a proclivity intensified by the turbulent politics that followed the Republican capture of the Congressional majority in 1994. In this "adhocracy" (a label coined by Roger Porter, a senior White House staff member in three Administrations) entrepreneurship was rewarded. The National Economic Council seems to have taken better advantage of this environment than the National Science and Technology Council, in part due to the personality and experience of its leader and in part due to the fact that it lacked some of the more mundane responsibilities that burdened the OSTP and NSTC.

The most important resource in the Administration is the President's time and attention. The President has little more than the "power to persuade" (as Richard Neustadt has put it) in our system of government, and the value of this power is inversely proportional to the number of items on which it is used. The more priorities the President has, the less he will get done. The White House staff can play a critical role in focusing the President's energy. Similarly, those people and organizations that focus on what the President cares about will gain his time and attention. In the case of the first four years of the Clinton Administration's technology policy, NEC was more conscious of this lesson than OSTP and NSTC. The latter tried to do too much and wound up without much access to the President—by the end of the Administration, they had become peripheral. This outcome was unfortunate for the advocates of the Clinton technology policy strategy, because NEC was too small to initiate a second phase of policy innovation once the major ideas inherited from the campaign had been worked through. A tighter alliance between OSTP and NEC would have strengthened the capacity of the White House in this policy area over the long term.

More generally, for the OSTP and the science advisor to be influential, they need to build alliances with more powerful bodies in the White House, like OMB and NEC. The concept of an NSTC analogous to the NSC had little chance to succeed. Such a body will inevitably provoke turf conflict. More importantly, it presumes that science and technology (which are after all but means to desired ends) deserve the same status as security or economic prosperity (which are ends that Presidents desire to achieve). Means and ends ought not to be confused, and indeed, President Clinton did not make the mistake in this instance, relegating NSTC to the important but less glamorous role of coordinating interagency science and technology policy efforts.[2]

---

[1] This case draws heavily on David M. Hart, "Managing Technology Policy in the White House," in Lewis M. Branscomb and James H. Keller, *Investing in Innovation* (Cambridge: MIT Press, 1998).

[2] The NSTC's immediate predecessor in this regard was the federal Coordinating Committee for Science, Engineering and Technology (FCCSET), which it came to resemble.

IX. PRESIDENTIAL CONTINUITY: THE USE OF INDIVIDUALS ACROSS ADMINISTRATIONS

The Mansfield Transition

By Don Oberdorfer

Former Senate Democratic Majority Leader Mike Mansfield had been President Jimmy Carter's Ambassador in Tokyo for four years and was preparing to return home when he was awakened past midnight by a telephone call from President-elect Ronald Reagan asking him to stay on in his Administration. This was a welcome surprise to many people, including to Senate Democrats, to whom Reagan announced the news in a get-acquainted luncheon in the Mike Mansfield Room of the Senate a few hours after the call on January 7, 1981. At the announcement, Democratic Senators gave Reagan a sustained and standing ovation and called it a masterstroke.

Beyond the domestic political advantages to the incoming Republican President, the decision to retain Mansfield was a boon to U.S.-Japan relations. The former Montana Senator was highly respected in Japan, first as an *omono*, or a big shot with supreme political connections, and second, as a lifelong Asia expert whose carefully considered and frankly stated views carried unusual weight in both Tokyo and Washington. The news that Mansfield was staying drew a spontaneous standing ovation from 2,000 Japanese business executives and government officials—in what one participant called an "electric" atmosphere—when it was announced at a reception he was attending in Tokyo.

Mansfield's reappointment as Ambassador did not solve the myriad issues between the United States and Japan, but his steady hand at a key juncture in the relationship contributed to years of civility and stability in the face of many challenges. In one area, defense, Mansfield personally and immediately contributed to a beneficial change in U.S. policy after his retention. On January 26, 1981, less than a week after Inauguration Day, Mansfield proposed in a classified cable to President Reagan and Secretary of State Alexander Haig that the United States should "re-focus our defense discussions" on substantive requirements such as military roles and missions, and "back away gracefully from an essentially unproductive debate over the percent of Japan's GNP or national budget devoted to defense." Upon reading the cable, Reagan approved the idea, which had been discussed but not adopted in the Carter Administration. An excerpt from Mansfield's cable was circulated within the new Administration, with Reagan's endorsement, as a directive to government departments. The change in policy led quickly to Japan's adoption of an expanded view of its military responsibilities in the Pacific—and eventually led to increases in its military forces and expenditures to meet those responsibilities.

Mansfield's retention by Reagan was not entirely the spur-of-the-moment move that it appeared to be. While on a visit to Tokyo in 1978, then-Governor Reagan had met Mansfield for the first time, and discovered to his surprise that he liked and respected this former leader of the Democratic opposition. After Reagan's nomination in August 1980, his foreign policy aide Richard Allen, who was present at the 1978 meeting and who would go on to be Reagan's first White House National Security Adviser, privately sounded out Mansfield about his willingness to serve in a Reagan Administration if asked. After Reagan's election, Mansfield decided he would like to stay on in Tokyo and asked former President Gerald Ford and Democratic Senator Henry M. (Scoop) Jackson to intercede with Reagan on his behalf. Reagan's decision came in a conversation with Allen the morning of the luncheon with the Senate Democrats.

Nobody, including Mansfield, anticipated that he would remain in Tokyo for all of Reagan's two terms, which in addition to his service for Carter made him the longest-serving Ambassador to Japan in U.S. history. However, he retained the confidence of both the U.S. and Japanese leadership throughout his nearly 12 years in the post. When economic disputes between the two countries mounted in the mid-1980s, and some in the U.S. Administration advocated replacing Mansfield, Reagan refused to consider such a change (and Secretary of State George Shultz continued to be a Mansfield backer). On January 19, 1989, his last full day in the Presidency, Reagan awarded the Presidential Medal of Freedom, the nation's highest civilian award, to "two remarkable Americans," George Shultz and Mike Mansfield. Even today, a decade after his retirement from government, the 97-year-old Mansfield continues to be a legend in Japan—and his office in the Washington headquarters of Goldman, Sachs is a port-of-call for senior Japanese officials visiting the United States.

Reagan's Democrat: Max Kampelman

By Lou Cannon

Max Kampelman, a onetime aide and longtime friend of Hubert H. Humphrey, was President Carter's Ambassador to the Conference on Security and Cooperation in Europe (CSCE) when Ronald Reagan was elected President in 1980. He submitted his resignation, as Ambassadors do when a new President is elected.

But Kampelman had won the respect of Secretary of State Alexander Haig at the CSCE conference in Madrid for speaking out against the Soviet Union on military and human rights issues. He had the backing of Richard Allen, Reagan's first National Security Adviser, who had served with Kampelman on the Committee on the Present

Danger. And Kampelman had met Reagan, who shared his opposition to Soviet participation in the Middle East peace process. So Kampelman became, with Mike Mansfield in Japan, one of two Democrats who were asked to remain as Ambassadors in the new Republican Administration.

When the CSCE talks ended, Kampelman returned to his Washington law practice where he continued to perform special assignments for the President and for Secretary of State George Shultz, who had replaced Haig. In 1985, Paul Nitze told Shultz that his wife's illness made it impossible for him to continue as the head of U.S. arms control negotiators in Geneva. As Kampelman remembers it, he was awakened at 5 a.m. on January 5, 1985, with a call from a TV network news correspondent asking for his comment on a report that he would be Nitze's replacement. Kampelman didn't consider himself technically qualified for this difficult assignment and so informed Shultz through a mutual friend. But Shultz called him to say that he was the President's choice and that Reagan would be calling to offer him the job.

"I couldn't turn down the President," Kampelman said.

Shultz announced the appointment on January 18. When he was asked why Kampelman, who lacked arms control experience was chosen, Shultz said, "He's smart. And he's a good negotiator. And he's experienced. He did an outstanding job in his [CSCE] work in Madrid."

Backed up by technical support, Kampelman also did an excellent job in the long arms control negotiations that followed in Geneva. After the dramatic summit between Reagan and Soviet Premier Mikhail Gorbachev in Iceland, Kampelman's skill led to the breakthrough of the Intermediate-Range Nuclear Forces treaty, the first U.S.-Soviet arms pact to reduce nuclear arsenals.

In retrospect, both the original decision to keep Kampelman and his selection as Nitze's successor speak to the merit of valuing competence over partisanship, particularly in foreign policy. Shultz had been right in seeing that Kampelman's negotiating skills more than compensated for any lack of technical expertise.

On a personal note, let me add that there were many occasions when, as a reporter assigned to Hubert Humphrey, I put questions to Kampelman about some sensitive matters. He was invariably helpful and sensible, the qualities for which he was prized by Senator Humphrey and President Reagan during Kampelman's long and productive career.

Staying the Course: Paul Volcker

By Lou Cannon

Ronald Reagan did not beat around the bush. Three days after he became President, he walked from the White House to the Treasury Department for lunch with Paul Adolph Volcker, the embattled Chairman of the Federal Reserve Board. Without wasting time, Reagan raised a favorite theme of iconoclastic conservatives who believed that private banks could do better than the federal government in regulating currency. "Why do we need the Federal Reserve?" he asked Volcker. According to Martin Anderson, Volcker's face muscles went slack and his jaw sagged. "It is a good thing Volcker had not had time to light one of his long cigars because he might have swallowed it," Anderson later wrote. But Volcker recovered and patiently explained to Reagan how the Fed had contributed to economic stability.

This meeting was the beginning of a tacit and significant alliance that helped steer the U.S. economy through the storm of the nation's worst economic downturn since the Great Depression. Volcker, a big man in more ways than one, was six foot seven and one-half inches tall and towered a half-foot over Reagan. He had served in the Nixon Administration and was Chairman of the New York Federal Reserve Bank when President Carter made him Chairman of the Fed in 1979. Volcker, a Democrat, called himself a "pragmatic monetarist" and had worked hard to stem the tide of rising inflation during the last two Carter years. But he came under attack in his own party and, as economist William Niskanen observed, was "whipsawed" by Carter into adopting credit controls that didn't work and were soon abandoned.

Reagan, despite his initial skepticism about the need for the Fed and deeper doubts about the wisdom of Wall Street, allowed Volcker more leeway than the President who had appointed him. As the nation slipped into recession in 1981, Volcker stubbornly insisted that higher interest rates were needed to break the back of inflation. This position did not endear him to Reagan's Cabinet or Republican Congressional leaders, who feared that tight credit and rising unemployment would hurt the GOP in the midterm elections, as it did. "Volcker's got his foot on our neck, and we've got to make him take it off," said Republican Senate leader Howard Baker.

But Reagan, whose approval rating slumped to a low of 35 percent in January 1983, resisted the pressure from his party to ask Volcker to ease interest rates. He respected the independence of the Fed and Reagan accepted the need of harsh measures to tame inflation after what he called a long "binge" of government spending. "Stay the course" became Reagan's mantra as the nation rode out the recession—and in 1983 entered a long period of prosperity that lasted well into the Bush Administration. These words also described the policies of Volcker, who shared with Reagan an awesome stubbornness and the courage to do what he believed was right.

★ ★ ★ ★ ★

Back to the Future: Alan Greenspan

By Lou Cannon

Success for President Bill Clinton begins with his economic policies, which boasted credit for the nation's remarkable prosperity. Clinton's critics for the most part acknowledge the success of these policies but claim that President Ronald Reagan was the real architect of the boom. This debate is often conducted along partisan lines, but there is a firm link between the policies of Reagan and Clinton, who were otherwise alike only in their political skills. The link is named Alan Greenspan, a onetime disciple of radical capitalist Ayn Rand, whose name has become synonymous with fiscal prudence.

Because of his access to Presidents and his key role as Chairman of the Federal Reserve Board, Greenspan is the most politically influential economist of the last quarter of the 20th century. As a loyal Republican, he stuck with President Gerald Ford in 1976 against a significant challenge from Reagan for the GOP Presidential nomination. But in 1980 Greenspan became an adviser to Reagan. With Martin Anderson he crafted Reagan's major economic speech of the campaign, a Chicago address to the International Business Council that attempted to reconcile the differences between supply-siders and traditional economists.

As President, Reagan entrusted Greenspan with the sensitive task of chairing the bipartisan National Commission on Social Security. Making any change in this most popular of all New Deal programs is always politically delicate—it was particularly so in 1983 after the Democrats had used the issue to score points in the midterm elections. But the Commission proposed increasing Social Security taxes and raising the retirement age in the future. These changes were incorporated into a bill that was shepherded through a skeptical House by Speaker Thomas P. (Tip) O'Neill and signed into law by Reagan—the last reform of any consequence made in the Social Security system.

In 1987, when Paul Volcker turned down a request to serve a third term as Chairman of the Federal Reserve Board, Reagan looked to Greenspan, who continued on the Reagan-Volcker path of treating inflation as Public Enemy No. 1. Although the Fed under Greenspan largely abandoned the Volcker policy of trying to control the money supply, it raised interest rates in 1987 and again in 1988. By then, a bipartisan consensus accepted the necessity of such periodic increases to restrain inflation. The Fed has continued the policy ever since under Greenspan, who was reappointed both by President George Bush and by Clinton.

It is frequently said that the Fed has served as a national economic stabilizer during a period when the United States has become the leader of a globalized economy. If this view is accurate, than Alan Greenspan deserves commendation. So, too, do Reagan, who appointed Greenspan, and Clinton, who kept him. Partisanship aside, the credit for prosperity must be shared.

A Case of Presidential Continuity: Dennis Ross

By Stephen S. Rosenfeld

The use of a special representative by the President or Secretary of State to deal with thorny issues of national policy is a familiar feature of American governance. Ambassador Dennis Ross, a national security policy expert with a political operator's bent for maneuvering and discretion, took the position to an early 21st century peak before departing at the end of the Clinton presidency. Operating from the State Department, Ross was for 12 years, the point man for the Middle East peace talks conducted by Presidents from both major American parties, Israeli democratic governments of different parties, and autocratic Arab regimes. His service provides an example of how a new President might organize his Cabinet to deal not just with the Mideast (an issue that is volatile in its region and in Washington, too). It can also help guide a new President in the varied forms and uses of preventive diplomacy as an essential tool of American policy in a turbulent post-Cold War world.

Not that the performance of Dennis Ross, and of American Mideast diplomacy overall, is beyond cavil. The "Special Middle East Coordinator" is criticized for supposedly becoming a captive of the incrementalist "peace process" (whose principal manager he is), to the detriment both of presumptive American favor for Israel's security interests and of the broader interests of the United States in the region. It is only fair, however, to note the improvements that took place in the Bush and Clinton administrations—Ross's time—in easing tensions in the region, and in reducing the sprawling Arab-Israeli confrontation to the issues imbedded in the core Palestinian-Israeli dispute.

Not withstanding the 11th hour collapse of peace talks, we would not be surprised to learn that we have not seen the last of Dennis Ross. The point man's experience in dousing the region's regular fires has made "Dennis" a familiar name on the street in the Middle East. In Washington, he is on the list of American figures (such as Max Kampelman and Mike Mansfield in foreign policy and Paul Volcker and

Alan Greenspan in the economic realm) who have served multiple Presidents with distinction across party lines.

Military intervention gets priority attention in American national security policy, while diplomatic intervention often is neglected. Yet in a world where American military resources, including funds, may be increasingly inadequate to support the full range of American global interests and aspirations, diplomacy becomes increasingly necessary to fill part of the gap. It requires a major review of national security policy, including the budget, to make this happen. It also requires a sensitivity to the value of the human talent available to any President ready to receive it on a bipartisan basis.

X. PRESIDENTIAL CRISES: WATERGATE, IRAN-CONTRA, AND IMPEACHMENT

Presidents in Crisis: Watergate, Iran-Contra, and President Clinton's Impeachment

By James P. Pfiffner

Three major crises of confidence have shaken the modern Presidency—Watergate, Iran-Contra, and President Clinton's impeachment. Each of the crises was caused not by external threats but by Presidential decisions. Each of them led to serious consideration of impeachment and removal of the President from office. Richard M. Nixon resigned in the face of virtually certain impeachment, Ronald Reagan saved himself by getting the truth out, and Bill Clinton was impeached although not removed from office.

The cases will be examined individually from the perspective of the President's motives, what happened in the crisis, and its consequences. The three cases will then be compared with respect to the key Presidential decisions, the ironies of the outcomes, the personal culpability of each President, and finally the relative threats to the Constitution and the polity presented by the crises. The conclusion will be that each of the three Presidents was guilty of serious missteps, but that President Reagan handled his crisis better by taking concerted action to get the truth out and that President Clinton's transgressions did not present as serious a threat to the Constitution as the other two crises.

Watergate

President Nixon's Motives

The deeper roots of Watergate can be found in Richard Nixon's early resentment against those who grew up in privileged circumstances and did not have to work as hard as he did to achieve success. In Nixon's mind those of privilege became associated with people who thwarted him in his career in politics and included the "eastern establishment elite," intellectuals in general (especially from Harvard and the Ivy League), and the media (in particular *The New York Times* and *The Washington Post*). President Nixon's resentment also focused on the Democratic political party, the Democratic control of Congress, "the bureaucracy" of career civil servants, think tanks (especially the Brookings Institution), anti-war protesters, and civil rights activists.

Although Nixon was paranoid (in the non-technical sense of the word) in that he attributed to his "enemies" powers greater than they had and saw threats greater than existed—he did in fact have political enemies. Certainly the Democrats wanted to embarrass him and see him defeated; certainly those who disagreed with his policies wanted to thwart him. But that is the nature of politics, and in a democracy fights over policy and political power are appropriate and necessary. But in Nixon's mind the distinction between the loyal opposition and enemies of the state blurred, and he thus felt justified in using the power of the government to "screw our enemies" (in White House Counsel John Dean's terms). Nixon justified his action by arguing that Democratic Presidents had used various unethical means to their political advantage. But the scale, scope, and means of Nixon's abuse of power were much broader than those of any of his predecessors.

What Happened

One key turning point came early in the Nixon Administration when Daniel Ellsberg, a former defense analyst, leaked to the media a lengthy internal analysis of early U.S. policy toward Vietnam. The collection of documents became known as the "Pentagon Papers" and were all concerned with policy making before Nixon became President. Nixon decided that the release of the documents was an unacceptable breach of security and ordered his aides to do something about it. In 1969 he told John Ehrlichman to establish "a little group right here in the White House. Have them get off their tails and find out what's going on and figure out how to stop it."[1] This "little group" became the "Plumbers" who would figure out how to stop leaks and carry out other tasks of political intelligence and sabotage.

In order to discredit Daniel Ellsberg, Nixon operatives broke into the office of his psychiatrist in Los Angeles. Although they did not find anything useful, their intention probably was to find and release embarrassing information about Ellsberg in order to affect his trial for violating security regulations. Breaking and entering is, of course, a crime—and this attempt to deprive Ellsberg of his civil rights was included in Article II of the House Judiciary Committee's impeachment charges. Nixon also encouraged breaking into the Brookings Institution to seize documents of those individuals he thought were working on the Pentagon Papers.

The Plumbers, who were paid from campaign funds and through the Committee to Reelect the President (CREEP), were to undertake a number of political intelligence operations including the bugging of the office of Lawrence O'Brien at the Democratic National Committee (DNC) headquarters in the Watergate office building. The national headquarters of political parties are not the most likely place to find valuable political intelligence, and the Nixon people probably were more interested in finding an illegitimate connection between Larry O'Brien and millionaire Howard Hughes. After the election in 1968 Nixon had received an illegal campaign contribution from Hughes. But at the same time Hughes also paid Larry O'Brien on retainer. Thus information about the O'Brien-Hughes connection could be used to counter any Democratic disclosure or condemnation of the Nixon-Hughes connection.[2]

On the night of June 17, 1972, five of the Plumbers, under the direction of Howard Hunt and G. Gordon Liddy, broke into DNC headquarters in the Watergate to repair a listening device they had previously set. After they were discovered and arrested, the trail led back to CREEP and the White House. The cover-up of this break-in was what eventually brought down President Nixon.

In addition to these events, the Nixon White House and reelection campaign undertook a number of other measures that are broadly covered under the rubric of Watergate. Among these were "dirty tricks" to affect the 1972 Democratic Presidential primary elections. Since Nixon judged that Senator Edmund Muskie of Maine would be his strongest opponent, his operatives tried to undermine Muskie's campaign by disrupting campaign rallies, forging letters, and financing his opponents.[3] White House officials tried to get the IRS to undertake audits on Democratic opponents and their supporters. A plan for political intelligence and operations, the "Huston Plan," was approved by Nixon but was never implemented. Nixon's counsel, John Dean, and others drew up lists of political "enemies" who were to be the targets of political retaliation.

Among all of these illicit activities, what eventually brought down President Nixon was his involvement with the cover-up of the crimes. Nixon never seemed to consider seriously the possibility of denouncing the break-in and promising that the White House would not conduct any such activities in the future. Nixon's lawyer, Leonard Garment, recalled:

> The transition from bungled break-in to cover-up took place automatically, without discussion, debate, or even the whisper of gears shifting, because the President was personally involved, if not in the Watergate break-in then by authorizing prior [Charles] Colson and Plumber activities like the Ellsberg break-in and a crazy Colson plot to firebomb the Brookings Institution in order to recover a set of the Pentagon Papers. These were potentially more lethal than Watergate. Other factors contributed to the cover-up, but I have no doubt that the main motive was Nixon's sense of personal jeopardy. His decision was not irrational, though it turned out terribly wrong.[5]

In retrospect, Nixon argued that the actions in the Watergate were minor, but that the cover-up was his big mistake.[6] But he was wrong— the illegal activities, including breaking and entering, conducted by a secret White House intelligence unit were serious abuses of power. This is why Nixon felt that the Watergate break-in had to be concealed at all costs. A thorough investigation of Watergate would have opened up the whole "can of worms" that included the other illegal abuses of power in the Nixon White House. And that, in fact, is what did happen.

The Consequences

When the Watergate burglars were arrested, they did not admit that they were working for Nixon's reelection campaign because they had been assured by Gordon Liddy that they would be taken care of and their prisons sentences would be minor if it came to that. But Judge "Maximum John" Sirica gave them long prison sentences because he suspected that their silence was protecting their superiors. This led to John Dean's discussion with Nixon about hush money for the jailed Plumbers. Dean told the President that it might cost $1 million to buy their silence. Nixon replied, "We could get that. On the money, if you need the money you could get that. You could get a million dollars. You could get it in case. I know where it could be gotten."[7] John Dean testified that $500,000 did go to Liddy and his men.[8]

The Senate Watergate Committee investigated many aspects of the White House activities and found out that President Nixon had set up a taping system in the White House. The tapes were subpoenaed by the Special Prosecutor and the House Impeachment Committee. Nixon sent to the committee transcripts of the tapes, but they had been altered in key places. Finally, the Supreme Court ruled that Nixon could not withhold the evidence on the tapes. The turning point in the House came when the "smoking gun" tape was discovered. Until that time, many Republican members of the committee had argued that the evidence against Nixon was not conclusive and that impeachment was so serious a step that only conclusive proof of a crime was sufficient to vote in favor of impeachment.

In the tape of a conversation on June 23, 1972, just five days after the Watergate break-in, H.R. Haldeman told the President that FBI agents were tracing the money carried by the Watergate burglars and were about to discover that it had come from CREEP and White House safes. He suggested that the way to stop the investigation would be to have the CIA tell the FBI that further investigations would jeopardize CIA operations and that they should drop the money trail. Haldeman suggested, "That the way to handle this now is for us to have Walters [of the CIA] call Pat Gray [Director of the FBI] and just say, 'Stay the hell out of this...this is ah, business here we don't want you to go any further on it'." After this suggestion, Nixon told Haldeman to tell CIA Director Richard Helms that, "the President believes that it is going to open the whole Bay of Pigs thing up again. And...that they [the CIA] should call the FBI in and [unintelligible] don't go any further into this case period!"[9]

The release of the tapes and their damning evidence provided the final impetus for the House Judiciary Committee to vote Articles of Impeachment. Article I charged the President with failure to fulfill his oath of office and obstruction of justice. It mentioned specifically the break-in of Ellsberg's psychiatrist's office, misuse of the CIA to obstruct the Justice Department investigation, withholding evidence, and counseling perjury, among other things. Article II charged the President with failing to faithfully execute the laws by using the IRS to harass his political opponents, by using the FBI to place unlawful wiretaps on citizens, by maintaining a secret investigative unit in the White House that was paid with campaign funds, and by impeding criminal investigations, among other things. Article III charged the President with refusing to honor Congressional subpoenas lawfully issued by the House Judiciary Committee and impeding the Congress from constitutionally exercising its impeachment powers.

Two other articles were debated by the committee but rejected. One would have charged that the President, through the secret bombing of Cambodia during the Vietnam War, undermined the constitutional powers of Congress. The other article would have charged the President with income-tax evasion when he backdated his report of the gift of his Vice Presidential papers to the National Archives.[10] But before the articles could be presented to the full House for action, President Nixon resigned and left office on August 9, 1974.

Iran-Contra

President Reagan's Motives

President Ronald Reagan did not suffer from the resentment of "the establishment" that had characterized Richard Nixon, and he did not have a similar hatred of his political enemies; he was not paranoid about his political enemies, and he did not seek their destruction. His own motives and personal predispositions, however, did contribute to the Iran-Contra affair that seriously damaged his Presidency. Reagan held strong convictions about his political values and goals, but he did not often inquire into the implications of the actions necessary to carry out his objectives. His tendency to delegate to his subordinates the responsibility to implement his goals was in some cases good management practice. But in important issues of state and major policy his refusal to look more closely into the means that would be used to accomplish his ends could be seen as an abdication of his responsibility as President.

In the Iran part of the Iran-Contra affair, President Reagan let his personal concern for the U.S. citizens taken hostage in Iran to override his own stated convictions and the policy of the government that giving in to terrorists will only lead to more terrorism. This inconsistency on the President's part is understandable and in some ways admirable—his concern for the human beings involved overrode his rational mind. He might have taken more seriously, however, the concern of his Secretary of Defense that sending arms to Iran was a breach of the law.

On the Contra part of the Iran-Contra affair, President Reagan's personal ideological convictions were that the Sandinista government of Nicaragua was a threat to U.S. national security interests and that the Contras should be supported by America. There is nothing wrong or sinister about these convictions, but his concerns set a tone in the White House that led his national security staff to break the law in order to carry out what they were sure were his wishes. Here, the President's failure to inquire more closely into how his White House aides were carrying out his policies can be seen as a serious problem.

If the diversion of funds had been framed as a question and he had been asked by his aides whether or not to break the law, President Reagan would almost certainly have said no. (Although he was willing to break the law to free the hostages.[11]) But if the diversion issue was framed as "we're taking care of the Contras," Reagan might not have inquired too closely as to exactly how it was being done.

What Happened

In 1984 and 1985, seven U.S. citizens were kidnapped in Lebanon by Shiite Muslims closely connected to the leaders of Iran. Iran and Iraq were at war, and Iran had a desperate need for military equipment and spare parts to fix its weapons, many of which had come from the American government during the period it supported the Shah of Iran. Intermediaries proposed a deal that would include the release of the hostages in exchange for the United States supplying spare airplane parts and missiles to Iran.

President Reagan had become extremely concerned with the plight of the hostages, one of whom was a CIA station chief. His concern was reflected by National Security Council (NSC) staff, who made arrangements to exchange U.S. arms and spare parts for Iranian intervention to have the hostages in Lebanon released. NSC aides also argued that it was important to try to reestablish ties to moderates in Iran, so that when the Ayatollah Khomeini died, the U.S. government would have some influence there. The United States did not want Iran to fall under Soviet influence. Israel also wanted to support Iran in its war with Iraq because Israel considered Iraq to be a greater security threat. So Israel agreed to ship arms to Iran, which would then be replaced by the United States. The U.S. government also shipped TOW missiles and HAWK missiles directly to Iran.

President Reagan's decision to trade arms for hostages can be questioned on several grounds. First, the surface rationalization for the policy was to open relations with "moderates" in Iran. But it is doubtful that there were any moderates in powerful positions in Iran at the time. It was the CIA's judgement that Khomeini was in charge and that no one else would be allowed to negotiate with the Americans, especially about weapons.[12] Second, the United States had a firm policy not to negotiate with terrorists. In a 1985 speech President Reagan said that Iran was part of a "...confederation of terrorist states...a new international version of Murder Inc. America will never make concessions to terrorists."[13] The Reagan Administration had launched "Operation Staunch," a diplomatic campaign to stop U.S. allies in Europe from selling arms to Iran or Iraq.[14]

In a number of meetings in the White House, Secretary of State George Shultz and Secretary of Defense Caspar Weinberger argued strenuously against trading arms for hostages (for example, on August 6, 1985, December 7, 1985, and January 7, 1986)[15] Although Weinberger and Shultz may have been right on the merits of the arguments, the President was elected and clearly had the authority to set policy in the Executive Branch. Members of the Cabinet are merely advisors to the President and implementers of policy, and the President has no obligation to take their advice. On the other hand, sending arms to Iran raised the issue of the Arms Export Control Act of 1976 that prohibited the sale of U.S. arms to nations designated as sponsors of terrorism. Iran had been so designated since 1984. George Shultz asked his legal advisor, Abraham Sofaer, to consider the legality of the arms sale, and Sofaer concluded that such a sale would not be legal.[16] In the December 7, 1985 meeting with the President and top aides, Casper Weinberger argued against the sale of arms, saying that it would violate the Arms Export Control Act.[17]

In addition, the National Security Act governing covert actions specified that they were to be taken only after an official "finding" by the President that such actions are important to national security.[18] National Security Advisor Admiral John Poindexter testified before Congress that President Reagan had signed such a finding for the earlier approaches to Iran, but that he (Poindexter) had later destroyed it to save the President from possible embarrassment. President Reagan also signed a finding on January 17, 1986 that authorized U.S. direct arms sales to Iran. The law provides that Congress is to be notified before covert actions are undertaken, or if that is impossible, "in a timely fashion."[19] Congress did not learn of the arms for hostages initiatives until they were disclosed in the Lebanese newspaper, *Al-Shiraa* on November 3, 1986.

The Reagan Administration's actions to gain the release of the hostages over the course of several shipments of arms turned out to be futile. A few of the hostages were released, but three more hostages were captured. The courting of "moderates" in Iran was not successful because first, there were no moderates in power, and second, some of the missiles were inferior equipment for which they had charged artificially high prices.

In the Contra dimension of the Iran-Contra affair, White House aides (particularly National Security Advisor Poindexter and staff member Oliver North) undertook to use the "profits" received from the sale of missiles to Iran to aid the Contras in Nicaragua. The problem was that Congress had passed, and President Reagan had signed, a law prohibiting U.S. aid to the Contras. The Boland Amendment included in the law stated:

> During fiscal year 1985, no funds available to the Central Intelligence Agency, the Department of Defense, or any other agency or entity of the United States involved in intelligence activities may

be obligated or expended for the purpose of which would have the effect of supporting, directly or indirectly, military or paramilitary operations in Nicaragua by any nation, group, organization, movement or individual.

—Public Law 98-473, 98 Stat. 1935, sec. 8066

The law had not been passed without due deliberation in Congress. From the beginning of the 1980s, the Reagan Administration had felt that the Sandinista government of Nicaragua posed a serious threat to U.S. national security interests, and support of the Contra opposition was a high priority of the White House. Financial and operational aid were provided to the Contras by the Administration, but military aid was subject to a series of limitations written into law between 1982 and 1986. Despite the best arguments of the White House, Congress was dubious of the wisdom and efficacy of continuing to arm the Contras. Thus the Boland Amendment was passed for FY 1985.[20]

Despite the law, the Administration was committed to continuing support of the Contras. President Reagan told National Security Advisor Robert McFarlane to keep the Contras together, "body and soul."[21] NSC staff member Oliver North proposed the "neat idea" of using the money received from the sale of arms to Iran to support the Contras by diverting the money from the U.S. Treasury where it should have gone. To carry this out, North and his associates set up secret bank accounts to handle the money.

The Consequences

The secret attempt to fund the Contras was in direct violation of public law and a serious threat to the Constitution. The President's aides decided that what they could not achieve through the public constitutional process (continuing aid to the Contras) they would accomplish through secret means. There was no doubt about what the law prohibited. There had been a high-level public debate over aid to the Contras throughout the 1980s, and the Administration had not been able to convince a majority of the Congress that continued military aid to the Contras in 1985 was essential to U.S. security. But White House staff decided that aid to the Contras ought to continue. There is no question that President Reagan strongly supported aid to the Contras and that he communicated this directly to his staff. Reagan, however, denied any knowledge of the diversion of funds to the Contras, and there is no evidence that he knew about it before it was discovered by Attorney General Edwin Meese.

Revelation of arms for hostages deals and the diversion of funds to the Contras threw the Administration into chaos for a number of months. Opinion polls showed that most Americans believed that President Reagan was not telling the truth when he denied that he had traded arms for hostages, and public approval of the President and his Administration dropped significantly. George Shultz, Reagan's Secretary of State concluded that Poindexter and North:

...had entangled themselves with a gang of operators far more cunning and clever than they. As a result, the U.S. government had violated its own policies on antiterrorism and against arms sales to Iran, was buying our own citizens' freedom in a manner that could only *encourage* the taking of others, was working through disreputable international go-betweens, was circumventing our constitutional system of governance, and was misleading the American people—all in the guise of furthering some purported regional political transformation, or to obtain in actuality a hostage release. And somehow, by dressing up this arms-for-hostages scheme and disguising its worst aspects, first McFarlane, and then Poindexter, apparently with the strong collaboration of [CIA Director] Bill Casey, had sold it to a President all too ready to accept it, given his humanitarian urge to free American hostages.[22]

Congress held hearings on what had occurred, and concluded that the affair was a disaster:

In the end, there was no improved relationship with Iran, no lessening of its commitments to terrorism, and no fewer American hostages.

The Iran initiative succeeded only in replacing three American hostages with another three, arming Iran with 2,004 TOWs and more than 200 vital spare parts for HAWK missile batteries, improperly generating funds for the Contras and other covert activities (although far less than North believed), producing profits for the Hakim-Secord Enterprise that in fact belonged to the U.S. taxpayers, leading certain NSC and CIA personnel to deceive representatives of their own Government, undermining U.S. credibility in the eyes of the world, damaging relations between the Executive and the Congress, and engulfing the President in one of the worst credibility crises of an Administration in U.S. history.[23]

Although the possibility of impeachment was discussed in both the Executive and the Legislative Branches, it was not pursued by Congress. The feeling in Congress was that the country was not ready to go through another trauma so soon after Watergate. In addition, there was no evidence that President Reagan knew about the diversion of funds to the Contras before it happened, which would have been the most likely grounds for impeachment. The other aspects of the opening to Iran, despite possible illegality, were not serious enough for impeachment proceedings. In addition, Reagan did not stonewall the investigation, as Nixon had done and Clinton would do in the future.

President Reagan established the Tower Board to investigate the matter and testified personally. On December 26, 1986 he called David Abshire back from Europe to act as his "Special Counsellor" with Cabinet rank. Abshire was given a staff of lawyers completely independent of White House Chief of Staff Donald Regan. Abshire and his aides ensured that there was full cooperation with the investigations and an honest internal process. President Reagan refused to claim

Executive privilege and turned over documents to the Independent Counsel and Congressional investigators. When Howard Baker became Chief of Staff, there was another exhaustive internal investigation.[24] Thus Ronald Reagan salvaged his Presidency from what might have been much worse consequences.

President Clinton's Impeachment

President Clinton's Motives

For all of his talents and electoral victories, President Bill Clinton still felt like a victim. When the press wrote stories about his past sexual affairs, Clinton believed that the press and his enemies were out to thwart him and ruin his career. According to his long-time associate and advisor, Dick Morris, Clinton "...was constantly trying to escape blame for anything. Denial spread into a ubiquitous pattern where everything that went wrong was somebody else's fault. Never his."[25] According to Stephen J. Wayne, "When things do not go right, Clinton tends to see himself as victim. He rarely blames himself, however. Clinton not only lashes out at his staff, but also demonizes his opponents."[26]

On January 17, 1998, Clinton testified in a deposition in the Paula Jones case against him that he had not had sex with Monica Lewinsky. On January 21 the story was made public in *The Washington Post*. After the story broke about Clinton's affair with Monica Lewinsky, the President's first instinct was to deny the relationship, as he had the allegations about many other sexual affairs in his past. But he asked Dick Morris to conduct a poll to see what public reaction would be if he admitted to having had an affair with Lewinsky. Morris reportedly found that the American people would be relatively forgiving of an extramarital affair, but if the President lied about it or encouraged others to lie, the public would be unforgiving. Clinton's reaction was, "Well, we just have to win, then."[27] This seemed to be the turning point when Clinton decided to lock himself irrevocably into lying about his relationship with Lewinsky. Clinton's motives were to avoid personal embarrassment and to maintain his standing with the public. As he later considered whether to admit that he had lied in the Paula Jones deposition, the President's motives came to include avoiding the legal ramifications of admitting that he had broken the law.

What Happened

Shortly after graduating from college in June 1995, Monica Lewinsky came to work in the White House as one of many interns. According to her account, she and the President began having an affair in November of that year, and she received a salaried position in the Office of Legislative Affairs. By April 1996 some on the White House staff felt that Lewinsky was seeing the President too often and had her transferred to a public affairs job in the Pentagon. Over the next 21 months White House logs recorded that she was cleared to enter the White House 37 times.[28] While at the Pentagon, Lewinsky made friends with a former White House secretary, Linda Tripp, who also now worked in the Pentagon. Tripp had been the source for a news story about the sexual advances that the President made in an encounter with Kathleen Willey in the White House. When Tripp's credibility was questioned by the President's lawyer in the fall of 1997, she began to tape her phone conversations with Lewinsky. The tapes contained assertions by Lewinsky about her relationship with the President and her frustration because he was not calling her.

In the meantime, the suit brought against the President by Paula Jones had been underway for several years. Jones alleged that in a 1999 encounter in a Little Rock hotel room then-Governor Clinton had crudely propositioned her and that she had turned him down. The suit was a civil action alleging sexual harassment (Jones was a state employee). In the course of building their case, Jones's lawyers were gathering evidence about other women with whom Clinton might have had relationships over the years in order to demonstrate a pattern of sexual harassment.

The President gave a deposition in the Paula Jones lawsuit on January 17, 1998. With knowledge of the Tripp-Lewinsky tapes, the lawyers for Paula Jones asked Clinton if he had had sex with Lewinsky. When asked about an affair, Clinton denied a sexual relationship, providing the grounds for charges of perjury and eventual impeachment if Special Prosecutor Kenneth Starr could prove that, in fact, there had been a sexual relationship between the President and Lewinsky. Having sex with an intern is not illegal (however wrong it might be), but intentionally lying about it in a civil deposition could constitute perjury. Thus the question by Jones's lawyers about Lewinsky set Clinton up for a possible perjury charge. Based on the tapes, Starr suspected that Clinton might have tried to illegally cover-up the Lewinsky affair.

On January 21, 1998, the story of the tapes and Lewinsky's conversations with Tripp became public, and the media began a feeding frenzy about all aspects of the scandal. President Clinton, pointing his finger angrily, in a strong statement publicly denied that he had a sexual relationship with Lewinsky. "I want you to listen to me. I'm going to say this again. I did not have sexual relations with that woman, Miss Lewinsky. I never told anybody to lie—not a single time, never. These allegations are false. And I need to go back to work for the American people."[29]

Starr's investigation of Clinton continued through the spring and summer of 1998. In July Starr came to an immunity agreement with Monica Lewinsky, assuring her that she would not be prosecuted based on her testimony about her relationship with Clinton. Lewinsky testified in detail about their relationship and provided evidence that convinced the grand jury that she and Clinton had had a sexual relationship. Based on evidence from the Lewinsky testimony, Starr sought to subpoena the President to testify before a grand jury.

The Consequences

In the face of the subpoena, President Clinton agreed to testify "voluntarily" before Kenneth Starr's grand jury on August 17, 1998, about his relationship with Monica Lewinsky. During four hours of close questioning by Starr's lawyers, President Clinton carefully answered most questions but still maintained that he had not lied in his denial of a sexual relationship with Lewinsky. The President was clearly equivocating in his answers to some questions about their relationship.

In the evening after his deposition, the President made a statement in a nationally televised broadcast about his testimony. In his statement Clinton told the nation that he regretted his relationship with Lewinsky and its consequences. "Indeed, I did have a relationship with Miss Lewinsky that was not appropriate. In fact, it was wrong. It constituted a critical lapse in judgment and a personal failure on my part for which I am solely and completely responsible....I know that my public comments and my silence about this matter gave a false impression. I misled people, including even my wife. I deeply regret that." In his statement Clinton also criticized Kenneth Starr for his relentless pursuit of evidence, saying "It is time to stop the pursuit of personal destruction and the prying into private lives and get on with our national life."

Several weeks later on September 9, Kenneth Starr sent his report to Congress concerning possible impeachable offenses by the President. The list of charges included allegations that Clinton had lied under oath in his deposition in the Paula Jones sexual harassment case and in his testimony on August 17, that he had urged Lewinsky and his secretary to lie under oath, that he had tried to obstruct justice by having his secretary hide evidence, and that he had tried to get Ms. Lewinsky a job to discourage her from revealing their relationship.

On October 5 the House Judiciary Committee voted 21-16 along party lines to recommend impeachment hearings. Three days later, on October 8, the full House voted 258-176 (with 31 Democrats voting in favor and no Republicans against) to open an impeachment inquiry. On December 11 and 12 the Judiciary Committee voted along party lines in favor of four Articles of Impeachment. A Democratic motion to censure the President was easily defeated by committee Republicans, and the articles were reported to the full House.

The formal impeachment debate opened on December 18 on the floor of the House of Representatives, with the Republicans arguing that Clinton had corrupted the rule of law by committing perjury and obstructing justice. The Democrats argued that the President should be censured but not impeached. Democrats and moderate Republicans who felt that Clinton's actions were reprehensible, but not impeachable, wanted to vote to censure Clinton. Censure language was proposed by Democrats that harshly condemned Clinton for making "false statements concerning his reprehensible conduct" and that he "violated the trust of the American people, lessened their esteem for the office of the President, and dishonored" the Presidency.[30] But the motions for censure were not successful.

The House of Representatives met on December 19, 1998, and adopted two Articles of Impeachment. Article I charged that President Clinton "willfully provided perjurious, false and misleading testimony to the grand jury" on August 17, 1998, concerning his relationship with Monica Lewinsky and his attempts to cover it up. Article III charged that President Clinton "prevented, obstructed, and impeded the administration of justice" in order to "delay, impede, cover-up, and conceal the existence of evidence and testimony" in the Paula Jones case by encouraging a witness to lie, by concealing evidence, and by trying to prevent truthful testimony by finding a job for Lewinsky. Each of these articles concluded that "William Jefferson Clinton has undermined the integrity of his office, has brought disrepute on the Presidency, has betrayed his trust as President, and has acted in a manner subversive of the rule of law and justice, to the manifest injury of the people of the United States." The two articles charging perjury in the Paula Jones deposition of January 17 and failure to respond adequately to Congressional inquiries were defeated.

The trial in the Senate opened on January 7, 1999. The House impeachment brief argued that the President had indeed committed the crimes charged in the two articles—that he lied under oath before the grand jury investigating him on August 17, 1998 (Article I), and that he attempted to obstruct justice by encouraging Lewinsky to lie about their relationship, concealing evidence, and getting her a job. On February 12, 1999, the final votes were taken, and both article failed to receive the two-thirds majority necessary for conviction and removal from office.

Comparing Three Presidents in Crises

Each one of these Presidents, when faced with potentially damaging public revelations about his behavior, acted initially to limit the political damage to himself and his Administration—and each chose a path of behavior that would threaten his Presidency. Admitting to the truth of the alleged improper behavior would have been bad, but failure to respond truthfully led directly to much worse damage being done.

At a deeper level each President could not initially admit to himself that he had done anything wrong. Richard Nixon rationalized the actions of his Administration by arguing that Democratic Presidents had done the same thing and that his enemies were out to destroy him. Ronald Reagan rationalized his trading of arms for hostages by arguing that the hostages were merely a side issue in a strategic opening to Iran. Bill Clinton rationalized his lies by arguing that his enemies were out to get him, that other Presidents had done worse, that his private life was not the public's business, and that he was technically telling the truth. These rationalizations allowed each President to choose the path that would end up damaging him more than the initial admission would have.

The Key Decisions

Each President made initial key decisions that reflected character flaws that got him into trouble.

When he first heard about the Watergate break-in Richard Nixon did not hesitate—he followed his first instinct, which was to limit the political damage and cover-up the incident. His decision was based in part on a rational calculation that publicity about the incident would hurt him politically and that the revelation might uncover other damaging evidence of illegal behavior by other White House and reelection committee aides.

Ronald Reagan's initial reaction was that there was no problem when the McFarlane trip to Iran was disclosed, since the actions of his highest aides were merely intended to bring about an opening to Iran. He knew that he did not approve of trading arms for hostages, so Reagan concluded that he could not have done so. After weeks of publicity and press reports, and after strong prodding by David Abshire and George Shultz, the President finally was convinced that he had to tell the truth. Reagan saved himself from further damage about the diversion of funds to the Contras by fully cooperating with the investigations, refusing to invoke Executive privilege, and turning over requested documents. Reagan thus stemmed the damage to his Presidency in a way that the other two Presidents did not. Although the diversion of funds was a grave constitutional issue, it was done without President Reagan's knowledge.

Bill Clinton's first instinct was to deny his sexual relationship with Monica Lewinsky, just as he had with all previous allegations of sexual impropriety. He did seem to consider the possibility of telling the truth after the allegations became public, but following the poll by Dick Morris, Clinton concluded that confessing to the lie would hurt him too much politically; and so he embarked upon the firm policy of denial that resulted in his impeachment.

Ironies

The initial irony is that each President was hurt more by the denial and cover-up than he would have been if he had immediately admitted the truth about his previous behavior. The cost would have been quite high for each, but the truth did come out in the end and caused more harm at that late stage than an early admission would have.

The more profound irony is that none of the three breaches of trust by the Presidents or their aides was necessary or achieved the goals they wanted.

Richard Nixon did not need a lot of illegal help to get reelected in 1972. Even if Edmund Muskie was the Democratic candidate, Nixon's foreign and domestic policy record was sufficiently popular to put him in a strong position. Thus the actions that led to the cover-up were unnecessary—it was only Nixon's paranoia and the tone he set that encouraged his aides to undertake the actions that eventually brought him down.

Ronald Reagan's selling of arms to Iran did not free the hostages—those that were freed were replaced by others. The selling of inferior arms at inflated prices did not endear the United States to Iran. Iran also had its own security reasons for not wanting to be pulled into the Soviet orbit. The diversion of funds from Iran to the Contras did not make a big difference in the rebels' ability to overthrow the government of Nicaragua. Only a small percentage of the funds intended for the Contras actually got to them.

Bill Clinton did not need to lie in his deposition in the Paula Jones case. The judge dismissed the case several months later even though it had become public knowledge that Clinton had lied. Neither did he need to lie directly to the American people in his finger pointing statement. As became evident after his lies were revealed, public support for him was strong enough to weather the storm. Clinton's highest public approval ratings came during his impeachment and trial. The President's treatment of Kenneth Starr as his nemesis became a self-fulfilling prophecy when Starr pursued Clinton and disclosed his most private and embarrassing actions.

They Did It to Themselves

Each President felt that his political enemies and the press were the cause of his troubles, but in fact each caused his own problems.

Richard Nixon had developed deep suspicions about his political enemies and the tactics they would use to get him. But these suspicions were often projections of the tactics he used to get his enemies. Certainly Nixon did have political enemies and they wanted to beat him politically, but that is the nature of politics. Nixon's overreaction and actions against his enemies were the very things that accomplished what his enemies never could have—his resignation from the Presidency in disgrace. Nixon's epiphany came in the last moments of his Presidency in his farewell remarks just before leaving for California, "...always remember, others may hate you, but those who hate you don't win unless you hate them, and then you destroy yourself."[31]

Ronald Reagan felt that the press was guilty of embarrassing him and undermining his attempts to repair relations with Iran. He felt that Congress tried to obstruct his policies and was generally irresponsible. Certainly Congress had different policy preferences than Reagan and passed laws of which he did not approve. But it was not the media or Congress that began the doomed arms for hostages initiative, and it was not their fault that North and Poindexter decided to break the law. It was Ronald Reagan's decision to trade arms for hostages. And it was his approach to policy direction and managing his White House that allowed Reagan's subordinates to pursue their illegal actions.

Bill Clinton had long blamed his enemies for working to bring him down. He felt that the press was hostile to him, and his wife blamed a "vast right wing conspiracy" for attempting to orchestrate his downfall. Certainly Clinton had political enemies who were doing their best to undermine him. But it was not his political enemies who initiated his affair with Monica Lewinsky or led him to lie about it. It was his own denial of his actions and refusal to take responsibility for his behavior that caused the disaster.

---

[1] Quoted from Stanley I. Kutler, *The Wars of Watergate* (NY: Alfred A. Knopf, 1990), p. 112. On May 16, 1973, Nixon, in a conversation with Alexander Haig, said, "The Ellsberg thing was something that we set up. Let me tell you. I know what happened here and Al knows what happens. We set up in the White House a independent group under Bud Krogh to cover the problems of leaks involving, at the time, of the Goddamn Pentagon papers; right?...the plumbers operation." Tape transcript in Stanley I. Kutler, *Abuse of Power: The New Nixon Tapes* (NY: The Free Press, 1997), p. 514.

[2] Fred Emery, *Watergate* (NY: Times Books, 1994), p. 30.

[3] See Stanley Kutler, *Abuse of Power*, p. 33.

[4] Of the Huston Plan, Nixon said, "Well, then to admit that we approved...illegal activities. That's the problem." Also, "I ordered that they use any means necessary, including illegal means, to accomplish this goal." Quoted in Kutler, *Abuse of Power*, p. xxi.

[5] Leonard Garment, *Crazy Rhythm* (NY: Times Books, 1997), p. 297.

[6] See Kutler, *Abuse of Power*, p. xxi.

[7] The New York Times, *The White House Transcripts* (NY: Vintage Books, 1973), pp. 146-147; (March 21, 1973).

[8] See Michael Genovese, *The Nixon Presidency* (NY: Greenwood Press, 1990), p. 190.

[9] *The White House Transcripts*, quoted in Larry Berman, *The New American Presidency* (Boston: Houghton Mifflin, 1987), p. 189.

[10] See Kutler, *The Wars of Watergate*, pp. 431-434.

[11] Secretary of Defense Casper Weinberger and Secretary of State George Shultz argued that selling arms to Iran might break the Arms Export Control Act in meetings with the President. "I felt that as far as being the President that a thing of this kind to get back five human beings from potential murder, yes, I would violate that other—that law," Reagan is quoted as saying. Bob Woodward, *Shadow* (NY: Simon and Schuster, 1999), p. 164. See also pp. 109-110, 137, 155.

[12] George Shultz, *Turmoil and Triumph* (NY: Charles Scribner's and Sons, 1993), p. 824. After reviewing the CIA analysis, Shultz concluded, "Khomeini was firmly in power, and Rafsanjani was carrying out the ayatollah's resolute policy of opposition to the United States; recent events in Iran suggested that no Iranian leader other then Khomeini has the power to initiate a rapprochment with the United States or even to offer such a suggestion for debate."

[13] Quoted in William S. Cohen and George J. Mitchell, *Men of Zeal* (NY: Viking, 1988), p. xx.

[14] See George Shultz, *Turmoil and Triumph*, pp. 237, 239, 785. Shultz was angered that he was told by White House aides that the United States was not selling arms to Iran and that he assured our European allies of it at the same time that America was in fact selling arms to Iran. See pp. 783-924, passim.

[15] See the chronology in William S. Cohen and George J. Mitchell, *Men of Zeal,* pp. xix-xxxi.

[16] See Shultz, *Turmoil and Triumph*, p. 811.

17 See Theodore Draper, *A Very Thin Line* (NY: Hill and Wang, 1991), pp. 225-226, 247-248. See also Bob Woodward, *Shadow*, p. 137. White House Counsel Peter Wallison also reported to Chief of Staff Donald Regan that the shipments were likely violations of the Act. See Woodward, *Shadow*, p. 109.

18 See Schultz, *Turmoil and Triumph*, p. 804.

19 See the discussion of the law in Cohen and Mitchell, *Men of Zeal*, pp. 12-13, 279-288.

20 For an analysis of the Boland Amendment and its application to the National Security Council staff see, *Report of the Congressional Committees Investigating the Iran-Contra Affair* (Washington: Government Printing Office, November 1987), pp. 41-42.

21 See Draper, *A Very Thin Line*, p. 33.

22 Shultz, *Turmoil and Triumph*, p. 811.

23 *Report of the Congressional Committees Investigating the Iran-Contra Affair*, p. 280.

24 See David Abshire's account of his experience in the Reagan White House, *To Save a Presidency: The Curse of Iran-Contra* (NY: Oxford University Press, forthcoming). On the internal Baker investigation, see Bob Woodward, *Shadow*, p. 151. Baker's investigation included 13 interrogations of the President, a staff of 67 in the White House, and an examination of more than 12,000 documents.

25 Dick Morris, *Behind the Oval Office* (Los Angeles: Renaissance Books, 1999), p. xxiv.

26 Stephen J. Wayne, "Presidential Personality: The Clinton Legacy," in Mark J. Rozell and Clyde Wilcox, *The Clinton Scandal* (Washington: Georgetown University Press, 2000), p. 217-218.

27 Jeffrey Toobin, *A Vast Conspiracy* (NY: Random House, 1999), p. 244.

28 *The Washington Post* (February 8, 1998), p. A20.

29 Quoted in Jeffrey Toobin, "Circling the Wagons," *The New Yorker* (July 6, 1998), p. 29.

30 *Congressional Quarterly Weekly Report*, December 22, 1998, p. 3324.

31 Richard Nixon, *RN: The Memoirs of Richard Nixon* (NY: Grosset and Dunlop, 1978), p. 1089.

CONTRIBUTORS

Stephen Barr — Writer, *The Washington Post*, "Federal Diary" column, and former editor and reporter for the Metro News, Style and National News departments.

Charles Bartlett — Newspaper columnist and co-author of *Facing the Brink*.

Michael Beschloss — Award winning Presidential scholar, historian, and author of *The Crisis Years: Kennedy and Khrushchev, 1960–1963, Kennedy and Roosevelt: The Uneasy Alliance, Mayday: Eisenhower, Khrushchev, and the U-2 Affair*, and *Taking Charge: The Johnson White House Tapes, 1963-1964*.

Larry Bland — Managing editor of the *Journal of Military of History*, author of *George C. Marshall: Soldier of Peace*, and editor of *George C. Marshall Interviews and Reminiscences* and *George C. Marshall's Mediation Mission to China*.

Robert Bowie — Dillon Professor of International Affairs (emeritus), founding Director of the Center for International Affairs at Harvard University, former Director of Policy Planning at the State Department, member of the NSC Planning Board under Eisenhower, and author of *Waging Peace: How Eisenhower Shaped an Enduring Cold War Strategy*.

John P. Burke — Professor of Political Science at the University of Vermont, recipient of the Richard Neustadt Award (1990) for *How Presidents Test Reality*, and author of *Presidential Transitions: From Politics to Practice, Bureaucratic Responsibility,* and *The Institutional Presidency*.

Stanton H. Burnett — Author of *Investing in Security: Economic Aid for Non-economic Purposes* and *The Italian Guillotine: Operation Clean Hands and the Overthrow of Italy's First Republic* (with Luca Mantovani.)

James MacGregor Burns — Pulitzer Prize-winning author of *Roosevelt: The Soldier of Freedom* and author of *Roosevelt the Lion and the Fox* and *Dead Center: Clinton-Gore Leadership and the Perils of Moderation* (with Georgia J. Sorenson).

Carl Cannon — White House correspondent at the *National Journal*, monthly columnist of "White House Watch" for *George*, and winner of the Gerald R. Ford award (1999) and the Pulitzer Prize (1989).

Lou Cannon — Author of *President Reagan: The Role of a Lifetime, Official Negligence: How Rodney King and the Riots Changed Los Angeles and the LAPD, Reporting: An Inside View,* and *Reagan*.

Timothy Conlan — Associate Professor, Department of Public and International Affairs, George Mason University, author of *Taxing Choices: The Politics of Tax Reform* and *New Federalism: Intergovernmental Reform from Nixon to Reagan*.

John Milton Cooper — E. Gordon Fox Professor of American Institutions, University of Wisconsin, and author of *The Warrior and the Priest: Woodrow Wilson and Theodore Roosevelt* and the forthcoming *Breaking the Heart of the World: Woodrow Wilson and the Fight over the League of Nations*.

George C. Edwards III — Director of the Center for Presidential Studies and Jordan Professor of Liberal Arts, Texas A&M University, editor of *Presidential Studies Quarterly*, and author of *Presidential Leadership: Politics and Policy Making*.

Genene Fisher — Ph.D. candidate in atmospheric and space science and master candidate in public policy at the University of Michigan and former researcher at Arecibo Observatory in Puerto Rico and the Polar Cap Observatory at Resolute Bay, Canada.

David Gergen — Editor-at-large, *US News & World Report*, Professor, John F. Kennedy School of Government, Harvard University, former White House advisor to Nixon, Ford, Reagan, and Clinton, and author of *Eyewitness to Power: The Essence of Leadership—Nixon to Clinton*.

John Goshko — Former diplomatic correspondent with *The Washington Post* covering foreign policy and national security affairs at the State Department and White House, and recipient of the Maria Moors Cabot Gold Medal Award and Edwin Hood Memorial Award.

Michael Green — Olin Senior Fellow for Security Studies at the Council on Foreign Relations, author of "The Forgotten Player" (*The National Interest*, Summer 2000), and co-author of *The U.S.-Japan Security Alliance in the 21st Century: Prospects for Incremental Change*.

Fred Greenstein — Professor of Politics and Director of the Woodrow Wilson School Research Program in Leadership Studies at Princeton University, and author of *The Hidden-Hand Presidency: Eisenhower As Leader* and *The Presidential Difference: Leadership Style from FDR to Clinton*.

David M. Hart — Associate Professor of Public Policy, Harvard University, and author of *Forged Consensus: Science, Technology, and Economic Policy in the United States, 1921-1953*.

Gina Marie Hatheway — Foreign policy advisor to Senator Mike DeWine, contributed to such legislation as "The Western Hemisphere Drug Elimination Act" and "The Controlled Substances Abuse Act of 1998," and former Professional Staff Member of the Senate Foreign Relations Committee.

Lee Huebner — Professor of Communication Studies and Journalism at Northwestern University, chair of the Center for the Study of International Communication in Paris, former Special Assistant to the President and Deputy Director of the White House Writing and Research Staff under Nixon, and publisher and CEO of the Paris-based *International Herald Tribune.*

Robert E. Hunter — Senior advisor at the RAND Corporation, member of the Defense Secretary's Defense Policy Board, vice chairman of the Atlantic Treaty Association, former U.S. ambassador to NATO, representative of the United States to the Western European Union, and author of *Security in Europe* and *Presidential Control of Foreign Policy.*

Dwight Ink — President of New York Institute of Public Administration, former assistant general manager of the Atomic Energy Commission (1958-1965), executive director of the Anderson Commission (1964), chairman of the White House Task Force on Education, former acting head of the General Service Administration and senior policy advisor to President-elect Reagan's transition team.

Charles O. Jones — Hawkins Professor of Political Science (emeritus), University of Wisconsin, nonresident Senior Fellow in Governmental Studies at the Brookings Institution, and author of *Clinton & Congress* and *Separate But Equal Branches: Congress and the Presidency.*

Lawrence Kaplan — Author of *The Long Entanglement: NATO's First Fifty Years, NATO and the United States: The Enduring Alliance,* and *The Warsaw Pact: Political Purpose and Military Means.*

Sherman Katz — Holder of the Scholl Chair in International Business and Director of International Finance and Economic Policy at the Center for Strategic and International Studies and author of several articles in *Journal of Commerce, National Law Journal,* and *The Wall Street Journal.*

James Kitfield — National security and foreign affairs correspondent for the *National Journal,* recipient of the Edwin M. Hood Award (2000) for diplomatic correspondence, two-time recipient of the Gerald R. Ford Award, and author of *Prodigal Soldiers.*

Fredrik Logevall — Associate Professor of American History at the University of California, Co-director of the Cold War History Group, co-winner of the Stuart L. Bernath Book Award (2000), and author of *Choosing War: The Lost Chance for Peace and the Escalation of War in Vietnam.*

John R. Malott — President of the World Affairs Council of Orange County, former ambassador to Malaysia (1995-1998), Director and Deputy Director of the State Department's Japan desk, Deputy Assistant Secretary of State for South Asia (1992-1993), author of *Partners: An American Diplomat Talks Frankly About the Future of U.S.-Japan Relations*.

John McGinn — Diplomatic historian and defense policy analyst, Associate Policy Analyst at the RAND Corporation specializing in European security, the Balkans peace operations, and national military strategy formulation, and author of "The Politics of Collective Inaction: NATO's Response to the Prague Spring" (*Journal of Cold War Studies*, Fall, 1999).

Richard Neustadt — Douglas Dillon Professor of Government (emeritus), John F. Kennedy School of Government, Harvard University, author of *The American President, Presidential Power and the Modern Presidents*, and *Thinking in Time: The Uses of History for Decision Makers* (with Ernest May).

Don Oberdorfer — Journalist-in-Residence and Adjunct Professor in International Relations, The Paul H. Nitze School of Advanced International Studies, Johns Hopkins University, and author of *The Turn: From the Cold War to a New Era* and *The Two Koreas*.

Henry David Owen — Senior Advisor at Salomon Smith Barney, former Ambassador-at-Large in the White House for International Economic Affairs, and former Director of Foreign Policy Studies at the Brookings Institution.

Bradley Patterson — Senior Fellow, National Academy of Public Administration, former National President of the American Society for Public Administration, and author of *The White House Staff: Inside the West Wing and Beyond*.

Rudy Penner — Senior fellow at the Urban Institute, former Director and Chief Economist of the White House Office of Management and Budget, and director of the United States Congressional Budget Office (1983-1987).

Geoffrey Perret — Author of *Eisenhower, Ulysses S. Grant: Soldier & President, Old Soldiers Never Die: The Life of Douglas MacArthur, Winged Victory: The Army Air Forces in World War II*, and *Days of Sadness, Years of Triumph: The American People, 1939-1945*.

James Pfiffner — Professor of Government and Public Policy, George Mason University, vice-chair/coordinator of the Council of Scholars, Center For The Study of the Presidency, and author of *The Strategic Presidency: Hitting the Ground Running, The Modern President* and *The President, the Budget, and Congress: Impoundment and the 1974 Budget Act*.

William Piez — Senior Associate at the Center for Strategic and International Studies, former Deputy Assistant Secretary of Commerce for Planning in the International Trade Administration, and Deputy Assistant Secretary of State for East Asian and Pacific Affairs.

Bill Quandt — Professor of Government and Foreign Affairs, University of Virginia, nonresident Senior Fellow, Brookings Institution, and author of *Peace Process: American Diplomacy Toward the Arab-Israeli Conflict Since 1967, Camp David: Peacemaking and Politics, Saudi Arabia in the 1980's,* and *Revolution and Politics Leadership: Algeria 1954-1968.*

Peter W. Rodman — Director of National Security Programs at the Nixon Center, former Deputy Assistant to President Reagan for National Security Affairs, and author of *More Precious than Peace* and *Uneasy Giant: The Challenges to American Predominance.*

Stephen Rosenfeld — Former editorial page editor of *The Washington Post*, co-author, with his wife, of *Return from Red Square* and author of *The Time of Their Dying.*

Mark Rozell — Associate Professor of Politics and Director of the Graduate Program in Congressional Studies at The Catholic University of America, and co-author of *Interest Groups in American Campaigns: The New Face of Electioneering* and author of *Executive Privilege: The Dilemma of Secrecy and Democratic Accountability.*

Michael Schaller — Professor of History at the University of Arizona and author of *Altered States: U.S.-Japan Relations Since the Occupation, The American Occupation of Japan: The Origins of the Cold War in Asia* and *Present Tense: The United States Since 1945.*

Roy C. Smith — Professor of Finance and International Business at The Stern School of Business, New York University, author of *The Money Wars: The Rise and Fall of the Great Buyout, The Global Bankers,* and *Comeback: The Restoration of American Banking Power in the New World Economy.*

Anne G. K. Solomon — Senior Associate at the Center for Strategic and International Studies, former Senior Policy Analyst for International Affairs in the White House Office of Science and Technology Policy under President Carter, and Deputy Assistant Secretary of State for Science, Technology, and Health.

Theodore C. Sorensen — Senior Counsel at Paul, Weiss, Rifkind, Wharton & Garrison, former Counsel and Advisor to President John F. Kennedy, and author of *Kennedy* and numerous articles in *Foreign Affairs* and *The New York Times.*

Charles Sorrels — Author of *U.S. Cruise Missile Programs: Development, Deployment & Implications for Arms Control*, and several government studies on defense and intelligence, and first budget examiner in OMB for the National Reconnaissance Program. Dr. Sorrels has taught a course at Yale College on Presidents in crises.

Elizabeth Spalding — Director and Visiting Assistant Professor of Government in Claremont McKenna College's Washington Program, teacher, Catholic University graduate program in International Relations, author of several articles in *Presidential Studies Quarterly*, the *Encyclopedia of Religion in American Politics* and *American Enterprise,* and a forthcoming book on *Truman and Containment.*

Sidney Weintraub — Holder of the Simon Chair in Political Economy at the Center for Strategic and International Studies, Dean Rusk Professor (emeritus) at the Lyndon B. Johnson School of Public Affairs, University of Texas, and author of *Financial Decision-Making in Mexico: To Bet A Nation.*

John C. Whitaker — Former Under Secretary of the Interior, senior advisor to the President's Commission on American Outdoors, member of the Chairman's Committee for the National Fish and Wildlife Foundation, and author of *Striking a Balance: Environment and Natural Resources Policy in the Nixon and Ford Years.*

Howard Wiarda — Senior Associate, at the Center for Strategic and International Studies, Professor of Political Science and Comparative Labor Relations, Leonard J. Horwitz Chair of Iberian and Latin American Studies at the University of Massachusetts, and author of *European Politics in the Age of Globalization* and *Introduction to Comparative Politics.*

Samuel R. Williamson — Professor of History, Vice-chancellor and President (emeritus), The University of the South, author of *Austria-Hungary and the Origins of the First World War, The Origins of U.S. Nuclear Strategy; 1945-1953*, and recipient of the George Louis Beer Prize for *The Politics of Grand Strategy: Britain and France Prepare for War, 1904-1914.*

Philip Zelikow — Director of the Miller Center of Public Affairs, White Burkett Miller Professor of History at the University of Virginia, and author of *Germany Unified and Europe Transformed: A Study in Statecraft, Essence of Decision: The Cuban Missile Crisis* (with Graham Allison), and *The Kennedy Tapes: Inside the White House During the Cuban Missile Crisis* (with Ernest May).

Barry Zorthian — Communications consultant in Washington DC, formerly with Voice of America and the United States Foreign Service, former President of Time- Life Broadcast, Vice President for Government Affairs, Time Inc., member of the Board for International Broadcasting, and recipient of the U.S. Army Distinguished Civilian Service Medal.

ACKNOWLEDGMENTS

Arie and Ida Crown Memorial

Arthur Ross Foundation

PaineWebber, Inc.

Richard Lounsbery Foundation

Smith Richardson Foundation

The Henry Luce Foundation

United States-Japan Foundation

W. M. Keck Foundation

William H. Donner Foundation

BIBLIOGRAPHY

Compiled by James P. Pfiffner

Abshire, David. *Preventing World War III*. New York, NY: Harper & Row. ,— *Foreign Policy Makers: President vs. Congress*. Thousand Oaks, CA: Sage, 1979.

Adler, David Gray, and **Larry N. George**, eds. *The Constitution and the Conduct of Foreign Policy*. Lawrence: University Press of Kansas, 1996.

Allison, Graham. *Essence of Decision: Explaining the Cuban Missile Crisis*. Boston: Little, Brown, 1971.

Ambrose, Stephen. *Eisenhower: Soldier and President*. Carmichael, CA: Touchstone Books, 1991. —. *Nixon: The Triumph of A Politician 1962-1972*. NY: Simon, 1989.—. *Nixon: Ruin and Recovery, 1977-1990*. NY: Simon, 1991.

Anderson, Patrick. *The President's Men*. New York: Doubleday, 1968.

Arnold, Peri E. *Making the Managerial Presidency*, 2nd ed. Lawrence: University Press of Kansas, 1996.

Barber, James David. *The Presidential Character: Predicting Performance in the White House*. 3rd ed. Englewood Cliffs, NJ: Prentice-Hall, 1985.

Barilleaux, Ryan J., and **Barbara Kellerman**. *The President as World Leader*. NY: St. Martin's Press, 1991.

Bennett, Anthony. *The American President's Cabinet: From Kennedy to Bush*. NY: St. Martin's Press, 1996.

Berger, Raoul. *Impeachment: The Constitutional Problems*. Cambridge, MA: Harvard University Press, 1973.

Berman, Larry. *Planning a Tragedy: The Americanization of the War in Vietnam*. NY: Norton, 1982.—. *Lyndon Johnson's War*. NY: Norton, 1989.—. *The New American Presidency*. NY: Little Brown, 1987.

Beschloss, Michael R. *The Crisis Years: Kennedy and Khrushchev, 1960-1963*. NY: HarperCollins, 1991.—, *May-Day: Eisenhower, Khrushchev and the U-2 Affair*. NY: Harper and Row, 1986.

Blakesley, Lance. *Presidential Leadership: From Eisenhower to Clinton*. Chicago: Nelson-Hall 1995.

Bland, Larry I. and **James B. Barber**. *George C. Marshall: Soldier of Peace*. Baltimore: Johns Hopkins University Press, 1997.

Bond, Jon R., and **Richard Fleisher**. *The President in the Legislative Arena*. Chicago: University of Chicago Press, 1990.

Bose, Meena. *Shaping and Signaling Presidential Policy: The National Security Decision Making of Eisenhower and Kennedy*. College Station, TX: Texas A&M University Press, 1998.

Bowie, Robert and **Richard H. Immerman**. *Waging Peace: How Eisenhower Shaped an Enduring Cold War Strategy*. NY: Oxford University Press, 1997.

Brace, Paul, and **Barbara Hinckley**. *Follow the Leader: Opinion Polls and the Modern Presidents*. NY: Basic Books, 1992.

Binkley, Wilfred E. *President and Congress*. NY: Vintage, 1962.

Brody, Richard A. *Assessing the President: The Media, Elite Opinion, and Public Support*. Stanford, CA: Stanford University Press, 1991.

Bryce, James. *The American Commonwealth*. NY: MacMillan, 1888.

Buchanan, Bruce. *The Citizen's Presidency*. Washington: CQ Press, 1987.

Burke, John P. *The Institutional Presidency*. Baltimore: Johns Hopkins University

Press, 1992.—, *Presidential Transitions: From Politics to Practice.* Boulder, CO: Lynne Rienner, 2000. and **Greenstein, Fred I.** *How Presidents Test Reality: Decisions On Vietnam, 1954-1965.* Russell Sage Foundation, 1989.

Burnett, Stanton and **Luca Mantovani**. *The Italian Guillotine: Operation Clean Hands and the Overthrow of Italy's First Republic.* Lanham, MD: Rowman and Littlefield, 1998.

Burns, James MacGreor. *Leadership.* NY: Harper & Row, 1978.—*Deadlock of Democracy.* Englewood Cliffs, NJ: Prentice Hall, 1963.—*The Power to Lead: The Crisis of the American Presidency.* NY Simon & Schuster, 1984.

Campbell, Colin. *Managing the Presidency.* Pittsburgh: University of Pittsburgh Press, 1986.

Campbell, James E. *The American Campaign.* College Station, TX: Texas A&M University Press, 2000.

Cannon, Lou. *President Reagan: The Role of a Lifetime.* NY: Touchstone, 1991.

Cohen, Jeffrey. *The Politics of the U.S. Cabinet.* Pittsburgh: University of Pittsburgh Press, 1988.

Conlan, Timothy, Margaret T. Wrightson, and **David R. Beam**. *Taxing Choices: The Politics of Tax Reform.* Washington: CQ Press, 1990.

Conlan, Timothy. *From New Federalism to Devolution.* Washington: Brookings, 1998.

Cooper, John Milton. *The Warrior and the Priest: Woodrow Wilson and Theodore Roosevelt.* Cambridge, MA: Harvard University Press, 1985.

Corwin, Edward S. *The President: Office and Powers.* 5th ed. NY: New York University Press, 1984.

Covington, Cary R., and **Lester G. Seligman**. *The Coalitional Presidency.* Chicago: Dorsey Press, 1989.

Cox, Gary W., and **Samuel Kernell**, eds. *The Politics of Divided Government.* Boulder, CO: Westview, 1991.

Crabb, Cecil V., and **Pat Holt**. *Invitation to Struggle: Congress, the President, and Foreign Policy.* 3rd ed. Washington: Congressional Quarterly Press, 1989.—, and **Kevin V. Mulcahy**. *American National Security: A Presidential Perspective.* NY: Harcourt Brace, 1990.—, *Presidents and Foreign Policymaking.* Baton Rouge: Louisiana State University Press, 1986.

Cronin, Thomas E., ed. *Inventing the American Presidency.* Lawrence: University Press of Kansas, 1989.—*The State of the Presidency.* 2nd ed. Boston: Little, Brown, 1980.—, and **Michael Genovese**, *The Paradoxes of the American Presidency.* NY: Oxford University Press, 1998.

Dallek, Robert. *Hail to the Chief: The Making and Unmaking of American Presidents.* NY: Hyperion Books, 1996.

Destler, I. M. *Presidents, Bureaucrats, and Foreign Policy: The Politics of Organizational Reform.* Princeton, NJ: Princeton University Press, 1972.

Dickenson, Matthew J. Bitter Harvest: FDR, Presidential Power and the Growth of the Presidential Branch. NY: Cambridge University Press, 1997.

Draper, Theodore. *A Very Thin Line: The Iran-Contra Affairs.* NY: Hill and Wang, 1991.

Durant, Robert F. *The Administrative Presidency Reconsidered.* Albany: State University of New York Press, 1992.

Edwards, George C. *At the Margins: Presidential Leadership of Congress.* New Haven, CT: Yale University Press, 1989.—, *The Public Presidency.* NY: St. Martin's Press, 1983.—, and **Stephen Wayne**. *Presidential Leadership: Politics and Policy Making.* 5th ed. NY: St. Martin's Press, 2000.

Emery, Fred. *Watergate: The Corruption of American Politics and the Fall of Richard Nixon*. NY: Random House, 1994.

Farrand, Max. T*he Records of the Federal Convention of 1787*. New Haen, CT: Yale University Press, 1966.

The Federalist Papers. NY: New American Library. 1961.

Fenno, Richard F., Jr. *The President's Cabinet*. NY: Vintage, 1959.

Fishel, Jeff. *Presidents and Promises*. Washington: Congressional Quarterly Press, 1985.

Fisher, Louis. *The Constitution Between Friends*. NY: St. Martin's, 1978.—. *Presidential Spending Power*. Princeton, NJ: Princeton University Press, 1975.—. *Constitutional Conflicts Between Congress and the President*. Lawrence: University Press of Kansas, 1991.—. *The Politics of Shared Power: Congress and the Executive*. 4th ed. College Station, TX: Texas A&M University Press, 1998.—. *Congressional Abdication on War and Spending Power*. College Station, TX: Texas A&M University Press, 2000.

Gaddis, John Lewis. *Strategies of Containment: A Critical Appraisal of Postwar American National Security Policy*. NY: Oxford University Press, 1982.—. *We Now Know: Rethinking Cold War History*. NY: Clarendon Press, 1997.

Garrison, Jean A. *Games Advisors Play: Foreign Policy in the Nixon and Carter Administrations*. College Station, TX: Texas A&M University Press, 1999.

Gelb, Leslie H., with **Betts, Richard K**. *The Irony of Vietnam: The System Worked*. Washington: Brookings, 1979.

Genovese, Michael A. *The Presidential Dilemma: Leadership in the American System*. NY: HarperCollins, 1995.—**The Nixon Presidency: Power and Politics in Turbulent Times**. Westport, CT: Greenwood Press, 1990.—. *The Presidential Dilemma: Leadership in the American System*. NY: HarperCollins, 1995.—. *Power and the American Presidency, 1789-2000*. NY: Oxford University Press, 2000.

Gergen, David. *Eyewitness to Power: The Essence of Leadership from Nixon to Clinton*. NY: Simon & Schuster, 2000.

George, Alexander. *Presidential Decisionmaking in Foreign Policy: The Effective use of Information and Advice*. Boulder, CO: Westview Press, 1979.

Glennon, Michael J. Constitutional Diplomacy. Princeton, NJ: Princeton University Press, 1990.

Greenstein, Fred I. *The Hidden-Hand Presidency: Eisenhower as Leader*. NY: Basic Books, 1982.—, *Leadership in the Modern Presidency*. Cambridge, MA: Harvard University Press, 1988.—, *The Presidential Difference*. NY: The Free Press, 2000.

Grossman, Michael B., and **Martha Joynt Kumar**. *Portraying the President*. Baltimore: Johns Hopkins University Press, 1981.

Halberstam, David. *The Best and the Brightest*. NY: Random House, 1969.

Hargrove, Erwin C. *The President as Leader: Appealing to the Better Angels of Our Nature*. Lawrence: University Press of Kansas, 1998.

Hart, David M. *Forged Consensus: Science, Technology, and Economic Policy in the United States, 1921-1953*. Princeton, NJ: Princeton University Press, 1997.

Heclo, Hugh. *A Government of Strangers: Executive Politics in Washington*. Washington: Brookings, 1977.—, and **Salamon, Lester**, eds. *The Illusion of Presidential Government*. Boulder, CO: Westview, 1981.

Hart, John. *The Presidential Branch*. 2nd ed. Chatham, NJ: Chatham House, 1995.

Henkin, Louis. *Foreign Affairs and the Constitution*. NY: Free Press, 1972.

Hess, Stephen. *Organizing the Presidency*. Washington: Brookings, 2nd ed. 1988.

Hoff, Joan. *Nixon Reconsidered*. Boulder, CO: Basic Books, 1995.

Hoxie, R. Gordon. *Command Decision and the Presidency*. NY: Reader's Digest, 1977.— and **Ryan J. Barileaux**, eds. **The Presidency and National Security Policy**. NY: Center for the Study of the Presidency, 1984.

Jamieson, Kathleen Hall. *Packaging the Presidency*. NY: Oxford University Press, 1996.

Janus, Irving. *Groupthink: Psychological Studies of Policy Decisions and Fiascoes*. 2nd ed. Boston: Houghton Mifflin, 1982.

Johnson, Richard Tanner. *Managing the White House: An Intimate Study of the Presidency*. NY: Harper & Row, 1974.

Jones, Charles O. *The Presidency in a Separated System*. Washington: Brookings, 1994.—. *Separate But Equal Branches: Congress and the Presidency*. Chatham, NJ: Chatham House, 1995.

Kaplan, Lawrence S. *The Long Entanglement: NATO's First Fifty Years*. Westport, CT: Praeger, 1999.

Karnow, Stanley. *Vietnam: A History*. NY: Viking Press, 1983.

Kellerman, Barbara. *The President As World Leader*. NY: St. Martin's, 1991.

Kernell, Samuel M. *Going Public*. Washington: Congressional Quarterly Press, 1993.—, and **Pokin, Samuel L.** eds. *Chief of Staff: Twenty-five Years of Managing the Presidency*. Berkeley: University of California Press, 1986.

Kitfield, James. *Prodigal Soldiers*. Washington: Brasseys, 1997.

Koh, Harold Kongju. *The National Security Constitution: Sharing Power After the Iran-Contra Affairs*. New Haven, CT: Yale University Press, 1990.

Kutler, Stanley K. *The Wars of Watergate*. NY: Knopf, 1990.

Labovitz, John R. *Presidential Impeachment*. New Haven, CT: Yale University Press, 1978.

Landy Marc, and **Sidney M. Milkis**. *Presidential Greatness*. Lawrence: University Press of Kansas, 2000.

LeLoup, Lance T., and **Steven A. Shull**. *Congress and the President: The Policy Connection*. Belmont, CA Wadsworth, 1993.

Leuchtenburg, William E. *In the Shadow of FDR: From Harry Truman to Ronald Reagan*. Ithaca, NY: Cornell University Press, 1983.

Levy, Leonard W., and **Fisher, Louis**, eds. *Encyclopedia of the American Presidency* (NY: Simon and Schuster, 1993. 4 vols.

Light, Paul C. *The President's Agenda*. Baltimore: Johns Hopkins University Press, 1982.

Lowi, Theodore J. *The Personal President*. Ithaca, NY: Cornell University Press, 1985.

Logevall, Fredrik. *Choosing War: The Lost Chance for Peace and the Escalation of War in Vietnam*. Santa Barbara, CA: University of California Press, 1999

Maltese, John. *Spin Control: The White House Office of Communications and the Management of Presidential News*. Chapel Hill: University of North Carolina Press, 1992.

Mann, Thomas E., ed. *A Question of Balance: The President, the Congress, and Foreign Policy*. Washington: Brookings, 1990.

Mayhew, David. *Divided We Govern*. New Haven, CT: Yale University Press, 1991.

Mezey, Michael. *Congress, the President*, and Public Policy. Boulder, CO: Westview, 1989.

Milkis, Sidney M. *The President and the Parties*. NY: Oxford University Press, 1993.

Miroff, Bruce. *Icons of Democracy*. NY: Basic Books, 1993.

Nathan, Richard. *The Administrative Presidency*. NY: John Wiley and Sons, 1983.

Nelson, Michael, ed. *Guide to the Presidency*. 2nd ed. Washington: CQ Press, 1996.

Neustadt, Richard E. *Presidential Power*. NY Wiley, 1960.—, *Presidential Power and the Modern Presidents*. NY: Free Press, 1990.—, and **Ernest R. May**. *Thinking in Time: The Uses of History for Decision Makers*. NY: Free Press, 1986.

Oberdorfer, Don. *The Turn: From the Cold War to a New Era*. NY: Basic Books, 1999.

Patterson, Bradley. *The White House Staff*. Washington: Brookings, 2000.

Penner, Rudolph. *Broken Purse Strings: Congressional Budgeting*, 1974-1985. Washington: Urban Institute, 1988.

Perret, Geoffrey. *Eisenhower*: NY: Random House, 1999.

Peterson, Mark A. *Legislating Together*. Cambridge, MA: Harvard University Press, 1990.

Pfiffner, James P. *The President, the Budget, and Congress: Impoundment and the 1974 Budget Act*. Boulder, CO: Westview Press, 1979.—, ed. *The President and Economic Policy* ed. Philadelphia: ISHI Publications, 1986.—, *The Strategic Presidency: Hitting the Ground Running*, 2nd ed. Lawrence: University Press of Kansas, 1996.—, *The Managerial Presidency,* ed. 2nd ed. (College Station, TX: Texas A&M University Press, 1998).—, *The Modern Presidency, 3rd ed.* New York: Bedford-St. Martin's Press, 2000.—, and R. Gordon Hoxie, *The Presidency in Transition*. NY: Center for the Study of the Presidency, 1989.—, and Marcia Whicker and Raymond Moore, eds, *The Presidency and the Persian Gulf War*, Westport, CT: Praeger Publishers, 1993.—, *and Roger H. Davidson. Understanding the Presidency*, eds. 2nd. *Ed.* NY: Addison Wesley Longman, 1997.

Pious, Richard. *The American Presidency*. NY: Basic Books, 1979.—, *The Presidency*. Boston: Allyn and Bacon, 1996.

Polsby, Nelson. *Congress and the Presidency*. 4th ed. Englewood Cliffs, NJ Prentice-Hall, 1986.

Ponder, Daniel E. *Good Advice: Information and Policy Making in the White House*. College Station, TX: Texas A&M University Press, 2000.

Porter, Roger. *Presidential Decision Making: The Economic Policy Board*. NY: Cambridge University Press, 1980.

Quandt, William and **Bruce Maclaury**. *Peace Process: American Diplomacy Toward the Arab-Israeli Conflict Since 1967*. Washington: Brookings, 1993.

Ragsdale, Lyn. *Presidential Politics*. Boston: Houghton Mifflin, 1993.

Robinson, Donald L. *"To the Best of My Ability": The Presidency and the Constitution*. NY: Norton, 1987.

Reedy, George E. *The Twilight of the Presidency*. NY: World Publishing, 1970.

Rehnquist, William H. Grand Inquests. NY: William Morrow, 1992.

Richardson, Elliot L. *The Creative Balance*. NY: Holt, Rinehart, and Winston, 1976.—. *Reflections of a Radical Moderate*. NY: Pantheon Books, 1996.

Rockman, Bert. *The Leadership Question: The Presidency and the American system*. NY: Praeger, 1984

Rossiter, Clinton. *The American Presidency*. Baltimore: Johns Hopkins University Press, 1987.

Rozell, Mark J. *Executive Privilege*. Baltimore: Johns Hopkins University Press, 1994.

Rozell, Mark J. and **Wilcox, Clyde**. *The Clinton Scandal and the Future of American Government*. Washington: Georgetown University Press, 2000.

Schlesinger, Arthur M., Jr. *The Imperial Presidency*. Boston: Houghton Mifflin, 1973.—. *The Cycles of American History*. Boston Houghton Mifflin, 1986.

Shull, Steven A., ed. *The Two Presidencies: A Quarter Century Assessment*. Chicago: Nelson-Hall, 1991.

Simonton, Dean Keith. *Why Presidents Succeed*. New Haven: Yale University Press, 1987.

Smith, Hedrick. *The Power Game: How Washington Works*. NY: Ballantine, 1998.

Smith, Roy C. The Money Wars: The Rise and Fall of the Great Buyout. NY: Beard Group, 2000.

Skowronek, Stephen. *The Politics Presidents Make*. Cambridge, MA: Belknap, 1993.

Sorley, Lewis. *A Better War: The Unexamined Victories and the Final Tragedy of America's Last Years in Vietnam*. New York, NY: Harcourt Brace, 1999.

Sorrels, Charles. *U.S. Cruise Missile Program: Development, Deployment and Implications for Arms*. Washington: Brasseys, 1983.

Spitzer, Robert J. *President and Congress: Executive Hegemony at the Crossroads of American Government*. NY: McGraw-Hill, 1993.—, *The Presidential Veto: Touchstone of the American Presidency*. Albany, NY: State University of New York Press, 1988.

Stockman, David A. *The Triumph of Politics: How the Reagan Evolution Failed*. NY Harper and Row, 1986.

Stuckey, Mary E. *The President as Interpreter-in-Chief*. Chatham, NJ: Chatham House, 1991.

Sundquist, James L. *Constitutional Reform and Effective Governance*. Washington: Brookings, 1986.

Tatalovich, Raymond, and **Bryon W. Daynes**. *Presidential Power in the United States*. Belmont, CA: Brooks/Cole, 1984.

Thurber, James A., ed. *Divided Democracy*. Washington: CQ Press, 1991.—, ed. Rivals for Power: Presidential-Congressional Relations. Washington: CQ Press, 1996.

Tower, John; Muskie, Edmund; and **Scowcroft, Brent**. *The Tower Commission Report: The Full Text of the President's Special Review Board*. NY: Bantam, 1987.

Tulis, Jeffrey K. *The Rhetorical Presidency*. Princeton, NJ: Princeton University Press, 1987.

Walcott, Charles E., and **Hult, Karen M.** *Governing the White House: From Hoover Through LBJ*. Lawrence: University Press of Kansas, 1995.

Warshaw, Shirley Anne. *Powersharing: White House-Cabinet Relations in the Modern Presidency*. Albany: State University of New York Press, 1996.—. *The Domestic Presidency*. Boston: Allyn and Bacon, 1997.

Waterman, Richard W. *The Presidency Reconsidered*. Itasca, IL: F.E. Peacock, 1993.—. *Presidential Influence and the Administrative State*. Knoxville: University of Tennessee Press, 1989.

Wayne, Stephen J. *The Road to the White House, 2000*. NY: Bedford-St. Martin's, 2000.—. *The Legislative Presidency*. NY: Harper and Row, 1978.

Weintraub, Sidney. *Financial Decision-Making in Mexico: To Bet A Nation*. Pittsburgh: University of Pittsburgh Press, 2000.

Weko, Thomas J. *The Politicizing Presidency: The White House Personnel Office, 1948-1994*. Lawrence: University Press of Kansas, 1995.

Wiarda, Howard. *American Foreign Policy: Actors and Processes*. NY: Addison Wesley, 1996.

Williamson, Samuel R. *Austria-Hungary and the Origins of the First World War*. Boston: Bedford Books, 1991.

Wilson, Robert A., ed. *Character Above all: Ten Presidents from FDR to George Bush.* NY: Simon & Schuster, 1995.

Zelikow, Philip and **Condoleeza Rice**. *Germany Unified and Europe Transformed: A Study in Statecraft.* Cambridge, MA: Harvard University Press, 1997.

INDEX

TRIUMPHS AND TRAGEDIES OF THE MODERN PRESIDENCY

Security and Cooperation in Europe, Conference on, 279-280
Security Council, National (NSC), 29-30, 107, 124, 152-154, 219, 274-275, 291, 294
    Executive Committee (ExCom), 185, 187
    Operations Coordinating Board, 219
    Planning Board of, 152-154, 219
security, military, 157-159
security, U.S. national, 108, 152-154, 166-167, 180, 185, 222, 283-284, 291, 293
Seidman, William, 141-142
Senkaku/Diaoyutai Islands, 201-202
Serbia, 170, 179, 236-240
sexual harassment, 296-297
Shevardnadze, Eduard, 211
Shocks,
    auto, 127-129
    China, 118-121, 196
    Dollar, 121-124
    economic, 121-129, 139
    surcharge, 125-127
    soybean, 126-127
Shultz, George, 132, 204-206, 208, 210, 279-280, 292, 294, 299
Simon, William, 141-142
Singapore, 143
Smithsonian Agreement with Japan, 121-124, 126
Social Security, 129-131, 282
Social Security, National Commission on, 129-131, 164, 282
"Solarium Exercise," 154
Somalia, 205, 226-232, 241
Sorensen, Theodore, 23, 184
South Korea, 119, 143, 178, 196, 200, 203
Soviet Union (*see also* Russia), 204, 273, 279-280, 291, 300
    Bay of Pigs invasion and, 182-183
    China and, 118-120, 195-197
    Cuban Missile Crisis and, 184-187
    disinformation campaign, 155
    "evil empire," 156, 209-210
    influence in Asia, 167
    Japan and, 118-120, 167, 206-207
    Korea and, 178
    national security and, 154, 162
    NATO and, 174-176
    public diplomacy and, 154-156
    space program and, 82
    Superconducting Supercollider, 98

unification of Germany and, 217, 219
space program,
    International Space Station, 99-101
space race, 81-83
Space Studies Board (*see* National Research Council)
Special Prosecutor, 289, 295
    Jaworski, Leon, 95-96
    Starr, Kenneth, 296-297, 300
Special Representative for Trade Negotiations (STR), 115-116, 124
SS-20s, 155-156
Staats, Elmer, 248, 257
Stalin, Joseph, 154, 209
Starr, Kenneth, 296-297, 300
"Star Wars," 210
State, Department of, 118-119, 156-157, 165, 167, 172-173, 177, 283
    Foreign Service Officers, 156
    Okinawa reversion, 191-195
    Panama, 213, 216
Secretary of, 118-119, 132, 141, 164, 169, 178, 202, 204-206, 208, 217, 222, 234-235, 278-280, 283, 292, 294
stock markets, Asian, 143-144
"stove piping," bureaucratic, 109
Strategic Arms Reduction Talks (START), 162-163
Strategic Defense Initiative (SDI), 210
Strategic Forces, President's Commission on (Scowcroft Commission), 160-163
Strauss, Robert, 164
    as USTR, 116-117
Structural Impediments Initiative (SII), 132-133, 137
Summers, Lawrence, 138, 148
summits,
    Brussels, 175
    Camp David, 197-199
    Madrid, 176
    Moscow, 209-210
    Reykjavik, 209-210
Superconducting Supercollider (SSC), 97-99
Supreme Court, 91, 93, 289
surcharge on imports to United States, 121-129
Syria, 204-205

Taiwan, 143, 196-197